MW00995341

War
Elephants

John M. Kistler

Foreword by Richard Lair

University of Nebraska Press
Lincoln and London

Manufactured in the United States of America
(∞)
First Nebraska paperback printing: 2007
Library of Congress Cataloging-in Publication Data
Kistler, John M., 1967–
War elephants / John M. Kistler; foreword by Richard Lair.
p. cm.
Includes bibliographical references and index.
ISBN 978-0-8032-6004-7 (pbk.: alk. paper)
1. Animals—War use—History. 2. Elephants. I. Title.
UH87.K57 2007
355.4'24—dc22   2007008358

Frontispiece: XXVIA.102 © The Board of Trustees of the Armouries. The only surviving set of elephant armor in the world, circa 1600 A.D. The large circular gaps near the top of the head probably held shielding to protect the rider from enemy fire.

I dedicate this book to the Thai Elephant Conservation Center, where the innovative and traditional have met to improve the lives of elephants and people.

I am proud to have survived the ten-day mahout training course, under the careful tutelage of Sidoyai, the Casanova of Thailand's tuskless elephants, and his mahout Jaran.

Thanks also to Richard Lair for his expert assistance.

Contents

CONTENTS

Foreword

Before addressing the many intriguing questions about the elephant as an individual fighter, as a scientist and conservationist, I am obligated to consider the big picture. To the elephant expert, reading a book as panoramic as this—the multitudes of animals and the vast expanses encompassed—is staggering. Today we have become accustomed to thinking of small and shrinking populations of three Endangered Species (only about forty thousand wild Asian elephants remain, and the two African species have declined dramatically though they still number 440,000–600,000).

Until recently the modern literature has referred to only two species, the Asian elephant (*Elephas maximus*) and the African elephant (*Loxodonta africana*), conventionally described as comprising two subspecies, the savannah elephant and the forest (or pygmy) elephant. In 2004 taxonomists determined that, beyond significant morphological differences, the two subspecies did not interbreed to any significant level and thus each was a full species; the African savannah elephant remained *L. africana* while the African forest elephant became *L. cyclotis*. The distinction transcends academic quibbling because, of the two African species, almost certainly only the forest elephant ever fought in wars. Forest elephants are much smaller than their savannah cousins, about the size of the Asian elephant and sharing with it some characteristics that many biologists believe to show a high degree of convergent evolution.

At the time the battles in this book were fought, North Africa and the Middle East still had abundant grasslands. African forest elephants certainly reached the shores of the Mediterranean and even the Asian elephant came very close. A sobering thought today is that—whether through hunting or habitat destruction or climate change—elephants have become extinct over nearly all the huge swaths of land that hosted so many battles and campaigns.

The wild elephant populations required to supply the armies of this book must have comprised a huge supply pool. Wilderness is key to elephant warfare because it is safe to assume that nearly all of the elephants ever used in warfare were wild-caught. A close examination of surviving traditional elephant-keeping cultures shows a virtually universal preference for captured elephants for two reasons. First, wild elephants are favored in the subjective belief—perhaps containing a degree of truth—that a wild elephant that has been strongly broken will always fear man, whereas a calf born in captivity will never fear man and therefore will never be truly trustworthy to humans.

Second, on purely practical grounds, wild animals were preferred because an elephant takes twenty years to reach maturity and the strength to do productive work; thus, every year of age an elephant is at capture is one less year that it does not require intensive care from humans. Further, there is no need to take pregnant cows off of work for three years. Preferring wild elephants is basic economics: Why go to the trouble and cost of breeding when it is not necessary?

Where there is very little breeding, however, it necessarily follows that there can be little or no selective breeding. One perplexing fact is that the elephant, the only animal that humans ever used systematically and at large scale as a fighter, is an animal that humans never domesticated. Surprisingly, none of the three elephant species—the lack is most conspicuous in the Asian elephant—was ever bred selectively over many generations so as to produce a superior, modified animal. Thus, genetically and even behaviorally, the elephant remains a wild animal, exactly like the rhinoceros or water buffalo or gaur. The dog and the horse, the only other two animals to ever play extensive combatant roles in human conflict, have both been domesticated for over four thousand years. The dog, however, mostly pulled guard duty and never performed on the field of battle. A well-trained war horse was taught to collide and perhaps to kick, but the horse was never a fighter but rather the vehicle for the human warrior.

In Asia, most of the elephants employed in warfare were laborers rather than fighters. The most basic non-combatant job was simply carrying supplies and occasionally people. In areas where elephants were plentiful and easily fed and watered, they routinely performed such mundane work. (As late as the Vietnam War elephants were used as pack animals, a job condemning them to be deemed, grotesquely, legitimate targets for American air attack.) The elephant's unique value, however, came with transporting objects so massive—for example, siege engines and, later, cannons—that only dragging would suffice. A specialist job requiring even more highly-trained elephants can only be described as 'engineer.' In the remote jungles of Burma in World War II, for example, both the

British and Japanese armies highly valued logging elephants as builders of wooden bridges strong enough to carry tanks and railroad locomotives.

The elephant's role as an actual fighter, however, is what fascinates. Why the elephant? When considering or analyzing which animals might be employed in war, three factors might especially recommend the elephant: size, weaponry, and controllability. As for size, beyond an initial element of intimidation, pure bulk seems to never have conferred an overwhelming advantage. As for weaponry, tusks were undoubtedly useful and unique weapons (quite unlike the teeth and talons of other animals), but tusks never did make the elephant 'the queen of the battlefield.' As for controllability, elephants are easily trained, suggesting the ability to learn and, thus, intelligence. The elephant's intelligence is often considered to fall in the range of cetaceans and the higher primates, placing these impressed warriors firmly amidst the most intelligent animals known to man.

Having considered the species, I finally can muse about 'elephant nature' or temperament, leaving academics behind to draw on nearly thirty years spent with individual elephants. The first question to occur to most readers is probably: Can the elephant be a gifted warrior?

Answering that question, however, requires noting that all fighting elephants were males (and probably all tuskers). This preference came mostly because of the male's undoubtedly more stalwart and pugnacious nature but also partly from the sexism—in modern eyes—embedded in virtually all traditional cultures. Whatever the reason, when discussing the nature of war elephants, we are talking about the male of the species.

Five times I have witnessed an elephant try to kill a human and many more times have attended funerals to hear first-hand accounts of the death of a mahout (by far the most frequent victim). The natural attack is to knock the victim to the ground and then finish the job. The onslaught is very fast and incredibly athletic. Books often create neat lists of the means of attack as separate moves (goring, trampling, kicking, biting, grabbing with the trunk, and more), but when trying to recall an actual attack, the impression is more of a rapid blur of disparate movements, like a cartoon of Sarge bashing Beetle Bailey. The last attack I witnessed was in a curious way the most enlightening; for no apparent reason an eleven-month-old calf (and, ironically, a female) knocked a seventy-year-old woman, a tourist, to the ground and then relentlessly head-butted her as if going for the coup de grace. What was startling here was how a 'cute little calf' illustrated just how deeply innate are the elephant's offensive capabilities.

That insight begs the question of how effectively those fighting instincts could have been channeled or harnessed to the formal battlefield. The closest surviving analogy to a war elephant is a logging elephant, combining extraordinary strength and intelligence augmented by great skill instilled through training. What the martial arts sports are to human combat, the dangerous work of elephant logging is to elephant warfare. People lucky enough to see an elephant at work (dragging, pushing, lifting, and stacking huge logs) are amazed at how much the animal can do on its own, but astute observers will also note that the mahout operates the elephant just as if it were a machine. Master mahouts issue a rapid and continuous stream of orders through voice commands, kicks behind the ear, touches with the hook, and even whole body moves; the mahout's actions mirror the bewildering flurry of hand and foot movements of an expert bulldozer operator. The best battle elephants were undoubtedly trained to a similar degree of perfection.

The ideal war elephant, not unlike the perfect soldier, thus embodies two apparently conflicting characteristics, being an instinctive, natural-born killer but one responding perfectly to commands to perform behaviors ingrained through years of rigorous drills. The provocative word 'killer' might not be anthropomorphizing. Many scientists have noticed that wild elephants have elaborate death rituals, including sometimes covering their fellows' corpses and making annual visits to 'graves.' Some observers have even boldly speculated that elephants might be the only animals apart from man to have an understanding, a concept, of death. If this is true, then the war elephant would not fight simply as a programmed automaton but rather with conscious intent to kill. Clearly, the battle elephant was not John Donne's "An elephant; the only harmless great thing" but rather a creature bent on violence, enabled by nature but enhanced with skills most cleverly and laboriously taught by man.

There remains an obligation. Having paid homage to the skills and spirit of fighting elephants, I must also acknowledge that Donne's paean of peacefulness holds great truth. In times and places where wild elephants are unthreatened by humans, the females are on balance highly tolerant of people and even the males are not usually aggressive. Many captive cows, and even some bulls, are as sweet natured as the gentlest of horses. In the end, any large population of elephants contains the equivalents, in human terms, of everything from saints to ax murderers. For war, humans selected the prime males for both physique and temperament and then transformed them into killing machines the likes of which will, blessedly, never be seen again.

Richard C. Lair

Introduction

...elephants, which are wonderful animals both in form and in ways. If in respect of size I liken them to a mountain in order to describe them to those who have not seen them, I do not succeed in my attempt, for where is account taken of their beauty of form, and where is their swiftness? Or if I liken their speed and fury to the wind, how is their wrath depicted at the time of their o'erthrowing the firm-footed on the field of battle? If I compare them for foresight, intelligence, and sagacity to the horse, the real thing is not said. A separate volume would be required to describe their ferocity, their revenge, and their wondrous deeds. Such a work might be written by a sage without the adornments of fine writing. Eloquence and fluency alone are not sufficient for such a great subject being treated of in its entirety. In addition to true wisdom there must be a long life spent in the company of experienced men who have learnt the ways of this wondrous-looking, mighty-formed, highly intelligent, mountain-demolishing, horseman-throwing, army-confounding animal, and thereby acquiring knowledge of the marvelous, awe-inspiring, astonishment-producing creature.[1]

These accolades for the elephant, penned several hundred years ago, represent the feelings that any person might develop upon seeing the elephant at war. Similar awe comes from the experience of living among "working elephants," whose gentleness and wisdom inspire trust rather than fear.

War Elephants represents the first book on the subject of pachyderm warfare written in English. Colonel P. Armandi penned *Histoire Militaire des Elephants* in 1843, but no translation exists and copies are extremely rare.[2] H. H. Scullard produced the most useful tome for research on the elephant in ancient Greece and Rome but left all the rest of human/elephant history untouched. Dr. G. N. Pant published a beautifully illustrated work, *Horse and Elephant Armour*, which provides many important insights on Asian elephants in combat in India. However, *War Elephants* is the first work to provide coverage for all of the elephant's uses in warfare from ancient to modern times.

War Elephants focuses most carefully on ancient Near Eastern and Asian history because that is where the pachyderms lived and fought most frequently. Aside from tenuous claims that a handful of Mongol elephants landed in South America, based on some odd sculptures, the giants created their legacies in the 'Old World' and not the New.

This book contains an almost exhaustive account of war elephants in the ancient western world but cannot claim the same thoroughness for the Asian sphere. The author has no background in Asian languages or history and therefore has relied entirely upon English translations and histories. Since only a fraction of original Indian and Chinese documents have been translated, there must be many gripping tales of elephants that remain unknown to the West. Perhaps in the future an Asian scholar, who loves both history and pachyderms, will cast light on those hidden treasures.

The reader may wonder about the author's personal views on elephants as warriors. The dramatization of the violence in war may seem to be a glorification of that violence, which is not intended. However, the long history of elephants in warfare is impressive. Pachyderms are strong and intelligent, loyal and creative, in peace and war. There are proper times for war; the author is not promoting pacifism as a reaction to animal suffering. Nor can armies be blamed for seeking every means at their disposal to protect themselves and their countries. However, just as ethics encompass our treatment of persons and nations, they must also speak for animals and the inanimate world.

In respect to intelligence and emotional responses, the author believes that elephants come closer to a likeness of humanity than any other land animal. If 'rights' or simple moral consideration is to be based upon a species' capacity to think and feel, then pachyderms will be very high on the waiting list for that consideration.

Your first impression when standing before an elephant is awe. You cannot avoid this feeling; it must be genetically reflexive to fear a creature larger than yourself. Whether the pachyderm is gentle or wild, he is significantly more massive than you and has the natural strength to destroy you. Try to remember that the men who fought with or against elephants in combat knew very little about them. The learning process was largely trial and error. Even after thousands of years of study, scientists have not solved many riddles of elephant life! Only in the last decade or two did we discover that elephants communicate sub-sonically, below the human range of hearing.

Because elephants have been employed by armies for thousands of years on a fairly continuous basis, *War Elephants* is, to a degree, a history of warfare. Elephants have seen the advent of the wheel, the growth of archery, the birth of metallurgy, the organization of armies and logistics, and much more.

My hope is that *War Elephants* will remind the world that elephants and man share a long and intricate relationship and awaken further efforts to renew that relationship toward the survival of both species.

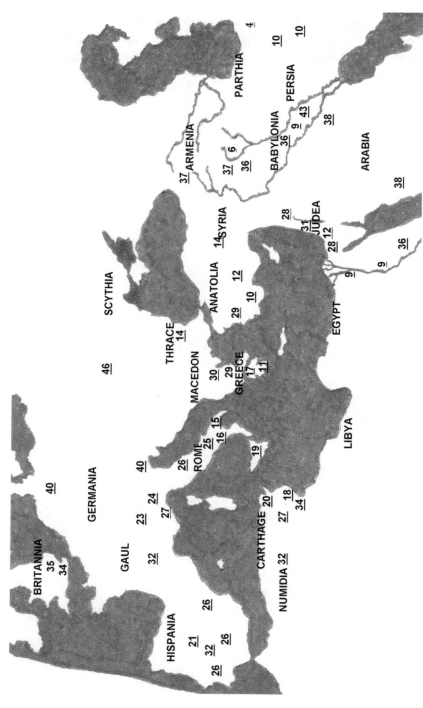

The numerals on the map show the chapter numbers where detailed descriptions of the war elephant battles may be found. These numbers are placed in the approximate location where the battles occurred.
[Photo by the author.]

1
Useful Orphan

Five thousand years ago, a lonely and hungry Asian elephant calf wandered into a village, sparking the first domestication of a pachyderm. By feeding the baby and providing social stability, *Homo sapiens* became her surrogate family. She learned to carry people on her back and to pull logs. As people in other villages saw that the elephant could be friendly and useful, they tried to catch young pachyderms for use in their towns. When certain men proved to be adept at capturing and training the beasts, they traveled afar to sell their expertise where needed.

This is conjecture, because no written records detail the first friendly encounter between humans and elephants, but the orphaned-calf theory is the most likely scenario for our initial cooperative contacts with the species, says Richard Lair.[1]

Thousands of years before humans adopted that calf, our ancestors killed her ancestors, mammoths and mastodons, for food.

From about 2600–1900 BC, the people of the Indus Valley hunted elephants with poisoned arrows and spears. They used detachable poisoned points on the projectiles so that even if the elephant pulled out the shaft, the barbs and poison remained in the wound. The hunters tracked the beast until it fell, carved out the area of poisoned meat, and butchered the carcass for food.[2] There is no consensus on the taste of pachyderm flesh. One writer opines, "Elephant meat is as tough as a tire...they smoke the meat for months before they eat it."[3] Reverend J.G. Wood, however, says that "slices of elephants trunk broiled are considered wonderful delicacies, and are unrivalled except by the rather superior flavour of the feet when baked."[4] An ancient Chinese said that "elephant trunk tastes like piglet, especially when made crispy by roasting."[5] Tasty or not, elephants were not usually killed for their meat.

Elephants were once common throughout Asia (including China), the Middle East, and North Africa.[6] Their disappearance from this vast expanse comes not from a human desire for elephant steak, but for their long ivory teeth. *Loxodonta*, our name for the African elephant, means

1

long teeth (Asian elephants are *Elephas maximus*). Called "white gold" by artisans and hunters, ivory is fine material for carving decorative objects.

Egyptians of the second millennium BC completely exterminated the elephants living in the Nile Delta, seeking their ivory. The town of Elephantine in southern Egypt "...undoubtedly received its ancient name, *Abou* (elephant town), because of the vast quantities of ivory that it sent to the Egyptian capitols."[7] The herds of elephants in Syria and Mesopotamia were nearly gone by eighth century BC.[8]

As for those people who preferred living elephants to dead ones, the earliest physical evidence of the human elephant relationship comes from an ancient Mesopotamian plaque dated to around 2000 BC showing an Asian elephant ridden by a man.[9] That this piece represents a custom of elephant riding, and not just a freak event, is implied by the detail of a

Asian armies believed that old bulls with tusks were best for warfare: experience overshadowed simple power. [*J.A. Hammerton, editor. Wonders of Animal Life, London: Waverly Book Co. circa 1930, no date. Volume 4, page 1429.*]

strap or rope which the human has put on the beast, perhaps to help him hold on.[10] Similar artifacts of a slightly later date have been unearthed in Pakistan.

Riding elephants caught on quickly in western China (Shensi) by 1100 BC, where pachyderms were so abundant that most people "had one!"[11] The region of southern Ho-nan of China became known as the "Country of Docile Elephants."[12]

The first step in taming an elephant is acquiring one. Although elephants have no innate fear of humans, they do learn caution once humans begin chasing or killing them. Capturing an elephant is not easy.

Elephants have immense strength to match their immense frames. Every year at the Surin elephant roundup in Thailand, the champion bull elephant engages in a tug-of-war contest with a row of humans pulling a rope, where he pulls down as many as one hundred people. A simple rope snare will not usually hold a pachyderm!

Some cultures use the pit method: covering large holes in the ground with branches and then chasing an elephant herd toward the pits, hoping that a few will fall and be trapped. Unfortunately, pits may injure the beasts, and getting them out of the holes can be a challenge.

Once you have obtained a few elephants and tamed them, it is possible to capture others more easily. Tamed elephants used to capture and control wild elephants are called *Koonkies*. The target elephants do not notice the men on the back of the Koonkie until rope nooses have tightened around his neck or feet![13] Remarkably, wild elephants do not attack the men or the Koonkies, although they could easily do so.[14]

While the wild elephant's senses of smell and sound are highly acute, their eyesight is not especially good. It seems that pachyderms cannot see a man more than fifty yards away.[15] By masking his smell and keeping quiet, a hunter can approach a herd of elephants without disturbing them.

The Koonkie method of capturing wild pachyderms is very effective, but obtains only one or two beasts at a time, since the rest of the herd flees when the new captive begins to squeal about the ropes.

The most frequently used strategy, capturing whole herds at once, is called the *keddah* or *kraal* method. One of our earliest descriptions comes from Megasthenes (350–290 BC), a Greek ambassador to India after Alexander the Great's conquests.[16]

A keddah is a corral or enclosure to trap elephants, usually having a wide opening that gradually narrows to a gate leading into the holding pen. You might think of an hourglass that is open on one end. You can pour sand into the open end, which will slowly seep through the narrow spot and then fall into the large area below. People build the enclosure while the elephants are grazing in other areas, but where the herd is known to often return.

There are two common methods of getting elephants into the keddah. Fire or loud noises may be used to drive the herd into the funnel where they are trapped. Another variant is to use tamed elephant cows inside the trap, enticing virile males. Some wild bulls often go right in and then the humans close the narrow doorway.

Typically, the successful *Homo sapiens* do not keep the entire herd. The elephants are chosen based on their age, sex, and beauty, depending on what role they are to play for their captors. If the beasts will serve as loggers, large bulls, and young males are chosen. Tuskless bulls, while they lack the advantage of tusks to balance logs upon, are believed to have much stronger trunks. If pack animals are needed, then the calmer females are chosen. Calves are prized because they are easily trained, but this requires a long-term commitment for training and caring for the animal. One key reason why people have used elephants for thousands of years is because some of them can be trained even as adults.[17] Most other species, having grown up in the wild, do not accept the transformation to captivity.

The most common use for a trained elephant, in ancient times and modern, was simple transportation. The jungles and forests of Asia, particularly during the long monsoon seasons, are practically impenetrable. Elephants are quite comfortable moving through the brush and mud, thus providing people with a means of getting around and carrying a load for trading with other villages.

Riding on an elephant takes some getting used to. From the elephant's neck, a fair sense of balance and stability can be achieved, but from the elephant's back, the nearest approximation of the experience is sitting in a rowboat in heavy waves. Here is another description:

I paid my rupees and climbed the ladder that led to the howdah; on the way to Amber I discovered that elephant-back was the most damnably uncomfortable mode of travel that I had ever experienced...an elephant has four legs and what might be called independent suspension for each of them; I remembered too late the peculiar character of the elephant's walk, which is that it raises each foot from the ground separately and slowly, and puts it down with great deliberation before the next mighty foot is lifted. That meant that on my ride I had four separate shocks and a tilt in four directions for each complete pace the animal

took. Worse still was that the howdah in which I was sitting was a kind of box…
uncovered and uncushioned, and very hard indeed.[18]

Trained elephants provide other services for humans. Possessing great
strength, an elephant can drag heavy logs or rocks easily out of a path or
to a work site. Their immense appetites reduce the dense foliage around a
village, making it harder for tigers or cobras to lurk out of sight. Elephants'
frequent use of the local rivers sends crocodiles fleeing. Farmers use
elephant dung for fertilizer. Humans had discovered a biological tractor
that required only food, water, and training to be of great service to the
community.

The reader should not get a false impression of the human elephant
relationship because of poorly chosen words. Left undefined, words such
as "domesticated" or "tame" can be misleading, especially to modern
Americans or residents of wealthy countries. Most Americans live and
work far away from animals. The only animals that frequent our lives are
"pets," which we refer to as domesticated and tame. This is very different
from the meaning of the words when related to elephants. Elephants are
not pets, even when trained and relatively tame.

Elephants are not tamed or domesticated to the same degree that
household pets have been. Humans have been selectively breeding dogs
for many centuries, and thus brought about the variety of dogs that we see
today. Bull dogs and Chihuahuas are not indigenous dog types found
living wild in some region of the Earth. We have bred one style of dog for
its color and size with another style of dog possessing a desirable temperament, thus creating a new breed.

Humans have not had success breeding elephants, let alone selectively
inbreeding special traits. Tame elephants, in fact, are only tame in the
sense that they cooperate with their riders. Most "tamed" elephants eat
and sleep in the forest and simply "come to town" with their riders for a
handful of hours each day! The tamed elephant is not so different from
the business person, who gains some rewards by working several hours a
day and then returning home to do whatever she wishes. The "domestication" of elephants is simply a forced cooperation exchanged for food
and social contact. Yes, it is possible to enslave an elephant and forcefully
require it to work longer hours. However, this breaks the sense of bonding
that the elephant might feel to its rider, and either the pachyderm will die
of overwork or kill its tormentor. So, do not think of elephants as pets, but
more as companions or hired laborers. In exchange for special foods and
good scrubbing baths in the river, the elephant will do some work for the

humans. Do the elephants actually think this way? Scientists may argue about this specific point, but there is no way around the simple truth that this is how the human elephant relationship works.

2
Early Contests

A caravan of twenty trained elephants walked quietly in a single-file line under the heavy canopy of the teak forest. Each beast carried a mahout on its neck and five hundred pounds of food and supplies for the army. The elephants were nervous. The leader kept stopping and opening his ears wide to listen and snaking his trunk upward to sniff the air. His rider signaled for some of their infantry escort to spread out and look around the west side of the trail to see what might be alarming the animals.

Soon the scouts are shouting, and the sound of running through the brush is clearly heard. Enemy soldiers speed toward the caravan with spears and wooden shields in hand. Ten of the elephants are frightened and run off into the forest away from the noise, ignoring their riders' commands. Seven pachyderms are alarmed, but obey the riders and stay on the trail. But three of the elephants, including the male leader, react quite differently. They are angered by the confusion and noise and turn to fight.

The first enemy to crash through the underbrush, expecting to find a line of human foes or supply carriers, instead is confronted by a massive elephant. He sticks his spear quickly forward to stab the charging beast, and the weapon wounds its trunk, but this simply infuriates the animal. It grabs the man around the chest and bashes him hard against the ground and then crushes him underfoot. As a modern hunter describes an elephant's means of attack:

He defends himself often with his trunk, and picks up and squeezes the life out of a man, or throws him against trees, or puts his foot on him and with his trunk tears him in two, or holds him in his trunk and batters him against any hard substance near at hand. The trunk, which is constantly used for heavy work, is very highly developed, muscular, massive, and very active, quite different from the flabby, wizened trunk seen in a zoo.[1]

The three angry elephants stomp and toss their attackers mercilessly until the rest of the dispirited foes turn and flee for their lives.

It took two hours for the caravan to recall its panicked members and treat the wounds of the combatants before they could renew the journey. The wounded infantry escorts rode atop the elephants, while a few were pulled behind on bamboo-pole mats.

Upon reaching the army camp, the commander saw that the convoy had been attacked and demanded details on the size of the enemy force. He was surprised to learn that three elephants actually fought decisively to save the caravan and supplies!

The commander has discovered that some elephants are good fighters, although many preferred flight. Over the coming years he would watch for brave elephants because they could serve his army well!

The transition from using elephants for constructive purposes, such as riding or hauling, to destructive purposes, such as combat, did not tarry long. The dramatization just given is a possible scenario for the initial discovery of elephant combat abilities. The intimidating size and strength of their now-tamed behemoths must have been obvious to humans from the beginning.

Which nation invented elephant warfare? We cannot be sure. War elephants appeared in Syria at around 1500 BC,[2] whereas the Shang Dynasty of China (1723–1123 BC) also employed them, although the dates are uncertain.[3]

The Sanskrit epic called the *Mahabharata* was long believed to tell a story from about 3000 BC, but recent studies push it forward by one or two millennia. Still, it may reflect the oldest mention of elephants in war.

In the *Mahabharata*, armies feared the male elephant in *musth* more than any other. This word "is a corruption of the Urdu word *mast* meaning intoxicated."[4] During its adult life, the bull elephant periodically goes berserk, literally, when hormones provoke it to mate with females and fight with other bulls. To use a popular cultural parallel, think of Mr. Spock from the *Star Trek* original series, whose normal demeanor collapsed under the hormones of the "pon farr" so that he had to mate and fight. The bull elephant is overwhelmed by his changed body chemistry and may attack anything, even a helpless tree! Glands on the sides of his head produce a pungent-smelling oil that drips down, and elephant riders know that the male in musth must be dealt with very cautiously.

Of course, since this happens naturally in the bull elephant only once or twice a year, the question is, how could armies make use of "rutting bulls" for battle? After all, battles are not usually scheduled by the hormonal cycles of male pachyderms! Mahouts discovered that this dangerous anger of bull elephants could, to a degree, be provoked (or inspired) by various means. Drugs, alcohol, loud noises, and music were used to arouse the males to action. In later chapters we will see specific cases of these methods in use before combat.

The *Mahabharata* of India also tells of one dramatic confrontation in battle with elephants, cavalry, and men. One large musth elephant crashed through the enemy and killed a set of chariot horses. The chariot driver threw his iron lance at the mahout, killing the elephant's rider, and then with a mighty sword blow severed the trunk from the elephant's head. The beast shrieked and died.[5]

Because archaeology indicates that India first gained iron-smelting technology at about 1000 BC, the use of iron lances and weapons in the *Mahabharata* is an indicator that the story may date from the first millennium before Christ.[6]

The earliest attempts with elephants in battle were primitive compared to the sophisticated tactics and armor presented in later millennia. The first war pachyderms bore no protective armor and only carried a single mahout/rider on his neck. One ancient text says that elephant riders would sometimes climb down on to the elephant's tusks to kill enemy soldiers and horses.[7] This would be necessary because the mahout sits on the elephant's neck some six to ten feet off the ground, and thus could not reach foes below.

Surprisingly, it was the older elephants who were most prized for combat. The oldest elephants had the most experience and the least fear, and thus were confident enough to stand firm in battle. This belief is confirmed in modern times by the popular colonial sport of tiger hunting. Elephants are innately afraid of tigers, one of the few predators capable of harming an elephant. Only with years of training do the pachyderms learn to overcome their fear, to pursue the colorful cats. Although the years between twenty-five and forty are when an elephant's strength is at its peak, its mental discipline improves with age.[8] With long experience they learn more voice and signal commands from their mahouts.[9]

Training elephants for war is a long process, requiring great patience. Most pachyderms are too skittish and nervous for the martial lifestyle and are only used for carrying supplies in an auxiliary role.

Before the invention of howdah towers, warriors rode directly on the elephant's back. The mahout rider almost always rode on the beast's neck. [*Illustration copyright © Ian Heath, from 'Armies of the Macedonian and Punic Wars' by Duncan Head (WRG 1982).*]
Source: Ian Heath.

In the centuries BC, the Indian military had seven specific courses of training for the war elephants, as described by Kautilya Arthasastra. In combat, these orders could be given to the elephant squadrons by the use of flags.

1. *Upasthana*: rising and jumping over fences and other obstacles.
2. *Samvartana*: sitting and leaping over pits. The words "jumping" and "leaping" are somewhat misleading, as elephants cannot jump or leap. What they can do is rear up on their hind legs and then lunge forward to take a giant step over an obstacle such as a ditch or a short fence. Trenches are an effective obstacle against elephants, used in modern zoos.
3. *Samyana*: marching straight or zigzag.
4. *Vadhavadha*: trampling under foot horses and foot soldiers.
5. *Hastiyddha*: pitting elephants against one another.
6. *Nagarayana*: rushing against forts and buildings.
7. *Samgramika*, used in open warfare.[10]

The training of war elephants probably parallels the training of pachyderms for tiger hunting, because it involves gradually increasing familiarity with feared sensations while heightening aggression and courage. J.G. Wood offers a very detailed account of teaching an elephant to lose its fear of tigers so that it will carry men to hunt the cats.

The first step is to introduce the beast frequently to a tiger skin, even encouraging the elephant to step on it. Later, a stuffed tiger is placed in tall grass and the elephant learns to walk past it. Eventually, a small boy wears a tiger skin to animate the feared object. Finally, a small cow is wrapped in the tiger's hide, and the elephant is encouraged to attack it with its tusks and kill it.[11]

Only a fraction of trained elephants can overcome their fear of tigers, and likewise, not all trained pachyderms can become war elephants.

Perhaps the most important element in the creation of a successful war elephant is not the strength of its legs or trunk, but the strength of its relationship with the mahout. Even a fearless musth bull needs a rider who can control or direct it, otherwise it is only a good individual warrior and not a part of the strategy of the army as a whole. The undisciplined elephant may end up deep inside enemy lines, surrounded on every side by foes and doomed to a quick death. The mahout understands the signals of the commanders (by flag and drum) and recognizes battlefield dangers to employ the elephant effectively. The rider intimately knows the idiosyncrasies of his elephant: that it turns more slowly to the left than to the right, that it is terrified by flaming arrows, and so on.[12] The mahout is, really, the elephant's greatest protection. He assesses dangers and makes decisions to the benefit of both human and animal. The mahout, also called "oozie" in Burma, learned to carry a long spear so that he could strike at foes that threatened the elephant.

A modern elephant rider training manual offers this brief list of qualifications:

Mahouts should have stamina, quick reflexes, sense of discrimination, and most of all patience, perseverance and responsibility. Common sense and a sharp mind are essential qualities for a mahout to handle in a crisis. A short tempered person must not enter this profession. [13]

The most common way to teach elephants not to fear military noises was quite simple: repeat the sounds over and over again until the beasts become accustomed to the noise. One might think of National Football League players holding practice sessions with loudspeakers blaring crowd noise from the sidelines to prepare them for the sensations of the big game. Mahouts had drums and other instruments beaten nearby, while men practiced their combat skills. Such sound as sword clashing against shield, lance striking armor, arrows flying into targets, and frightened horses neighing were all introduced to the trainee elephants so they would not become confused and frightened during the real battle.

Not only were the sounds and smells of battle simulated for the pachyderms, the animals themselves learned different ways to attack and defend themselves. Teaching the elephant to use its trunk as a weapon is not simple. Just as a human protects his eyes, intuitively, when a threat emerges, so the elephant innately desires to protect its trunk.[14] Even when in musth and crazed by their hormones, the bulls will often be seen fighting with their tusks and bodies, but holding their trunks well out of harm's way. Obviously the army does not want the elephant's trunk to be wounded, but often the way to avoid a wound is to strike out at the threat. By attaching a shield to the elephant's trunk and having men jab their spears toward the trunk, the elephant begins to understand that it can block or strike at the weapons effectively.[15]

Elephants never carried shields into battle because the army wanted their trunks to swing as weapons. If the trunk carries a shield, it cannot grab foes. Only thousands of years later would men teach elephants to swing weapons in their powerful trunks.

As early as the 600s BC, elephant soldiers lived in villages together as a group.[16] These would be relatively small groups of elephants, as the beasts eat a lot of local resources. The importance of keeping men and their elephants in groups was twofold. They could be gathered up rapidly if a military need arose and they could learn from each other, the veterans teaching the recruits.

Commanders soon recognized that even brave elephants are affected by pain in different ways. Some beasts would become vicious when wounded, attacking more vigorously, whereas others would flee when pierced by arrows or spears. Most fled.

To reduce the number of retreating pachyderms, gradual improvements in armor were added to the elephant's regalia. Early elephant armor consisted of layers of ox hide, sometimes decorated with snakeskins.[17] Later, it was discovered that leather could be moistened, shaped, and fire-hardened to create a perfect fit on each individual pachyderm, which provided good protection to the elephants' head, trunk, and front shoulders. Full-time elephant veterinarians joined the army to heal the wounded animals.[18]

Elephants became such a prized part of Asian armies that foreign invaders were forced to make unusual preparations, as the Assyrians would learn in 800 BC.

3
Beauty and the Beasts

Ancient records frequently mix legend and history. Stories about Semiramis, the famous queen represented in operas by Rossini and Rossi, are a case in point. One source claimed that doves raised the infant Semiramis when her mother turned into a fish.[1] Ignoring the plainly mythological tales, several scenes from the scribes of antiquity have the ring of truth and may in fact provide us with the first detailed sketch of a battle with elephants.

The most plausible candidate for the model of Semiramis was the Assyrian Queen Sammu-ramat, who reigned in Babylon about eight hundred years before Christ.[2] Semiramis possessed fabulous beauty, and she may have been a royal prostitute before catching the eye of King Shamshi-Adad V and bearing him a son. We are told that the queen convinced her husband to take a break and allow her to rule for just five days. On the very first day, while she wore the royal robes and carried the king's scepter, she convinced the Assyrian generals that she would be a better ruler.[3] They deposed the king and named Semiramis empress.

Semiramis' love/hate relationship with men did not stop with the death of her husband the king, according to our sources. When feeling amorous, the empress would invite a handsome soldier for a long night of passion. In the morning he was put to death to preserve the queen's reputation from vicious gossip.[4]

Perhaps as a favor to the generals who elevated her to power, the queen agreed to prepare the army for an invasion of India. Semiramis wisely gathered information about her distant enemies, perhaps with spies disguised as traveling merchants. The reports were alarming: King Stabrobates of India suspected that Assyria would attack, and he was already collecting a huge force of war elephants to defend his lands.[5]

One interesting detail from the spy report was that the Indian king was capturing these elephants from the forests for his army. Certainly this is a misunderstanding by people unfamiliar with war elephants. These pachyderms were not "new captures." It takes years to train war elephants, and

An Execution by an Eliphant.

An ancient form of execution: dismemberment by elephant. [*Robert Knox, An Historical Relation of the Island Ceylon, London, 1681.*]

sending out parties to capture new recruits would be quite belated if Stabrobates suspected an imminent attack. The truth is that elephants eat far too much to leave standing around in an army camp: they are set free in the jungle to forage until needed. So the mahouts were simply going out into the forest and bringing back the already trained beasts in expectation of the coming war.

The queen recognized that the force of elephants would pose a major problem for her army. The simplest solution would be for the Assyrians to collect elephants of their own to counter the enemy. Unfortunately, all of the elephants from Iran to Syria had been slaughtered for ivory and sport over the previous centuries! A completely different plan would be needed to deal with the Indian beasts.

Semiramis delayed the attack on India for two full years, while crafts-men, tailors, and soldiers labored feverishly to prepare the queen's anti-elephant weapons. The army assembled and marched eastward, probably along the same route through modern-day Afghanistan that Alexander the Great would follow four centuries later.

News of the invasion force came to King Stabrobates, who called up his army and took up a strong position to await the intruders. We are told that he was supremely confident that his thousands of ele-phants would overrun the enemy. The arrival of the Assyrian force did not worry the Indian king, although the sight of thousands of camels surprised him. Camels had never been a particularly menacing weapon of war, and Stabrobates must have wondered what purpose they would serve.

Late into the night, while the Indians slept, the queen ordered her secret weapons to be made ready. The camels bellowed noisily at first, but were soon quieted. Semiramis believed wholeheartedly in her plan, but many of her soldiers did not. Fearing the morning, when they would struggle in close quarters with the giant elephants of India, some soldiers fled into the night. Knowing they would be killed for desertion if captured by their Assyrian leaders, many surrendered themselves to the Indian sentries, hoping for mercy on their defections.

The high-ranking defectors offered information about the empress' secret strategy in exchange for their lives, but the Indian generals found the defectors' stories to be simply unbelievable, not worthy of waking the king. As morning approached, the elephant riders brought grass, sugar-cane, and wine to their nervous elephants. The smell and noise from the enemy camels disturbed them because it was unfamiliar.

As the sun began to lighten the sky, Indian scouts sprinted to the command tent, where the generals gathered with the king. Perhaps in disbelief, the high-ranking entourage found an overlook point to see the enemy positions.

The Westerners had thousands of elephants, with a rider on each one!

King Stabrobates was astounded and speechless. One of the Assyrian defectors was dragged before the king and ordered to tell the king his story. The soldier must have said something like this:

Two years ago, the queen ordered that every dark-haired ox found in the empire be butchered and the hide sent to Babylon. We collected tens of thousands of ox hides. These were sewn together in the shape of elephants. Craftsmen built wooden platforms to set on the backs of camels. We trained the camels to carry the platform and later added the elephant costumes over the frames. One man walks in front of the camel under the costume and swings the trunk. He also gives food and water to the camel while she walks. This practice took one year. Then we spent one year training our horses not to fear the camel weapons.

Now the Assyrian army began to form into ranks in the distance, and the Indian king could hear the sound of consternation and confusion in his own army. Stabrobates ordered his leaders to inform the army that the Assyrian elephants were only a trick: camels under gray cloth. He instructed the cavalry to immediately charge at the enemy elephant puppets and destroy a few to show the army that they were harmless toys. It was too late to rearrange the Indian formations, and the morale of his army was already on the decline.

Semiramis ordered the Assyrian army to march straight ahead toward the enemy. Delay would only give the Indians more time to discover her deception. She stationed thousands of the camel-driven devices on both the right and the left wings of her formation with her cavalry behind. When the Indian cavalry ran from the puppets, her own cavalry would come around behind the enemy infantry.

As the Assyrians approached, the commanders of the Indian cavalry prepared to charge, to follow the king's orders, but they could not. Their horses were terrified by the smells and sounds coming from the elephant-shaped camel puppets. Seeing that a charge was impossible, the leaders ordered a slow reverse, not a panicked retreat.

King Stabrobates was now running out of options. If he did not do something quickly, he would lose all cavalry support on the wings. Using flags and horns, the king's new orders were sent to the elephant riders: attack the enemy contraptions!

The Indian elephants rumbled forward and diagonally to meet the unusual threat. The real pachyderms were somewhat reticent at first because of the novelty of the enemy both in shape and in smell. The strategy of using strange figures (dummies and so on) against elephants is successful because elephants are frightened by almost anything that is new and unknown.[6] But the Indian mahouts were confident, and the behemoths below trusted their human friends, so they shook off their hesitation and plowed into the puppets.

The elephants wrapped their trunks around the fake noses and tore them off. They bashed the wooden platforms, which toppled from the fleeing camels' backs. Like a wave of gray pebbles rolling in the tide, the camel squadrons pivoted and sped away, leaving their hideous costumes behind. The success of the elephants restored the morale of the Indian infantry and cavalry, which now attacked en masse.

As Diodorus tells us,

...the army of Semiramis withstood the onslaught of these monsters for only a short time; for these animals are of incredible ferocity, and relying on their inherent physical strength they easily slaughtered everyone who opposed them. A prodigious killing then took place, and death took many forms, as some fell beneath their feet and others were torn apart by their tusks, while yet others were tossed about by their trunks. Multitudes of corpses soon lay about in heaps.[7]

Stabrobates gained the victory, driving Assyria completely out of India and Pakistan. Queen Semiramis went back to Babylon and did not reign for very long after this defeat.

The empress' plan, while seemingly ridiculous from the outset, was a clever and nearly successful stratagem. Facing an enemy that possessed weapons that Assyria could not counteract using natural means, she used artificial means. She astutely recognized that the effectiveness of ele-phants showed itself best against enemy horses and, further, she trained her own horses not to fear them. A military unit composed of horses and elephants working cooperatively would be very powerful, although in this instance, it was horses working with costumed camel puppets.

This would not be the only time in history that puppets were used to imitate elephants or to frighten elephants, but it was the earliest and grandest attempt.

4
Fill of Blood

The Bible book of Daniel describes the Babylonian empire under Nebuchadnezzar and his sons, and the fall of Babylon to Cyrus the Great of Persia. Cyrus left trusted advisors in charge of his conquests (like the city of Babylon) but wished to continue expanding his territories. Several ancient chroniclers detail the story of Cyrus' demise, although there are minor differences in the tales. Some modern scholars are skeptical of the accounts of Ctesias and Herodotus because they include elephants in the enemy army.

The identity of Cyrus' foe is the major difficulty because every ancient source seems to have a different name for the tribe. Whether they are called the Massagetae, Derbices, Dahae, or Sarmatians, this tribe controlled territory north of India.[1] Since specifics are helpful to the reader, the Massagatae of Herodotus will be the designation for the remainder of this chapter.

The Persians loved both art and money, and the ivory trade was quite lucrative in Babylon.[2] Importing African elephant tusks from Ethiopia cost a fortune, and if the Persians took control of the Indus valley, the cost of ivory would certainly decrease. However, Cyrus and his men may not have really known what elephants looked like, nor that India used them as weapons. The tuskers of India, in fighting Cyrus, may have unwittingly been protecting their own ivory!

It seems that Cyrus initially sought to make an alliance with the Massagatae, as he asked their Queen Tomyris to marry him. Presumably this wedding would give the Persians control of the important road to India, but the royal lady spurned the great king. Allies from India sent troops and a number of elephants to oppose the Persians and to support Tomyris.[3]

Resorting now to treachery, in 529 BC, Cyrus invited the Massagatae to a feast, perhaps pretending that he still hoped to win Tomyris over to his proposal. She did not attend, but sent her oldest son to hear the Persian offer. The Persians either ambushed the Massagatae delegation or got them drunk and held them prisoner. Rather than be held as hostage, the prince stabbed himself and died. When Queen Tomyris received the bloody body of her son, she sent a message to Cyrus that since he loved blood so much, she would see that he would drink his fill of blood.[4]

As the Persian forces crossed a river with King Cyrus and his cavalry in the front, the Massagatae attacked. The Asian elephants terrified the Persian cavalry, and the horse of Cyrus reared up and threw him. Here Cyrus received a deadly wound, but the accounts vary.[5] The Persian version says that the king was carried from the battlefield but his men won the victory and then Cyrus died of his wounds. Other sources say that Cyrus perished immediately after falling from his horse and that Queen Tomyris took his head and dipped it in gore, saying "I give thee thy fill of blood."[6]

Cyrus was buried in Persia, so some historians doubt the veracity of the head-hacking accounts. However, Queen Tomyris may have left the body behind once handling the skull of her enemy sated her vengeance.

In later centuries, the Persians held an extremely negative view of elephants, and their religious Zoroastrian traditions viewed them as demons![7] Perhaps episodes like the death of Cyrus helped shape those early attitudes.

As for the fear of horses in the presence of elephants, at least in the case of war elephants, this apprehension is justified. Elephants do in fact have the strength to knock a horse over with its trunk or tusks. One pachyderm escaped from a traveling circus in the United States in the nineteenth century and went on a rampage, overturning wagons and killing horses. One witness said that the behemoth "shook and tossed [his] horse on its tusks just as a terrier shakes and tosses a rat."[8]

The son of Cyrus, named Cambyses, may have given up on conquering India but continued to seek nations with ivory. He took a large army south and west, and conquered Egypt. However, the adventures of Cambyses in southern Egypt and Nubia ended in defeat. The Nubian failure "unhinged his mind" and he killed himself.[9]

Only a few years later, in about 520 BC, King Darius fought against an army with war elephants, and purportedly saddled his own camels with bushels of flammables on their backs and sides to scare the elephants away.[10] This may not have been a success, as Persia continued to import its ivory from Cush (Libya) rather than the east.[11]

Persistence eventually paid off. The Persian empire annexed the regions of Afghanistan and northwestern India in about 500 BC under a general/admiral named Skylax.[12] The fertility of the soil and abundance of wildlife brought great wealth to the Persians for nearly two hundred years.

5
Improvements

Although the Shang Dynasty of China utilized war elephants before 1000 BC, this knowledge was localized. One good example comes from the land of Ch'u, which is geographically within China's modern borders, but at the time was inhabited by an ethnically non-Chinese people.

The neighboring Wu army assaulted Ch'u with great success in 506 BC and surrounded the fortified city in siege. The Ch'u owned hundreds of trained elephants, for riding and hauling, but had never attempted to use them in combat. In desperation to break the siege, the Ch'u attached lighted torches to the tails of many elephants, which in panic charged out of the gate and through the enemy blockade.[1] The plan did cause some consternation and confusion, but did not break the siege. Some two thousand years later, the same stratagem did work, killing over a thousand of the besiegers, but the attackers used several hundred elephants.[2]

The use of elephants for war in China faded rapidly because of population growth and its accompanying destruction of the forests. As the elephant populations moved south, the Chinese could not gather enough pachyderms to make them a useful part of their combat schemes.[3] By 300 BC, elephants were rarely found in China.[4]

India, however, had a massive supply of elephants. Greek historians cited the rich soil of India for providing plants in "unsparing profusion" as the reason that Asian elephants were larger and stronger than African pachyderms.[5] With a plentiful supply of pachyderms, India would always remain the world's central hub for producing war elephants.

According to early Buddhist texts, King Bimbisara of Magadha (558–491 BC) possessed a well-trained elephant corps bearing leather armor and wearing metal spikes on their tusks.[6]

The technology and organization of elephant warriors continued to grow in Asia. Plate metal, like that of medieval knights, was prohibitively expensive (to cover an elephant) and had numerous other disadvantages.[7] Metal is heavy, hinders normal movements, and traps in heat. The poor pachyderms overheat under metal! Thus, only the forehead and

Generals discovered that they could see the battlefield and command their troops more effectively from elephant-back. *[Photo by the author]*

upper trunk commonly held iron plates. However, by combining the sciences of textile and metallurgy, an excellent composite armor was invented. By taking heavy cloth and sewing pieces of metal into it, quilted armor appeared on the battlefield. It contained the flexible and relatively well-ventilated qualities of cloth with the solid properties of metal. It proved to be a good compromise between foolproof protection and practical needs.

Mahouts also improved their own protection. The mahout sat on the elephant's neck but now carried a small shield in his left hand, and could reach for the quiver of javelins near his right hand to hurl at the foes on the ground. His bronze helmet had a brim in the back to guard against sunburn and a cloth wrapped around the helmet reduced heat. Because mahouts had quickly become "hot shots" like modern fighter pilots, they were seen as high-class warriors. This meant they could wear bright colors and dye their beards brightly![8] The mahout used his feet and an ankhus to direct the elephant, as his voice might not be heard in the din of combat. He kicks or taps with his feet under the elephant's ear to give basic orders, such as turn right or stop.

The primary tool used by the elephant rider is known by many names, but chiefly as the ankhus, which looks something like a sharp hook on a pole. While riding, the mahout carries the short ankh, perhaps fourteen inches long, while from the ground he would hold a hook on a pole five feet in length.[9] The hook is quite sharp, but it is mainly used for emergencies, e.g., if the elephant becomes angry and threatening to the rider or other people. In noisy combat, the hook could also signal commands when the mahout's voice could not be heard. It would be foolish for a mahout to often use the hook to hurt the elephant, because eventually the elephant would find a way to hurt his tormentor![10] During my weeks with the elephants and mahouts at the Thailand Elephant Conservation Center, the hooks were only used to scrape mud off the elephants' backs before their morning baths.

One clever army commander must have realized that if the "draught" elephants carrying supplies could carry an oozie plus five hundred pounds on their backs, a combat elephant could carry more than one rider on its back. What else would you want to put on an elephant? What does the army always want? More firepower! That meant more men.

By the sixth century BC, four men were riding on the elephant, with others below guarding the beast's feet.[11] On the elephant's back was a wicker or wooden box, open at the top, secured to the elephant's body with a girth around its belly, and ropes around its neck and legs. Three riders could hurl javelins or shoot arrows at the foe, seated or crouching in a tower, using its walls for protection.[12]

The old flag system of communication between the leaders and the army improved by getting elephants into the act. The signal flags could be seen more easily by the allies if they waved from the tall back of an elephant. Furthermore, by adding the element of sound, the flagmen could get more attention. During the battle, the soldiers might be too occupied with combat to continuously look back to see what the flags might say. To reduce the distraction of frequent looking back for orders, one in ten elephants became a signal elephant. Behind the mahout, the signal elephant carried a pair of large drums on his sides and a small platform or tower with the signalman and his flags.[13] By beating the drums, the signalman announced that the soldiers and mahouts should look back at the flags for new orders.

While technology and planning made elephants into better warriors in the east, the rest of the world had only myths and legends to remind them of elephants.

Europe had largely forgotten elephants because they were long absent. Driven to extinction by over-hunting and climate change, only rumors from the east kept the idea of pachyderms alive in Greece.

An ancient myth, that Dionysus led war elephants to fight the Amazons, explained how elephant bones jutted from the ground on the Isle of Samos (although in fact these were mastodon fossils).[14] Because these fossil beds lay in earthquake-prone terrain, the legend of the Neades grew: giant noisy elephants caused the earth to open and devour them.[15] Pliny took a somewhat more reasonable view, although still incorrect, that elephants bury their tusks to hide them because so many tusks were found under the ground.

The legends and tall tales just mentioned were based on the correct identification of the bones as belonging to elephants (or their ancestors). Of course, many people would not know an elephant bone from a cow bone! One theory says that the myth of the gigantic one-eyed Cyclops originated from an elephant skull, which has a large central sinus cavity in the forehead and no obvious eye sockets.[16] Reconstructing a skeleton without the advantage of seeing a live specimen led the early fossil hunters to stand the mastodon bones upright, forming a gigantic biped!

6
The Elephant Mystery

The Persian empire ruled from Anatolia (Turkey) and Egypt in the west all the way to northern India in the east under the watchful eyes of "the Great King." Persian armies repeatedly ravaged Greece, but the rebellious Europeans could not be subdued.

King Philip of Macedon spent decades upgrading his armored infantry (*hoplites*) to strike back. When Philip died at the hand of an assassin in 337 BC, his impetuous twenty-year-old son, Alexander, decided to conquer the world.

Thirsty for revenge and glory, Alexander led his troops into Persian territory in 334 BC. The Greeks used a *phalanx*, a rectangular formation of hoplites marching in lock-step together, carrying 16-foot-long *sarissae* spears, which proved impenetrable to the enemy.[1] The Macedonians swept aside the Persian defense forces of Anatolia, and then dismembered the vast army of Darius III at Issus. Rather than pursue the Great King, Alexander moved south to subdue the enemy's naval bases and gain control of Egypt's riches.

Darius fled to his Iranian capitol and summoned warriors from the loyal *satraps* of his eastern kingdoms. Amid the myriad soldiers and horses that journeyed toward Babylon over the next year, a squadron of fifteen Indian elephants traversed the mountains of Afghanistan to defend the empire. Sambus, a Persian "agent" in the India province, may have encouraged the local rulers to send the elephants to the Great King.[2]

The arrival of pachyderms initially alarmed the Persians, whose Zoroastrian scriptures called them "creatures of Ahriman...," basically demons.[3] However, Iranian generals recognized that, demons or no, Ahriman's brutes could be useful against the Greeks. With Alexander finishing his diversion in Egypt, the elephant force could not be incorporated into the Persian cavalry. Horses despise elephants, and need many months to grow accustomed to the giants.[4] The commanders suggested to Darius that the behemoths might punch holes in the mighty Macedonian

25

phalanxes. Perhaps unspoken, they also hoped that putting elephants in the front and center would keep the Greek cavalry from charging at the panicky Darius, whose flight at Issus prevented an orderly retreat.

Avoiding one of his mistakes at Issus, Darius chose a wide flatland for the battle, with plenty of room for forty thousand Persian cavalry and four hundred thousand foot soldiers to surround Alexander's meager seven thousand horsemen and forty thousand infantry.[5] The contest between east and west would be decided on the plain of Gaugamela, also called Arbela.

The plan of battle for Darius placed the fifteen elephants in the front line, with one hundred scythed chariots on each side of them. Scythed chariots used sharp blades (projecting from the sides of the cart) to cut their enemies apart, while archers and javelin hurlers in the cart fired arrows and spears. The elephants would each run between the two wings of chariots. For weeks, Iranian engineers flattened every bump and rise on the field to ensure that the spinning scythes on the chariot wheels would not break off or become stuck in the dirt.[6] One might suppose that the lumbering behemoths would fall behind the horse-drawn chariots during this charge, but over short distances an elephant can sprint at fifteen miles per hour! Because they would run at the enemy, the elephants did not carry towers or howdahs on their backs. It would be an unnecessary hindrance. The men in a tower could not throw weapons with any accuracy during the charge. Instead, these soldiers would sit directly on the pachyderm's back, tuck their legs under a strap or rope around its waist, and hang on for dear life. Once the elephant broke through the enemy phalanx they could hurl their weapons at the foe, replenishing their javelins from quivers of ammunition hanging from the elephant's sides.

On the last morning of September, 331 BC, scouts informed the Great King that the Greek army approached. Alexander always took the initiative by attacking first, before his enemies were fully prepared. Remembering Alexander's penchant for swift attack, Darius moved the enormous battle lines into position. As was their custom, the Indian mahouts gave each elephant a significant drink of wine to stimulate them before battle.[7]

Darius may well have been correct that the Greeks would begin the assault immediately. However, that did not happen. Macedonian scouts saw something that worried them, and when Alexander heard their reports, he did something completely unexpected.

He hesitated.

Never a cautious man, the pause of Alexander deserves discussion. The vast numerical superiority of the Persian army cannot have been his concern, since he had faced a similar situation at Issus and took no pause. One intriguing speculation is that the scouts had seen the discoloration of the ground where Persian engineers had flattened the ground and supposed that spikes or pits might be hidden to hinder the Macedonian charge.[8] However, Alexander and his captains would recognize that traps would harm the Persians more than the Greeks. Scythed chariots are useful only when moving at high speed, which meant that the Persians intended to charge. Spikes and pits would hinder the horses and chariots, ruining their rapid attack.

The only new element seen by Alexander's reconnaissance on the field at Gaugamela was the squad of Ahrimans's devils: elephants in the front line.

As a boy, Alexander studied under Aristotle, the pupil of Plato. Aristotle wrote *Historia Animalium*, and from this work Alexander may have read some lore of the Indian elephant. Even Aristotle's knowledge of elephants was very sparse, however. The young conqueror would not have learned much more than this from *The History of Animals*:

Elephants fight fiercely with one another, and stab one another with their tusks... Indians employ these animals for war purposes, irrespective of sex; the females, however, are less in size and much inferior in point of spirit. An elephant, by pushing with his big tusks, can batter down a wall, and will butt with his forehead at a palm [tree] until he brings it down...[9]

Alexander had no experience with elephants and therefore had no idea what threat they might pose to his cavalry or infantry. Darius was now safely ensconced behind a line of behemoths, ruining the tried-and-true assault on the center. In the distance, Alexander could see their gleaming tusks: they wore bladed spikes on their ivory to repel enemies and reduce tusk damage.[10] Alexander sent the army into camp and spent hours revamping his strategy.

That morning, the Persians were excited about the coming conflict, but their energy faded as they stood for hours in the sun. The region of Iraq is extremely hot from April through October, with practically no precipitation. This long day was simply hellish for the Indian elephants, which were wearing fire-hardened leather or quilted armor, and perhaps iron head/trunk caps.[11] The mahouts and servants brought buckets of water for the elephants to drink and to splash on themselves all afternoon.

To protect the elephant's vulnerable legs from enemy axes, guards marched alongside. [Photo by the author]

The unexpected delay puzzled the Great King. Darius concluded that Alexander spent the day resting his army as a prelude to a surprise night attack. An assault under cover of darkness was a common way for a smaller army to defeat a larger force, and at least one Greek general was recommending exactly that.[12] Alexander refused, saying he would not "steal a victory."

Alexander and the Macedonians took the field on the morning of October 1, 331 BC, while their foes, both human and animal, stood exhausted. Darius had kept them awake and in formation all night long, fearing a sneak attack.[13]

Alexander used an unusual oblique front: his troops marched in a diamond formation and diagonally *away* from the enemy center where the elephants would charge. As they drew near the Persian forces, Alexander found that the elephants were gone!

Alexander was not the only one surprised by the absence of the elephants. Historians have been puzzling over it for thousands of years. Why do ancient writers tell us that at Gaugamela the Persians had fifteen elephants in the front line, but then tell us that the beasts were all captured in the Persian camp, far from the battle?

Some theorize that at the beginning of combat, when the scythed chariots rushed ahead, the elephants panicked and ran back to the baggage train. Certainly not! Armies of India used chariots more often and in greater numbers than the Persians. The Persian chariot horses were more likely to run from the elephants than the elephants were to run from the chariots![14]

The dark night of September 30 dealt the logistical blow to Darius' elephant scheme. Fatigue, among both the horses and elephants, led to the pachyderm retreat in the darkness.

Elephants are acutely habituated to routines. When their normal activities are changed, they become confused or belligerent. Even the skills of the mahouts were rendered useless by the long hours broiling in the sun. Although elephants can sleep in a standing position, they cannot stand all day in the hot sun, then all night, and then again the next day, particularly in armor. They also may have been drunk: it was a common Indian tradition to "excite" the beasts before battle with rice wine.[15] In the line they were unable to "comfort and allay each other's anxiety under stressful and traumatic conditions by various sounds and by placing their trunk into each other's mouth."[16] So, separated from their companions, forced from their routines, and intoxicated with wine, Ahriman's creatures became quite ill-tempered. On the eve of battle, when darkness settled, the elephant squadron was probably in a state of chaos.

The elephants were not the only cranky creatures at Gaugamela. Surely the chariot horses were tired of being harnessed to their chariot bars, especially with pachyderms standing nearby. Darius had little time to prepare the chariot horses and elephants for this formation. Even if the species had learned tolerance during training, who could predict that they might have to stand together in the darkness? It is one thing for the horses to tolerate the pachyderms in daylight, when the behemoths could be cautiously watched. It is quite another thing to expect the horses to stand all day and night, exhausted, with recently acquired huge monsters grunting, munching, and defecating in close proximity, unseen in the dark!

Forced to remain in formation by the Great King, the elephants at Gaugamela became increasingly noisy throughout the night. As the elephants became loud, the horses were spooked, and the front line was in danger of collapse. Darius was forced to send the pachyderms away during the early morning hours of October 1.

We will never know whether the elephants might have turned the battle for Persia. Alexander's tactics ruined the chariot charge. He drove a wedge of heavy cavalry through the Persian center, where the elephants should have been, to attack the Great King. When Darius fled, his immense army disintegrated.

Where were the fierce, or perhaps drunken, pachyderms? General Parmenio, a Macedonian commander, captured them in the baggage train, with the camels.[17] Any shame felt by the mahouts for ejection from the Persian front must have been short-lived. After all, they survived the conflict without injury and were offered a place in the Greek army.

Alexander examined the captured elephants and interviewed their mahouts. A nearby city, hearing of Darius' defeat, immediately sent twelve more elephants as a gift to Alexander; these apparently belonged to the Great King but may have been part of a local zoo and were not trained for combat.[18] Perhaps the conqueror even sent a pachyderm home to Aristotle.

The first encounter between the hoplites of the west and the terrible beasts of the east ended not with a bang, but a whimper.

The horror would come, and it would be vicious.

7
The Horror

After conquering Persia's armies, Alexander spent years chasing the elusive Darius III and appointing bureaucrats to administer the new empire. We are not told what became of all fifteen elephants from Gaugamela, nor the twelve surrendered by a nearby Iraqi city. There is a story told by the ancient historian Pliny that tells the sad fate of one:

When Alexander the Great was on his way to India, the king of Albania had presented him with one dog of unusually large size…[Alexander] ordered an elephant to be brought in, and no other show ever gave him more delight: for the dog's hair bristled all over his body and it first gave a vast thunderous bark, then kept leaping up and rearing against the creature's limbs on this side and that, in scientific combat, attacking and retiring at the most necessary points, until the elephant turning round and round in an unceasing whirl was brought to the ground with an earth-shaking crash.[1]

Alexander and his associates enjoyed the same style of entertainment that would enthrall the Romans in future spectacles.

Still hungry for glory, Alexander mobilized his army for a march to India in the spring of 327 BC.[2] The Macedonians pushed across northern Iran and then south through Afghanistan and Pakistan. As Alexander approached India, King Omphis surrendered his city, Taxila, near modern Islamabad.[3] Elephants were still a native species in this fertile region between the Indus and the Hydaspes Rivers.

When the Greek army arrived at the Hydaspes River of India in May or June of 326 BC, a tall king named Porus was waiting with his army. Porus offered to pay the Macedonians to leave his land unharmed. Alexander did not want money, but conquest, and refused.

Although the armies of Porus and Alexander were similar in number, Porus had two hundred colorful pachyderms lined up along the river's edge. Before weddings and wars, Indian mahouts paint bright colors and geometric shapes on the elephant's head and trunk. By grinding mineral

King Porus of India opposing the forces of Alexander in northern India. The Macedonian cavalry would not approach the elephants, making this scene unlikely. [*John Frost. Pictorial Ancient History of the World. Philadelphia, Walker & Gillis, 1846. Page 233.*]

crystals and mixing the powder with vegetable dyes, the colors remain visible for weeks.[4]

Porus' army remained on the riverbank to prevent Alexander's forces from crossing the Hydaspes. Alexander, looking across the river at the line of elephants, recognized that his nervous cavalry could not launch a frontal assault on Porus' army. Carrying the horses across a swollen river on rafts would be difficult enough, but the horses would panic when they found their path barred by pachyderms and archers. Alexander was so dazzled by this new challenge that a companion heard him say, "I see at last a danger that matches my courage. It is at once with wild beasts and men of uncommon mettle that the contest now lies."[5]

Porus sent requests to his allies for reinforcements. In a short time he would have more troops and elephants ready to oppose the invaders. Furthermore, when the heavy monsoon rains arrived in July, the enemy would be unable to ford the Hydaspes even if they obtained boats.

Alexander had his carpenters build boats sixteen miles to the east of his army. During a reconnaissance he noted that this spot in the river was shallow and that the thick tree cover would hide the carpenters' work from enemy scouts. Alexander could not wait long to attack, as he learned about the approach of reinforcements for Porus.

One dark night the sky crashed with lightning and monsoon rains. Although this rain caused the river to rise, Alexander took advantage of the thunderous noise to screen the sound of fifteen thousand troops moving to the east. He took five thousand cavalry and ten thousand infantry. The rest of the army (including his elephants) stayed behind with General Craterus, in camp. The young conqueror even left an imposter in his armor so that enemy scouts would see Alexander in his normal routines the following morning!

The monsoon rains had begun. The Hydaspes, while not yet at its peak, moved violently. The Greeks arrived at the crossing point well after midnight. In the darkness the rafts and boats carried the army across, but lightning struck and killed several men.[6] The nasty weather slowed their progress, and Alexander's men reached their destination at sunrise, where they were spotted by Porus' scouts.

The scouts rushed to the Indian camp to inform Porus, but neglected to determine the size of the amphibious force in the east. Porus had no idea how large this opponent might be, although the scouts claimed Alexander led the cavalry. This river crossing in the darkness, under cover of a thunderstorm, showed the ingenuity of Alexander. Porus knew that Alexander's maneuver would be difficult to counter. If the Indian army moved to intercept Alexander's advance, the infantry of General Craterus would cross the Hydaspes to flank them. However, if Porus stayed in position at the river, Alexander's cavalry would flank them. Either way, the Indians had been outmaneuvered.

Porus, hoping that the enemy assault force was only a small cavalry contingent, sent out his son with two thousand cavalry and 120 war chariots to delay or repel Alexander's advance.[7] Porus stayed to ascertain the number of forces remaining across the river from him.

Porus' son arrived to repel the Greeks while some were still slogging across the river. The Indians gained the initial advantage, and Alexander's beloved old horse, Bucephalus, was fatally wounded. Nevertheless, the Indian momentum failed when the muddy ground hindered the chariots.[8]

Macedonian archers killed the chariot drivers and then the cavalry routed the Indians. Porus' son died.

Survivors of the doomed mission returned and reported the losses to Porus. He had to put aside his grief for his fallen son to save his country. Recognizing that Alexander had crossed with a large force, the Indian king divided his army, taking more than two-thirds to stop Alexander and leaving less than one-third to keep Craterus' soldiers from crossing the river. The majority of war elephants, cavalry, and infantry left the riverbank and headed east.

About five miles to the east, Porus found some wide, level ground where the cavalry and elephants could fight easily in the open. They formed their battle line. We do not know if the sun broke through the clouds, but the air was steamy after the night's rains. The ground was slippery with mud, affecting both footing and visibility for the troops. Muddy ground would be an advantage to Porus' light infantry, and an Indian writer of the time said that "muddy ground is the ideal environment for war elephants."[9]

Alexander kept his cavalry hidden in the jungle while he let the infantry catch up and rest. They had, after all, marched sixteen miles during the night and then ten more miles that morning.

The Indian line stretched at least two miles from north to south, with cavalry at each side, and infantry and elephants mixed in the center. MacMunn describes the appearance of an Indian army formation:

Masses of spearmen and archers, gaudy colours, plenty of banners as each chieftain led forward his henchmen—the great elephant tanks in the intervals, the whippets of the chariots waiting to gallop forward en masse—plenty of color, steel helmets, bright scarves and baldricks, axe and lance and mace.[10]

Porus stood with twenty-five thousand troops, while Alexander commanded about fifteen thousand. The war elephants waited at intervals of fifty feet, with ground troops between and behind them to protect their vulnerable flanks. Perhaps 10 percent of the elephants carried drums and flags, which their riders used to pass orders from King Porus to his army.[11]

All of the elephants wore fire-hardened leather and quilted armor for protection. Their foreheads and trunks bore iron plate to block against enemy arrows.

Most of the elephants carried wooden towers with a trio of archers or javelin hurlers. King Porus rode an elephant, but did not use a howdah. He wore a remarkable suit of armor and did not need the extra protection of a tower. Arrian implies that elephants with wooden howdahs were placed at the wings because Alexander had more than one thousand horse-mounted archers. Porus wanted his archers in the elephant towers to keep the Greek horse archers from threatening the flanks.

Alexander spent hours devising a plan while his men rested. If his horses would not confront the elephants, what good would his five thousand cavalry be? Alexander wanted to surround and harass the enemy with his horses, but with the enemy line so wide and with Indian cavalry protecting the wings, how could he do this? With guile.

The Greeks marched out of the jungle with "all" the cavalry on one side and infantry on the other. This meant that all of the cavalry on one of Porus' wings would have no role in the battle, so the Indian drums and flags instructed them to all line up in one spot against Alexander's horses. Now, seeing that his cavalry greatly outnumbered the Greeks, Porus ordered a charge.

However, this was not all of Alexander's cavalry. Coenus' division remained hidden in the forest.[12] Once the cavalry forces engaged, Coenus' group rode out and attacked the Indians from the side. Surprised and outmaneuvered, the Indian horses fled into the line of infantry and elephants. Porus' horses were accustomed to elephants, and thus they could mingle. However, the addition of thousands of horses into the formation of infantry and elephants brought chaos to the Indian line.

Seeing the confusion, Porus ordered the elephants to advance, to drive away the Greek horses. With Porus' flanks now unsupported by cavalry, Alexander led his horsemen to attack from the sides, leaving the infantry to face the elephants.

The foot soldiers of Macedon became the first warriors from Europe to face war elephants in combat. The struggle was brutal.

The elephants stormed deep into the Macedonian formations, causing great destruction, but the farther the elephants moved into the enemy, the farther they were from support troops who protected their legs. The historian Curtius, who studied eyewitness accounts, wrote:

...the elephants, applying to good use their prodigious size and strength, killed some of the enemy by trampling them under their feet, and crushing their armour and their bones, while upon others they inflicted a terrible death, for they first lifted them aloft with their trunks, which they had twined around their bodies, and then dashed them down with great violence to the ground. Many others they deprived in a moment of life by goring them through and through with their tusks.[13]

A more common means of death by elephant has been observed even in modern times, especially in circus or zoo elephants "gone mad." The beast grasps a man with his trunk, forces him to the ground, and then kneels down and crushes the man under its head. One fanciful account claims that Alexander brought up super-heated statues of men so that the elephants grabbed the hot bronzes, were badly burned, and then refused to grab any soldiers![14] Neither elephants nor their mahouts would mistake a statue for a real man.

The violence done to the elephants by the Macedonian soldiers was equally horrific. Alexander ordered the light infantry to aim their javelins at the mahouts and the elephants' eyes.[15] With a range of only twenty yards, the soldiers had to approach the enemy to toss their weapons. Once blinded or leaderless, the elephants would be easier targets for the armored infantry.

The heavy infantry carried two-sided axes and scimitars to hamstring the elephants.[16] While one group of soldiers distracted the elephant and mahout by chopping at the pachyderm's trunk, other men rushed to the unfortunate creature's sides to hack between its front and back legs, cutting its tendons and crippling it.

As the Greek cavalry surrounded the enemy and Craterus crossed the river with his half of Alexander's army, the Indian forces became more and more compacted until they could hardly fight. To quote from Arrian's "Anabasis of Alexander,"

The elephants were now crowded into a narrow space, and their own sides were as much damaged by them as the enemy, and trodden down in their turnings and jostlings...most of the drivers of the elephants had been shot down, some of the elephants had been wounded, others were weary and had lost their drivers, they no longer kept their separate formation in the battle but, as if maddened by suffering, attacked friends and foes alike and in all sorts of ways kept pushing trampling, and destroying...As the beasts wearied and no longer made vigorous charges, but merely trumpeted and gradually retired like ships backing water...[17]

King Porus fought so bravely that Alexander admired him and wished to save his life. Porus repeatedly led charges from his elephant to drive back the enemy, receiving many wounds from arrows and javelins, despite his armor. The elephant of Porus fought bravely as well. Plutarch, an ancient biographer, wrote that Porus' elephant

during the whole battle, gave many singular proofs of sagacity and of particular care for the king, whom as long as he was strong and in a condition to fight, he defended with great courage, repelling those who set upon him; and as soon as he perceived him overpowered with his numerous wounds and the multitude of darts that were thrown at him, to prevent his falling off, he softly knelt down and began to draw out the darts with his probiscis.[18]

Such stories are not preposterous. Elephants do form intimate bonds with their human riders and have been known to protect their human friends, and may even die of grief when their partner is lost. Megasthenes, a contemporary of Alexander, attests to both.[19]

His army surrounded, and himself suffering from wounds, Porus surrendered. When Alexander asked him how he should be treated, Porus replied, "as a king." Alexander made him regent of the land, and Porus remained loyal until his death. The victor also honored the king's elephant, naming him Ajax.

Of Porus' two hundred elephants, eighty died in battle. The rest were captured. Many more probably died of wounds or had to be "put down." The Indian army did pay professional horse and elephant veterinarians to treat nonfatal wounds and they certainly saved many wounded animals.

Hundreds of years after the Battle of Hydaspes, a Greek named Apollonia visited Taxila in northwest India. He saw an old elephant bearing gold rings on his tusks with the inscription "Alexander, the son of Zeus, dedicates Ajax to the Sun." The people were anointing the elephant with myrrh, draping garlands over its neck, and treating it like a god. They claimed that the aged elephant was Ajax who fought against Alexander and that he had been alive for more than four hundred years.[20]

Alexander did name Porus' elephant Ajax and created gold rings for his tusks, but the life span of an elephant cannot surpass one hundred years. Still, this beast of Taxila may have descended from that great Ajax of Hydaspes, and the honor of Alexander remained long with his kin.

8
Alexander's Opinion

The remarkable victories of Alexander deserve admiration, at least at the military level, whether we admire or vilify his character. His tactics, strategies, and opinions on military matters are worth consideration. If Alexander had something to say about elephants as warriors, we should listen.

According to Quintus Curtius, after the battle at the Hydaspes, Alexander said this:

I have always so little esteemed them, that when I have had plenty of them, I would never use them, knowing very well, that they are more dangerous to such as imploy them, then to their enemies.[1]

Many historians have seized upon this statement as evidence that the "best" generals, such as Alexander, viewed elephants as unpredictable and poor weapons. However, there are several problems with the famous statement. Curtius probably lived in the time of Emperor Claudius, almost four hundred years after Alexander had died. It would be odd if Curtius had discovered some quotations from Alexander that were not known earlier, from Ptolemy, for instance. H.H. Scullard calls the purported speech of Alexander "nonsense."[2] Also, this statement has been taken out of its obvious context and ignores Alexander's prior and subsequent efforts to obtain elephants for his army.

Pliny's account of Alexander's march toward India indicates that he had elephants in the army, as one fell victim to a large and clever hound for entertainment. When the troops left Babylon, he could include two dozen pachyderms in the column. During the journey Alexander made every effort to obtain more elephants. When he learned that the small city of Assacenia owned thirty pachyderms and set them out to graze every night, he paid local "elephant hunters" to capture the creatures. Two of the elephants panicked when the strangers tried to catch them, running over a cliff to their deaths, but the rest became part of the Greek column.

When we consider the nature of traveling elephants—their voracious appetite, enormous thirst, tendency to frighten allied cavalry horses, expensive armor, and the long-term commitment to their training and care—one must conclude that Alexander had big plans for them.[3] One does not simply "pick up" some elephants as if adopting pets. In fact, the origin of the modern phrase "white elephant" comes from Asia and refers to the actual gift of an elephant to a rival. In Nepal, they have an adage,

'To take revenge on an enemy, buy him an elephant.' At first the recipient of your gift will be humbled by your generosity. Then he will be made a pauper as the elephant eats him out of house and home.[4]

As Alexander crossed Pakistan, Omphis of Taxila surrendered and donated eighty-six elephants to the growing Macedonian army. Assuming that even 10 percent of his elephants died crossing the Hindu Kush, Alexander possessed as many as 130 elephants before the contest with Porus. This herd must have been enough, as he refused thirty elephants offered by a local tribe.

When Alexander reached the Hydaspes River where Porus opposed him, the Greeks had more than one hundred elephants and at least a handful of elephant handlers.[5] The obvious question is: why didn't Alexander use his elephants in this important battle?

Alexander's elephants were outnumbered by at least 35 percent, as Porus fielded two hundred. The twenty-eight pachyderms from Assacenia were captured in the field without their riders and armor, and thus would require new trainers and gear. We do not know whether the elephants given by Omphis came with mahouts and armor or if they were trained for war. Outnumbered, and perhaps less experienced, Alexander's elephant force was inferior to that of Porus, increasing the risks.

Second, we cannot be certain that his cavalry had been sufficiently trained to work with elephants. Although he possessed the captures from Gaugamela for a few years, he spent much of that time marching in Bactria in pursuit of Darius III and the elephants probably did not participate in that campaign.

The major reason why Alexander did not deploy his own elephant squadrons for the battle of the Hydaspes is much more mundane. He could not get them across the river.

Although the monsoon rains had not yet come, the Hydaspes was running swiftly. Even if Alexander had boats and rafts capable of carrying elephants across, to do so in the face of the enemy under a withering hail of arrows and javelins would be foolish. Also, the Greek night march under cover of a storm to reach their boats (sixteen miles distant) was supposed to be a surprise: they left an Alexander look-a-like in camp and fires burning so the Indians would not be suspicious. It is easy to imagine that the enemy scouts might notice the noisy departure of 130 elephants even under the flickering visuals of a lightning storm.

Alexander did not use elephants at the Hydaspes because it was logistically too difficult to get them across the river.

The assault against Porus' elephants traumatized the Macedonian infantry. As military historian W.W. Tarn wrote,

This was quite unlike Alexander's other battles; as untrained horses will not face elephants he was unable himself to help his army, beyond defeating Porus' cavalry and preventing them from interfering. In most of his battles he saved his men all he could by using his brains...but against the two hundred elephants of Porus he had no choice; all he could do was to put some of his best infantry in line and leave it to them. They did defeat the elephants, but it was evidently a fearful struggle. The men were never quite the same again...[6]

Alexander did not truly view the elephants as easily defeated. According to Lucian, immediately after the battle, a writer flattered the Macedonian king by inscribing for posterity that Alexander killed an elephant with a single javelin throw. Alexander threatened the writer for his stupidity and threw the document into the Hydaspes river.[7]

After the horrendous conflict, in which the Macedonian army suffered more casualties than all its previous fights, Greek spies reported that Porus was only a minor king with a small army. One of the major kings who waited ahead, Xandrames, was mobilizing four thousand elephants to oppose Alexander![8] As the bad news spread throughout his camp, Alexander sought to discredit the information, thinking it must be an exaggeration. He called in Porus and Omphis for second opinions. Far from negating these negative reports, the Indian allies confirmed that Xandrames could indeed field four thousand pachyderms.

To the Greek soldiers, who had narrowly defeated the two hundred behemoths of Porus, marching against four thousand was nothing short of suicide.[9] The men sent their officers to beg Alexander to take the army home, but he stubbornly insisted that he would vanquish all foes as far as the Great Sea.

After many years of loyal service, the army of Alexander mutinied. He begged, cajoled, and wept to change their minds. Is it any surprise then that Alexander would offer his "low opinion" of war elephants? It was one of many arguments he made to manipulate the army into continuing to advance, despite the enemy having thousands of elephants. Alexander fudged the truth, and his men could see the lie. He had been collecting elephants all along the trip to India. They just fought a horrific struggle with these supposedly worthless creatures! It might even be seen as an insult to those men who lost friends on the elephants' tusks at Hydaspes.

Perhaps arriving at a bad time, the reinforcements that Porus had called arrived and surrendered, offering Alexander seventy more elephants as a gift.[10] Unable to convince the men to battle their way across India, he agreed to return to Babylon.

In 325 BC, when Alexander the Great returned to Babylon from India, he surrounded himself with elephants. During the eastern campaigns, Alexander had acquired hundreds of pachyderms. The fearsome beasts encircled his pavilion headquarters in Babylon, "fully equipped."[11]

Not all two hundred war elephants stood together for guard duty, except in emergencies. The elephants would work in shifts throughout the daylight hours, possibly using canopies to shade them from the blazing Iraqi sun. The pavilion must have been surrounded with frightful sounds and smells. This may have been Alexander's goal—to cause fear in those who came to visit his golden throne. In India, elephants had been kept by kings for centuries, but in Iraq, these armored elephant sentries would be an impressive and new symbol of power.

Alexander appointed an "elephantarch" or "commander of the ele-phants."[12] Alexander officially incorporated the war elephants into the Macedonian army. The only factor in Alexander's nonuse of elephants was his premature death, not a general disdain for the beasts.

When Alexander died on June 13, 323 BC, elephants took part in his funeral procession.[13] Although horses drew the carriage holding his body, the carriage itself was painted with war elephants and Macedonian riders, showing that the Greeks were already preparing the beasts for war.

9
Death on the Nile

Alexander collected hundreds of elephants, set them around his palace in Babylon, and appointed a military commander to oversee their training.[1] He died before he could use them.

Elephants presented unusual problems for the army. Aside from the vast quantities of fodder required by a division of elephants, the beasts also produced a massive amount of biological waste. The elephants' primitive alimentary system digests less than half of the food eaten: the rest is deposited unceremoniously on the ground.

Recently, the frequency and amounts of urine and dung excreted by the average elephant were calculated. An elephant urinates every two hours, in the amount of five to ten liters each time. It defecates every one hundred minutes, five to seven boluses (lumps) each time, evacuating a total weight of approximately two hundred and fifty pounds per day.[2] If two hundred elephants maintained an adequate diet and normal rate of secretion, a full twenty-five tons of manure would have to be hauled away from Alexander's pavilion every day! Presumably, the pack animals assigned to elephant duty were laden with elephant food for the journey into Babylon and were burdened with elephant dung upon their departure. It may well have been sold as fertilizer.

When Alexander died in June of 323 BC, he left behind a bastard son, a retarded half-brother, and two pregnant wives, but no obvious heir.[3] This led his generals to fight a long civil war known as the "War of the Diadochi," or War of the Successors. The history of these wars becomes quite complex because of the numerous participants and their ever-changing alliances. The author will attempt to avoid less relevant details to focus mainly on the role of the elephants under each general. Trautmann declares that "the wars of the successors inaugurated what might be called the arms race of the fourth and third centuries, which was a struggle to acquire superior forces of elephants."[4]

Perdiccas had the early advantage because he was Alexander's second in command. Perdiccas expected the other generals to elect him as sole ruler. Instead, the generals argued that they should just divide up the world between them and not elect a leader.[5] Meanwhile, the Macedonian infantry surrounded the meeting hall, demanding that Alexander's retarded half-brother, Philip III, be named king. After accepting a compromise, Perdiccas set a trap: he surrounded the soldiers with cavalry and elephants and forced the surrender of the rebellious ring leaders. Between thirty and three hundred Macedonians (the sources vary) were trampled to death by the elephants on the spot.[6]

Without a real agreement, the generals carved up Alexander's empire. Each of the Diadochi ruled a different region (satrapy) of the conquered world from which to draw money and hire mercenaries.

One striking aspect of the wars of the Diadochi was the speedy incorporation of war elephants into combat formations. In India, the elephants of King Porus had nearly beaten the Macedonian army, leading to a mutiny in the proud Greek infantry. Having seen the impact of war elephants, the generals sought to develop elephant corps of their own.[7] Those who had fought against the Asian elephants alongside Alexander included Ptolemy, Perdiccas, Lysimachus, and Seleucus.[8] Three of these would become generals with war elephants in their armies. According to historian W.W. Tarn, "…the impression made on the generals…was that elephants were an arm to be obtained at any price, and after Alexander's death every one of the contending generals got all the elephants he could."[9]

Perdiccas, because he controlled Babylon and the elephants, took custody of both "kings," Philip III and Alexander's newly born son, Alexander IV.[10] Perdiccas still hoped to consolidate power and to rule the world, in time.

Ptolemy received the rich and easily defended satrapy of Egypt. His descendants would form a long-lasting dynasty to rule Egypt and, within decades, would begin capturing African elephants for warfare.

Perdiccas' friend Eumenes became satrap of Turkey. A close friend and personal secretary of Alexander, he would soon command dozens of war elephants. This was a slap in the face to Antigonus the One-Eyed ("Monophtalmos"), who had governed Turkey for a decade on Alexander's behalf. Perdiccas accused Antigonus of treason and summoned him for trial, but the One-Eyed fled west and convinced the ruler of Greece, Antipater, to oppose Perdiccas.[11]

The "trigger" for the Successor Wars came through an unusual example of political scheming. General Ptolemy of Egypt became a body snatcher!

The Macedonians expected a new ruler to bury his predecessor, and so Perdiccas planned to bury Alexander in Macedon, paving the way to

Elephants love the water, and require a considerable supply. *[Rev. J.G. Wood. The Romance of Animal Life. New York, Thomas Whittaker, 1894. Page 199.]*

take charge.[12] This made Alexander's body extremely valuable to ambitious generals! Perdiccas sent the body with a military escort toward the Mediterranean, to send it home by ship. General Ptolemy paid informants to learn the exact route of the convoy and sent an army north to capture Alexander's body![13] The corpse temporarily rested in Memphis, Egypt, while Ptolemy fashioned a magnificent tomb in Alexandria.

This theft was a major setback to Perdiccas' ambitions. He also heard that Antigonus One-Eyed and Antipater would soon invade his lands from Greece. Perdiccas asked his friend Eumenes to delay the Greeks as long as possible. Gathering his own army, and forty elephants, Perdiccas rushed to Egypt. He hoped to quickly crush Ptolemy, regain Alexander's body, and then return to fight in the north and west.

To guard Babylon during his absence, Perdiccas put his assistant Seleucus in charge. Five years earlier, Seleucus had commanded infantry and personally faced the elephant attack at the battle of the Hydaspes. Seleucus would soon become a major player in the Successor Wars.

Why did Perdiccas take only forty elephants to Egypt and not two hundred? The roads to Egypt passed through desert country, and provisioning even forty elephants with food and water on the journey would be difficult!

In May 321 BC, Perdiccas arrived in Egypt to kill Ptolemy and reclaim Alexander's corpse. Ptolemy hurried with reinforcements to a fortress near the Nile called Castellum Camelorum, or Fort Camel.

Perdiccas attacked with a force of several thousand infantry, cavalry, and forty elephants.[14] Perdiccas had the best infantry in the world, Alexander's old corps of Silver Shields. These men were literally in their fifties and sixties, but their experience and camaraderie made up for any loss of youthful vigor.

Elephants, ladder carriers, and infantry led the assault on the Camel's Fort. The task of the war elephants was to rip up the palisades: fences made of sharpened wooden posts meant to stop the invaders from reaching the fort. By grappling a post with its trunk, an elephant could use its weight and strength to wrench the stake from its moorings, thus clearing paths for the soldiers behind. The elephants made quick work of the palisades and were soon dismantling the parapets along the walls.[15]

Showing himself brave, Ptolemy rallied the defenders on the walls. Writes Diodorus:

Ptolemy...wished to encourage the other commanders and friends to face the dangers, taking his long spear and posting himself on the top of the outwork, put out the eyes of the leading elephant, since he occupied a higher position, and wounded its Indian mahout...Following his example, his friends fought boldly and made the next beast in line entirely useless by shooting down the Indian who was directing it.[16]

Ptolemy imitated the orders of Alexander at the Hydaspes: impale the elephant's eyes or its rider. Disabling the leading beasts caused the rest to panic, and the whole squad of elephants stormed away from Camel's Fort. Perdiccas' discouraged army withdrew.

Despite this setback, Perdiccas did not abandon the campaign. Even if he could not capture or kill Ptolemy, Perdiccas needed to retake Alexander's corpse. The army moved south along the Nile river toward Memphis, where Alexander had been temporarily interred. Although the Nile was not in flood, the river was quite deep, up to the men's necks. With little or no wood in the region to be cut, his army could not build a bridge or boats.

Perdiccas devised a unique, but risky, plan. The elephants waded into the Nile in a line stretching the full width of the river, standing trunk to tail, to act as a breakwater, slowing the current! As a backup measure, the cavalry horses were placed nose to tail, down river, so that any soldiers swept away by the current could grab onto the horses.[17] This clever idea worked for a short time, but all of the activity stirred up the sand from the bottom and the river became deeper. The biographer Kincaid describes the horror of the deepening water:

This was to send all but the strongest swimmers to certain death...others threw away their arms and armour and tried to swim, but the undertow sucked many of them below the surface. Their corpses were carried down stream and drew to the spot quantities of crocodiles, probably sacred animals fed daily by the Egyptians, and these attacked the swimming soldiers. Before the eyes of their panic-stricken comrades, the horrible beasts pulled down man after man....No less than two thousand perished in the crossing, of whom one thousand were the prey of the crocodiles.[18]

Later commanders in India, for instance, used elephants as breakwaters in rivers in a more methodical way. They made two strings of elephants: one group upstream to slow the water and another group connected by ropes, downstream, to catch any men or horses being washed away.[19]

These two defeats in the summer of 321 BC, at Camel's Fort and the Nile, led Perdiccas' officers to stab him to death in his tent. The assassins made quick peace with Ptolemy, gave him the elephants, and led the remnants of their army back to Babylon.[20]

10
Elephants Marching

While Alexander's second in command was murdered in a mutiny at the Nile, his friend Eumenes won a surprising victory against the Macedonians in Asia Minor. Many military people despised Eumenes as a weakling, since he had not been a lifelong soldier.[1] Antipater and Antigonus ignored Eumenes while they hurried to Babylon to ensure that the empire did not fall apart after the death of Perdiccas. The mutinous army of Perdiccas surrendered.

Antipater quickly sorted out the management of Alexander's empire. Antipater left half of the royal army for Antigonus to use against Eumenes. Because this half included seventy war elephants, we know that there were only 140 war elephants available in late 321 BC. Forty had gone to Egypt with Perdiccas and twenty probably died of natural causes.

Antipater left Seleucus in charge of Babylonia province. Antipater took half the army, seventy war elephants, and the two potential kings (Alexander IV and Philip III) back to Greece.

Antigonus Monophtalmos had lived for more than sixty years and fought for both Philip of Macedon and Alexander. He lost an eye to a catapult missile, probably during the siege of Perinthus in 339 BC with Philip. Antigonus refused to allow doctors to remove the arrow until the battle ended![2] Antigonus was a notably large man, over six feet tall. He loved to tell jokes and laugh with his soldiers. He led seven thousand hoplites into Asia with Alexander and fought at the Battle of the Granicus. Alexander appointed Antigonus as ruler of Turkey, an important post, meant to keep supply and communication lines with Macedon open while he fought in the east. Antigonus successfully stopped all Persian resistance in Asia Minor.[3]

Antigonus the One-Eyed now had to face two rebel armies: one led by Eumenes and one commanded by Perdiccas' brother, Alcetas. The two enemies waited on opposite ends of Turkey. Antigonus split his army, sending forty elephants and half his troops to shadow Alcetas, while he pursued Eumenes himself.

Antigonus took thirty war elephants with his army to attack Eumenes. Using formation tricks and false signals, Antigonus' army pretended to expand with thousands of fresh reinforcements. This deception led most of Eumenes' soldiers to defect. Eumenes and a few loyal followers fled to the east.

Antigonus left some men to pursue Eumenes. Hoping to surprise the distant rebel army of Alcetas, Antigonus planned the swiftest march ever made by elephants. His army moved three hundred miles in only one week, averaging about forty-five miles per day![4] This trek killed five of the pachyderms, and only sixty-five of the original seventy reached their destination. Although never recommended, the elephants are capable of it. Even with a young calf, a herd will travel up to fifty miles in one day, if they are in desperate need.[5]

Alcetas realized that the enemy had arrived when he heard the trumpeting of Antigonus' elephants on the ridge above. Bravely, Alcetas tried to give his army more time to create its formations. He charged up the hill with a small cavalry force, hoping that Antigonus was not ready. Antigonus cut off Alcetas' charge with his own cavalry and sent the whole line of sixty-five elephants rumbling down the hill to crush Alcetas' infantry. Understandably intimidated, they immediately signaled their surrender.[6] Alcetas killed himself.

Eumenes' tiny army escaped in the east, hoping to find support among the Persian and Babylonian satrapies. They needed money and troops to destroy Antigonus. Along the way, Eumenes hired many of Alexander's veterans, including the famed Silver Shields.

The best stroke of luck for Eumenes came in the form of a treacherous Greek named Eudamos. Eudamos had been working with King Porus in India, but he murdered Porus and took all 125 of his elephants.[7] Eumenes paid Eudamos two hundred talents for the beasts and named him "master of the elephants."

Antigonus caught up with Eumenes at Paraetacene, on the border between Media and Persia, in the late summer of 317 BC. Antigonus had thirty-eight thousand infantry, 8500 cavalry, and sixty-five elephants. Antigonus was surprised to see that his enemy, practically overnight, had obtained double his own number of elephants! Eumenes lined up thirty-five thousand infantry, 6100 cavalry, and 125 elephants.[8] This would be the first battle in the western world between two armies using war elephants.

Eumenes set forty-five elephants on his left flank with 150 Persian slingers, archers, and javelin throwers between each beast.[9] He stationed forty elephants in the center in front of the infantry and forty elephants on the right flank. W.W. Tarn explains the strategy:

The battle which ought to throw most light on the use of elephants is Paraitakene...for both Antigonus and Eumenes had a strong force of Indian elephants...both generals meant to use their elephants as screens against the enemy cavalry, and perhaps to threaten that cavalry in return.[10]

Antigonus' twenty-year-old son Demetrius joined him on the right flank for his first battle. Because Antigonus had chosen higher ground, he studied Eumenes' movements and set his army's strengths and weaknesses against that of the enemy. Instead of dividing his smaller force of elephants evenly, Antigonus put thirty in his right wing, twenty-five in front of his infantry, and only a handful with Peithon's on the left wing.

Antigonus controlled his own right wing; he ordered Peithon on the left wing to simply hold his position against his more numerous opponents. Peithon ignored the order; he wanted to fight! Peithon sent his cavalry around the flank of Eumenes' elephants and harassed them with arrows, causing great damage. When Eumenes saw his right wing crumbling, he detached and led some of his own cavalry to bolster it. This action drove Peithon into retreat, but weakened the left wing of Eumenes' army. Antigonus took advantage, charging into a gap between the infantry and cavalry, causing Eumenes' left wing to flee.

The overall battle was indecisive, although Eumenes' famous Silver Shields infantry had forced Antigonus' men to retreat. With darkness falling, the generals each decided to withdraw to winter camp and try again the next year, or so it seemed.

In December of 317 BC, Antigonus chose to gamble. Assuming that the campaign season was over, Eumenes had broken his army into six detachments so that they could forage enough food for the men and animals.[11]

Rather than taking the road, a twenty-five-day march, Antigonus led his army on a nine-day hike straight across the Iranian desert, intending to surprise and destroy Eumenes' six detachments one at a time. Despite Antigonus' orders that there be no fires, the fifth-consecutive freezing night led many of his troops to light campfires for warmth.[12] Eumenes' scouts spotted the fires and reported that Antigonus' forces were only four days away.

The generals after Alexander designed heavy-armor to protect the elephant's legs and trunk. Tower-archers and javelin-throwers made war-elephants into a mobile artillery platform as well as a shock weapon. [*Courtesy of artist Louie Hays, Reprinted with permission.*]

These scouts saved Eumenes from disaster, but not completely. His elephant corps was now dangerously close to Antigonus' army and did not know it.

At night, Eumenes sent a fast force of cavalry to light hundreds of fires near Antigonus' army. Antigonus believed that Eumenes had discovered the winter march and had drawn up his whole army to fight. This deception delayed Antigonus for a couple of days.

Finally recognizing the trickery, Antigonus sent his cavalry to capture Eumenes' elephants. Antigonus' cavalry found the elephant division moving quickly toward Eumenes' army, but with only a small screen of horsemen for defense. Diodorus explains what happened:

...the commanders of the elephants arranged them in a square and advanced, placing the baggage train in the centre and in the rear the cavalry that accompanied the elephants, consisting of a force of not more than four hundred men. As the enemy fell upon them with all its weight and pressed ever more heavily, the cavalry was routed, overwhelmed by numbers; but those who were in charge of the elephants resisted at first and held firm even though they were receiving wounds from all directions and were not able to injure the enemy in return in any way. Then when they were now becoming exhausted, the troops sent by Eumenes appeared and rescued them from their danger.[13]

The mahouts certainly had swords, but such weapons were useless against Antigonus' cavalry, which used javelins and arrows. The mahouts, refusing to surrender, were ready to die protecting their elephants. They were saved by the arrival of friendly cavalry.

Although Antigonus' attack failed to capture the elephant corps, the elephants were terrified and many mahouts were wounded or killed.[14] Eumenes' elephant corps was thus traumatized by the encounter with Antigonus' cavalry and fought poorly in the coming battle.

Having lost the element of surprise, Antigonus would be tempted to retreat, but he could not retreat easily across the desert, should Eumenes decide to pursue. So the two forces again lined up for combat at Gabiene, on a dry salt plain.

Plutarch says that the elephants of Eumenes at Gabiene bore towers.[15] This is the earliest recorded battle of the western world naming towers on elephant back as a weapons platform. Since the Indians had used towers on elephants, it should be no surprise that these beasts stolen from King Porus would use howdahs as well.

The formations at Gabiene were nearly identical to the prior battle: elephants across the front lines, with light troops between them, and cavalry and infantry following behind. Diodorus says that Eumenes set "the weaker of the cavalry and of the elephants...whom he ordered to avoid battle" on his right wing.[16] Since there is no such mention of "weaker" elephants in the first battle, presumably these weaker elephants are those who lost mahouts or were injured during Antigonus' desert raid. It takes some weeks for an elephant to trust and obey a new mahout, as is commonly known among elephant trainers.[17] These beasts could still stand on the right wing to hinder the enemy horses from a direct charge, carrying new riders, but they were ineffective for any offensive duties without their trusted mahouts.

When the elephants and armies began their charge across the dry salt plain, dust billowed into the air, hampering visibility on the battlefield.[18] Sensing an opportunity, Antigonus ordered a small detachment of cavalry to swing around the whole melee to capture Eumenes' camp, about half a mile in the rear. The guards were no match for the horsemen, who took the camp easily and escorted prisoners and valuables to Antigonus' camp, undetected.

Eumenes wanted to kill Antigonus and end the war, so he changed the order of battle on his left wing. He outnumbered Antigonus' elephants about three to one on the left. Eumenes' elephants had lined up diagonally to prevent any flanking maneuvers. Eumenes' order to charge could only be obeyed gradually, with elephants arriving one at a time because of their varying distances from Antigonus' line.[19] Eumenes' wing charged into Antigonus' smaller wing, where a fierce battle erupted between the Asian elephants.

In elephant versus elephant combat, a pair of beasts use their heads and trunks to wrestle. The struggle continues until one elephant turns to flee; the victor sticks his tusks up into the stomach or between the rear legs of his opponent, seriously wounding or killing the beast. Eumenes' lead elephant was gored and fell down dead.[20] Deprived of their leader, the remainder of Eumenes' elephants fled from the left wing. Despite a three-to-one advantage, Eumenes' elephants were defeated.

Eumenes' veteran infantry again routed Antigonus' foot soldiers. It looked as if another indecisive battle had been fought, with neither side able to deliver the knockout blow. However, the blow had fallen, unknown to Eumenes.

Antigonus showed the enemy infantry, the Silver Shields, that their families and property had all been captured. Eumenes had failed to adequately guard his soldiers' treasures.[21] Eumenes' men, fearing that Antigonus would kill their captured families, agreed to exchange Eumenes for their camp. Eumenes called them cowards, saying "you deliver up your general to redeem your stuff."[22] This antagonized the old soldiers even further, forcing Antigonus to send ten elephants and a division of cavalry to save Eumenes from his own men. Later, Eumenes and Eudamos, the "elephantarch", were strangled. The commander of the Silver Shields died more painfully: he was thrown into a pit and burned alive.[23]

"To the victors go the spoils." Antigonus took Eumenes' army and elephants. Elephants had transformed warfare in the post-Alexander world, according to Bosworth.

The campaign was also notable for its use of elephants. Prodigious efforts and resources were expended to keep them fit and active under the most unfavourable climatic conditions, and they were consistently placed in front of the line of battle....There is no evidence of the beasts attacking enemy infantry, as Porus' elephants had done at the Hydaspes. Perhaps the dangers of their being wounded in the eyes or trunk were too acute.... Accordingly, elephants tended to be used against each other or to keep cavalry at bay. Their usefulness was limited, but they clearly had a mystique, a psychological advantage for their army.[24]

With the defeat of Eumenes, Antigonus controlled much of Alexander's empire. The battles between Antigonus and Eumenes demonstrated that elephants and cavalry could be combined in formations effectively: war elephants were not just a "gimmick weapon."[25] Horses continued to fear elephants, but could stand within a reasonable distance for mutual support. Elephants had become nearly as important to Hellenistic armies as cavalry.[26]

Antigonus decided to allow no men of ability, who might pose competition, to live.[27] Seleucus, governor of Babylon, fled to hide with Ptolemy. Antigonus stationed his son Demetrius over the defenses in Palestine to keep Ptolemy in Africa.

Antigonus moved into Asia Minor, planning to invade Europe. Now that he had a large army and control of much of the empire, Antigonus grew ambitious. Will Durant cleverly wrote that "Antigonus I ('Cyclops') dreamed of uniting all of Alexander's empire under his one eye."[28]

With a huge army and 150 elephants trained to work with his cavalry, Antigonus might soon rule the western world.

11
Siege

In 319 BC, while Antigonus fought the rebel armies of Eumenes and Alcetes in Turkey, Antipater, the old regent of Greece, died. Antipater had brought seventy elephants back with him from Babylon two years earlier and left his ambitious young son Cassander as a cavalry commander for Antigonus the One-Eyed.

When his father died, Cassander returned to Macedon to take power, but instead, an old general named Polyperchon had taken command of Greece and Antipater's elephants. A charismatic leader, Cassander had many allies in Greece. The whole country divided into cities supporting Cassander and cities favoring Polyperchon.

Polyperchon quickly moved to subdue the southern Greek cities that supported Cassander. In 318 BC, Polyperchon's army advanced against Megalopolis accompanied by sixty-five elephants.

Megalopolis prepared itself for the attack with the help of a veteran of Alexander's army named Damis. The townsfolk dug a moat and used catapults against Polyperchon's besieging force, but Polyperchon used *sappers* to dig mines that undermined part of the city wall. The elephants probably assisted the siege engineers by lifting timber and pulling siege engines for the assault.

Late one evening, a large section of Megalopolis' wall collapsed into the sappers' tunnels. With no way to build an effective wall in a single evening and knowing that Polyperchon would rush through the opening with superior forces in the morning, the city called on Damis for advice. Surprisingly, he ordered the people to clear the rubble out of the street, creating a path for the enemy to rush into the city! As the classical historian Diodorus wrote:

...Damis, who had been in Asia with Alexander and knew by experience the nature and the use of these animals, got the better of him [Polyperchon] completely. Indeed, by putting his native wit against the brute force of the elephants, Damis rendered their physical strength useless. He studded many

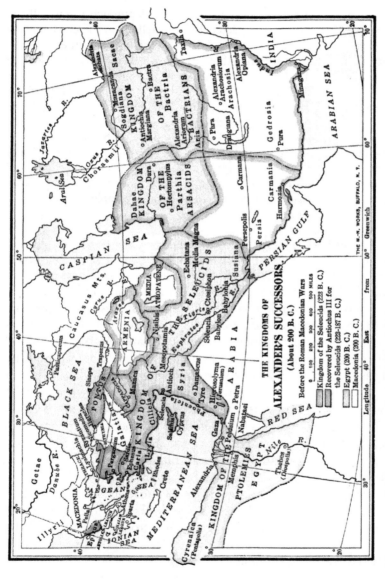

The empire of Alexander as it had stabilized after the battle of Ipsus. [M.L.W. Laistner. *A Survey of Ancient History to the Death of Constantine. Boston, D.C. Heath and Company, 1929. Plate map on page 347.*]

great frames with sharp nails and buried them in shallow trenches, concealing the projecting points; over them he left a way into the city, placing none of the troops directly in the face of it, but posting on the flanks a great many javelin throwers, bowmen, and catapults. As Polyperchon was clearing the debris from the whole extent of the breach and making an attack through it with all the elephants in a body, a most unexpected thing befell them. There being no resistance in front, the Indian mahouts did their part in urging them to rush into the city all together; but the animals, as they charged violently, encountered the spike-studded frames. Wounded in their feet by the spikes, their own weight causing the points to penetrate, they could neither go forward any farther nor turn back, because it hurt them to move. At the same time some of the mahouts were killed by the missiles of all kinds that poured upon them from the flanks, and others were disabled by wounds and so lost such use of the elephants as the situation permitted. The elephants, suffering great pain because of the cloud of missiles and the nature of the wounds caused by the spikes, wheeled about through their friends and trod down many of them. Finally the elephant that was the most valiant collapsed; of the rest, some became completely useless, and others brought death to many of their own side.[1]

This is the earliest recorded use of *caltrops*, or ground traps, against elephants. Hiding the nail-studded boards in the rubble of the streets proved an effective ruse to draw the pachyderms into a trap and stop them. The elephant's feet are extremely sensitive and would feel much the same as a human would upon stepping on nails: inestimable pain.

While the beasts roared and struggled to free themselves, the citizens of Megalopolis deluged the mahouts and elephants with javelins and arrows, effectively destroying the cohesion of the elephant corps. One frequently exploited weakness of war elephants is the vulnerability of their riders. Because mahouts control the elephants using their toes and a stick (voices being too soft to be heard in battle), they are primary targets.[2] Polyperchon's soldiers followed close behind the elephants into the breach. When the wounded beasts got free from the spikes, they turned to flee and ran over Polyperchon's soldiers.

Megalopolis was a major defeat, and Polyperchon retreated.

In the spring of 317 BC, Cassander won a victory against Polyperchon and captured some of his elephants. Cassander built barges specifically designed to carry pachyderms and took them across a small part of the Aegean Sea with his army.[3] Cassander may have been the first westerner to design elephant-transport craft.

Cassander pressed Polyperchon hard in the west. Desperate, Polyperchon asked for the help of Olympias, the mother of Alexander, not realizing that she presented dangers of her own.[4]

Olympias raised an army in Greece, and while Polyperchon was away fighting, she decided to ensure that her grandson, Alexander IV, would have no rivals. She murdered the retarded Philip III and executed Cassander's brother and one hundred other nobles. This barbarity shocked the allies of Polyperchon and sent Cassander into a rage. He rushed north to kill Olympias. Olympias fled, taking Alexander IV and Polyperchon's war elephants with her. They took refuge in a fortified city called Pydna.

Cassander formed a secure siege. The people of Pydna resorted to cannibalism to survive. Not able to spare any food for the elephants, Olympias tried to keep them alive by feeding them sawdust.[5] They "pined away for want of food" and died; a sad end for the magnificent beasts of King Porus.[6]

The city surrendered in the spring of 316 BC. After a brief trial, she was executed.

Cassander's army and elephants pacified the rest of Greece that same year. Believing rumors that his old mentor Antigonus Monopthalamus intended to invade Europe to take Greece, Cassander joined a coalition to oppose the One-Eyed.

12
Cavalry Killers

Antigonus the One-Eyed was a notably large man, over six feet tall, and possessing a constantly expanding waistline. By defeating Eumenes in 316 BC, Antigonus ruled ancient Iran, Iraq, Syria, and Turkey. Aside from the sheer volume of Antigonus' estates, he owned the largest army, controlled the largest squadron of war elephants, and clutched the biggest war chest for hiring troops. Antigonus fielded about 170 war elephants, including sixty from Alexander's old division and more than one hundred captured from Eumenes' army at the Battle of Gabiene.

Seleucus, the long-time governor of Babylon, had been one of Alexander's commanders. The Babylonians and Persians respected him. Antigonus recognized that a popular ruler in Babylon could undermine his own power. When Seleucus learned that the One-Eyed intended to execute him, he fled with his family to Ptolemy, in Egypt.[1]

Antigonus marched with a massive military force into Turkey, planning to enter Europe to destroy his Greek rivals. The escape of Seleucus from Babylon foiled Antigonus' surprise. Seleucus not only warned Ptolemy, but sent friends to warn the Greeks by fast ship.

The One-Eyed received messengers in Turkey informing him of an alliance of Ptolemy of Egypt, Seleucus, Cassander of Macedon, and Lysimachus of Thrace.[2] These rulers sent an ultimatum full of incredible demands. Although they had contributed nothing to help Antigonus during the war against Eumenes, they demanded that Antigonus surrender Turkey, Syria, Babylon, and lots of money...or face their combined wrath.[3]

Antigonus flew into a rage and chose not to negotiate. In 314 BC, the One-Eyed began his war against the overconfident allies. To weaken Cassander, Antigonus funded rebels in southern Greece. The One-Eyed and his son Demetrius pushed Ptolemy out of Palestine and back into Egypt. Antigonus paid maritime nations a small fortune to construct a huge fleet. By 313 BC, Antigonus' navy ruled the Mediterranean Sea.

Antigonus planned to harass Cassander and Lysimachus in Asia Minor, so he left twenty-four-year-old Demetrius behind in Palestine, with some experienced advisors, to keep Ptolemy trapped in Egypt. Many ancient sources call Demetrius the most handsome, charming, and daring man of the era, but the same sources add that his character flaws matched his virtues.[4] He loved wine and women, and usually too much of both!

In late summer 312 BC, a large army left Egypt to attack Demetrius at Gaza. Ptolemy and Seleucus believed that this was an excellent chance to retake Palestine and Phoenicia, while Antigonus the One-Eyed remained distant in Turkey. Antigonus' advisors pleaded with Demetrius to avoid battle until reinforcements could arrive. The Egyptians fielded 30 percent more infantry, but Demetrius felt that his forty-three war elephants would carry the day.

Both Ptolemy and Seleucus were highly experienced leaders, trained by Alexander himself. As historian Billows recognizes, war elephants only made effective attacks against inexperienced armies:

As a screen from behind which to charge with one's cavalry, elephants had proved useful at Paraitakene and Gabiene...but as an attacking force in themselves, elephants were effective in ancient warfare only against enemies who had not encountered them before and were overawed by their size and strength. Seleukos and Ptolemy had encountered elephants before.[5]

Why didn't the Egyptian army bring elephants to fight at Gaza? The Egyptian industry of capturing African elephants for warfare would not begin for another twenty years. However, Ptolemy had probably captured thirty to forty pachyderms from Perdiccas in 321 BC.[6] Natural deaths could not claim all of those beasts in nine years; Ptolemy should have been able to produce at least twenty elephants for battle. There is no certain solution as to why Ptolemy brought no elephants to Gaza. Perhaps he did not want to take his elephants across the desert because of the vast supplies of food and water they would require on the march.

The traditional military method for dealing with enemy elephants was to send in soldiers to disable the beasts by chopping their legs and trunks with axes. Demetrius planned to protect his animals by stationing javelin throwers and slingers between the elephants.

Ptolemy, however, brought some new tactics to anti-elephant combat at Gaza. He intended to capture, not kill, the pachyderms. Ptolemy ordered his own "light troops" to aim their missiles at the mahouts, not the elephants. Perhaps his ally Cassander had told Ptolemy about the major success of spiked traps in the siege at Megalopolis; Ptolemy unveiled a new version of caltrops at Gaza.

Teams of men carried out long chains of connected iron spikes, laying them in front of their right wing, as a trap for the beasts. Military historian Delbruck (always the skeptic) scoffs at the tale as "a silly guard room story," saying that Demetrius or his men would see the trap being laid out and avoid it.[7] However, that assumption depends on a number of factors. Could the enemy see a narrow object, like a chain, at a distance? Seeing it, would they decide that it presented some sort of danger? Demetrius had never seen caltrops in battle. Diodorus' statement that Ptolemy and Seleucus sent out scouts to determine the exact setup of Demetrius' forces tells us that they were not near enough to see the enemy troop dispositions, so how could Demetrius' then see small traps in the dirt?[8]

This chain of spikes proves Ptolemy's ingenuity. Caltrops and spikes were the most effective ancient device against elephants.[9] Caltrops of this type are used against elephants even today. Humans often protect their crops using boards filled with nails, buried around their fields.[10]

The biggest drawback to the use of caltrops is the same as that of modern landmines. If mines are not retrieved after the fighting, they remain on-site forever and may harm friendly troops (or civilians) when forgotten. Ptolemy's connecting of these traps by chain solves the problem of picking them up and allows the caltrops to be moved very easily.[11] Another problem with the use of caltrops is accurately predicting the path of the enemy elephants. At Megalopolis a few years earlier, the citizens cleared a path so that Polyperchon's elephants would run down the streets where the traps were hidden. Ptolemy's moveable spike chains would allow the carriers of the device to move it to another sector of the battlefield, should enemy movement differ from the initial assessment.

The Battle of Gaza played out on Demetrius' left wing, where he stationed the majority of his elephants and cavalry. Demetrius planned to charge his forty-three pachyderms and cavalry against Ptolemy's horsemen. When the Egyptian horses fled the field from the elephants, his own cavalry could surround and destroy the more numerous Egyptian infantry.

Ptolemy's plan was the better one. When the elephants charged forward to frighten the Egyptian horses, they ran into Ptolemy's spikes. Diodorus writes:

And now, when the fight between the horse had been a long time doubtful, the elephants, forced on by the Indians, made so terrible an onset, that it appeared impossible for any force to have stood against them. But when they came up to the palisado, the darters and archers sorely galled both the beasts and their riders; and being still forced on, and whipped by the Indians, some of them stuck upon the sharp points of the palisado, with which, besides the multitude of the darts and arrows that galled them, they were in such pain and torment, that they caused a horrible tumult and confusion....upon which the greatest part of Demetrius' horse were in such a consternation, that they forthwith fled.[12]

Because elephants are heavy, they cannot simply jump up to free themselves from traps holding two feet: normally they only lift one foot at a time. When two feet are impaled, an elephant is trapped in place. The screaming of the wounded elephants caused the unharmed pachyderms to flee, disrupting Demetrius' own cavalry horses. Ptolemy sent his archers and javelin throwers forward to kill the mahouts, clearly intending to capture, and not kill, the elephants. Seeing this major set-back, and fearing that their horses might step on more of these traps, Demetrius' cavalry fled the field, and his infantry joined them in full flight.

The psychological impact of hidden ground-traps is discussed at length by Robert Reid:

After Alexander's death, his self-appointed successors struggled for supremacy and territory within the vast empire they had helped to conquer. In the ensuing wars between the various Hellenistic monarchies, extensive use was made of wooden balls armed with metal spikes, which formed a valuable component in field and camp defenses. Although not immediately lethal, the devices caused wounds that sapped an enemy's morale. The sight of injuries inflicted on horses or comrades by caltrops made infantry and even more, cavalry uneasy about advancing over ground that might be strewn with the insidious devices....[13]

All forty-three of Demetrius' Indian elephants were captured. So complete was the panic of Demetrius' infantry, that the fortified city of Gaza was taken. Demetrius' fleeing soldiers rushed the gates, and the human mass would not allow the gates to be closed.

Ptolemy's army continued to pursue Demetrius to the north. Seleucus, fighting beside Ptolemy, recognized an opportunity to return to his satrapy of Babylonia.[14] Ptolemy gave him one thousand infantry and three hundred cavalry to rush to Babylon.

Seleucus was no amateur. He became a junior general under Alexander and eventually commanded the Royal Hypaspists heavy infantry division. Seleucus governed Babylonia for five years before Antigonus forced him to flee in 316 BC.

Seleucus added two thousand more soldiers to his force on the road to Iraq and easily retook Babylon. This brave but risky adventure would start a "new front" against the strong central position of Antigonus the One-Eyed.

Antigonus underestimated his new opponent. The One-Eyed dispatched a force of ten thousand infantry and seven thousand horse to squash Seleucus' three thousand soldiers. Seleucus sprang a night ambush on the sleeping enemy, forcing their surrender in 312 BC. Three years later, Antigonus decided to deal with Seleucus in person, but he again misjudged his enemy. Seleucus launched an early morning assault on his sleeping enemies. Although Antigonus' army was not completely routed, Antigonus cut a deal with Seleucus, promising to leave Iraq alone if Seleucus would stay east of Syria.[15]

Now safe in the west, Seleucus went east, to take back the rebellious provinces of Bactria and India. His men began to call him "Seleucus Nicator," the Victorious.[16]

Antigonus grew sickly in his late seventies. He had to rely on Demetrius to lead the troops. This was not a foolish policy, according to Griffith:

Defeat was not annihilation so long as Demetrius survived, for Demetrius could make poor tools do more and better work than any man living: even when he later became king, he remained the adventurer par excellence, and he was by temperament probably the greatest leader of mercenaries who ever commanded Greek soldiers.[17]

His defeat at Gaza was the exception and not the rule. In June of 307 BC, Demetrius launched a brilliant naval attack to capture Athens. He easily overran southern Greece, depriving Cassander of much revenue and manpower. Demetrius sailed to Cyprus in 306 BC, taking it from Ptolemy.

Antigonus hoped that Ptolemy's heavy losses in Cyprus had seriously weakened Egypt. The One-Eyed arranged for Demetrius to meet him at the mouth of the Nile with the navy. Antigonus led eighty thousand infantry, eight thousand cavalry, and eighty-three elephants to the Nile.

Demetrius arrived with the fleet to ferry Antigonus' soldiers across the Nile, but storms and disorganization caused many of his ships to sink or run aground. Ptolemy fielded an army only one-fourth the size of Antigonus' force, but Antigonus' soldiers were all mercenaries. Mercenaries fight for money, not loyalty. Ptolemy also employed mercenaries, but he paid them better and gave them land in Egypt, essentially making them loyal citizens. Ptolemy sent small boats into the Nile to shout offers

An escaped circus elephant shook and tossed this horse 'like a terrier shakes and tosses a rat,' said a witness. [*Wood, J.G. Sketches and Anecdotes of Animal Life, second series. London: G. Routledge, 1858. Page 27.*]

of money to any soldiers who would defect.[18] Hundreds of Antigonus' men swam to these boats so that Antigonus had to place archers, slingers, and even catapults on the beaches to kill defectors.[19] Seeing no way to cross the Nile, and losing troops to defection every day, Antigonus withdrew.

Demetrius returned to his sea-going adventures and spent a whole year in a spectacular siege at Rhodes. He built one machine called a Helepolis: nine-stories high, on wheels, with artillery on the lower floors and catapults to shoot men on the city walls. Although he failed to conquer the city, he earned the nickname Poliorketes, the Besieger. The Rhodians took the monstrous Helepolis and melted it down, using the metal to build one of the wonders of the ancient world, the Colossus of Rhodes.[20]

With Antigonus honoring the truce in the west, Seleucus could freely move eastward to reclaim the defecting provinces of Afghanistan, Pakistan, and India. Few ancient sources offer details of this campaign, but it seems clear that Seleucus hoped to capture elephants for his army during the campaign. Instead, Seleucus suffered a huge defeat at the hands of the Indian king Chandragupta Maurya in 304 BC.

Chandragupta Maurya was a very able ruler and administrator. According to one popular legend, Chandragupta caught his own war elephant. He called to the beast, and it instantly kneeled and accepted the king as its rider.[21]

Defeated, Seleucus was forced to retreat back through the mountains of Afghanistan. Seleucus asked for a peace treaty and reached a mutually beneficial agreement with Maurya. Seleucus gave one of his daughters to marry Chandra Gupta and surrendered most of Pakistan, Afghanistan, and India.[22] In return, Seleucus received five hundred war elephants, including their mahouts and other staff.[23]

Why did Seleucus want war elephants? Twenty years earlier, with Alexander the Great, he led the Royal Hypaspist infantry attack on King Porus' elephants at the Battle of the Hydaspes river. Historian W.W. Tarn wrote that the elephant battle marked Seleucus: "...the impression made on the generals, and particularly upon Seleucus, who had led the line, was that elephants were an arm to be obtained at any price...."[24] Seleucus wished to lead an armada of elephants against Antigonus' eighty beasts.

Skeptics scoff at the "five hundred" elephants account, thinking it to be an exaggeration. However, several ancient sources tell us that Seleucus used between four hundred and 480 elephants in battle two years later, so it is difficult to justify the skeptical view. Maurya of India would have no difficulty in giving up five hundred elephants, as he and his successors frequently fielded thousands of war elephants for combat. Maurya himself owned at least three thousand war elephants.[25] In fact, Maurya may have been delighted to give up hundreds of elephants, as he would have fewer pachyderms to feed during the march home through arid Pakistan. Five hundred elephants would require a daily diet of 110 tons of fodder![26]

Elephants intended for war are usually captured and begin training before age five, but they are not large enough to train for war until in their teens. The elephants reach full size in their twenties, and Indians believe they are in their prime in their thirties and forties. Elephants in the wild die in their sixties, when their teeth are all worn down and they cannot eat, but elephants in captivity rarely live past their forties. Although older male elephants do not have the strength and youthful vigor of their younger counterparts, their tusks tend to be longer and their wisdom of experience enables them to fight with good effect.

These Indian elephants may well have used metal sheaths, or even spikes, on their tusks, as had been an Indian tradition.[27] Tusks, although dangerous weapons, are not highly durable and can be broken in combat. The use of armor on tusks was to protect the elephants more than to threaten the enemy.

Demetrius overran most of central Greece, taking it from Cassander, in 303 BC, but also spent a lot of time with women and drink rather than finishing his conquests. Worried that Demetrius would soon control Greece, the allies (Ptolemy, Seleucus, Lysimachus, and Cassander) renewed their cooperation pact and made plans for simultaneous invasions against Antigonus. In essence, this multinational effort would be similar to the movements of the allies in World War II, who converged on Germany from multiple theaters of operation.

Lysimachus invaded northwestern Turkey with help from Cassander's troops, Ptolemy moved up through Palestine, and Seleucus marched westward from Babylon.

Antigonus learned of these multiple invasions and had no choice but to recall Demetrius, only days or weeks before a likely conquest of Greece. Antigonus hoped to engage the invaders one army at a time and not allow them to mass together. Lysimachus refused to fight and continually moved back whenever Antigonus approached for battle. This was a true strategic withdrawal, as his own forces could never defeat the massive army of Antigonus alone.[28]

Antigonus the One-Eyed had constructed many small fortresses along the major roads throughout his empire and hoped that these forts would delay Seleucus in the east and Ptolemy in the south. Rather than be delayed by the fortresses, Seleucus journeyed on a slower, more treacherous mountain road that was undefended.[29] Plutarch wrote that Seleucus could bring only four hundred elephants to the battle because twenty had to be left behind on the mountain trail, exhausted during the hard march, and eighty others were too weak upon arrival to fight.[30]

Antigonus' scheming, or Ptolemy's sense of self-preservation, did succeed in putting Ptolemy out of the coming battle. Rumors of Lysimachus' retreat in Asia Minor led Ptolemy to believe that nothing would be gained by joining this apparently failed alliance. Ptolemy took his army home to Egypt. It is not clear whether Ptolemy had taken any of his elephants along for the conflict, but because Egypt remained safely away from the incessant fighting, "the cultural center of the Hellenic world was shifted to Alexandria" under Ptolemy I and II.[31]

Seleucus reached Lysimachus before the combined forces of Demetrius and Antigonus could block the path. The armies met in central Turkey in a place called Ipsus.

Demetrius joined his father, now eighty years old. On the day of battle, in early summer of 301 BC, Antigonus stumbled while exiting his tent, falling on his face. This seemed to be a bad omen to Antigonus' men. He did not improve morale by praying aloud for the gods to kill him rather than allow him to survive a defeat.[32]

The lines of battle formed while the young brother-in-law of Demetrius watched: Pyrrhus of Epirus.[33] In a decade, Pyrrhus would be using elephants in his own armies.

The allies, Seleucus and Lysimachus (with reinforcements from Cassander), fielded sixty-four thousand infantry, 10,500 cavalry, four hundred war elephants, and one hundred scythed chariots. Antigonus and Demetrius brought up seventy thousand infantry, ten thousand horses, and seventy-five elephants.[34]

Seleucus provided one hundred elephants for Lysimachus, who commanded the infantry. Lysimachus put all one hundred beasts in the center, in front of the phalanx infantry. With the one hundred elephants in the center, Antigonus had no choice but to put his seventy-five beasts in front of his own infantry, lest his own men panic. Antigonus might also have seen that Seleucus kept three hundred elephants in reserve behind the army, and pondered the meaning of this. Why wouldn't Seleucus, with a vast superiority in elephants, put all four hundred in the front? Perhaps the pachyderms were not well trained or reliable? Elephant warfare in the western world was such a new concept that all of the possible tactics for their uses in combat had not yet been discovered.

Demetrius commanded the right wing of Antigonus' heavy cavalry, facing Antiochus, the twenty-three-year-old son of Seleucus. Demetrius the Besieger planned a charge on the right, intending to flank the infantry of Lysimachus.

Seleucus seems to have expected this; his left wing collapsed (or withdrew), allowing Demetrius to move deep behind the infantry. Demetrius followed the enemy cavalry, but Seleucus then moved three hundred elephants *behind* Demetrius' cavalry. The Besieger, turning to attack the infantry, could not approach the wall of elephants!

In the center, Antigonus' seventy-five pachyderms struggled with the one hundred beasts of Lysimachus.[35] Diodorus wrote that at Ipsus, "the elephants of Antigonus and Lysimachus fought as if nature had matched them equally in courage and strength."[36] While the elephants wrestled in the center and Demetrius tried to find a way around the column of Seleucus' elephants, Seleucus took his horses around the unprotected enemy flank and behind Antigonus' infantry. He offered an honorable surrender to any who wished to quit the fight, and many divisions laid down their arms. A few groups who were loyal to Antigonus begged him to flee, but he kept crying aloud, "Demetrius will come and save me."[37] As the enemy closed in, Antigonus the One-Eyed fell in a hail of javelins.

Demetrius, seeing that the battle was lost and his father was dead, escaped to his fleet and returned to Greece.

At Ipsus, the elephants played a decisive role. Gaebel calls Ipsus the "greatest achievement of war elephants in Hellenistic military history." [38]

Major General J.F.C. Fuller declares that the employment of elephants as a "shock arm" was the "greatest innovation of all" in the Greek/ Hellenistic development of warfare.[39] War elephants hastened the demise of cavalry formations in the post-Alexander years, according to military historian Pierre Ducrey:

After the death of Alexander, the cavalry gradually lost its importance as a tactical arm. There are a number of reasons for this: one was the growing weight and size of the phalanx, increasingly monolithic and apparently invincible; another, the appearance and widespread use of the war elephant. Like the cavalry and chariots, the elephants were regarded as a mobile unit, capable of a number of maneuvers, including surprise attacks and, above all, encirclement.[40]

Elephants made enemy cavalry useless because the horses ran away in terror.

After Ipsus, Demetrius' drunken friends began referring to Seleucus as Master of the Elephants, or the "elephant king."[41]

13
The Elephant Industry

The Battle at Ipsus, won by the clever deployment of hundreds of Seleucus' Indian elephants, killed Antigonus the One-Eyed, sent his son Demetrius into flight, and ended any immediate hope of a unified Macedonian empire. Alexander's squabbling commanders realized that none "could afford to leave elephants out of its armament programme."[1]

Among the keepers of war elephants in the western world are many now familiar names. Cassander kept about forty in Macedonia, and Ptolemy stabled a similar number in Egypt. Seleucus, now called "Master of the Elephants," possessed nearly five hundred in Syria. All of these beasts were Indian elephants, captured and transported from India to the west.

The reader may wonder why these desperate generals did not embark on elephant breeding programs to create new generations of war elephant stock. Bar-Kochva summarizes the reasons very well:

As to the possibility of a new generation of elephants, bred at Apamea, there is some reason to suppose that the elephants of Ipsus were all bulls. The bull-elephant is taller, heavier, and stronger, and, what is most important, has a long tusk, while the cow has a small tusk or none at all. These advantages are decisive in a battle between elephants, and indeed only bulls are represented on Seleucid monuments, terracottas, and coins. Although allowance should be made for the possibility that the bulls alone were depicted just because of their impressive appearance and did not in fact comprise the whole herd, on the other hand, the Indian kings are likely to have tried to preserve their monopoly over the supply of elephants by offering only bulls. I would not deny the possibility that Seleucus had some Indian cow-elephants, as Antigonus and Pyrrhos apparently had, but they...were too few to produce a new herd, especially as elephants rarely breed in captivity....[2]

First of all, the beasts bought, captured, and collected from India were desired for war, which meant male elephants, for the most part. Without females, breeding would have been impossible. Female elephants only breed every four years, and the pregnancy lasts nearly two years.[3] Because female elephants do not have the temperament for fighting, they were rarely used for war.[4] As the generals became desperate for war elephants, they did use females, but with mixed results. Males bore tusks, grew larger, and were more desirable in every way to warring generals.

Second, elephants are notoriously difficult to breed in captivity. Even in modern zoos, multiple techniques are being devised for artificial insemination because there has been little success with captive births. The *Cincinnati Enquirer* of May 3, 2003, happily announced the successful birth (via artificial insemination) of only the twelfth African elephant born in the United States since 1995, half of which died within their first year.[5] This good news is darkened by the fact that captive elephant births are so rare that they make headlines. The Seleucid rulers did run a breeding program at Apamea, yet had to capture new stock frequently.[6] Thus, the fighting Macedonian commanders had no choice but to obtain wild captures from India and train them for war on a continuous basis. Unlike typical "domestic" animals, elephants throughout history have been captured from the wild and tamed rather than "bred."[7]

After the Battle of Ipsus, Seleucus became very angry with his former allies, Cassander, Lysimachus, and Ptolemy. They decided that with Antigonus gone, Seleucus had become the strongest and so they formed a new alliance against him.[8]

Seleucus started a construction program to solidify his positions against possible invasion. He established his imperial military headquarters in northern Syria at Apamea, where the military training school and war elephants were stationed. Along with five hundred war elephants, Apamea housed thousands of cavalry horses. The cavalry horses may have been garrisoned in close proximity to the elephant stables to allow the equines and pachyderms to train together.[9] Apamea was a perfect location for both cavalry and elephants because, unlike most of Syria, Apamea had plentiful water.[10]

Elephants became a symbol of the Seleucid empire. The imperial mint began issuing coins that showed Seleucus in a chariot pulled by elephants.[11]

Worried about Seleucus' growing elephant corps, Ptolemy decreed that African elephants should not be killed because the ruler wanted them for the army. This decree must have been intended for the Ethiopians and Nubians, whom he did not directly control, because elephants became extinct in Egypt before 2600 BC.[12] The early Pharaohs' obsession

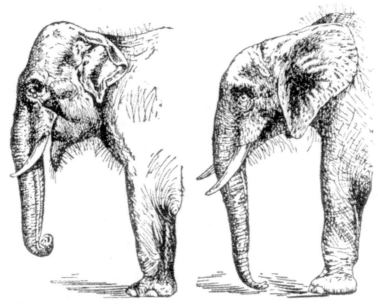

Asian elephant on the left compared with the African elephant on the right.
The most obvious difference is the size of the ears. *[Webster's New International
Dictionary of the English Language, G.& C. Miriam and Co., Springfield, MA,
1911, p. 710.]*

with ivory, along with changing climatic conditions, had driven indigenous elephants completely out of the Egyptian territories. When Ptolemy I
learned that the lands south of Egypt contained elephants, he began
preparations to collect and train his own indigenous elephant force.[13]

Elephants by this time were essential war machines, the armoured tanks of their
day already employed by the hostile Seleucid armies of Western Asia. The
Seleucids controlled the land routes from India where elephants could otherwise
be obtained. The ability to independently obtain elephants in Africa was therefore a great advantage to the early Ptolemies....[14]

Ptolemy's first son, Keraunos (meaning Thunderbolt), was a rash and
imprudent young man and was banished. Ptolemy I died in 283 BC, at the
age of eighty-four, passing the kingdom of Egypt to Ptolemy II Philadelphus. Philadelphus became most famous in future millennia for founding
the great Library of Alexandria.[15] He also took up the collection of war
elephants.

The home base for the future elephants would be at Memphis, not Alexandria, the capital. At Memphis, the Nile was one large river, while at Alexandria the Nile is split into several smaller rivers. It would be much easier to transport elephants across the Nile at Memphis than at Alexandria if enemies invaded from the east.[16]

Elephants were plentiful to the south of Egypt, in the lands of modern-day Sudan, Ethiopia, Eritrea, and Somalia, even into nineteenth century AD.[17] The easiest way to transport the elephants to Memphis was along the Nile River, either on land or by boat. Unfortunately for the Ptolemies, several powerful and hostile African tribes controlled the upper Nile.[18] This forced the expeditions to travel and hunt only along the coasts of the Red Sea and eastern shores of Somalia.

The Kushites (Ethiopians) used war elephants long before Macedon, according to Arrian.[19] The giant temple complex of Musawwarat es Sufra has numerous paintings and relief sculptures of elephants and riders, while an art relief shows an elephant holding the rope of a line of bound prisoners.[20] The Sufra Great Enclosure may have been a center for training war elephants, as there are ramps allowing them to move easily between buildings.[21] Unfortunately, our understanding of the Kushites is sparse and few records exist. As to the time when Kush used war elephants, the evidence cannot prove a pre-Ptolemaic tradition of the practice.[22]

Ptolemy Philadelphus sent scouts to find the best sites for hunting elephants. Two of the most important ports were built on the west coast of the Red Sea: Ptolemais Theron and Berenice Troglodytica. An inscription on the famous "Stele of Pithom" (264 BC) mentions the founding of Ptolemais Theron where "the Egyptian admiral hunted many elephants."[23] Elephants were unloaded at the Red Sea ports and then walked by road to ports on the Nile: all of these ports had specially built docks and ramps to accommodate the heavy elephant cargo.[24]

Hundreds of men boarded ships in the Red Sea for the trip to Eritrea, to hunt the elephants, in the early years. The Egyptians had to establish new bases further and further south during the reigns of Ptolemy Euergetes and Philopater, as elephant populations dwindled near northern bases. These expeditions could last for a year, and to attract workers, the Ptolemies had to pay very well. The men sent to capture the elephants were soldiers, but during these expeditions they were called "hunters."[25] The task before the men, to capture elephants, was no simple task.

When we consider the enormous strength of the elephant, which enables him to break through all ordinary means of confinement, and, at the same time, regard not only his ability to resist any violent attack, but his sagacity to elude any common stratagem, it must be evident that the business of his capture must be a task requiring equal courage and activity....[26]

Because of their size and cleverness, elephants are difficult to capture. Most of the local people were accustomed to killing and eating elephants, not capturing them.

The most adventurous method of killing an elephant in ancient Africa was described by Pliny and Diodorus. An African rubs himself with elephant dung to mask his scent, then hides in the trees about ten feet up. When the beast passes under the trees, the warrior jumps down and grabs the elephant's tail with one hand and braces his legs against the elephant's rear end.[27] Using an axe, he hacks at the elephant's legs until the tendons are cut and the beast cannot run. Then the rest of the tribe gathers to cut the elephant up for eating. Less strenuous and dangerous methods are also mentioned by Strabo and Pliny, including the use of poisoned arrows or stabbing them in the neck with spears.[28]

The Ptolemies did not want elephant steaks; they wanted living war elephants.

The Kushites may have given the Ptolemies a big boost in expertise in the handling and training of elephants, but the Kushites were too few.[29] Ptolemy II sent a representative to India to recruit mahouts and trainers, along with interpreters.[30] The Red Sea ports could send and receive Indian cargo and men, but that type of shallow-hulled vessel was incapable of carrying elephants in the Indian Ocean.

Ptolemy's naval engineers designed special boats called elephant carriers. Unlike warships, these vessels used sails rather than oars and were designed for use in shallow water. A similar vessel was apparently "reinvented" in the seventeenth century for elephant transport, as described in Ceylon in 1703:

But there is lately invented...a big Vessel, flat bottom'd, cover'd with Planks like a floor, so that this floor is almost of the height of the Key, then the side of the Key and the Vessel are adorned with Green Branches, so that the Elephant does see no Water till he be in the Ship.[31]

Because these ships used wind rather than man power, their travel times were determined strictly by the seasons. The elephant carriers traveled south from Egypt from June to September, and north to Egypt between October and May.[32] Travel in either direction would take one or two months, depending on the strength of the wind.

The Egyptian expeditions learned the Indian method of elephant capture because the African method of pitfalls and ditches was often fatal, or at least wounded the beasts unnecessarily.[33] A large group of horsemen would drive a herd of elephants into a man-made gorge, and then specialists would enter the gorge to catch young beasts and calves.[34] Often, tame elephants assisted in the capture of wild elephants; this often helped calm the frightened elephants. Presumably, the rest of the elephants were freed.

Because travel by ship is not natural to the elephant, the beasts probably received basic training before attempting to march them aboard the transport. If the elephants became panicked, even while restrained, they might damage the ship and sink it. To help the process, the bases were equipped with corrals, sheds, and elephant trainers who would take the initial steps of "breaking" and training of the animals before sending them north to Memphis.[35]

The voyage up the Red Sea was a perilous business. There were dangerous reefs and shallows along the coast, and we have an account of how the elephant-transports, riding deep in the water and propelled by sails, not by oars, might easily run aground by night and become total wrecks. Night-sailing on these voyages may have been due either...to the strength of the wind making it impossible to put into shore or anchor for the night, or to the fact that in the sultry heat of the Red Sea sailing by day was injurious to the health of the elephants; for in sailing ships the wind that helps progress diminished ventilation. The beasts would stand on the bottom of the vessel, uncovered except by light sheets to protect them from the sun.[36]

Once the elephants were delivered to Memphis, trainers would teach the beasts the arts of war for many years. Ptolemaic war elephants wore armor. Five plates of iron, joined by rings, were fastened around each elephant's head and ears with chains. He carried a castle on his back with several archers or spearmen.[37] One interesting historical piece shows an "open" howdah, meaning that the walls of the tower were not solid, but slatted, with gaps.[38] Such a howdah might have been intended only for parades, not battles, since it offers little protection.

The Ptolemaic training program was successful. Although the numbers may be somewhat inflated, two ancient commentators say that Philadelphus raised a force of three hundred to four hundred African elephants. This number seems reasonable, accepting that a high percentage of the animals became simple supply carriers.

Ptolemy II's elephant commanders must have learned a lot from the Indian advisors, as some of their mammoth learners were obeying Greek commands rather than Indian ones. Aelian writes that Ptolemy II was given a young elephant that "was brought up where the Greek language was used, and understood those that spoke to it. Up to the time of this particular animal it was believed that elephants only understood the language used by Indians."[39] In the early years, Ptolemy may have relied on Indian mahouts, thinking that only they were "qualified" to train elephants effectively.[40]

It goes without saying that people love to see elephants on parade, and the Egyptian rulers recognized the morale value of pachyderms. The behemoths marched in public festivals, on one occasion pulling a golden effigy of Alexander the Great in a chariot through the streets of Alexandria.[41]

14
Unmitigated Gauls

Lysimachus of Thrace, one of Alexander's longest surviving commanders, believed that Seleucus' army was weak. He died during an invasion of Turkey that proved the faultiness of his premise. With no rivals left, King Seleucus of Syria had only to march to Macedon to become king of Greece. He would rule Alexander's whole empire except for Egypt and India.

Seleucus moved into Thrace with a very small escort, expecting to be hailed king. While he stopped to have a look at a famous monument, Ptolemy's disgruntled and banished son, Keraunos (Thunderbolt), found King Seleucus alone and stabbed him in the back.

After killing Seleucus, Thunderbolt leapt on a horse and declared himself king of Greece. Many of Seleucus' troops in Turkey, now leaderless, decided to support him. Ptolemy Keraunos inherited at least a few dozen of Seleucus' war elephants. He soon gave (or sold) most of the beasts to King Pyrrhus of Epirus, who wanted to invade Italy.

One year after naming himself king of Greece, Ptolemy Keraunos ran into a major problem. The Gauls invaded in May of 279 BC.[1]

Gauls periodically appeared as raiders throughout Europe. Although not familiar with "modern" military tactics, they were fierce warriors. Their preferred armor for battle was their own skin: Galatian swordsmen fought naked until second century BC![2] Ptolemy Thunderbolt's officers begged him to avoid the invading Gauls until his own reinforcements arrived, but he did not listen.

Ceraunos commanded in person in this conflict. He rode into the field at the head of his troops, mounted on an elephant. In the course of the action he was wounded, and the elephant on which he rode becoming infuriated at the same time, perhaps from being wounded himself, threw his rider to the ground. The Gauls who were fighting around him immediately seized him. Without any hesitation or delay they cut off his head, and, raising it on the point of a pike, they bore it about the field in triumph.[3]

The backstabber of Seleucus met a rather poignant end of his own, literally.

With Pyrrhus away, pillaging southern Italy, Antigonus Gonatas, the son of Demetrius the Besieger, became king of Macedon in 276 BC.[4]

Antiochus succeeded his murdered father, Seleucus, in ruling Syria, Iraq, and Iran. Much of Seleucus' army had defected to Keraunos. Ptolemy Philadelphus attacked from the south, and the Syrian military headquarters of Apamea declared its independence. This defection of his cavalry fortress took away his elephants and horses with one stroke. Antiochus would have no easy time restoring his father's empire.

After defeating Ptolemy Keraunos, the Galatian raiders wandered, looking for new targets. Ptolemy Philadelphus bribed them to push further into Turkey against Antiochus. This distraction was intended to keep Antiochus busy in Turkey, while Philadelphus invaded southern Syria. However, Antiochus saw through the scheme and drove the Egyptians back out of Syria before tackling the Gauls.[5]

In 276 BC, Antiochus ordered an eastern ally to quickly collect some war elephants to use against the Gauls. The ally succeeded in obtaining twenty, presumably purchased from India. This exchange was the first of many good contacts between Antiochus and the second Indian emperor, Bindusara.[6]

The twenty war elephants reached Babylon in the early spring of 275 BC and were sent west to Antiochus. It is not clear what happened to the five hundred elephants that had been stationed at Apamea, Syria, before the city declared its independence. If Chandragupta Maurya of India had given old elephants ("past their prime") to Seleucus in 303 BC, then most of them would have died in the subsequent twenty-eight years. Otherwise, the rebels sold, or killed, the elephants.[7]

Antiochus led a rather small and tired army into Turkey to meet the Gauls and found himself seriously outnumbered.

As Lucian wrote:

Antiochus' heart failed him as the battle drew on. The host of the Galatians counted forty thousand horses and a great array of chariots, eighty of them scythed, and against all this he had only a small body of troops to set, hastily collected and for the most part light-armed. But the tactician, Theodotas of Rhodes, bade him be of good cheer. The King had sixteen elephants, and Theodotas instructed him to set these in the fore-part of the battle. For when the elephants moved out, the Galatian horses became mad with fear and swerved backwards. The scythed chariots tore their own ranks. The Macedonians and Greeks followed up with an immense slaughter. Only a few of the Galatians escaped into the hills...but the eyes of Antiochus were full of bitter tears. 'Shame, my men,' he broke out, 'is all that we have got this day. Our deliverance we owe to these sixteen brutes. But for them, where should we have been?' And the King commanded that the trophy should bear nothing but the figure of an elephant.[8]

Lucian's account may exaggerate the numbers of the Galatian raiders, but the outcome of the battle is accurate. The people of western Turkey celebrated Antiochus' "elephant victory" heartily and left statues to commemorate the event. In 1881, archaeologists found a five-inch-tall terra cotta sculpture in the region of an Indian elephant.[9] This statue shows many intriguing details that must be discussed.

The beast bore a howdah tower and mahout on his back, wore a bell around his neck, and trampled on a Galatian soldier.[10] A puzzling feature of this elephant is the very strange shape of the ears, which are shaped like a fish fin! Some details imply armor on its trunk, and circular bands of metal may have been used to protect its legs.[11]

The bell around the elephant's neck is interesting. The common use of bells on war elephants is clearly affirmed by coins and sculptures of the day. An interesting analysis comes from Arthur Pease, who offers some possible explanations as to why war elephants would wear bells.

That little bells like these should have been used with any intention of terrifying the enemy is almost preposterous. The two most reasonable theories are these: (1) that this bell has, like so many others, some superstitious significance; (2) that its purpose is entirely practical, namely, to give warning to people of the elephant's approach, that they may not be trampled upon.... If it be objected that elephants used in war were intended to trample upon the enemy, and that it would therefore be absurd to have their approach thus advertised, two answers may readily be given: (1) that the approach of a crowd of elephants would surely be known by the enemy, even if there were no bells to apprise them of the fact, while single elephants, accidentally let loose and wandering about their own camp, might easily do damage if no warning was given of their approach....[12]

More likely, the custom of bells on elephants rose from simple habit: the elephants to this time had all been born and trained in India, where they wore bells. During peace time, Indian elephants had to forage food for themselves each night, and their mahouts needed those ringing bells to find the beasts in the forest each morning. Bells are used on elephants to this day for the same reason.

The most unusual ears of the Turkish war elephant statue, shaped like a fish, can only be explained by theorizing that the artist failed miserably in

The generals after Alexander used extended head-pieces on the elephant to help protect the mahout while metal bands protected the beasts legs. *[Illustration copyright © Ian Heath, from 'Armies of the Macedonian and Punic Wars' by Duncan Head (WRG 1982).]*

depicting his model's ears. One scholar believes that because the elephant's ears are "its most vulnerable part," the elephant riders trimmed and cut the ears down to a smaller size.[13] This interpretation is difficult to accept: the elephants use their large ears to cool themselves, and although the ears are sensitive, they are hardly so touchy as to require docking.

Perhaps these elephants wore armor over the ears, and so the actual shape of the beasts' ears was unseen by the artist.

The leg armor of circular bands for the elephants was an important innovation for protecting the animals. Alexander and many subsequent commanders ordered their men to go for the pachyderms' eyes and legs. The leg armor would have to be segmented armor to allow them to walk.

The accounts about the Gaulish adventures against war elephants are puzzling for one reason. Why would the Galatian raiders handily defeat Ptolemy Keraunos while he rode on a war elephant in the front of his army, while the Galatians fled in terror from Antiochus' elephants in front of his army?

First, the Galatian raiders were not just one group, but many. Perhaps the tribe that killed Thunderbolt and his elephant in Thrace did not participate in the later advance into Turkey.

Second, Ptolemy Keraunos had only one elephant, whereas Antiochus had sixteen. This, in combination with the Galatian formation, was key. The description of Thunderbolt's demise has Gauls lopping off his head and carrying it around on a pike: this implies infantry, not cavalry. Against Antiochus, the Galatian scythed chariots and cavalry intended to charge when sixteen elephants charged at them instead, sending the horses back into their own infantry. Elephants are much more effective against cavalry than against infantry.

With Antiochus' successes against both Egypt and the Gauls, Ptolemy II asked for an end to the war in 271 BC.

15
The Elephant of Surprise

The Greek shall come against thee,
The conqueror of the East;
Beside him stalks to battle
The huge earth-shaking beast,
The beast on whom the castle
With all its guards doth stand,
The beast who hath between his eyes
The serpent for a hand.[1]
[Macaulay—a fictional prophecy of Pyrrhus for ancient Rome]

The first true elephant adventurer came from an unlikely place: Epirus, an ancient kingdom in modern-day Albania, northwest of Greece. The country was small and possessed no elephants, either indigenous or imported. In 319 BC, while Antigonus the One-Eyed sought to reunite the empire of Alexander the Great, Pyrrhus was born.

Pyrrhus was a second cousin of Alexander, and he seems to have inherited many of Alexander's qualities, ambitions, and vices.[2] Pyrrhus nearly died at the age of two because of his family's loyalty to Alexander. Pyrrhus' father died trying to save Queen Olympias, Alexander's mother, from Cassander who wished to rule Greece. When Cassander's assassins stormed the palace of Epirus to murder Pyrrhus, loyal nurses escaped with infant Pyrrhus and his sister.

Pyrrhus had a pair of unusual physical features. His upper teeth looked like they were fused together, with no spaces, as if they were one continuous mass.[3] And, according to popular legend, Pyrrhus healed people of "spleen problems" by touching them with his big toe![4] Statues show him as a handsome young man, displaying neither his teeth nor his toes.

Pyrrhus became king of Epirus at age twelve, but Cassander's army again forced him to flee. At seventeen, Pyrrhus traveled to southern Greece to join Demetrius the Besieger (son of Antigonus the One-Eyed) against Cassander. In Demetrius, Pyrrhus had an expert teacher in the use of cavalry and horsemen in combat.

Pyrrhus assisted Demetrius the Besieger in the cavalry wing at the Battle of Ipsus in 301 BC. Pyrrhus fought bravely and defeated the opponents facing him, but the vast number of enemy elephants sent Demetrius and Pyrrhus into retreat.[5] Pyrrhus went to Egypt as a hostage for Demetrius, to be sure that the Besieger would obey certain conditions after the Ipsus defeat. Ptolemy I discovered that Pyrrhus was a young man of many talents and could be a valuable ally. Ptolemy ensured that Pyrrhus received an excellent military education and training in wrestling and other activities. There were a few dozen Indian elephants in Egypt, captured from Perdiccas, and so Pyrrhus may have worked with the beasts in Alexandria.[6]

The treaty with Demetrius collapsed, and Ptolemy decided to install Pyrrhus as his new ally in Greece. Ptolemy gave one of his daughters to marry Pyrrhus and sent him with a small army and navy to retake Epirus in 297 BC.[7]

For fifteen years, Pyrrhus grew more and more competent in the arts of war, defeating Demetrius' units. His people nicknamed him "the Eagle." But when Demetrius was finally defeated, Pyrrhus became restless. He loved adventure and war.

In 283 BC, messages came from Tarentum, a Greek city in southern Italy, begging for Pyrrhus' help against "the wolves of Italy," the Romans.[8] The Romans were an unknown quantity in the Mediterranean world at the time, slowly usurping more and more of Italy, but until this time, staying out of Greek affairs. Pyrrhus wanted to give the wolves a hard lesson.

Pyrrhus' neighbors were all too happy to see Pyrrhus leave the region and offered him substantial help to get him on his way. The son of Demetrius (Antigonus Gonatas) loaned ships to take Pyrrhus across the Adriatic, and Ptolemy Keraunos loaned Pyrrhus nine thousand men and fifty elephants.[9] That left one fewer rival for the warring Greeks to worry about in eastern Europe.

There is disagreement on the source of Pyrrhus' elephants. Some historians claim that Ptolemy Keraunos (Keraunos means Thunderbolt) provided them, whereas others say that Pyrrhus captured them from Demetrius.[10] By considering the chain of ownership of each "herd," we can arrive at a probable solution. The basic question is: how old were these elephants?

The first option would be if Pyrrhus wrested the elephants from Demetrius. Going backward in time, the previous owners of this herd

HOISTING ELEPHANTS ON SHIPBOARD.

The hoist method of getting an elephant aboard a ship. The ancients probably had to walk the elephant up a strong ramp. ["Gleason's Pictorial Drawing Room Companion" June 21 and 28, 1851.]

had been Demetrius, Cassander, Polyperchon, Antipater, Alexander the Great, and finally King Porus of India. The training of Indian elephants usually begins between ages three and five, but military training does not begin until age ten. Elephants are not combat ready until they are between fifteen and twenty years old, fully grown. Since Porus used these elephants against Alexander in 326 BC, the beasts must have been born before 340 BC. So in 280 BC, when Pyrrhus went to Italy, elephants captured from Demetrius would be at least sixty years old! Sixty years old is nearing the maximum average age for elephants.[11]

However, if Pyrrhus acquired his elephants from Ptolemy Keraunos... the prior owner was Seleucus, who got them from Chandragupta Maurya in 305 BC. Adding fifteen years for growth and training would mean that these beasts would have been born before 320 BC. Therefore, the elephants from Keraunos would be in their forties and up rather than in their sixties. In Asia today, prime elephant working years are considered to be from age twenty through fifty.[12] Since elephants in good health live about sixty years, it is probable that Pyrrhus received the "younger" elephants of Ptolemy Thunderbolt.

Thirty-seven-year-old Pyrrhus ferried his army across the Adriatic Sea to southern Italy in 280 BC. It is not clear why he took only twenty of the fifty elephants, although there are two possibilities: (1) Perhaps thirty of the animals were "mere" haulers and not real combat elephants and thus, were not needed or, (2) the trip across the sea claimed some of the ships, and the elephants with them.

What about the ships used for transport? Ptolemy II Philadelphus had specially-designed elephant carriers built for the shallow waters of the Red Sea and the Nile river.[13] Pyrrhus' ships were not custom built for elephants; Antigonus Gonatus provided them on loan. Sea-going vessels could hold plenty of weight, although the average cargo ship of the day displaced only three hundred tons; some larger vessels could carry 1,300 tons.[14] The average male Asian elephant weighs less than five tons, so even twenty elephants at one hundred tons could conceivably be carried in an average cargo vessel. It is doubtful that all the elephants traveled in the same ship, however. Not only would their large bulk require a very spacious cargo hold, but should the ship sink, the whole elephant corps would be lost! As for the space needed, military analysts say that eight horses take up the same amount of cargo space as forty men.[15] There is no data for the stowage requirements of elephants, but perhaps one pachyderm would need the same amount of floor space as eight horses.

The biggest challenge to the sea transport of elephants would certainly be the loading and unloading of the beasts. Were cranes or reinforced ramps used? In Ceylon in the eighteenth century, when a heavy dock (or deep channel) was unavailable, the following method was used:

When the Elephants are put on board the Ships, there is a thing prepar'd of fifteen or twenty double Sailcloath, which is laid about his Breast, Belly and Sides, and is tyed together upon his Back, whereunto Ropes are fastened; then he is led into the Water betwixt Elephants bred for the purpose, upon which a Man sits to govern him, and another Elephant (upon which sits a Man) goes behind the Elephant that is to be shipp'd, and when this Elephant is unwilling to enter the Water, the Elephant that is behind puts his Head to the foremost's hinderparts, and presses him forward, which will cause any person to laugh to behold the same; when he is got deep enough in the Water he is tyed to the Boat, the other Elephants return, and he swims after the Boat to the Ship, where he is hauled over into the Ship.[16]

To paraphrase this old English...a strong cloth is fastened around the elephant and tied securely at the top of his back. Three elephants with riders force the beast into the water alongside a boat, and the elephant is guided along (swimming) to the ship in deeper water, where a crane or pulley system is attached to the ropes on his back and he is hoisted up to the deck of the ship. A method of this sort could have been used in the ancient world on ships that had heavy-duty winch systems. Another possible method is explained in Chapter 34 during Julius Caesar's invasion of Britain.

The ancient record of Pyrrhus' landing in Italy may provide the clue regarding how the elephants traveled by sea. As the fleet approached Italy, a storm came up and scattered the ships. Pyrrhus and his men, fearing their flagship would sink, jumped into the ocean to swim to the nearby shore. Interestingly, Pyrrhus was able to collect two thousand men, a few cavalry, and two elephants at this landing place.[17] How did the elephants get ashore during the storm? Certainly elephants are strong swimmers, but how would they get out of the ship? They must have been standing on the main deck when the ship sank beneath them. It seems that Pyrrhus must have kept the elephants on the deck of the ships, making their loading and unloading substantially easier. The storm itself was only a small danger to the swimming beasts, as we may infer from the gale that swept an elephant off a ship in 1856. The creature simply swam the remaining fifty kilometers to South Carolina![18] What a sight that would have been, to see the fleet of Pyrrhus sailing along with pachyderms under the masts!

The chaos from the storm was an inauspicious beginning to the adventure, but Pyrrhus became the first man to invade a country by sea with war elephants.[19]

Within a few days, more ships arrived and safely deposited the army and pachyderms in southern Italy. It is possible that Pyrrhus lost more than half of his elephants to the storm, if he had sailed with fifty and arrived with only twenty.

The Romans had advance warning and arrived quickly to attack, hoping to keep Pyrrhus from gaining any reinforcements from the Greek cities. They met for battle at Heraclea in 280 BC.

Pyrrhus watched the Romans line up and was impressed with their discipline and armor, but believed that his phalanx with its long spears would crush the legions. Having only twenty elephants, he kept them in reserve to see how the rest of the battle progressed. Pyrrhus personally led the three thousand Thessalian heavy cavalry on the left wing, but the Roman cavalry outnumbered the Greeks and were beginning to push them back.

...Pyrrhus raised the signal for the elephants. Then, indeed, at the sight of the animals, which was out of all common experience, at their frightful trumpeting, and also at the clatter of arms which their riders made, seated in the towers, both the Romans themselves were panic-stricken and their horses became frenzied and bolted, either shaking off their riders or bearing them away. Disheartened at this, the Roman army was turned to flight, and in their rout some soldiers were slain by the men in the towers on the elephants' backs, and others by the beasts themselves, which destroyed many with their trunks and tusks (or teeth) and crushed and trampled under foot as many more. The cavalry, following after, slew many; and not one, indeed, would have been left, had not an elephant been wounded, and not only gone to struggling itself as a result of the wound but also by its trumpeting thrown the rest into confusion. This restrained Pyrrhus from pursuit...[20]

Roman historian Lucius Florus wrote that between the "ugliness" of the roaring elephants and neighing of the frightened cavalry horses, the battle at Heraclea had "turned the battle into a wild-beast show."[21]

The military historian Delbruck, always skeptical, says that the Romans greatly exaggerated the power and effectiveness of the elephants just to excuse their losses against Pyrrhus.[22] Such is not a fair assessment. Pyrrhus was developing new tactics for elephants. Individually, the elephants were simply heavy cavalry, but wearing towers with archers on their backs turned them into mobile artillery platforms, which surprised the Romans.[23]

Cassius Dio's story contains one curious element: "the clatter of arms which their riders made, seated in the towers." In prior chapters we noted the use of bells around the necks of war elephants, but here we are told that the howdah soldiers were making a lot of noise as well. Perhaps Indian traditions continued with this elephant squadron, with some of the elephants carrying signal drums to deliver orders to the other riders; or the riders may have beaten their spears against the walls of their howdahs to draw the Romans' attention toward the coming monsters. Whatever the purpose of the howdah-generated noise, Cassius Dio agrees that it helped to terrify the Romans.

The injured elephant that brought disorder into the allied cavalry died of his wounds. Pyrrhus had only nineteen elephants in the next battle.[24]

There are several reasons why the early Roman legions had so much trouble against elephants. First, there was the terror of seeing an entirely new thing. Romans had never seen an elephant before. Commanding generals often calmed their soldiers' fears of cavalry horses by reminding them that horses do not kill, only the man on the horse's back can kill.[25] This is not, however, true of elephants used as cavalry. Pachyderms did kill, and so the fears of infantry soldiers facing them would not be allayed so easily.

Second, the early Republican Roman armies were not professional soldiers: the legionaries were simply called up for duty when an army was needed. Full-time professional Roman legions were still more than two centuries in the future.

Finally, the Romans were armed with short stabbing swords. In fighting elephants, these are inadequate. Although it is possible to cut off an elephant's trunk with the Roman gladius, to do so requires the soldier to avoid the enemy guards at the elephant's sides and approach within striking distance of elephant tusks and trunk! The Greeks had used long spears, axes, and machetes against elephants, not short swords.

The future rulers of the world, the Romans, seemed to have met their match.

16
Flaming Pigs

Pyrrhus marched straight to Rome with his victorious army, hoping that the Romans would grant the Greek cities full independence. Several southern Italian cities joined his cause, but Rome was stubborn in negotiation. In the seventeenth century, Edward Topsell translated Plutarch's story about the unusual tactic of Pyrrhus to convince the Roman ambassador to give in.

When Fabritius was sent by the Romanes to King Pyrrhus in Ambassage, Pyrrhus offered to him a great summe of money, to prevent the Warre, but he refused private gain, and preferred the service of his Country: the next day he brought him into his presence, and thinking to terrifie him placed behind him was a great Elephant, shadowed with the cloth of Arras; the cloth was drawne and the huge beast instantly laid his trunke upon the head of Fabritius, sending forth a terrible and direfull voice: whereat Fabritius laughing, perceiving the pollicy of the king gently made this speech; Neque heri aurum neque hodie bestia me promovit. I was neither tempted with thy Gold yesterday, nor terrified with the sight of this beast today...[1]

A year later, the Romans had produced more legions to oppose Pyrrhus, causing the general to remark that "the Roman legions when cut to pieces grew whole again, hydra-fashion."[2] For the battle of Asculum, the persistent foes had invented some anti-elephant weapons, according to Dionysius of Halicarnassus:

Outside the line they stationed the light-armed troops and the waggons, three hundred in number, which they had got ready for the battle against the elephants. These waggons had upright beams on which were mounted movable transverse poles that could be swung round as quick as thought in any direction one might wish, and on the ends of the poles there were either tridents or swordlike spikes or scythes all of iron; or again they had cranes that hurled down heavy grappling-irons. Many of the poles had attached to them and projecting in front of the waggons fire-bearing grapnels wrapped in tow that had been liberally daubed with pitch, which men standing on the waggons were to set afire as soon as they came near the elephants and then rain blows with them upon the trunks and faces of the beasts. Furthermore, standing on the waggons, light-armed troops—bowmen, hurlers of stones and slingers who threw iron caltrops; and on the ground beside the waggons there were still more men.[3]

These wagons, if the description is accurate, were chock full of elephant-harming devices. The Romans had caltrops for the elephants' feet, swinging blades to cut trunks, fiery grappling hooks to tether and burn the beasts, and archers and spearmen to shower the pachyderms with darts; it was quite a kaleidoscope of weaponry in the wagons!

As often happens, reality gets in the way of well-laid plans. The Romans put the wagons on the wings of the legions, where the elephants had been at Heraclea. Rather than obliging the enemy, Pyrrhus placed the elephants in the center, far from the strange wagons.[4] Next, the Greek general attacked the anti-elephant carts by sending archers and slingers to kill the men inside. The elephants again rumbled through the legions, routing them.

Although the Romans fled, one legionary cut off the trunk of an elephant.[5] Pyrrhus may have lost a few elephants at Asculum, along with thousands of men, and he famously said "Another victory like this and I shall be ruined!"[6] The origin of the phrase "Pyrrhic victory" comes from this statement of Pyrrhus. A Pyrrhic victory is a win that is so costly that it seems like a loss. The Romans could continue to raise reinforcements, while the Greeks had very little hope of raising more troops or elephants.

The two consecutive defeats at the hands of Pyrrhus, at Heraclea and Asculum, shook the Romans. Rome began to panic and even considered Pyrrhus' demand to leave southern Italy alone. However, just as the Roman Senate prepared to vote on reaching an agreement with Pyrrhus, some representatives of Carthage arrived.

Carthage, a rich port city in North Africa, had a huge navy. They also owned most of Sicily and feared that Pyrrhus would come to defend Greek cities in Sicily. So Carthage offered to use its navy against Pyrrhus if Rome would keep up the fight in Italy. The Romans agreed. In 279 BC, Rome and Carthage allied against Pyrrhus.[7]

As the Carthaginians feared, Pyrrhus decided to enter Sicily to defend the Greek cities and fight against the Carthaginian outposts. Carthage had been nearing complete victory in Sicily, but Pyrrhus' dealt them a serious blow.[8] In the summer of 278 BC, Pyrrhus took his army to Sicily. He won several easy victories, often without a fight.

The Carthaginian fear of the elephants was far greater than their fear of Greek troops. The latter they had often fought with success; but rumour had spread and magnified the terror of these mighty beasts with their strange, dark Indian mahouts. The Romans had faced them and died; the Carthaginians scampered off the field of battle.[9]

Pyrrhus did face one strong fortified city, called Eryx. Pyrrhus himself climbed a ladder up the battlements in the first wave of attack and won a great victory. When Pyrrhus seemed poised to take the whole island of Sicily, the Greek cities began to fear him more than they feared the Africans.

When the Greek cities began to turn against him, Pyrrhus decided to leave. While sailing back to Italy, Pyrrhus remarked, "What a fine battle-field we are leaving to the Romans and Carthaginians!"[10] This statement accurately predicted the upcoming Punic wars.

The Carthaginian fleet sank many of Pyrrhus' ships while he returned his army to Italy in 276 BC. On the spot where the surviving ships landed, an enemy army ambushed Pyrrhus, where he lost many men and two elephants.[11] This left Pyrrhus with perhaps fifteen elephants.

Pyrrhus faced two Roman armies and hoped to defeat them one at a time. In 275 BC, the Greek general attempted a very difficult night march to surprise the legions from behind at dawn. His forces became lost during the night and arrived late. The Romans were surprised, but they were already awake. At the Battle of Maleventum, Consul Manius Curius had the advantage against Pyrrhus' tired troops and new methods for dealing with elephants.

As Pyrrhus' forces fell back against the legions, Pyrrhus again sent in the elephants. As in the previous two battles, the Romans began to crumble before the giant beasts. Plutarch says that the Romans made an organized withdrawal behind some deep trenches, where the elephants were stopped by the ditches.[12] Then we have three different versions of the Roman counterattack against the elephants.

One author says that the legionaries used javelins and flaming arrows against the elephants, causing them to panic.[13] Another version claims that the Consul had armed his rear line of soldiers with flaming torches in the left hand and swords in the right because elephants fear fire.[14] During this counterattack by the Romans:

...when the elephants again moved forward into the front rank, a young one that happened to be among them was struck a heavy blow on the head with a spear and turned round; and when it was hurrying back through the confused mass of its fellows, trumpeting with pain, its dam recognized it and left her place to defend it, causing by her vast bulk as great a disturbance around her as if she were attacking the enemy. Thus the same beasts which deprived the Romans of their first victory and equalized the second battle, gave them undoubted victory in the third fight.[15]

Dionysius agrees with this story of Florus, saying that the Romans wounded an "elephant cub," leading to the rampage, and then captured eight elephants with their mahouts.[16] This story is entirely consistent with normal elephant behavior, as protective elephant mothers will crash through any barrier to help a calf.[17] In fact, the calf would even accompany the mother to battle, as they cannot be separated. There is also a famous plate that dates to this period and region showing an Indian elephant carrying a tower, with a small elephant calf trotting behind. The plate may refer to this story.[18]

The final version of the Roman counterattack against the elephants at the Battle of Maleventum tells of the "flaming pig" stratagem.

This time the war elephants were unable to force a victory. The Romans now drove them off using pigs coated with grease and pitch which they turned into live torches. Their shrill, dying squeals made the huge pachyderms panic and put to flight.[19]

This is not the only recorded example of the "flaming pig" tactic in use against elephants. Legend has it that King Porus taught Alexander the Great that elephants fear pigs, and set up a demonstration to prove it, after the Battle at Hydaspes.[20] According to both Aelian and Polyaenus, the son of Demetrius the Besieger, Antigonus Gonatas, besieged Megara with elephants in 266 BC. It seems that Gonatas tried to use the elephants in a rather Indian manner: as battering rams or "wall destroyers."[21] The people of Megara, doused pigs in oil, lit them, and then tossed the unfortunate squealers among the elephants.[22] After this debacle, Gonatas required his mahouts to always keep swine among the elephants to accustom them to the pigs![23]

A bronze coin from Italy from this time period shows an elephant on one side and a pig on the other, perhaps referring to this incident at Maleventum between the Romans and Pyrrhus' pachyderms.[24] The town producing the coin often produced coins with two different and yet related objects on each side, including a sword on the front and a scabbard on the back.[25] This coin might imply that the story of the elephants and the pigs at Maleventum was well known in Italy.

The armored elephants of Pyrrhus panicked the Roman cavalry in Italy. [*Attributed to T.H. McAllister, circa 1890s.*]
Source: George Eastman House.

Although there are many different versions of the Battle of Maleventum regarding the method used by the Romans to scare the elephants, all include the element of fire and all agree that the Romans won the day. They killed two elephants and captured eight, leaving Pyrrhus to escape with only a few.

Some writers ascribe Pyrrhus' failure to destroy Rome as the fault of the elephants.[26] The elephants brought victory in the first two battles and were defeated in the third; the theory of elephants as the failure behind Pyrrhus' departure from Italy seems farfetched. Pyrrhus failed to see that Rome was not just another Greek-style city-state, it was becoming a nation-state.[27]

Pyrrhus desired to stay in southern Italy to continue fighting the Romans but he had no money to pay for troops, and Antigonus Gonatas, King of Macedon, refused to send him any help. Pyrrhus' anger then turned against Gonatas instead of the Romans. Pyrrhus returned to Epirus with only eight thousand infantry and five hundred cavalry.[28] The fate of his remaining elephants Pyrrhus had taken to Italy is unknown: some say he took them back to Epirus, whereas others say the beasts were left behind.

Four of the war elephants captured by the Romans at Beneventum marched into Rome as part of Consul Manius Curius' triumphal parade in February of 274 BC. The people of Rome crowded the streets to see the amazing beasts with "a snake for a hand."[29] Florus describes the scene:

Rarely has a fairer or more glorious triumph entered the city....on nothing did the Roman people look with greater pleasure than upon those huge beasts, which they had feared so much, with towers upon their backs, now following the horses which had conquered them. The elephants came with their heads bowed low, and they were not wholly unaware that they had been captured.[30]

This conflict with Pyrrhus awakened the Roman people to the dangers posed by enemies outside of Italy, not to mention the tactics of Greek warfare and the use of war elephants. Likewise, the other nations of the earth learned of the Italians who defeated the great Pyrrhus, although they suffered much at the tusks of the war elephants.[31] Ptolemy II Philadelphus found the Roman strength impressive enough to establish diplomatic relations with Italy in 273 BC.[32] Within twelve years of Pyrrhus' retreat, Rome had taken practically the whole of Italy, lacking only the Po Valley, where Hannibal would invade in sixty years.[33]

With the Pyrrhic War, Rome faced for the first time an enemy from the civilized core of the Mediterranean world and, with his defeat, that world began to take notice of Rome.[34]

17
Chaos in the Streets

Pyrrhus' return to Epirus was no somber affair; the people viewed him as the savior of the Greek cities of the west. He had, after all, defeated the Romans and Carthaginians in most of their engagements. Now Pyrrhus wanted to deal with the new king of Macedon who had so ungraciously refused to help with the Italian campaign. His army was not large enough, however, so Pyrrhus had to hire many thousands of Gauls.

In 273 BC, Pyrrhus drove Antigonus Gonatas out of Macedon with only minimal fighting. A good speech by Pyrrhus, along with his unbeatable reputation, induced most of Antigonus' infantry to defect; then a quick strike forced Antigonus' elephant battalion to surrender.[1] Pyrrhus' control of his Gallic reinforcements left something to be desired. When the Gauls began to plunder Greek tombs and commit other atrocities, the Greek peoples quickly came to hate Pyrrhus.[2] As one writer put it, Pyrrhus was "the great general and the blind statesman."[3]

Following the fleeing Antigonus Gonatas, Pyrrhus took his army and twenty-four elephants to southern Greece in the spring of 272 BC.[4] Pyrrhus arrived late in the evening at the unprepared city of Sparta. Although encouraged by some to attack immediately, he wanted to wait for morning, assuming that the city could accomplish no reasonable defense in twelve hours. Pyrrhus knew that Sparta had very few men present because they had sent an army on an expedition far away. However, the women of Sparta were at home and were outraged to hear the city elders discuss surrender. The women, old folks, and children vowed to work all night to prepare defenses so that the few men could sleep and fight valiantly the next day. These unconventional support troops worked from dark until dawn digging a large trench, 1200 feet long, nine feet wide, and six feet deep! They also buried wagons down to their axles, to prevent easy removal, as primitive palisades. The trench and palisades proved to be excellent anti-elephant defenses. Pyrrhus and his forces threw themselves at Sparta repeatedly, but could not get through the defenders. According to Polybius and Frontinus, some elephants were

The Elephant rescuing a Soldier.

Based on a true story, when a man fell beneath the wheels of a heavy munitions-wagon, the trailing elephant quickly lifted it over the man, saving his life. *["The Intelligence of Animals with Illustrative Anecdotes, from the French of Ernest Menault." Charles Scribner & Co., New York, 1870. Illustrated Library of Wonders Series.]*

killed or wounded when they ran upon the ditch.[5] At last, reinforcements arrived to defend Sparta, so Pyrrhus gave up on the city.[6]

Having failed to capture Sparta, Pyrrhus moved toward the city of Argos, where Antigonus Gonatas held the city and its garrison. Some of Pyrrhus' allies opened the city gates in the middle of the night so his army could enter secretly and surprise the enemy. However, the army made a major miscalculation. The city gate had a low overhead, and the first pair of elephants bashed their howdah towers on the gate.[7] This forced the mahouts to remove the howdahs, using the various chains and straps around the elephants' bodies. The elephants became nervous, and the mahouts tried to calm them by singing to them quietly. Once inside the gate, the howdahs were put back on, making even more noise. This whole process awoke some sleeping citizens, who looked out and saw the beasts in the streets and sounded the alarm.

...while they [elephants] could usefully be used to help to demolish strongholds, it was a risky experiment to try to use them in the cramped conditions within a town, and it is strange to find a professional soldier of the stature of Pyrrhus failing to foresee the problem of getting them through the gates.[8]

The garrison of Argos awakened, and Antigonus quickly organized his army to drive the invaders out.

At dawn, Pyrrhus could see how small a portion of his army had safely come inside the city walls. He could also see the large number of Antigonus' soldiers approaching. Pyrrhus sounded the retreat and sent a messenger to his young son outside the gates of Argos to stop sending any more troops. But the boy misunderstood the order, and ordered the rest of the Epirot army to rush into the city with more men and elephants.[9] Now total chaos reigned at the gates of Argos as part of the army tried to escape and the rest strove to enter.

To add to the confusion, the largest of Pyrrhus' elephants had fallen athwart one of the gates. Another elephant, whose name Nikon has survived, missed its mahout, who had been mortally wounded and had fallen off the beast's back. It dashed through the retreating force until it had found its master's dead body. Lifting it with its trunk, it put the body across its tusks, and wild with grief and rage, it charged in all directions, trampling down everyone whom it met.[10]

While the elephants ran angrily through the streets and blocked the gates, the soldiers of Antigonus Gonatas arrived. Pyrrhus, on his horse, was hit lightly by a javelin, thrown by a local boy, whose mother watched from a house above the street. When Pyrrhus spurred his horse angrily toward his assailant, the woman picked up a large tile and threw it at Pyrrhus. The tile crashed on Pyrrhus' helmet, knocking him unconscious for a moment, and he slipped from his horse. One of Antigonus' mercenaries rushed to the spot and hacked off Pyrrhus' head while he lay stunned.[11]

Pyrrhus died before the age of fifty.[12] Antigonus Gonatas had been a boyhood friend of Pyrrhus and granted him a royal burial in Argos. The monument at the tomb of Pyrrhus showed his famous elephants.

Pyrrhus, rather like Demetrius the Besieger, spent his life seeking adventures and fighting bravely, with no thought to settling down and ruling a kingdom. Sometime in the years before his ill-fated invasion of southern Greece, Pyrrhus published a memoir of his battle tactics in Italy and Sicily, explaining the battles of the Romans, Carthaginians, and his own army. This book had little "circulation," and copies have not survived to modern times. Plutarch used a copy of the book to help him write a short biography of Pyrrhus.

Another copy of Pyrrhus' tactics came into the hands of a young Carthaginian cavalry commander, who studied it carefully to learn about elephants and the Roman war machine. His name was Hannibal.[13]

18
War Elephants of Carthage

Hundreds of years before Rome became an important city, Phoenician sailors of the Middle East (modern Lebanon) explored the coasts of "the Middle Sea," the Mediterranean. Carthage, in modern Tunisia became a rich city by exploiting Hispania (Spain), where Celts and Iberians mined gold, silver, and tin.[1]

Carthage lay on the coast of northern Africa, only ninety miles from Sicily.[2] Carthage established colonies in Sicily and in Hispania. She boasted a skilled navy, but produced poor armies.[3] Carthage was an empire of merchants, not warriors.[4] Her neighbors hated Carthage because of the high taxes she imposed to keep up the mercenary armies and navies.[5]

While Carthage was not beloved, she did have lots of money. Carthage paid Africans, Spaniards, Gauls, Greeks, and Celts to do their fighting. The most famous of the mercenaries came from nearby Numidia, whose horsemen may have been the best light cavalry in the ancient world.[6] Numidians rode practically in the nude, wearing only a leopard skin over the shoulder like a sash.[7] Numidians were among the mahouts riding the war elephants in the wars against Rome, and an ancient coin seems to show that they rode the elephants seated in a sideways position![8]

Greek colonists in Italy tried to stifle the growing power of Rome by hiring a brilliant general, Pyrrhus. After defeating Rome in two major battles, Pyrrhus moved into Sicily to attack Carthaginian colonies, nearly driving them off the island. The combat with Pyrrhus from 278 BC to 276 BC was Carthage's first exposure to war elephants.[9]

When Pyrrhus left Sicily, Rome decided to move in and conquer the undefended Greek cities. Thus, as Pyrrhus had predicted, Rome and Carthage became neighbors and rivals.

Carthage took notice of the "new" weapon of war that had been so devastating to their own mercenary troops: the elephant.[10] The leaders of Carthage realized that northern Africa had plenty of elephants, and they prepared to deploy their own elephant squadrons.

Carthage paid professionals to capture elephants for them throughout north Africa, around the Atlas Mountains, Morocco, and Algeria.[11] The elephants caught here were the forest variety, like those captured by the Ptolemies' in East Africa; smaller than Asian and African Bush elephants.[12] Carthage built stables in the thick city walls capable of housing three hundred pachyderms and hired "Indian" mahouts. The term "Indian" became synonymous with elephant rider in ancient times, whether the rider was actually born in India or not.[13] During the early years of the elephant program, Carthage relied heavily on real Indian mahouts, hired and brought through Egypt.[14] In later years, certainly, many riders came from Egypt, Syria, and black Africa.[15] We know this because some of the artwork and coinage of ancient Carthage and Rome show elephant riders with African features.[16]

The First Punic War, between Rome and Carthage, lasted twenty-three years, from 264 BC to 241 BC.[17] During this conflict, Carthage started a military modernization program: replacing the horse-drawn war chariot with the war elephant.[18]

Rome sent legions into Sicily and laid siege to the Carthaginian city of Agrigentum in 262 BC. Africa sent an army of fifty thousand mercenaries, six thousand cavalry, and sixty elephants to break the siege. The African general did not know how to use his new weapon, the elephants, so he put them behind the army rather than in front. When the Romans routed the first line of mercenaries, the fleeing Africans ran into the elephants, panicking them.[19] Stampeding elephants threw the whole army into disarray, with the Romans killing eight and wounding thirty-three pachyderms.[20] Carthage's first attempt at elephant warfare had failed miserably.

For years, inconclusive fighting in Sicily dragged on. The Romans decided to try some new tactics. First, they built a navy. Some fleets were destroyed in storms, whereas others were ripped apart by the superior seamanship of Carthage's sailors. Once the determined Romans eventually took control of the seas, the Senate decided to send an army down to Africa to destroy Carthage. Sicily would fall to Rome by default.

Regulus took two legions to Africa in 256 BC, numbering about fifteen thousand men.[21] Carthage sent out a large army to oppose the Romans, but the inexperienced African general put his troops on a steep hill and lost the advantage of having cavalry. The Romans destroyed most of the infantry, while the horses and elephants fled back to Carthage.

The Suffetes, leaders of Carthage, realized that they needed a better general, so they hired a Greek named Xanthippus, from Sparta. He had personal knowledge of war elephants and knew the strengths and weaknesses of Roman formations.

Xanthippus had appreciated that the Carthaginians, although they possessed war-elephants, were ignorant of the tactical methods of employing them in the field. He proceeded to use them as no Carthaginian had ever been able to use them before...[22]

Where might Xanthippus have learned about war elephants? The city of Sparta defended itself mightily against the elephants of Pyrrhus in 272 BC, only fifteen years earlier. Xanthippus helped to defend Sparta against Pyrrhus and his elephants.[23]

Consul Regulus was confident that his Roman legions could again rout the poorly trained African soldiers, and he was in a hurry. He needed to make a name for himself before the next elections in Rome.[24] The legions, which would eventually conquer the western world, found success in combat for a number of reasons. They wore armor and marched together like the old Greek phalanx, but relied on swords (not spears) and operated in small groups for greater mobility.[25] Roman legions used a three-line system so that the first two lines of soldiers could alternate in the front as needed, while the third line protected the rear.

However, the Roman armies were not invincible; they had major deficiencies in this third century BC. Their leaders were elected by the senate, and did not necessarily know anything about military service.[26] Also, the Romans were seriously deficient in cavalry, making them susceptible to flank attacks by faster or more numerous opponents.[27]

In the spring of 255 BC, Xanthippus the Greek organized a formidable line of one hundred war elephants and set superior numbers of cavalry at each wing.[28] Behind the elephants, Xanthippus hid his phalanx infantry.

Consul Regulus made a strange decision. He set "his infantry massed thick and deep in the pathetic hope of stopping the elephants," as if to pierce like an arrow through the Carthaginian center.[29] The legionaries would only have to kill the several beasts in the center of the enemy formation to reach the weak African conscripts, Regulus thought. He completely ignored his weak flanks.

One hundred elephants charged. The Roman cavalry, unaccustomed to such huge creatures, fled without a fight. This left the Italian infantry unprotected on its flanks; the African cavalry and elephants turned in on the mass of Romans. In front, the elephants "functioned like massive bowling balls to mow down enemy lines."[30] They crushed many

legionaries, but the Romans did manage to battle through the center.[31]
Polybius says that the Romans perished in heaps piercing the elephant
line.[32]

However, upon achieving this small victory at the center, the Romans
found themselves facing a Greek-style phalanx: a densely compacted
line of heavily armored soldiers with long spears. Caught between elephants and heavy infantry, Regulus' soldiers died by the thousands.[33] Two
thousand Italians escaped to the African coast and found ships to go
home. On the way home, a storm sank most of their ships.

Regulus was captured. Although disputed by some sources, Diodorus
gave a detailed account of the Consul's last days.

Learn the fate that befell Marcus Regulus, the Roman general, after his capture
by the Sicels [Carthaginians]. They cut off his eyelids with a knife and left his
eyes open. Then, having penned him in a very small and narrow hut, they goaded
to madness a wild elephant, and incited it to draw him down under itself and
mangle him. Thus the great general, as though driven by an avenging fury,
breathed his last and died a most wretched death.[34]

Diodorus also says that out of envy, the "foul wretches" [Carthaginians]
put Xanthippus in a leaking ship so that he drowned on his way home to
Greece.[35]

The war in Sicily continued. The survivors from Regulus' army told
horror stories about the monstrous elephants that had defeated them, and
the Roman soldiers in Sicily became terrified of pachyderms. Whenever
a Carthaginian army put elephants in front, the Romans refused battle.[36]

19
Proud Mahouts

The first Punic War between Carthage and Rome continued. The Roman legions under Regulus invaded Africa but were pulverized by a Greek mercenary general and his one hundred war elephants. The few survivors described the monstrous elephants that had defeated them, and the Roman soldiers in Sicily became paranoid about pachyderms.

After the defeat of Regulus, the Romans were unwilling to give battle in open country, for fear of these monsters. Their vast size, their sword-like tusks, the astounding skill of their 'snake-like hand,' and their ferocious trumpeting, filled the soldiers with terror. To increase their almost supernatural reputation, the Carthaginians dressed them up and decked them out like actors. Their mahouts were doubtless dressed in Oriental garb and had Indian names, even when they were natives of Africa. To make them fiercer and more terrifying the elephants were given prisoners to trample to death...Their naturally thick hide was reinforced with armour, and turrets full of archers or slingers were perched on their backs.[1]

This success led the African commander in Sicily to become overconfident. He relied too heavily on his 140 elephants and stopped taking precautions.[2]

The Roman commander in Sicily, Metellus, recognized this overconfidence and hatched a clever plan. He filled the walled city of Panormus with a full legion of troops, knowing that the Africans would soon march by. The Romans dug a ditch in front of the city, not far from the walls, just as the Greek women had done at Sparta to stop Pyrrhus' elephants.

The Carthaginian general assumed that by placing his elephants near the city gates, the Romans would not come out and his columns could march safely past.

Metellus stationed lines of javelin throwers behind the ditch and archers on the city wall, and sent a few soldiers out to "harass" the elephants. Their only task was to taunt and annoy the beasts and their mahouts.[3] The Romans shouted insults at the Indian mahouts and tossed rocks at the pachyderms. The riders and their beasts became angry and charged toward the city to stomp on their tormentors. The Roman historian Polybius described the event:

...the drivers of the elephants were fired with the impulse to show off their prowess to Hasdrubal [the Carthaginian general]. They were anxious to play the leading part in the victory, and so, charging the front ranks of the light-armed troops, they easily drove them back and pursued them to the trench. But when the elephants attacked this obstacle, they were at once wounded by the archers who were shooting at them from the wall, while at the same time volleys of spears and javelins were poured upon them from the fresh troops who were drawn up in front of the trench. The animals found themselves pierced and riddled with missiles and before long they stampeded. They turned on their own troops, trampling and killing them, breaking their ranks, and throwing them into utter confusion.[4]

When the elephants threw the Carthaginian column into confusion, Metellus burst out of Panormus with his legion.[5] The Africans suffered heavy losses, including more than one hundred elephants, although most of their mahouts escaped. This disaster left Carthage with more than one hundred mahouts without elephants; they were sent back to Africa to capture and train new beasts for war.[6]

Metellus showed creativity not only in his decisive victory, but also in finding a way to transport the elephants from Sicily to Italy. He had no ships big enough to carry elephants. Metellus designed a large raft that floated on air-tight jugs; he topped it with a wooden surface, dirt, and plants.[7] This botanical trickery, with some coaxing from the captured mahouts, convinced the elephants to walk onto the raft. The troops then cut the ropes and the raft ferried the elephants across the narrow Strait of Messina to mainland Italy.

All of the elephants and ten mahouts marched to Rome to be part of Metellus' triumphal parade.[8] During the parade the captured elephants became unmanageable, so Consul Metellus offered pardon to any mahouts who could get control of the beasts; several came forward and calmed the behemoths.[9] They were paraded through Rome and then taken into the Roman Circus.[10]

There are two different versions of what happened in the arena. Pliny says that the elephants were shown to be "contemptible" by driving them around the stadium with blunted spears, whereas others said that they were killed in public with javelins.[11] Verrius wrote that the elephants perished because the Romans had no idea what else to do with them.[12]

20
Cruelty and Inhumanity

After several years of poor military leadership in Sicily, the leaders of Carthage sent Hamilcar Barca to regroup the army. The mercenary troops loved Hamilcar, and for seven years they held out against superior Roman forces. He may have had a few elephants, but the sharp crags of Sicily are a poor place to use cavalry or elephants. No records tell us that Hamilcar possessed elephants; we simply consider the probability based on his upcoming expertise and handling of Carthage's beasts during the Truceless War.

In 241 BC, the merchants of Carthage decided that the war was futile and sued for peace, giving Sicily to Rome. In many ways, this was just a temporary "armistice and not a permanent peace," as both sides were exhausted from the twenty-four-year war.[1] Rome lost four hundred thousand men to battle and sea, and yet survived the carnage.[2]

Hamilcar sent twenty thousand foreign mercenaries back to Carthage in small groups, to collect their earnings and be on their way, while he himself stayed to organize the evacuation of Sicily.[3] The soldiers respected Hamilcar, but they arrived in Africa to a much different kind of leadership.

The wealthy leaders of Carthage decided that since the mercenaries did not win the war, they could not expect full payment for their years of service![4] The Suffetes, leaders of Carthage's government, offered them a small percentage of their promised wages. The mercenaries, now a highly trained group of soldiers, became understandably upset. They started raiding nearby cities and looting to show their displeasure. The Libyans took advantage of the chaos to revolt against Carthaginian domination and gave the mercenaries as many as seventy thousand men.[5]

In the spring of 240 BC, Carthage sent out an army with one hundred war elephants. The elephants did heavy damage to the enemy, but the mercenaries regrouped on a hill and then surprised the African infantry.[6] Bitter beyond words, the mercenaries brutalized their prisoners without

Hannibal learned elephant tactics from his father Hamilcar. Hamilcar crushed the rebel mercenaries with elephants during the Truceless War. [*Henry Smith Williams*. The Historians' History of the World. *In 25 volumes. Vol. 5, the Roman Republic. London: Hooper & Jackson, 1909. Plate between page 234 and 235.*]

mercy, cutting off their limbs and dumping them in ditches to bleed to death.[7] The "Truceless War" had begun.[8]

When Hamilcar arrived in Carthage, he discovered that his men had gone wild. It was too late to negotiate; the war had already become nasty. Hamilcar was ordered by the Suffetes to destroy the army that he had trained for six years in Sicily.

Since Carthage had already lost its standing defense force to the mercenaries, Hamilcar Barca had only raw recruits for soldiers, but he did have about one hundred war elephants. He used them to great effect.

In Hamilcar's first battle against the mercenaries, his army was out-numbered twenty-five thousand to ten thousand and yet he crushed the enemy.[9] In a maneuver foreshadowing his son Hannibal's strategy at Cannae, Hamilcar faked a retreat with his center, leading the enemy to charge into his hidden phalanx and elephants, where they lost eight thousand men.[10] Shocked by the pachyderms, the rebel armies changed their tactics, staying largely on high ground to try to neutralize the effective beasts of Hamilcar's army.[11]

To avenge the merciless killings of Carthaginian captives, captured mercenaries were thrown to the elephants to be crushed or ripped apart.[12] It was these atrocities and counter killings that justified the Roman historian Polybius in writing that the Truceless War "surpassed all the wars we know of in cruelty and inhumanity."[13]

Battles raged in Libya and Tunisia for three years before the Truceless War came to a close in 237 BC.[14] To Hamilcar Barca and the war elephants, Carthage owed its thanks.

...in her war with the mercenaries the elephants were victorious again and again, and to them Carthage in no small degree owed her salvation.[15]

21
The Lion's Brood

Rome took advantage of the Truceless War. While the mercenaries and Carthaginians butchered each other, Rome decided to violate the peace treaty they had just signed.[1] During a surprise invasion, the Romans took Sardinia easily. When Carthage protested this breach of treaty, Rome threatened war and demanded more reparations for the war in Sicily.[2] Carthage had little choice but to agree, as they were still heavily engaged with the cruel mercenary war. Again showing deceit, upon receiving the amended treaty, the Romans invaded and stole the island of Corsica, further alienating the Africans.[3]

The losses of Sicily and Sardinia were a great blow to Carthage, as they had been profitable colonies, but Carthage could not yet go to war.[4] Now desperate for more money to pay their debts, the Suffetes accepted Hamilcar's offer to take an army into Hispania (modern Spain).[5]

Before departing in 237 BC, Hamilcar bade his young son, Hannibal, to make a vow.

...his father Hamilcar, after the campaign in Africa, was about to carry his troops over into Spain, when Hannibal, then about nine years old, begged, with all the childish arts he could muster, to be allowed to accompany him; whereupon Hamilcar, who was preparing to offer sacrifice for a successful outcome, led the boy to the altar and made him solemnly swear, with his hand upon the sacred victim, that as soon as he was old enough he would be the enemy of the Roman people.[6]

Hamilcar viewed Hispania to be not only a place of wealth and precious minerals, but a base from which to stage a land-based invasion of Rome. He took a small army, one hundred war elephants, and his family to Spain. By taking direct control of the Spanish tribes and their mines, Hamilcar made a lot of money.[7]

Hamilcar Barca shaped and trained an army, and raised his sons, Hannibal, Hasdrubal, and Mago, to be military leaders. The Barca boys became known as "the Lion's Brood." The Roman historian Valerius Maximus wrote that while Hamilcar watched his three boys play, he said, "These are the lion cubs I am rearing for the destruction of Rome."[8]

When Hannibal was seventeen years old, he and his brothers accompanied their father Hamilcar on a routine trip. They were ambushed by Iberian tribes. Hamilcar drew the attack away from his sons, and they were able to escape, but he perished.

Although the army wanted Hannibal to lead them, the rulers of Carthage ordered Hasdrubal the Handsome, Hannibal's uncle, to take over. Hasdrubal the Handsome spent nearly a decade using diplomacy (rather than brute force) to gain the allegiance of many Spanish tribes. In 229 BC, Hasdrubal the Handsome led fifty thousand men and two hundred war elephants to avenge the death of Hamilcar by destroying the responsible tribe.[9] This tells us that Hamilcar had doubled his elephant corps from its original one hundred.

The logistics of providing food and water for two hundred elephants in Spain must have been daunting. Although the average temperatures at Nova Carthago (modern Cartagena) are pleasantly warm, Asian elephants would be shocked by the arid climate, with an annual rainfall of only about forty inches. However, Carthage was capturing its own elephants from north Africa, and these beasts were accustomed to a semi-arid environment. Although Hamilcar's elephant squadron did include a few of the Asian species (probably purchased from Syria), a majority were north African forest elephants.

Hannibal, the oldest son of Hamilcar, proved to be an excellent horseman, becoming captain of the cavalry in 224 BC.[10] He trained the elephants and African horses in proximity so that they could work in formation against enemy cavalry. In theory, this would make the Carthaginian wings invincible: the enemy would flee before the elephants, while the African cavalry could fall upon the rear of the Roman infantry. Young Hannibal studied Pyrrhus' memoirs, learning about the tactics of Romans and war elephants.[11]

Hasdrubal the Handsome fell at the hand of an assassin, said to have been paid by Rome, in 221 BC.[12] Hannibal Barca, twenty-six years old, was unanimously proclaimed leader by the armies. His rise to power did not go without opposition in Carthage, however. One Carthaginian pacifist, Hanno, opposed this appointment, saying that "this small spark may one day kindle a great fire," as he feared that Hannibal would take revenge upon Rome for his father's sake.[13]

The mercenary army of Hispania adored Hannibal and said that surely Hamilcar had been reborn in the spirit of his eldest son.[14] Hannibal was fairly tall and had great physical endurance, enhanced by constant life with the army, and sharing in its privations.[15] Even his enemies spoke of him with respect, as seen in this passage from the Roman historian Livy:

Reckless in courting danger, he showed superb tactical ability once it was upon him. Indefatigable both physically and mentally, he could endure with equal ease excessive heat or excessive cold; he ate and drank not to flatter his appetites but only so much as would sustain his bodily strength. His time for waking, like his time for sleeping, was never determined by daylight or darkness: when his work was done, then, and then only, he rested, without need, moreover, of silence or a soft bed to woo sleep to his eyes. Often he was seen lying in his cloak on the bare ground amongst the common soldiers....Mounted or unmounted he was un-equalled as a fighting man, always the first to attack, the last to leave the field.[16]

Hannibal spent two years pacifying Celtiberian tribes. Hispania, his base of operations, had to be secure when the major offensive against Rome began. While campaigning in west central Spain, a massive army of Celts struck the African forces near the Tagus River. Although out-numbered, Hannibal cheered his men with a confident speech. They made a night crossing of the river so that the enemy would have to cross it in the morning. Archers, slingers, and javelin throwers killed thousands as the Celts slogged through the deep water. When the enemy managed to elude the missiles of Carthage, they faced a surprise. According to Polybius, "when the barbarians tried to force a crossing at various points, the greater number of them were killed as they left the water by the elephants, who followed the river's edge and attacked them as soon as they struggled up the bank."[17] The Numidian cavalry swung around behind, and the slaughter was complete.

In 219 BC, Hannibal and his army lay siege to the small city of Saguntum, known to be a friend of Rome. Elephants do not make good siege weapons, but they do make excellent siege laborers. It is likely that the pachyderms were used to carry or pull logs from Spanish forests to provide lumber for Carthaginian battering rams and siege towers. Rome sent formal protests to Carthage. The senate demanded that the Suffetes give Hannibal to Rome for trial as a war criminal. Upon their refusal, Rome declared war.

Little did the Romans know that Hannibal would appear very soon on Italian soil with his war elephants.

22
Dangerous Waters

Hamilcar Barca, considered a great general even by his enemies, was eclipsed by his son Hannibal. Hannibal took control of the Carthaginian army of Hispania, composed of mercenaries from a dozen nations, at the age of twenty-six. His charisma enabled him to lead a disparate army of men from many lands.[1]

Hannibal was a born fighter, and having been reared from boyhood in the practice of warfare and having spent many years in the field as the companion of great leaders, he was well versed in war and its struggles.[2]

Hannibal believed that the key to defeating his sworn enemy, Rome, lay in separating Rome from her allies in Italy.[3] Rome was strong because she could force all the cities of Italy to provide men for her legions. Hannibal hoped that the barbarian Gauls in north Italy would follow his banner and that the cities of southern Italy would defect from Rome, given the chance.[4] This was a reasonable belief, considering that Pyrrhus' two victories caused some of Rome's "allies" to change sides, sixty years earlier.[5] Once Rome's manpower was depleted, Hannibal could lay siege to Rome and destroy it forever.[6]

Hannibal's strategy included war elephants. He would take a substantial number of pachyderms with the Carthaginian army to confront a new generation of Romans. Pyrrhus made headway against the legions using only twenty elephants, and Hannibal planned to take double that number.[7]

Hasdrubal Barca, Hannibal's brother, remained in Hispania with a small army, four-dozen warships, and twenty-one war elephants.[8] Hannibal took ninety thousand mercenaries, twelve thousand cavalry, and thirty-seven elephants on a march across Europe: a distance of about 1,500 miles.[9] They left their base in early May of 218 BC.

Leading elephants on a long trek is difficult. An elephant may need more than 200–300 pounds of fodder, plus fruits and grains, each day. Carts must be lined up, full of food, to provide for them when they are not free to forage on fertile lands. The elephants require vast amounts of water, and the Middle Sea (Mediterranean) could not be the source because it is salty! Water had to be transported from rivers and creeks.

The British made some long journeys with elephants in recent centuries and found that pachyderms travel at a speed of three miles per hour and can cover fifteen to twenty miles each day while carrying a heavy load. In the grandest example of a forced march by elephants, Antigonus the One-Eyed crossed Turkey at an average of forty miles per day for one week of 319 BC (with no load carried), but that killed several of his beasts.[10] Hannibal's elephants averaged nineteen miles per day, without casualties, on the journey to Italy.[11] The army crossed Gaul and ran into their first major problem in late August, at the Rhone River.

Elephants love water, and do not fear it, when they have grown up with it. They are naturally good swimmers, as naturalists and historians attest.[12] Unfortunately, Hannibal's elephants did not grow up in the wild because they were captured as youngsters. Growing up in Hispania, with its paucity of rivers and lakes, did not prepare the beasts for distance swimming. The Rhone River was not very deep, but its breadth was at least three hundred feet.[13] Since elephants have poor eyesight, they could not see the other side. Being naturally nervous creatures anyway, the elephants were not in the mood to learn to swim in this large river.

Hannibal learned that the Roman legions of Scipio the Elder had just landed at Massilia, only a four-day march to his south.[14] Scipio's two legions did not pose any threat to the vast Carthaginian army, but even a quick battle would create a delay that might keep the Africans from crossing the Alps before the snows. Hannibal did not have time to waste in getting the beasts across the Rhone, but a large Gallic tribe waited on the other side to attack, refusing Hannibal's bribes.

Hannibal sent his cavalry north under cover of darkness to circle around behind the enemy for a surprise attack while the Gauls stood on the banks of the Rhone waiting for Hannibal's infantry to cross on rafts.

While Hannibal gave his cavalry time to set up their flank attack, he had the infantry build large, sturdy rafts for the elephants. The elephants were not going to walk willingly onto the rafts, and even brilliant generals discover that you cannot easily force an elephant to do anything; you must convince it to do what you wish. Hannibal took a hint from the old Roman commander Metellus from the first war between Rome and Carthage. Metellus had shuttled captured Carthaginian elephants across the Strait of Messina (between Sicily and Italy) on rafts by covering the planks with plants and dirt.[15] After early hints of elephant noncooperation, Hannibal tried disguising his rafts.

37

Hannibal's elephants did cross the Rhone River on rafts, but did not wear their howdahs nor did they carry soldiers at the time! [*Engraving by Henri-Paul Motte, owned by the author, circa 1880s.*]

The rear assault by the Spanish and Numidian cavalry utterly shocked the Gauls, and Hannibal's infantry crossed the Rhone without much difficulty. That plan worked well. The elephants-by-raft plan was not as successful. Polybius, who interviewed eyewitnesses, wrote about Hannibal's war and this crossing of the Rhone:[16]

As soon as they were standing on the last rafts, the ropes holding these were cut, the boats took up the strain of the tow-ropes, and the rafts with the elephants standing on them were rapidly pulled away from the causeway. At this the animals panicked and at first turned round and began to move about in all directions, but as they were by then surrounded on all sides by the stream, their fear eventually compelled them to stay quiet...but some became so ter-ror-stricken that they leaped into the river when they were half-way across. The drivers of these were all drowned, but the elephants were saved, because through the power and length of their trunks they were able to keep these above the surface and breath through them...In this way most of them survived and crossed the river on their feet.[17]

Livy has a somewhat different version of the Rhone crossing. Livy wrote that one mahout was beating his "ferocious" elephant, when she turned on him and attacked. He jumped into the river to escape, and she jumped after him. This led to a general stampede, so that many elephants charged into the river.[18]

A 1991 article by O'Bryhim suggests that Livy's "ferocious" elephant scene is the real truth of the Rhone crossing and that rafts were not involved.[19] He believes that Hannibal did not have time to build rafts with the Romans moving up from the south. Thus, Polybius invented the raft story based on the story of Metellus during the First Punic War.[20] O'Bryhim has assumed, however, that Hannibal waited to begin con-struction of the elephant rafts until after the hostile Gauls on the far bank of the Rhone had been defeated, a process that took a few days. It is hard to imagine that Hannibal would rely on such a flimsy plan: a mahout beats an elephant into a rage so that the whole herd will chase him into the Rhone? That is not a plan with much probability of success. The story of the ferocious elephant was probably part of the truth, but only one fragment connected with the raft story, not replacing it entirely. A combined version of events could say that Hannibal built rafts and got the elephants aboard. Halfway across the Rhone, one nervous pachy-derm was beaten by her mahout, and the scuffle started a general stampede into the river.

Because elephants are naturally good swimmers (even if they don't know it), they did not drown. They swam across. Fortunately for

Hannibal, they swam to the correct side. However, many mahouts drowned, swept away in the Rhone's current.[21]

...at last all thirty-seven elephants had been safely ferried across with the loss of some of their mahouts, who were drowned. This loss must have caused Hannibal some staff problems, since the mahouts must have been highly trained men and not easily replaceable.[22]

Because pachyderms grow emotionally attached to their mahouts, this was certainly a difficult time for them: combining the stress of this immense journey with the loss of their best friends. New riders would have to be brought quickly, perhaps trainees. The loss of the mahouts was a major blow to both Hannibal and the elephant battalion.

23
Treacherous Paths

Hannibal's invasion of Italy faced a critical delay at the Rhone River, where an enemy opposed his crossing and his elephants refused to board the rafts. The Carthaginian cavalry drove away their foes, solving one problem. Disguising the rafts enabled the mahouts to guide their elephants aboard, but the beasts panicked and plunged into the Rhone. Fortunately for Hannibal, the elephants all survived and reached the east side of the river, but most of the mahouts had drowned, leaving his army woefully short of experienced elephant handlers.

With a Roman army closing from the coast to hinder his invasion, the Carthaginians had to move quickly northward. Hannibal had no intention of engaging the Romans in Gaul because his army needed to cross the Alps before late October, when the heavy snows would fall. So the Africans hurried to meet the guides who would lead them into Italy.

The imposing mountains terrified many of the Celts, who threatened to mutiny. Rather than make matters worse and lose these men altogether, Hannibal told the men that if they wished to return, to guard Hispania from the invading Roman legions, they were welcome to go. More than ten thousand headed back.

They started up the Alps around October 14.[1] Light snow had already fallen and so plenty of water flowed down in streams along the paths. Thus, the troops had no need to rely on barrels of water carried by their 9000–10,000 pack animals.[2] However, elephants do not like cold water: bathing in it or drinking it can make them ill.[3] When the water is cold, elephants will take a few gallons and hold it in their trunks until it warms before drinking it. Of course, this water-warming process comes at the cost of body heat, and the elephants needed their body heat in the cold mountains.

Merely climbing, even on steep paths, is not a problem for elephants. Elephants are very sure-footed and not prone to falls.[4] As John Hoyte demonstrated by accompanying an elephant over the Alps in the 1950s,

Elephants have no difficulty traversing mountain terrain. [*Illustrated London News, August 21, 1846. Reprinted with permission of The Illustrated London News Picture Library.*]

the beast walked easily at two and a half miles per hour at a gradient of one in six, but became more cautious (and slower) at a slope of one in five.[5] In a similar experiment in Asia, "Working elephants were tested on smooth and rough terrain, both up and down steep gradients, over rocky surfaces and through deep rivers. They came through all these obstacles without any difficulty and we were convinced that the Alpine passes and the smaller rivers we had looked at would have presented no obstacle to well-trained elephants."[6]

The paths did present one major difficulty for the pachyderms. The Alps are strewn with sharp, jagged rocks. The soles of elephant feet have thick skin, but underneath are very soft and spongy. Sharp rocks can become lodged in the sole and drive themselves deep into the foot.[7] The beast will go lame if the mahout does not quickly notice the limp and remove the debris. Although the Carthaginian army included veterinarians, it is probable that the mahouts themselves had learned the most about elephant health care.[8] Unfortunately, most of the experienced mahouts were floating face down in the Rhone River!

Hannibal's guides were false. The next weeks in the mountains became a nightmare. One night, the guides vanished, and local tribesmen began appearing on cliffs high above the Carthaginian column.[9] Hannibal's marching column, twenty miles in length, attracted the mountain people as a great source of free supplies and these people constantly attacked.[10] When the army moved through a narrow defile, gigantic boulders crashed down the cliffs upon them, pushed by the tribesmen. Even rocks that missed caused terror in the pack animals: whole strings of mules ran blindly off the path, plunging into chasms below.[11]

The attack did not catch Hannibal by surprise, and his troops scaled the heights to stop the boulder hurling, but it was too late: most of the pack animals and supplies had already been lost.[12] Upon learning that the mountain people believed that the elephants were monsters or devils, Hannibal sent them to the front of the column to discourage any attempts to block the path. The tribes did attack the vanguard of the African column, but they ran when the elephants charged.[13]

Now, the army had climbed above the "treeline," meaning that the horses and elephants could not forage for food with any success. In modern journeys by elephant, it has been noted that thinner oxygen at altitudes over five thousand feet causes the beasts to slow down, and they have difficulty breathing.[14]

At the top, another light snow fell and froze, making the path slippery.[15] Despite this, the men cheered up when they looked down into Italy and saw that the rest of the journey was downhill.

The cheer was short-lived.

Toward evening, the column came to a halt. A titanic boulder, as big as a house, had blocked the narrow path. It was far too heavy to move. The slopes above and below the rock were too steep to go around. The Roman historian Livy describes the scene: "Four days were spent in the neighborhood of this precipice; the animals came near to dying of starvation, for on most of the peaks nothing grows, or, if there is any pasture, the snow covers it."[16]

The men and animals spent days in that spot, while engineers worked on the boulder. Happily, it did not snow on the army, but freezing temperatures and cold winds howled constantly on the narrow path. The elephants may have been helpful to some of the freezing men. Elephants sleep standing up. The mahouts would certainly cover their beasts with armor and blankets to help them stay warm. Men might sit under the elephants and blankets, safe from the wind and sharing their heat.

Hannibal sent cavalry back up the trail to find wood for building fires: not for the men, but for boulder demolition. Using a variety of methods, heating and freezing liquids in cracks on the rock, they were able to chip off large pieces and finally break it in half.[17]

Going down the Italian side of the Alps proved to be as treacherous as climbing the Gallic side. Ice on the paths and unsure footing sent many men and animals sliding away to their deaths. But the fifteen-day nightmare ended with the survivors resting in northern Italy.

Hannibal's army was a shambles. He lost two-thirds of his infantry and perhaps a third of the cavalry to the Alps, reaching Italy with only twenty-thousand infantry and six thousand cavalry.[18] Many authors assume that some of the elephants "must have died" during the trek, but all of the ancient sources say the elephants all survived.[19] Polybius admits that the elephants "were in a miserable condition from hunger," but insists that the beasts did fight in the first battle against the legions, before succumbing to the rigors of the journey.[20]

The Roman people were shocked by the arrival of Hannibal, as Florus wrote:

...the thunderbolt which had long been destined to fall upon the Romans, immediately, hurried along by some compelling force, it burst its way through the midst of the Alps and swooped down upon Italy from those snows of fabulous heights like a missile hurled from the skies.[21]

24
The Best Laid Plans

The Romans, who scoffed at the idea that an army could cross the Alps, did not allow their shock to slow a prudent reaction. Recognizing that Hannibal's forces would be tired and weak after the incredible journey, they sent legions north to attack.

Hannibal expanded his army with several thousand barbarians of northern Italy, who simply wanted to kill Romans. Hannibal used his elephants as a breakwater in a shallow stream to slow the current of the Po River for the infantry and horses to cross.[1]

In a skirmish at the Ticinus River, the African cavalry overwhelmed a Roman reconnaissance by Consul Scipio. He was injured seriously by a javelin and saved by his son Publius Cornelius Scipio, age seventeen, who would later become Scipio Africanus.[2] Another consul, Sempronius, arrived and took control of the legions for the wounded Scipio.

The legions blocked the main road to Rome, and Hannibal needed a good plan to give his small, tired army a chance against the heavy Roman infantry. The Africans could not simply avoid battle. With winter snows falling in Alpine Italy, there would not be enough food for the animals and men. Hannibal had to attack so that the army could move south to warmer climes.

The Romans built a fortified camp whenever they stopped marching. If the legions had been using a *castra*, a one-night camp, they dug a ditch only three feet deep and five feet wide around their palisades. That would not keep out an elephant attack. But the Romans built a *castra stativa*, meant for longer camping, with a ditch twelve feet wide and nine feet deep.[3] Elephants could not assault such a camp. Hannibal needed to draw the Romans out of their camp for battle.

Early one morning, while a light snow fell on the Trebbia River, the Numidian light cavalry charged to the Roman camp, shouting and hurling javelins over the palisade, to wake up the legions. The Roman Consul Sempronius was furious. He ordered the legions to pursue. While the African army ate breakfast and warmed themselves at their fires, the Romans marched six miles, crossing freezing streams, following the Numidian horsemen. The Italian army arrived on Hannibal's chosen battlefield, cold, tired, and hungry.[4]

Historians disagree on where exactly Hannibal stationed his elephants. The only thing we are sure of is that they were not in the center. Knowing that the elephants were weakened from the Alps passage, Hannibal did not attempt to use them as a front-line shock weapon. The thirty-seven war elephants were split evenly on the flanks, probably in a line (trunk to tail) between the infantry and the cavalry. Polybius wrote that the elephants were stationed on the wings of the infantry (not the cavalry); this is reasonable, as Hannibal already had major cavalry superiority but infantry inferiority.[5] The elephants would be more useful against the infantry, but in a flank attack rather than a frontal assault.

Did the elephants bear howdahs at the Battle of the Trebbia? Some doubt that Hannibal's elephants carried towers or were even capable of it. African Forest elephants, captured in northern Africa for use as war elephants in ancient times, were much smaller than the better-known African Bush elephant and a bit smaller than the Asian elephant.[6] We know that Hannibal's army did include some Asian elephants, purchased from Syria or Egypt.[7] The Roman poet Juvenal ascribed turrets to Hannibal's elephants.[8] We have coins from ancient Italy, from the time of Hannibal, showing elephants with howdahs; on one Roman coin, three human heads are seen peeking above the howdah wall.[9] A terracotta statue found at Pompeii shows an Asian elephant wearing a tower, bearing a mahout who is feeding bread to the elephant's uplifted trunk.[10] In the first century BC, the Roman writer Lucretius said, "In process of time the Carthaginians taught fierce elephants, with towers on their backs, and with snake-like proboscis, to endure the wounds of war, and to throw vast martial battalions into confusion."[11]

The main problem with a basic elephant attack is that the elephant can only harm enemies within reach of its trunk. When the beast is that close, the enemies can strike the elephant with spears or swords. Although the Carthaginians may have improved the defense of the elephant by "fixing iron points or spears on the tusks," an enemy this close is already a significant danger to the animal.[12] The addition of a tower with one or two archers would be highly desirable. The archer(s) provides a distance weapon and provides protection to the elephant if foes approach. Although the African Forest elephant is relatively small, it could surely carry one or two men in a small platform. Hannibal did have a few larger Asian elephants also, and no one can dispute their tower-carrying abilities.[13] It is likely that some of the elephants had howdahs with soldiers inside.[14] At the Battle of the Trebbia, Hannibal used the elephants as missile platforms (for archers and javelin throwers) and sent them to flank the Roman infantry as the battle progressed.[15]

At the Trebbia River, Hannibal fielded thirty-eight thousand infantry (eighteen thousand "unreliable" Gauls) and ten thousand cavalry against the Romans' forty thousand infantry and four thousand horses.[16]

The Roman system placed legionaries at the center and cavalry on the flanks. In the front row stood the *Velites*, quick troops, wearing wolf skins over their helmets, who would throw several light javelins into the enemy force and then fall back to safety behind the lines. At the Trebbia, however, the Velites had already thrown most of their javelins in pursuit of the Numidian cavalry and thus were useless when they reached the battlefield. The Romans formed three lines of heavy infantry behind the Velites.[17]

Hannibal, by design, possessed almost every advantage at the Trebbia. A light snow was falling when the Romans arrived, cold and hungry. The Roman cavalry horses heard the elephants and fled in haste. The Roman infantry may have successfully withstood the elephants on their flanks, but their Gallic auxiliaries on the opposite wing collapsed under the elephant onslaught.[18] Hoping to surround the enemy, Hannibal had set his brother Mago with one thousand infantry and a thousand cavalry in a nearby marsh, which the Romans passed without scouting.[19] Mago's men appeared in their rear when the battle commenced. If the legions had not been disciplined enough to cut right through Hannibal's Gauls at the center, they would have been annihilated. Several thousand legionaries escaped to a nearby Roman fortress, only because the falling snow prevented any organized pursuit.

Hannibal's first battle with Rome was decisive. With very few casualties, he had routed the Romans. The elephants had a large part in the victory, if only assisting to scare off the Roman cavalry and rout the Roman auxiliaries.

Pliny the Elder claims that Hannibal offered a deadly sport to his Roman prisoners: if a Roman could defeat an elephant in one on one combat, he would be set free. The soldier killed the elephant, but fearing that news would spread of the weakness of elephants, Hannibal ordered the Roman to be executed. The story is unlikely for many reasons. At any rate, Hannibal's elephants were already doomed.

Twenty-nine elephants died at the Trebbia. Whether they died of wounds from battle, sickness, or hunger from their Alps crossing, we do not know with certainty. Of the eight survivors, only one of Hannibal's elephants lived through the winter.[20]

His name was Surus.[21]

25
Stalemate

We might never have known the name of Surus, except that he became Hannibal's mount and thereby a part of history. While passing through the marshes of northern Italy, a four-day journey, Hannibal lost an eye to an infection.[1] His generals convinced him that with only one eye, he would be better off up high, where he could look around the battlefield.

The only surviving elephant, Surus, a huge Asian, made a very high platform. If the average Asian bull is seven feet tall at the shoulder, a very large Asian might be nine to ten feet high.

We learn from Roman writers and poets that Surus had only one tusk.[2] Cato named Surus as the bravest of the war elephants in his Annals.[3] Surus must have been a bull because female Asian elephants rarely have tusks and they never grow long, impressive tusks that Roman soldiers would talk about. It is possible that Surus lost a tusk in the battle at the Trebbia, or he might have only grown one tusk—not an uncommon trait in bull elephants. Roman playwright Plautus seems to refer to Surus wearing a red cloth, and a plate of the era shows an Asian elephant "in full battle-dress with a red saddle-cloth and a red shield painted on its tower."[4]

Because General Hannibal now organized his armies and gave orders from Surus, the last elephant, presumably elephants had no part in the next few battles. Hannibal crushed Roman legions (forty thousand men) at Lake Trasimene in "history's greatest ambush."[5] His greatest battle, called by some the most perfect battle ever designed, saw Hannibal's mercenaries defeat a Roman army almost double their number at Cannae on August 2, 216 BC.[6] So many tens of thousands of Romans died that when Hannibal sent home the plundered rings of the Romans, they were measured in "pecks and bushels" rather than by counting.[7]

However, one Roman poet, Silius Italicus, wrote that at Cannae the Romans attacked several howdah-bearing elephants with fire and sent them plunging into the nearby river. If true, it would imply that either Hannibal somehow received reinforcements, or that the report of only one surviving elephant at the marshes was false.

Many scholars fault Hannibal for not assaulting Rome itself after the major victory at Cannae. They have forgotten two critical problems. Hannibal's army was far too small to lay an effective siege line around a city like Rome, and he had not been able to bring any heavy siege equipment over the Alps to batter the immense Roman fortifications.[8] Also, Hannibal had no naval fleet to keep the Romans from sailing down the Tiber River with supplies for a besieged city.[9] Hannibal had no choice but to continue with his plans to wrest Italian cities from Roman control to enlarge his own army with Italians and Gauls.

Hannibal's strategy began to work: several southern Italian cities defected from Rome, including the large city of Capua. Because Romans wrote all of the surviving histories, we must take their statements about the viciousness of their enemy with a grain of salt. Perhaps Hannibal was cruel, perhaps not. One report said that when Hannibal entered Capua, he used an elephant to step on the heads of Roman sympathizers. If true, the elephant had to be Surus, as Hannibal did not get reinforcements for a couple of years.

Rome had learned its lesson: Hannibal was too skillful for them, even when they fielded superior numbers.[10] As the ancient Roman Cornelius Nepos wrote, "while Hannibal was in Italy, no one could stand up to him on the battlefield, and after Cannae no one camped in the same plain with him."[11] So they slowly rebuilt their legions under the watchful eye of Fabius (nicknamed the Delayer) and refused to fight.[12]

In 215–214 B.C., the Carthaginians managed to smuggle about forty elephants past the Roman naval blockade and into southern Italy for Hannibal.[13] Carthage usually sent reinforcements not to Italy, but to Hispania, where a pair of Roman legions were threatening the valuable Spanish mines.

Because the Romans refused to fight, the elephants were not terribly useful to Hannibal. However, when the Romans surrounded Capua and laid siege to it, Hannibal attempted to break the siege.

To keep the Capuans locked in and Hannibal locked out, the Romans constructed siege works on both sides of their legions. Hannibal sent the elephants against one weak-looking section of the defenses. The Romans were able to kill three of them at the perimeter, but apparently the dead elephants tumbled into the ditch, forming a nice bridge over the trench.[14] This allowed more elephants to swarm in through the breach, scaring the Roman horses out of their wits.[15] However, the legionaries knew that elephants hate fire and, by using javelins and fire, they herded the elephants back out the way they had come.[16]

Hannibal tried one more gamble to break the siege of Capua. He quickly moved on Rome. He had not yet attacked Rome, nor even seen it before. With his army made up mainly of cavalry, he could not successfully lay siege to the huge, fortified capital of Italy. Hannibal hoped, however, that the Roman senate would panic and order all the legions to return to defend their city. Hannibal strutted with his army outside the capital city, with thirty-three elephants, and the common people were terrified, but the bluff did not work.[17] The legions took Capua, and Rome ignored the African warriors outside the walls.

In the year 209 BC, the Roman Consul Marcellus had a small skirmish with Hannibal that grew into a battle, although neither side had planned for it. Marcellus was an old veteran of the First Punic War.[18] When the first Carthaginian war ended, he fought the Gauls and became only the third Roman general to kill an enemy king in hand-to-hand combat.[19] As the skirmish between Marcellus and Hannibal grew, the Carthaginian sent in the elephants. The elephants were creating much havoc on the Roman lines, when a tribune, Gaius Decimus Flavus, decided to intervene.

When the beasts, trampling upon many, soon caused disorder, Flavius, a tribune of soldiers, snatching an ensign, meets them, and wounding the first elephant with the spike at the bottom of the staff, puts him to flight. The beast turned around upon the next, and drove back both him and the rest that followed. Marcellus, seeing this, pours in his horse with great force upon the elephants... the elephants, wounded and running upon their own party, caused a considerable slaughter.[20]

Flavius took a group of soldiers into the fray, where they threw javelins at the elephants, and he struck the leading elephant with the sharp butt end of his Roman flag.[21] The elephants fled under the barrage of missiles, and five were killed.[22]

Marcellus was growing bolder with his small victories and hoped for a big battle, but one day he was doing a reconnaissance when Hannibal's Numidians sprang out in ambush and killed him.[23]

The Second Punic War had become a stalemate, with neither the Romans nor the Carthaginians able to deal a "knockout blow" to the opponent. Still, as in the First Punic War, Rome showed that it could absorb huge man-power losses and still raise more legions to survive.[24]

26
Hasdrubal

While Hannibal tried unsuccessfully to force battles with the cautious Italians, his brother Hasdrubal found himself facing major difficulties in Hispania. Hasdrubal, another of Hamilcar Barca's "Lion's Brood," was viewed as a great general by the Romans, second only to Hannibal.[1]

Hasdrubal intended to take his army over the Alps to reinforce Hannibal in 215 BC, but Roman legions intercepted and destroyed most of his army, delaying him for years. Four years later, Hasdrubal avenged the defeat by defeating those legions and killing their leaders, both the father and the uncle of Scipio Africanus.[2]

One problem for Hannibal and Hasdrubal was the stubbornness of the Suffetes in Carthage. Rather than send reinforcements to the Barcas, they sent new armies with new leaders, each having their own independent commanders. The merchants of Carthage did not trust the Barca family. This led to duplication of effort and lack of cooperation between Carthaginian forces in Hispania.

To make matters worse, a young Roman military prodigy, Scipio (the Younger), showed himself to be a fine tactician in Hannibal's class.[3] Busts of Publius Scipio show that he had a large Italian nose, deep-set eyes, and a jutting chin.[4] At the extremely young age of twenty-five, he was named Proconsul to Hispania. Using tactics similar to Hannibal's, with clever modifications, Scipio repeatedly defeated the Carthaginian armies of Hispania. Scipio recognized that cavalry was important, a revolutionary idea to the infantry-loving Romans.[5]

Scipio staged a remarkable surprise attack far behind enemy lines to capture the capital of Hispania, Nova Carthago.[6] This maneuver put Hasdrubal Barca completely on the defensive and cut him off from most of his supplies. Soon, Scipio's army lined up against Hasdrubal at Baecula, Hispania. Using brilliant infantry and formation tactics, Scipio refused to engage the strong Carthaginian forces in the center, while easily wiping out the weaker African troops on the wings. Hasdrubal had no choice but to retreat with his elephants and as many

soldiers as could escape the trap.[7] Hasdrubal gathered as many forces
as he could and marched across Europe to join Hannibal. Together, the
Barcas hoped they would have enough men to siege Rome and end
the war.

The Romans make an intriguing claim about Hasdrubal. They say that
he invented a procedure for killing elephants to keep them from turning
on their own troops.[8] Hasdrubal ordered the mahouts to carry a long spike
and a hammer, although the length of this spike is not known. If the
elephant panicked and turned into its own army, the rider was ordered to
pound this "iron instrument" into the elephant's neck, under the ear,
killing it.[9]

Modern sources confirm that African natives hiding in trees have often
dispatched elephants by sending heavy spears down into their necks.[10]
One report says the spike should go into the skull, near the eye, but it is
not easy to imagine a rider clinging to a panicked elephant leaning over
to accomplish that! Other sources imply that the spike severed a vertebra
in the elephant's neck. In any case, the method was not foolproof and was
a last resort.[11]

Hasdrubal took his small army and ten elephants across the Alps
without suffering any attacks or hardships. He planned to add some
Gauls into his army before heading south to meet Hannibal. He sent a
messenger to Hannibal, to announce his route and schedule.[12]

One version of the story says that the messenger had to memorize the
message so that if the Romans captured the rider, he could kill himself
and no message would be found in writing. As the rider neared Hannibal's
camp, a rattlesnake frightened his horse. The horse reared up, throwing
the messenger, who landed on a large rock, breaking his back! He could
not kill himself, and the Romans caught him and tortured him for the
message. Other versions simply say that Hasdrubal's messengers were
captured by a Roman patrol and gave up their information.[13] Thus,
Consul Nero learned that Hasdrubal had arrived in northern Italy and
would soon march south to join Hannibal.

Consul Nero (not to be confused with the later Emperor Nero), with
this information, hatched a daring plan of his own. He left most of his
army in front of Hannibal's camp, where it had been for months, while
Hannibal apparently waited for news from his brother. Nero took one of
his legions north that very night, traveling 250 miles in one week.[14]
There is much debate as to whether this speed on foot is possible, but this
march does admirably compare to other historic military journeys.[15] We
are told that the Romans traveled with nothing but armor and weapons,

relying upon forward scouts to enlist locals to provide food for the men as they marched. Nero met another Consul (with legions) on the way and together they met Hasdrubal Barca.

Hasdrubal saw that two consular armies now opposed him, but his latest reports said that one consul was shadowing Hannibal. Hasdrubal feared the worst, that his brother's army had somehow been destroyed. True or not, he was now outnumbered and so he retreated.[16] Hasdrubal's Gallic guides abandoned him, and his army became trapped against a large river and a hillside.[17] The Metaurus River was in flood, so they could not cross without a good bridge or shallow spot.

Hasdrubal put his unreliable Gauls on the steepest part of the hill on his left (where they couldn't run away) and his best men in the center and right. Although the Romans were more numerous, they could not flank Hasdrubal because of the hill on one side and vineyards on the other.[18]

Hasdrubal Barca set his ten elephants in front. The Romans had no choice but to march uphill to meet the enemy. When the Romans drew near, Hasdrubal ordered a charge, to give his army momentum moving down the slope. The useless Gauls stood on the hillside, not charging. This left Consul Nero unopposed. He left his position and moved behind the charging Africans.[19]

Until Nero arrived behind them, the Carthaginians were doing well. But the tide turned, as Polybius describes:

The elephants too had proved of no more service to the one side than to the other, for as they were hemmed in between the two armies and exposed to a hail of missiles, they threw both the Roman and the Spanish ranks into disorder.... Six of the elephants were killed with their mahouts, and the other four forced their way through the lines and were later captured alone, as their drivers had abandoned them.[20]

The Battle of the Metaurus ended the life of Hasdrubal Barca on June 22, 207 BC.

Nero rode quickly back to Hannibal's camp and tossed Hasdrubal Barca's head over the wall. When Hannibal looked into the eyes of his dead brother, he reportedly said, "I see there the fate of Carthage."[21]

In Hispania, the Romans under Scipio mopped up the last of the African armies. Hasdrubal Gisgonis placed thirty-two war elephants at his center in the Battle of Ilipa. To avoid the elephants, Scipio used the same Baecula tactic, spreading out his line to attack the flanks, while ignoring the center.[22] Gisgonis ordered the elephants to move to cover the flanks, but Scipio sent javelin throwers ahead and showered the beasts with spears. The elephants turned to flee among the African cavalry and made matters worse.[23] The Roman legions won again.

Spain belonged to Rome.

27
Rome's Genius

Scipio had accomplished his official mission: to take Spain away from Carthage. But he wanted more. He longed to defeat Hannibal, which no Roman had done. Scipio took part of his army to Africa, imitating Regulus, hoping that this would force Hannibal to leave Italy.[1]

Hannibal still had one remaining hope for destroying Rome, however. His youngest brother, Mago Barca, raised a formidable army of thirty-five thousand men and seven elephants. Mago planned to reinforce Hannibal, since Consul Nero had destroyed Hasdrubal's army at the Metaurus River. Roman legions again intercepted the army in northern Italy. Mago's center collapsed before the Romans, but his cavalry wings routed the Roman flanks. Unfortunately for Carthage, Mago was wounded in the battle and his army retreated.[2] Mago died of his wounds. This meant that Hannibal would never receive reinforcements, and the Italian campaign was a lost cause.

Hasdrubal Gisgonis, who had lost to Scipio at Ilipa, led an expedition in north Africa to capture more elephants. His expedition proved fruitful, as he brought 140 beasts to Carthage for training.[3] The army raised by Gisgonis dwarfed the Romans under Scipio. Scipio did what any out-numbered commander might do: negotiate. Pretending to make peace, Scipio had spies studying the camp of the Carthaginian army. With an excellent reconnaissance and the complete element of surprise, Scipio's legions attacked in the middle of the night, burning the barracks of the enemy soldiers and stables of horses and elephants.[4] As many as one hundred elephants perished in the flames, chained in their stables. Herbert writes of the Roman sneak attack, "Never perhaps in all the hideous annals of war, was such a horror."[5]

Finally recognizing that Gisgonis could not defeat Scipio, the Suffetes of Carthage begged Hannibal to return to Africa to save them. The Roman navy opened the blockade to let the Africans go; after sixteen years of terrorizing Italy, they were happy to see Hannibal leave.[6] During

Hannibal sent eighty elephants against the Romans at Zama. [*Archibald Wilberforce, The Great Battles of All Nations, vol. 1, Peter Fenelon Collier & Son, NY, 1900.*]

Hannibal's years of war, Rome had lost 25% of her population, four hundred towns, and 50 percent of her farmland.[7]

Although Scipio did not have a large army, he did skillfully augment it. He bribed and cajoled the Numidians to switch sides, promising them vast tracts of Carthage's land in exchange for their cavalry. Although Scipio did not win over all of Numidia, he did get six thousand men and four thousand cavalry from the traitor Massinissa.[8]

When Hannibal arrived in Carthage, he was welcomed as a hero and given large powers to prepare a defense. He had not seen the city in decades, since he was a boy of nine. Hannibal had only a core of good veterans from Italy, perhaps fifteen thousand, plus the small group of veteran cavalry he was able to get aboard the flotilla of Carthaginian ships.[9] He recruited locals into a militia and gave them basic training for a few weeks. Hannibal sent out teams of hunters to capture more war elephants, but these eighty had little time for training.[10] Still, eighty was the largest force of elephants Hannibal ever fielded and double the amount that Scipio had ever faced in combat.[11]

Howdahs were probably not used on the elephants for this battle because there had not been time to train the men or elephants in its use. Also, Hannibal planned to charge the elephants at the Roman legions. This running pace would make a howdah useless, as the archers could not aim with any accuracy. The elephants did wear colorful coverings, according to Appian, perhaps dyed leather armor.[12]

Scipio and Hannibal met face to face at Zama, for a few minutes, to talk. They each offered terms, but neither could accept. The battle of Zama would occur the next day, in October of 202 BC.[13]

Poorly trained war elephants are worse than no elephants at all in battle. Hannibal should have known this. Lucretius, a Roman writer, recognized this truth, "...as elephants even now, when imperfectly inured to weapons, flee hither and thither, after having inflicted much cruel damage on their masters."[14] It takes years to train war elephants. To send eighty fresh elephant recruits against a veteran Roman army was callous and foolish.[15]

The normal procedure would be to place the elephants on the flanks where they could disturb the enemy cavalry. However, Scipio had been fighting elephants for years in Hispania, and so his Roman riders knew them. Also, the traitor Masinissa from Numidia was an elephant expert himself! Hannibal hoped that the elephants might cause some problems for the Roman infantry, since Scipio's cavalry would know to avoid the beasts.

Contrary to scholars who think that war elephants are useless or even counterproductive, Consul Scipio arranged his entire veteran army in novel ways to counteract this dangerous piece of Hannibal's cavalry.[16] Instead of forming the normal checkerboard style of cohorts, he put the cohorts in rows with corridors between them so the elephants could run right on through.[17] This mirrored Alexander's strategy at Gaugamela, of letting the scythed chariots run through to the rear where they were no threat to his army.

The battle began with the elephant charge at the center of the Roman line.

...Hannibal ordered the drivers of his elephants to charge the enemy. But when the sound of trumpets and bugles pierced the air all around them, some of the animals panicked, turned tail and stampeded to the rear, colliding with the squadrons of Numidian cavalry which had come up to support the Carthaginians....The rest of the elephants charged the Roman velites in the space between the two armies and killed many of them, but also suffered heavy losses themselves. Then finally all the beasts took fright: some of them escaped by way of the gaps between the maniples through which the Romans allowed them to pass, while others fled toward the right wing where they met with volleys of javelins from the cavalry, and in the end stampeded clean off the battlefield.[18]

When the elephants approached, the soldiers blew their horns as loudly as possible, and those without horns were told to scream. This shocking racket, of perhaps thirty thousand voices and one thousand trumpets, frightened half of the elephants, who turned from the Roman infantry toward the Roman cavalry. Here, the cavalry and velites were waiting with javelins and arrows. They barraged the elephants with missiles, so the hapless beasts finally rambled back into their own cavalry.[19] As the African cavalry fell into disarray, the two wings of Roman horsemen charged to attack and the Africans' horses fled.

Scipio may have been pleasantly surprised at the effectiveness of his horn and scream ploy, but he also had plans for the remaining elephants. Some velites may have carried long poles with grappling hooks to pull the mahouts off the elephants, causing more confusion among the beasts.[20] One author says that Scipio used the flaming-pig method at Zama, but no ancient sources corroborate this.[21] The remaining elephants charged right on through the Roman lines between the cohorts, with Romans hurling javelins at them while they passed.[22] Eleven elephants died and the rest were later captured.[23]

In a very close battle of infantries, Hannibal had the initial advantage, but the bribed Numidian cavalry of Massinissa returned to attack Hannibal from the rear. Only two thousand legionaries died, while twenty thousand Carthaginians perished.[24]

Scipio won the battle, and Hannibal fled to Hadrumetum on horseback.[25] Why not to Carthage? Because the Suffetes had a habit of crucifying losing generals!

The author wonders if Hannibal had held the eighty elephants in reserve (as Seleucus did at Ipsus) to prevent the enemy cavalry from returning in the rear, whether Carthage may have prevailed.

Despite the loss, Carthage asked Hannibal to act as ruler and decide what they should do. He chose to accept Scipio's terms. Carthage would stay in Africa, without colonies, with only a handful of warships, and could keep or train no war elephants.[26]

Only eleven elephants died at Zama. A few escaped; most were captured. Scipio gave many to Masinissa the Numidian and took the rest of the elephants to Rome for his triumph.[27] His name became Scipio Africanus.

The importance of the Second Punic War can hardly be exaggerated. It was a turning-point in the history of the whole ancient world…. After it no power arose which could endanger the existence of Rome.[28]

Carthage had used war elephants frequently, with mixed results. Pachyderms were very effective against weak infantry or enemy cavalry. But the Romans rarely fielded weak infantry, and they learned how to deal with war elephants.

Carthage again grew prosperous, and the Romans eventually tired of Cato's incessant harping for the destruction of Carthage. They found an excuse to declare war, called the Third Punic War, and wiped out the city completely.[29] The Roman legions arrived in Africa quickly, and Carthage had no time to capture or deploy war elephants. In fact, in a bit of historical irony, the Romans used elephants to destroy the Carthaginian army at the battle of Nepheris in 146 BC.[30] The citizens of Carthage called out the names of their former war elephants, like Surus, hoping that the gods would send the beasts back from the dead to save their city.[31]

The Romans killed everyone in the city except for fifty thousand, who were sold into slavery. Only fifty years after surrendering her elephants to Scipio, Carthage burned for seventeen days and remained a heap for one hundred years.[32]

28
Africa versus Asia

Alexander's empire fragmented when his generals each claimed a kingdom and fought to steal pieces from the others. After the initial chaos, the empire settled into three semi-permanent rivalries. The Seleucids ruled Turkey, Syria, Iran, Iraq, and sometimes Afghanistan, Pakistan, and north India. The Ptolemies controlled Egypt, parts of Ethiopia and Sudan, and usually occupied Palestine. A variety of kings squabbled over control of Greece and Macedonia.

All of Alexander's successors desperately sought to obtain war elephants, but the Greek and Macedonian regions had no access to a regular supply. The Seleucids owned the roads to India for Asian elephants, and the Ptolemies controlled Ethiopia and Sudan for the African pachyderms. The Macedonians had to capture enemy elephants or perhaps purchase them through non-Egyptian ports, like Carthage.

The Ptolemies and Seleucids often fought over the ownership of Palestine.

The descendants of Seleucus were usually named Antiochus. Antiochus I died in 262 BC, leaving the kingdom to his drunkard son Antiochus II.[1] We know very little about Antiochus II or the major battle he fought in 246 BC, except that he lost Syria and his entire corps of Asian war elephants to Ptolemy III Euergetes of Egypt.[2] The only source extant is a basalt monument installed by Euergetes along the coast of Eritrea. Some details are intriguing:

The great king Ptolemy...set out on a campaign into Asia with military and cavalry forces and a naval armament and elephants both Troglodyte [Sudanese] and Ethiopic which his father and he himself first captured by hunting from these places and, bringing them to Egypt, trained them in military use.[3]

Ptolemy III hired Ethiopian and Sudanese mahouts to train and control the African Forest elephants caught along the Nile River. Unfortunately, we have no accounts of the battle and do not know how the elephant forces were deployed or fared in the battle. Ptolemy did "capture" and not destroy the enemy elephant corps, which shows the value commanders placed on the beasts.

Antiochus III became king of Syria in 223 BC, but immediately had to deal with rebels. The enemy forces, led by Molon, owned a large number of chariots. Antiochus astutely placed ten Asian elephants across the center of the frontline, causing the frightened chariot horses to turn aside, thus blunting the rebel advantage.[4] Antiochus was victorious and the rebel commander killed himself.

One account of the war elephants during this time period adds some details of the war elephant's appearance in the Syrian army.

The elephant was tricked out for battle with frontlets and crests; beside the Indian mahout who bestrode his neck, he carried upon his back a wooden tower with four fighting men. It would seem that before a battle the elephants were shown an imitation of blood made from the red juice of fruit, either to excite them or prevent their being alarmed by the real bloodshed.[5]

Frontlets are armor to protect the elephant's forehead and trunk, while crests are either simple decorative plumes, or perhaps armor extending upward from the beast's helmet to protect his vulnerable rider. It should also be noted in less than one century, the howdah tower used on the elephant back had grown from carrying one or two soldiers to three or four.[6] This would be possible by redesigning the howdah with lighter materials, such as hardened leather; reconfiguring the harness to better distribute the weight on the elephant's back; or lightening the soldiers by reducing their armor.

The description of presenting the elephants with fake blood to embolden them is unusual. In the case of the Seleucid army, the idea may have arisen from the apocryphal Bible book, I Maccabees 6:34, where the Seleucid war elephants are prepared for combat by "showing" them red grape juice and mulberry juice.[7] P.G. Maxwell-Stuart writes that a very slight scribal error in the Hebrew language could have accidentally changed "swilled" or "saturated" [drank] into "showed." If this were a Hebrew transcription error, the passage would indicate that the soldiers gave fermented red juice to the elephants to drink, not look at! "...[I]t is likely that the elephants were blind drunk before going into battle, a practice which can be amply illustrated elsewhere." [8]

III Maccabees 5:45. The superintendent of the elephants drove the beasts almost, one might say, to a state of madness with fragrant draughts of wine mingled with frankincense and equipped them with horrible implements [knives and scythes].[9]

Numerous ancient sources mention the practice of giving war elephants large amounts of wine before a battle. Whether intoxicating the corps of war elephants was in the best interest of the army is up to debate, as Ducrey questions:

...to increase their agressiveness [sic], they were plied with alcohol. The effect may indeed have been to increase their violence and ferocity, but in fact the uncontrollable side of their nature was even more affected. At times, they would turn on the soldiers of their own side.[10]

But elephants, like humans, are affected differently by alcohol. Alcohol and drugs affect humans and elephants in similar ways; some are pacified or calmed, whereas others become belligerent or combative. The mahouts would know if their elephants needed liquor to calm jittery nerves or to excite them to ferocity. When a group of Russian circus elephants became stressed because of a long train journey in 1999, the mahouts gave them liters of vodka, which calmed the beasts.[11] Considering that the Indian military practiced drugging or intoxicating elephants before battle for perhaps thousands of years, it seems unlikely that the practice provokes disastrous results.

Elephants love liquor. A herd of wild elephants raiding granaries for food in the Assam province of north India came upon supplies of home-made rice beer, enjoyed it immensely, and then went berserk, killing six people. "It has been noticed that elephants have developed a taste for rice beer and local liquor and they always look for it when they invade villages," explained an elephant expert to Reuters.[12]

Most scholars believe that "showing elephants the juice of grapes and mulberries" means the Seleucids got the elephants drunk before battle.[13] In Sri Lanka (Ceylon), elephant trainers of the sixteenth century slaughtered animals in front of new war elephants to "accustom these gentle giants to the noise and blood of war."[14] Perhaps both actions were practiced with war elephants: filling them with liquor and making them accustomed to the sight of blood.

According to Jewish tradition, Ptolemy IV Philopater (221–203 BC) tried to enter the Jewish temple but God struck him with sickness. Then Ptolemy desired revenge, ordering the Jews of Alexandria to be trampled by "a horde of elephants" but instead the beasts turned on the troops.[15] We are told that these elephants had been given wine and drugs before

At the Battle of Raphia, the Asian elephants had advantages of size and armor over the African forest elephants of Ptolemy. *[Illustration copyright © Ian Heath, from 'Armies of the Macedonian and Punic Wars' by Duncan Head (WRG 1982).]*

the planned execution, but there is no reason to believe that the intox-ication was the key factor in inducing the elephants to become angry. More likely, the elephants were not accustomed to killing quiet and frightened people standing in crowds.

On June 22, 217 BC, Antiochus III attacked an Egyptian army in southern Palestine at the Battle of Raphia. Both sides used similar numbers of infantry, including phalanxes of heavily armored foot soldiers. Heavy infantry could be a problem for war elephants, as Alexander had shown at the Battle of the Hydaspes one hundred years earlier. Both the Syrian and the Egyptian leaders knew that the elephants should not face heavy infantry. Antiochus put sixty elephants on his right wing and forty-two on his left wing: all Asian elephants. Ptolemy IV countered with forty African elephants on his left and thirty-three on his right wing.[16]

Antiochus commanded his own right wing and charged with the elephants. Polybius explains the battle between the African and the Asian elephants:

[O]nly some few of Ptolemy's elephants came to close quarters with their opponents, and the men in the towers on the back of these beasts made a gallant fight of it, lunging with their pikes at close quarters and striking each other, while the elephants themselves fought still more brilliantly, using all their strength in the encounter and pushing against each other, forehead to forehead.... Now most of Ptolemy's elephants were afraid to join battle, as is the habit of African elephants; for unable to stand the smell and the trumpeting of the Indian elephants, and terrified, I suppose, also by their great size and strength, they immediately run away from them before they get near them. This is what happened on the present occasion...[17]

Antiochus easily routed Ptolemy's left wing and pursued them off the field, but Ptolemy escaped to aid the central infantry when the wing began to collapse. The African elephants of Ptolemy's right wing refused to engage the Indian elephants across from them, but a shrewd commander led his cavalry and infantry around the Asian elephants and hit Antiochus' flanks.[18] Because Antiochus did not return quickly, Ptolemy defeated the enemy in the center and on the right.[19] So, Ptolemy won the battle, despite his own frightened elephants. Antiochus' elephants had been successful in their particular assignments, to stop the African elephants; but their success did not translate into an overall victory.

...at Raphia, the elephants were no longer used as cavalry screens; on the left wing they fought with each other, and the victorious Indian elephants of Antiochus passed on to break the Egyptian line. This is the only recorded battle in which Indian and African elephants ever met...[20]

Sixteen of Ptolemy's elephants were killed, while Antiochus lost only five.[21] Both the victors and the vanquished probably abandoned the battlefield soon after, because there is nothing pleasant about the corpses of elephants. One hunter says that if left for some hours in the heat of the sun, the body of the pachyderm will "...practically explode. The flesh very soon decomposes in a tropical sun and the gas generated distends the carcass to an enormous size, when it bursts, disclosing later a huge mass of maggots, and later again a swarm of flies."[22]

Perhaps realizing that his pachyderms were not useful against Seleucid beasts, Ptolemy IV sacrificed four war elephants to the sun and made bronze statues of them "to keep their memory alive forever."[23] Would he have killed the beasts if they had been victorious?

Changing his tactics after the loss at Raphia, Antiochus used large armies, bluff, and diplomacy to increase his empire in the east. In Afghanistan he began a siege but happily accepted the capitulation of the city in exchange for their sworn loyalty and their war elephants.[24]

In 207 BC the Seleucid ruler moved toward north India. The emperors of India had faded in power and their leader surrendered, offering treasure and elephants for peace.[25] Antiochus III returned to Syria with 150 elephants in his army. This "reconquest" of the east led his people to dub him Antiochus the Great.[26]

The Ptolemies had kept control of Palestine after Raphia, but Antiochus again sought to take it back. Only one fragmented account survives, from Polybius, regarding the Battle of Pania in 200 BC. The battle was fought on two different sides of a river and in mountainous terrain, with elephants taking a role in both arenas of combat.

Historian Bar-Kochba admirably sorts out the difficulties of the Polybius history. In the flat terrain north of the river, the Seleucid elephants formed a line in front of the phalanx to charge the Egyptian infantry. Here, Antiochus was entirely victorious. In the rugged southern battle zone, the elephants were stationed behind the Syrian phalanx. When the Egyptians succeeded in repelling the Seleucid infantry, they were unable to pursue the fleeing soldiers because they "were cut off by the living wall of the elephants."[27] The Syrians regrouped behind the elephants, and the Egyptians turned to flee.

War elephants played a decisive role in Antiochus' victory at Pania as the offense in the northern combat, and as the defense in the southern theatre. The Battle of Pania returned Judea to Syrian control.[28]

The Ptolemies were not having much success with the African elephants, and greatly reduced the use of war elephants in their armies.[29] The penetrating searches for pachyderms in the marshlands of Ethiopia came to an end.

The successes of Antiochus in the east and south increased his ambition. His eyes turned westward toward Turkey and Greece, toward a reunification of Alexander the Great's empire.

29
Day of Slaughter

Only months after Carthage and Hannibal were defeated in 201 BC, the Romans sought revenge against King Philip in Macedonia, who had allied with Hannibal.[1] The Italians blocked this alliance with an effective naval blockade of Philip's ports. Although Philip never actually helped Carthage, he had agreed to do so, and with Antiochus III expanding his empire in the east, the paranoid Roman Senate now feared that Greece would ally with Antiochus, allowing the Asians to invade Europe.[2] To prevent any such alliance, Rome invaded Greece.

After the wars against Carthage, defeating the famous elephants of Hannibal, many historians have joined together to sing the praises of the clever Romans who disdained "the dangerous use of elephants in war."[3] The widely held opinion of modern scholars is to discount the value of pachyderm squadrons, while they shake their heads in bewilderment that famed generals such as Pyrrhus and Hannibal would be foolish enough to use them. But even the skeptical Delbruck grudgingly admits that the Romans used elephants for combat.

The best testimony for their usefulness in combat still remains, however, the fact that even the great commanders always used them again and again, especially Hannibal and also Caesar....After the Second Punic War, when the Romans had established close relations with the Numidian kings, who provided them with these animals, they used them during the entire second century B.C...not only against the Macedonians but also in Spain, and against the Gauls.[4]

Livy says that in 199 BC, the Romans used the elephants captured at Zama to challenge the Greeks, but the Greeks would not leave their fortifications to fight.[5] Philip refused to engage the Romans there at Lyncestis, although he had superior numbers of infantry and cavalry. When the new consul, Flaminius, arrived to lead the Roman army, he immediately asked King Massinissa of Numidia to send more elephants.[6]

Flaminius was a very young man when sent to Greece, not yet thirty, but he was tactful and spoke Greek fluently. Flaminius had fought with the legions against Hannibal in southern Italy, and thus had experience fighting against elephants.[7] Now he wanted to employ them.

King Philip had faced years of civil war and had to enlist sixteen-year-old boys to form an army of just 23,500 foot and two thousand cavalry.[8] The opposing armies met on a foggy Spring day almost by accident, so the formations were not entirely ready.[9] The terrain was perfect for Philip, who had the advantage of the high ground. His phalanx took the initial advantage by pushing the Roman legions back, and it looked like a disaster for Italy. Consul Flaminius saw the danger and ordered his elephants against the Greek left, breaking it completely.[10] The Macedonian cavalry of Philip had not been trained to fight elephants and "could not be made to face them."[11] When the Macedonian troops on their flank fled from the elephants, the victorious Greek center was surrounded by the legions and cut to pieces.[12] Before leaving the region, Rome donated her elephants to a local ally, thinking that the wars were over.[13]

By 198 BC, Antiochus the Great had retaken most of Alexander's world. He also adopted an elephant as his own, and called it Ajax, probably because Alexander had honored the elephant named Ajax in north India. The ancient historian Pliny tells us a story about this new Ajax:

When Antiochus was trying to ford a river his elephant Ajax refused, though on other occasions it always led the line; thereupon Antiochus issued an announcement that the elephant that crossed should have the leading place and he rewarded Patroclus, who made the venture, with the gift of a silver harness, an elephant's greatest delight, and with every other mark of leadership. The one disgraced preferred death by starvation to humiliation; for the elephant has a remarkable sense of shame, and when defeated shrinks from the voice of its conqueror...[14]

The idea that elephants have a sense of honor and shame is true, but we can only hope that poor Ajax did not starve himself to death because he no longer wore the silver harness!

While the Roman elephants defeated Philip in Greece, Antiochus launched an offensive in Anatolia, modern Turkey. What really sent the Roman Senate into apoplexy was the appearance of their old nemesis Hannibal at the court of Antiochus. The Italians feared Hannibal, and his successful rebuilding of the Carthaginian economy after the Battle at Zama led the Romans to send assassins to kill him. Hannibal escaped to the east and warned Antiochus that the Romans would stop at nothing to control the world and that only an invasion of Italy would stop them. All of Antiochus' advisors scoffed at this idea and Hannibal was relegated to small military duties.[15]

The cities of Greece were on the edge of civil war, divided between pro-Roman and anti-Roman sentiments. King Philip, although not a lover of Rome, hated Antiochus more and so supported the Roman faction. In 192 BC, Antiochus invaded Greece with small force composed of only ten thousand infantry, five hundred horses, and six elephants.[16]

The Romans recognized that they should try to deal with Antiochus before he could take over Greece. The Roman consul in 191 BC, Glabrio, a friend of Scipio Africanus, obtained fifteen elephants from Massinissa for the Greek campaign.[17]

The legions pushed Antiochus' small army back until he halted at the historic strongpoint, Thermopylae, where the famed three hundred Spartans had deflected the Persians for many days.[18] Syrian archers, slingers, and javelin throwers on the heights pelted the Romans with missiles, and the legion could not penetrate the fortifications and phalanx. Eventually the Romans found a secret trail and surprised the Syrians at the rear. Antiochus was slightly wounded in the panicked retreat of his forces, but the Roman cavalry could not destroy the fleeing enemy because the Asian elephants of Antiochus hampered the pursuit.[19]

Antiochus retreated into Turkey, confident that he could hold Asia Minor. Rome, fearing that Hannibal might be put in charge of the Syrian army, elected Scipio Africanus as proconsul or commander in chief.[20] Rome's terms for peace were too severe for Antiochus' liking, and since he had twice as many soldiers (and three times as many elephants), he assumed he could defeat the legions. Hannibal either was not present or was not trusted by Antiochus to participate in the coming battle.

Scipio noticed that the Seleucid army relied heavily upon archers and that every time there was a rainstorm, the archers had to restring their bows.[21] This is a real factor in ancient bows, as "its composition made it very susceptible to moisture, which rendered it useless."[22] Scipio therefore planned to attack shortly after a heavy rain, to negate the enemy archers. The Battle of Magnesia took place in the winter of 190 BC.

We have detailed records of the formations used for this battle that help us understand the role of elephants. Antiochus unleashed a new weapon against the Romans at Magnesia, cataphract cavalry, which he had used in the east with good effect. Heliodorus describes a cataphract as a rider completely encased in plate armor who used a lance and looked very much like a medieval knight preparing for a joust.[23] The horse was also covered in armor, although its belly remained unprotected. The biggest problems for cataphracts were that the weight of the armor soon tired the horses and they could not easily turn to defend themselves.[24]

Antiochus put his phalanxes in the center, with sixteen elephants among them. On the wings he set chariots in the front, cataphracted cavalry in the second row, and sixteen elephants for a third row. The groups of sixteen elephants were not accidental: the Seleucids called eight elephants an *ile* (squadron) and sixteen behemoths an *elephantarchia* (herd).[25] Zeuxis and Philip the elephantarchos each commanded one squadron of elephants amid the central infantry formation. Since the battle plan of Antiochus did not include archers, Scipio's hope that the rain would nullify them seems to have worked.

The Romans used a nonstandard formation to great advantage. Scipio, by taking the initiative in attacking, must have ordered his archers to keep their equipment dry (while Antiochus, planning to defend, had his archers always ready). The proconsul stationed archers in front of his cavalry on each wing: a total departure from normal Roman deployments. The legions stood in the center. Where were Massinissa's donated elephants?

They placed sixteen elephants in reserve behind the triarii [rear Roman infantry], for, in addition to the fact that they seemed unable to face the greater number of the king's elephants—there were fifty-four of them—African elephants cannot resist even an equal number of Indian, whether because the latter are superior in size—for in fact they are far larger—or in fighting spirit.[26]

Livy's assessment is seconded by Appian, who agrees that Scipio kept the African pachyderms out of this battle because common wisdom said that African elephants were inferior both in number and in quality to the Asians.[27] Since the only actual test of this belief had been the Battle at Raphia, where the African elephants were outnumbered, the Romans evidently relied heavily on that single case! Nevertheless, Scipio's elephants were greatly outnumbered, and he was prudent in this case.

As at Raphia, Antiochus charged with his right wing successfully against the enemy left, but he did not return soon enough to save the rest of his army. Perhaps the chariots and cavalry on his side of the army were inspired by his presence. His left wing did not fare well.

The charge of chariots from Antiochus' left wing collapsed, as Roman archers pelted them with arrows. The wounded horses turned back into the Syrian cataphracts, sending the horses and sixteen elephants behind into disorder.[28] Taking full advantage, the Roman cavalry charged before the cataphracts and elephants could regroup. The whole Syrian left was neutralized and fled.[29]

With the Syrian left cavalry in flight and Antiochus in useless pursuit of Roman horsemen, the legions surrounded the phalanxes and the sixteen Asian elephants. When a phalanx is flanked, it reorganizes into a hollow square with the elephants in the center. The legions could not approach because the Syrians used twenty-foot-long spears, while they only carried the short gladius sword. So the Roman archers and javelin throwers took target practice on the elephants in the center, causing them to stampede in all directions, over their own infantry.[30] As these elephantine holes formed in the phalanx walls, the legionnaires broke through and the carnage began.

Antiochus lost fifty-thousand men, nearly the whole army. Only fifteen of Antiochus' elephants "escaped alive on that day of slaughter."[31]

30
Weapons of Massive Destruction

To gain peace with Rome after the battle at Magnesia, Antiochus the Great had to cede Turkey, pay a huge sum of money, and surrender all of his elephants. "The Romans insisted on this clause because they were well aware of what elephants were capable of...."[1] In modern times we call chemical, biological, and nuclear weapons "weapons of mass destruction" and try to keep them out of the hands of purportedly dangerous groups. Similarly, Rome attempted to restrict the spread of war elephants in their sphere of influence, although, of course, not denying their own right to possess them. Perhaps lacking the ships to transport the surrendered elephants of Antiochus back to Italy, the legions gave the beasts to an ally in western Turkey. The elephants were immediately useful in repelling a Gallic invasion only a year later.[2]

The Romans also insisted that Antiochus hand over the infamous Hannibal. Hannibal escaped and worked for a minor power near the Black Sea. Eventually Roman assassins caught up with him, and he took poison.

Antiochus tried to make the best of his defeat, claiming that "he was grateful to the Romans for saving him the trouble of ruling so large an empire."[3] Evidently, the Seleucids interpreted the treaty clause about surrendering their elephants as a one-time event because they immediately began collecting more![4]

After Magnesia many provinces defected from Antiochus, including Bactria, Parthia, Armenia, and more.[5] To pay the immense war reparation to Rome, Antiochus levied heavy taxes. He died, in fact, trying to collect the money at an unwilling temple in 187 BC.[6]

After about ten years, King Philip of Greece was beginning to doubt the benefits of his alliance with Rome. In secret (says Polybius), he built a strong army, but his death in 179 BC left the army to his half-brother Perseus.[7]

Perseus looked and acted like a strong king and became rather popular in Greece, causing Rome to fear a resurgent power. When Perseus married a daughter of the Seleucid king, the Senate feared once again that Greece might ally with the easterners.[8] Enemies of Perseus took advantage of the Roman paranoia and convinced them that Perseus was trying to poison several Roman senators. Rome declared war, invading in 171 BC.

The Romans sent a special commission to Numidia in northern Africa to ask for elephants and men from Massinissa for the Greek campaign. Twenty-two pachyderms, plus one thousand infantry and one thousand cavalry arrived in Greece to join the legions.[9] This was not enough for Rome. Polyaenus says that the Romans took back the twelve elephants that they gave to Pergamum after the Battle of Magnesia, twenty years earlier.[10]

Not surprisingly, when the elephants arrived, the Romans began to experience major supply problems, and the ships were unable to provide enough.[11] Romans, organized in all military matters, carried some fodder for the horses, but they could not carry all of it and there was not enough "pasturage" for the animals to graze in this region. Cavalry horses each required a normal ration of perhaps ten pounds of grains and twenty-five pounds of grazed fodder each day.[12] An elephant would need about ten times that amount! While horses might freely graze on short grass in Greece, the elephants would have great difficulty finding food tall enough to grasp with their trunks and eat.

The first small battle between the forces of Perseus and the Romans with elephants came at Phalanna. Details are very sketchy, but we do know that elephants were a major factor in the Greek defeat.[13] Considering the subsequent efforts of Perseus, we may confidently presume that the behemoths frightened away his cavalry at Phalanna.

Perseus recognized the danger of these elephants to his own cavalry, but had no elephants to use for training his horses. In a scene reminiscent of Queen Semiramis' invasion of India, Perseus constructed dummy elephants and tried to simulate their trumpeting.[14]

...in order to make sure that the beasts should not prove a source of terror to the horses, he constructed images of elephants and smeared them with some kind of ointment to give them a dreadful odour. They were terrible both to see and to hear, since they were skilfully arranged to emit a roar resembling thunder; and he would repeatedly lead the horses up to these figures until they gained courage.[15]

Horse expert Ann Hyland writes that some horses fear smells more than sights and sounds. "There is a saying that a horse can smell if a rider is frightened, and this is true. The explanation is that the odor which a frightened human emits, though not picked up by another human, is smelt by a horse. Fear in a rider...transmits itself to the horse who in turn becomes fearful...."[16]

Rightly worried that these simulated pachyderms might not adequately prevent his cavalry from panic, Perseus prepared some countermeasures to the Roman elephants.

Perseus had trained a brigade of 'elephant-fighters' (elephantomachai), who wore helmets with sharp spikes and carried shields with sharp spikes (Zon. 9.22); for the elephants at Cynoscephalae had caused much panic and damage.[17]

The Greeks prepared history's first corps of anti-elephant infantry! Their armor and weaponry were designed specifically to repel pachyderms, as the spiked helmets and shields would pierce the elephant's sensitive trunks if the beasts attacked these soldiers. In fact, if the men tossed their spiked shields on the ground in front of the elephants, the shields would act as a simple caltrop to wound the elephant's soft feet.

The following year, yet another gargantuan effort involving elephants took place, this time for the Romans. The new consul, Quintus Marcius Philippus, marched with the Roman army into high ground, but then could not penetrate the Macedonian forces holding the lower passes. In other words, the legions climbed a steep hill, but a Greek force cut off their exit. Supplies could not be hauled up to his elevated position.

Polybius, who knew some of the Romans from the incident, weaves a story that seems preposterous. Consul Philippus ordered his soldiers to build "collapsible wooden platforms" for the elephants to ride as they slid gently down to a lower level of the hill.[18] Polybius offers numerous details, and the idea is almost too strange to invent. However, elephants are famously sure-footed, and it is hard to imagine pachyderms unable to descend any terrain that a convoluted system of wooden platforms could surmount! An elephant descends steep hillsides by sitting down with forefeet in front and hind legs pulled up under him and then slides down using his front legs to slow or alter course as needed. The whole herd will follow the leader's chosen path.[19]

Furthermore, it is unclear how the consul found so much wood to make these platforms for sliding dozens of pachyderms down multiple levels of the incline. Polybius says that the elephants reached the base of the hill without injury, but their terrified trumpeting sent many pack animals into panicked flight.

The next year, a sixty-year old combat commander, Paulus, became consul.[20] Hammond says that Consul Paulus avoided a frontal assault against Perseus' fortified encampment because "he would not be able to use the arm which had been so valuable at Cynoscephalae, the squad of war elephants which had been provided by Massinissa."[21]

The decisive battle was enjoined on June 22, 168 BC at Pydna, beginning at three in the afternoon.[22] In a fashion similar to the fighting at Cynoscephalae under Philip, the Greek phalanx initially pushed back the Roman legions, but the consul sent in the elephants to flank the phalanx.[23]

[Paulus] sent a squad of elephants and some squadrons of allied cavalry against the cavalry and the light-armed of the Macedonian left wing. The untrained horses stampeded, the 'elephant-fighters' proved ineffective, and the light-armed troops were routed, so that the left-hand units of the phalanx line were turned and encircled.[24]

The elephants caused a similar riot in the Greek right wing, and the phalanx was utterly crushed. Some Macedonians escaped to the sea but when they tired of swimming and came near to shore, the mahouts had the elephants crush the enemy underfoot.[25]

In the East the critical Battle of Pydna which ended the Third Macedonian War was probably won by the allies, who with elephants crushed the left wing of Perseus and enabled the legionaries to split and outflank the Macedonian phalanx.[26]

Despite assessments like this, many historians downplay or even omit reference to elephants at Pydna. Plutarch, for instance, in glorifying Roman heroism, did not even mention elephants in his accounts of Cynoscephelae or Pydna.

After the Battle of Pydna, Rome was no longer in a forgiving mood and sold most Greeks into slavery. Rome broke up Greece into provinces and subsumed the whole country into the Roman empire.[27] The Romans stripped Greek cities of everything valuable, and this "booty" enabled the Roman republic to exempt Roman citizens from property taxes for four generations.[28] Paulus returned to Rome and held public games for celebration. He adopted a Carthaginian custom and had deserters trampled to death by elephants.[29]

In these two battles, at Cynoscephalae and Pydna, the Greek phalanx failed to defeat the Roman legions. Did the phalanx fail because the legions were more maneuverable? Perhaps. Yet few scholars have taken into account the elephant factor. War elephants were the weapon of choice when the Romans needed a strong assault on the flanks of the enemy.

31
Guerrilla War

After the death of Antiochus III "the Great," the once mighty Seleucid empire faltered under weak leadership. Antiochus IV lived in Rome for thirteen years as a hostage after the Battle of Magnesia to keep the eastern empire out of Rome's affairs.[1] When Syria neared collapse, Rome sent Antiochus IV back, hoping that he might put things in order and also be an ally, since he was well treated during his Roman captivity.

However, Antiochus IV was known by all, friend and foe, to be a bit odd. Almost immediately upon his return to Syria, he demanded that people call him "God Manifest," Epiphanes.[2] Sympathetic scholars say that "Illustrious" is an alternate translation and that Antiochus did not really demand recognition as a god.[3] However, because of his rather eccentric behavior, many called him Epimanes, rhyming from Epiphanes, meaning "crazy."[4]

It took the new king a while to reorganize his lands, but soon he was strong enough to expand the Seleucid realms. While the Romans used elephants to fight the Greek king Perseus, Antiochus IV invaded Egypt with his army and elephants.

Antiochus had the young Ptolemy and Egyptian leadership surrounded, and would soon have complete control of the wealthy African lands. In a famous story, a Roman legate sent by the senate arrogantly walked into the king's presence and drew a circle in the sand around Antiochus IV. The legate said that if Antiochus stepped out of that circle before promising to leave Egypt immediately, the legions would march into Syria and destroy his kingdom.[5]

The very angry Antiochus began the retreat to Syria, but rumors that he had been killed led Judea to revolt.[6] Antiochus lashed out at the Judeans vigorously. He stormed Jerusalem, took slaves, installed an idol of Zeus in the Jewish temple, and left Syrian governors to stamp out Judaism as a religion.[7]

An old Jewish man named Mattathias started the war that came to be known as the Wars of the Maccabees. Mattathias died shortly after

Eleazar Maccabeus bravely assaulted and killed the Syrian war elephant, but perished beneath the falling beast. [*Figures de la Bible. Illustrated by Gerard Hoet, and others. Published by P. de Hondt in The Hague (La Haye). 1728. Image courtesy Bizzell Bible Collection, University of Oklahoma Libraries.*]

starting the revolt against the Syrians, but left the conflict in the capable hands of his five sons, John, Simon, Judas, Eleazar, and Jonathan.[8] Judas Maccabeus (the Hammer) collected guerrilla warriors and went to war from the caves and hills.[9] Judas was strong, courageous, and a charismatic leader.

The Syrian leadership mistakenly believed that the Jewish revolt would be crushed easily and sent small armies with mediocre commanders to quell the uprising. Antiochus frittered away his time by throwing public festivals in Antioch in 165 BC, including thirty-six elephants in a parade, several of them pulling chariots.[10] He died shortly thereafter.

Rome must have heard about this parade, and immediately demanded that the new Syrian leadership kill all of their elephants.[11] The senate dispatched a commissioner, Cornelius Octavius, to enforce the Roman decree, but the people of Apamea saw this Roman and his soldiers hamstringing the war elephants and, in a fit of rage, lynched the Romans![12] The senate took no punitive action, and seemed to imply that Octavius had surpassed his orders by attacking the elephants himself, rather than just supervising.[13] The people of Apamea showed considerable empathy or concern for the war elephants in putting a stop to their executions.

Judas Maccabeus destroyed the first Syrian forces that attempted to restore order to Judea. By December of 164 BC, Judas had retaken Jerusalem and started the Hanukkah tradition by purifying the Temple.[14]

The Seleucid army returned with a larger and better-equipped army, including thirty-two elephants with howdahs and decorative royal armor. An escort of thirty-two special infantry guards called *stiphos* protected each elephant, in four rows of eight soldiers.[15] The books of the Maccabees claim that each elephant tower contained thirty-two men, but this is probably a corruption of the Greek letters delta and lambda, which, if corrected, would say four rather than thirty-two.[16] The only elephants capable of carrying thirty men exist in the fictional Middle Earth of J.R.R. Tolkien ("Oliphaunts").

The Syrian army met the forces of Judas Maccabeus in 162 BC at the Battle of Beth-Zacharias. In the mountainous terrain where the battle took place, this use of elephants was mainly psychological, since in a tight formation they could use neither their speed nor their physical power; the purpose was to frighten the Jews, who had never seen elephants before. The elephants also gave commanders a high platform to see the battlefield and issue orders more effectively. The Jewish fighters were terrified of the elephants, and so one of Judas' brothers wanted to show the beasts to be mortal.

...and Eleazar the son of Saura saw one of the beasts harnessed with the King's harness: and it was higher than the other beasts: and it seemed to him that the king was on it...and he ran up to it boldly...and he went between the feet of the elephant, and put himself under it: and slew it, and it fell to the ground upon him, and he died there.[17]

Eleazar ran beneath the elephant for a reason: the beast's armor did not protect its underside. He crouched under the elephant's front legs and drove his sword up into the animal's neck and throat. The pachyderm fell on him, and both elephant and attacker died together. This demonstration of the mortality of the elephant did not apparently fill the Jewish army with courage to imitate Eleazar, and Judas Maccabeus ordered a retreat.

The loss at Beth-Zacharias may have motivated Judas Maccabeus to seek allies. He sent a delegation to Rome asking for help, and the senate signed a treaty promising help if attacked. However, the Syrians brought another army with elephants, this time passing through some very narrow valleys in which the elephants had to walk single file. [18] At the Battle of Adasa, Nicanor the Elephantarch led the Seleucid army against the Jewish rebels and was soundly defeated, but we have no details on the role of the elephants. [19]

As each of the Maccabeus brothers died, the next effectively stepped in and kept up the revolt until they had achieved political independence. However, their alliance with Rome would bring serious consequences in about a hundred years.

The Seleucid royalty fell into disarray after Antiochus Epiphanes died, with numerous pretenders and weaklings ascending and falling from the throne. One of these unfortunate claimants met a fate similar to that of the Persian king Cyrus. Apparently while preparing his troops for a battle near Antioch, Ptolemy Philometer was on horseback when a screaming elephant frightened his horse. He was thrown off, cracking his head on the ground, and the attempted surgery to repair his skull killed him. [20] The next leader took that army formed by the deceased Philometer to fight against the Parthians in 140 BC.

The Syrians were indeed using African elephants rather than the Asian variety by this time; perhaps Egypt no longer viewed the Seleucid regimes as any threat. Because elephants were becoming harder to acquire, the Syrian military put a great deal of effort into improving the armor of the beasts. Innovations included armored leggings and scale armor with the plates facing upward, since attacks by soldiers against elephants come always from below. [21] Wall paintings found in the Marissa tomb show that the elephants' ears were painted red. The best illustration of war elephants of the late Seleucids comes from the Balustrade Reliefs in the Temple of Athena Polias Nikephoros in Pergamum, Turkey. The leather harnesses used to secure the tower to the elephant's back clearly show armor, to prevent enemies from hacking a strap and bringing down the howdah. These three straps go under the belly, under the chest, and under the tail. Most impressive is the elephant's helmet, looking like an American Indian headdress, which would help to protect the mahout from missiles. [22]

In 130 BC, Antiochus VII invaded Parthia in an attempt to reclaim lost Seleucid territory, taking ten African elephants with his army. However, the Parthian leader with his twenty Asian elephants caught the

Seleucid king by surprise in a winter attack, completely defeating the Syrians.

This is the last known appearance of elephants in the Seleucid kingdoms. Between the failure of the leadership to form stable governments and the inability to acquire elephants in meaningful numbers, pachyderms were relegated to the pictures on Syrian coinage.[23]

32
The Running of the Bulls

The Roman legions made good use of the African elephants captured from Carthage and donated by the Numidians in two campaigns against phalanxes in Greece. Known for exploiting effective military tactics and weapons, the Romans did not hesitate to send elephants to the western theatre of Spain.[1]

Rome learned of vast mineral wealth in central and northern Hispania and desired to raise auxiliary troops from the famous mountain warriors of Spain.[2] When Scipio Africanus first ejected the Carthaginians from Hispania during the war with Hannibal, the Iberian tribes were grateful. But in subsequent decades the Romans oppressed the people and caused revolts. Wars flared up intermittently from 195 BC to 133 BC. The Spanish learned not to trust Roman truces: when one tribe was promised clemency if they would lay down their weapons, the legion surrounded the tribe and hacked it to pieces.[3]

Spanish tribes united against Roman domination in the 150s BC, destroying the whole garrison in southern Spain. The new consul, Q. Fulvius Nobilor, waited in his fortified camp for ten elephants and three hundred Numidian cavalry, and only then dared to oppose the large Iberian army.[4] Apparently the general kept the elephants behind his troops, then opened up files and charged the elephants at the enemy through the rows.[5] Appian said:

The Celtiberians and their horses, who had never seen elephants before, were thunderstruck and fled to the city. Nobilor advanced at once against the city walls, where the battle raged fiercely, until one of the elephants was struck on the head with a large stone. He then became savage, trumpeted loudly, turned upon the Romans and began to destroy everything that came in his way, making no distinction between friend or foe. The other elephants, excited by his cries, all began to do the same, trampling the Romans under foot, scattering them this way and that."[6]

Appian comments that this disastrous incident shows that elephants are "the common enemy" on account of their fickleness.[7] However, it is unrealistic to blame the elephant hit on the head with a stone for this disaster. A ten-pound stone dropped from a wall of forty feet is "more than sufficient to kill" a man and would seriously wound an elephant.[8] The Roman commander should have studied the use of elephants in battle more carefully!

The elephant had three limited uses in ancient warfare: to act as a screen against enemy cavalry; to attack and penetrate the infantry mass; and to break into a fortified position; but, whenever employed in this last function it was generally unsuccessful.[9]

The confusion caused by the rampaging elephants gave the Celts a chance to counterattack. They killed three elephants and four thousand Romans.[10]

Far from abandoning the military use of pachyderms, Scipio Aemilianus stopped in north Africa to obtain more behemoths from Massinissa for the Spanish campaign.[11] These elephants lived in Hispania for at least ten years, since they appear in an ancient speech from 142 BC.

Apparently one selfish Roman mistreated his elephants for the sake of revenge and sabotage.

When he learned that his command in Spain was to be taken over by an enemy, Q. Pompeius, Macedonicus' response went beyond tears and bitter words. Valerius reports that he sabotaged the campaign by discharging any soldier who wished to leave service...by leaving the magazines unguarded and open to plunder by the enemy, by having the bows and arrows of the Cretan auxiliaries broken up and thrown into a river, and by refusing to feed the elephants...[12]

Another Roman had to bring new elephants and cavalry from Africa.[13] Some years later, Scipio Aemilianus returned to Spain to finish off the resistance by besieging the city of Numantia. He stopped again in Africa, obtaining a dozen elephants from Jugurtha, in 134 BC.[14]

Hispania is not the only western region to see Roman elephants stand with the legions. In Gaul, Ahenobarbus took several elephants to terrify the barbarians. At Vindalium in 121 BC the Romans fought a large battle against the Allobroges tribe and were victorious.[15] Proud of his achievements, Ahenobarbus henceforth rode through his captured province on the back of an elephant![16] The poet Juvenal wrote that Roman armies used turreted elephants, which would mean that they had adopted the use of howdahs and towers.[17]

Numidian kings of northern Africa (like Jugurtha) captured elephants using "pits," by having horsemen drive elephants into an artificial hollow surrounded by ditches and walls.[18] This method is entirely plausible and is similar to the *keddah* method used by the Indians for millennia. The Numidians had been the chief supplier of elephants to Rome. This changed in 111 BC when Jugurtha seized power in north Africa. He was a handsome and shrewd man, grandson of Massinissa, and an expert javelin thrower.[19] For many years Jugurtha was able to keep Rome from attacking by sending huge bribes to senators.[20]

Eventually the Romans decided to regain control of Africa by force. Jugurtha defeated the first Roman legion so badly that they surrendered and "passed under the yoke," the ultimate dishonor to an Italian army.[21] The African king knew Roman tactics, but was flexible, so when outmatched he took up guerilla warfare.[22]

The legions under Metellus fought against forty-four African elephants in 108 BC near the Muthul river, but it was a dismal affair. Perhaps hoping to ambush the Romans, the African infantry and elephant squadrons were ordered into an area of thick foliage. The elephants became entangled in the branches of trees, unable to maneuver. Their guards and the infantry panicked at the approach of the legion and fled. Without infantry support, the pachyderms were helpless. The Romans killed forty beasts and only saved four as prizes.[23]

Two Roman soldiers who would change the course of Roman history fought in Africa in the Jugurthine War. Gaius Marius burned most of Numidia until a traitor handed over Jugurtha to his assistant, Cornelius Sulla.[24] Both Marius and Sulla wanted credit for the capture of Jugurtha, and jealousy led to a rift and civil war between them.[25] The whole African affair greatly harmed the senate's reputation as its corruption and fraud was unmasked to the public eye; this would lead to the fall of the Republic.[26]

33
Pompey's Circus

The people of Rome loved a spectacle and had frequently seen captured elephants march through the city. The purpose of these displays, perhaps, was to show the populace that elephants were not invincible enemies; to keep up morale when faced with difficult foes.

Many books and papers have been written about the Roman mob, which seemed to enjoy bloody contests in the public Circus and Coliseum. Although public games are not specifically military in nature, the games involving elephants often took on a military aura, as combat was staged between man and pachyderm. Thus, some notice must be paid to the history of the games.

The first public fight between elephants thrilled the crowds in 99 BC. Pliny adds that the laws had to be changed to permit this: "There was an old Resolution of the Senate prohibiting the importation of African elephants into Italy...[the] Tribune of the Plebs carried in the Assembly of the People a resolution repealing this and allowing them to be imported for shows in the Circus."[1] The purpose of this law is not clear. Trophy elephants captured from Pyrrhus and the First Punic War had marched through Rome. It is especially odd because Pliny singles out African elephants, as if perhaps Asian elephants were permitted in Italy. At any rate, the shows began about one hundred years before Christ.

Gnaeus Pompeius, known later as Pompey the Great, was an officer who became powerful by crushing revolts in Spain and pirates in the Mediterranean Sea.[2] He had a large nose, athletic body, a lot of ambition, and was popular with troops.[3] He had no apparent experience with elephants until his troops campaigned in Africa in 81 BC. After his victory, he went elephant hunting and captured many in Numidia.

Pompey intended to celebrate his triumph in Rome by riding in a chariot pulled by four elephants side by side. It was widely believed that pachyderm chariots had pulled "gods" like Dionysus and Alexander, and so would be a great publicity statement.[4] This plan failed badly, and publicly, because no one thought to measure the width of the city gate and the elephants could not fit through it in harness![5] Embarrassed, Pompey had to abandon his chariot to enter the city.

Pompey did not dabble with elephants again for more than twenty years. In 55 BC he spent vast sums of money to hold fabulous public games in the Circus.[6] The main event on the fifth and last day would be the great finale, when criminals were pitted against twenty war elephants in a mock battle. The behemoths crushed the felons, and then the plan was that real experts, black warriors from Numidia, would kill the elephants to end the show.

One of the beasts tried to defend itself, although its legs had been disabled by hamstringing and it could only crawl on its knees. The soldiers were finally able to kill one by sticking a javelin into its eye.[7]

Then something very strange happened, as best described by Pliny.

There was also a wondrous sight when another elephant was killed by a single blow, for the javelin thrust under its eye had reached the vital parts of its head. All the elephants together attempted to break out from the iron barricades which surrounded them, and this caused anxiety among the people....But Pompey's elephants, when they had lost hope of escape, sought the compassion of the crowd and supplicated it with a kind of lamentation. There resulted so much grief among the people that they forgot the generosity lavished in their honor by General Pompey and, bursting into tears, all arose together and invoked curses on Pompey....[8]

The crowd that had come to the games for the purpose of seeing elephants kill and be killed had suddenly become sympathetic to the dying beasts. Many people of that time believed that elephants could understand human language well and be reasoned with. One of the rumors that had spread in Rome is that the mahouts had convinced the elephants to climb into the ships by promising that they would be safe and return home.[9] Now betrayed by Pompey, the pachyderms were calling upon the gods for revenge on injustice!

Once again, Pompey had twice hurt himself in the public eye by using elephants. The next leader of Rome would not make these mistakes.

34
The Herd of Julius Caesar

As the power of the Roman senate waned, generals became powerful. The main rival to Pompey's influence was the young Julius Caesar. He made a name for himself by leading legions against barbarians, Celts, Gauls, and Britons in western Europe.

Caesar was a slender man with black eyes, and he went bald early in life.[1] Caesar's charisma led his soldiers to follow him with absolute loyalty. Because he did not employ elephants in his early years, we jump ahead to Caesar's second invasion of England in 54 BC, where he first employed a pachyderm.[2] General Montgomery believes that the amphibious assault fleet of Caesar may have been the largest seen in the English Channel until World War II.[3]

As discussed briefly with Pyrrhus' elephant adventures on the sea, getting an elephant into a ship is no simple task. Here is one illuminating description into the ancient process:

An elephant has ventured on to the narrow bridge linking the ship with the land. Its feet, with the exception of the rear left, are firmly held by a rope. A group of men standing on the bridge above holds one of the ends, while a second group, on the land, holds the other. There is no mahout to help its advance; its progress, painfully laborious, is controlled by the pressures from above which drag it on to the ship while those below ensure that it does not miss its footing. Shackles in front forestall a mad charge and, for greater security, the ropes on which the slaves on the bridge are pulling are made fast to the bulwarks.[4]

While the march across Europe and passage over the English Channel must not have been particularly pleasant, the elephant might take some comfort from the fact that his role in the battle would not be terribly traumatic.

According to Polyaenus, in his "Eight Books of Stratagems":

Caesar attempting to pass a large river in Britain, Cassoellaunus, king of the Britons, obstructed him with many horsemen and chariots. Caesar had in his train a very large elephant, an animal hitherto unseen by the Britons. Having armed him with scales of iron, and put a large tower upon him, and placed therein archers and slingers, he ordered them to enter the stream. The Britons were amazed on beholding a beast till then unseen, and of an extraordinary nature. As to the horses, what need to write of them? Since even among the Greeks, horses fly at seeing an elephant even without harness; but thus towered and armed, and casting darts and slinging, they could not endure even to look upon the sight. The Britons therefore fled with their horses and chariots. Thus the Romans passed the river without molestation, having terrified the enemy by a single animal.[5]

The Thames River was perhaps five feet deep, so a difficult crossing for men on foot, but no problem at all for an elephant.[6] The pachyderm won the contest almost single-trunkedly!

Many skeptics discount this story because Caesar does not mention the elephant in his own writings, but C.E. Stevens, an authority on late Republican Rome, says that the story is probably true, omitted by Caesar from his books because there was no propaganda value in it.[7] As Gowers writes, "It seems conceivable that in his published *Commentaries* Caesar preferred to give the whole of the credit to his legionaries rather than to admit that he had made the task comparatively easy for them by scaring the simple savages out of their wits. Polyaenus was a writer of great repute in his day...it seems unlikely that he would have tried to foist on his public a brand new invention of his own."[8] A more concrete argument in support of the behemoth in Britain is that Caesar soon issued a coin with an elephant trampling a dragon. The dragon was used as a symbol of the region called Briton.[9]

In 50 BC the senate feared that Caesar would march on Rome as General Cornelius Sulla had done, so they stripped him of command and prepared for a trial of treason, leaving Caesar little choice but to march on Rome.[10] Pompey was named protector of the senate, but quickly retreated to Greece upon Caesar's fast march to Rome.

The civil war between Caesar and Pompey was played out in several arenas. King Juba of Numidia owed his throne to Pompey and also hated Caesar, who had once pulled his beard in a quarrel! Caesar sent an army to Africa under a subcommander, but Juba and sixty elephants defeated the Romans.[11]

At Pharsalia, in Greece, Pompey used elephants in his army against Caesar, but no record describes their role in the combat. After Caesar vanquished Pompey, the rest of the senatorial supporters waited in Africa, the only remaining haven from Caesar's control. Q. Metellus Scipio (Pompey's father-in-law) led fourteen legions, including four belonging to Juba. Caesar arrived with only eight legions.

While greatly outnumbered and waiting for reinforcements, Caesar's men prepared fortified positions around their camp, including traps and caltrops, to keep the elephants from ripping apart the palisades.

Florus notes that these elephants of Scipio were "unaccustomed to war and only recently brought from the woods...."[12] The fact that these animals were captured in "the woods" is another indication that these north African elephants were indeed of the forest variety and not the larger bush elephants.

Scipio meanwhile undertook the training of the elephants in the following manner. He drew up two lines of battle: one line of slingers, facing the elephants, to take the place of the enemy and to discharge small stones... and behind them drew up his own line so that, when the enemy proceeded to sling their stones and the elephants in their consequent panic wheeled round upon their own side, his men should receive them with a volley of stones, and so make them wheel round again away from his own line in the direction of the enemy. This method worked, though it was a difficult and slow process; for elephants are uncouth creatures, and it is difficult to get them fully trained even with many years' training and long practice; and if they are led forth to battle, they are, for all their training, equally dangerous to both sides.[13]

Scipio had good reason to train the elephants not to panic under a barrage of sling stones: both horses and elephants tend to run away when wounded. A horse will be turned by one arrow strike, thus removing it and its human rider from the battle.[14] Although elephants are superior to horses in regard to receiving missile fire, i.e., they can be hit a number of times by arrows or stones and still fight, eventually the repeated pains will cause the elephants to flee. Caesar recognized that slingers were especially good against elephants.[15] Vegetius wrote that the Greeks knew that sling stones "killed both the men who guided the elephants and the soldiers who fought in the towers on their backs."[16] Shot thrown by slings were often shaped with a wide head and narrow tail to allow "the tissue of the wound to close behind the missile and make extraction from the body very difficult."[17] Worse (for the enemy), Roman slingers qualified and practiced by striking a man-sized target at a range of six hundred feet!

The Roman poet Marcus Annaeus Lucanus wrote an unfinished piece on Caesar's battles, and this segment makes clear reference to our subject.

> Thus may an elephant in Afric wastes,
> Oppressed by frequent darts, break those that fall
> Rebounding from his horny hide, and shake
> Those that find lodgment, while his life within
> Lies safe, protected, nor doth spear avail
> To reach the fount of blood. Unnumbered wounds
> By arrow dealt, or lance, thus fail to slay
> This single warrior.[18]

Lucan's exaggerated belief in the impenetrable pachyderm skin lay quite far from the truth.

As for Caesar's opinion quoted earlier, that elephants are equally dangerous to both sides, he recognized that years of training were essential to incorporating the beasts into an army. Nevertheless, here in Africa, Caesar ordered his fleet to bring elephants from Rome. Just to practice with, of course!

[Caesar] had ordered elephants to be brought across from Italy to enable our troops not only to become familiar with them, but also to get to know both the appearance and capabilities of the beast, what part of its body was readily vulnerable to a missile and, when an elephant was accoutered and armoured, what part of its body was still left uncovered and unprotected, so that their missiles should be aimed at that spot. He had also this further object in mind, that his horses should learn by familiarity with these beasts not to be alarmed by their scent, trumpeting or appearance. From this experiment he had profited handsomely: for the troops handled the beasts and came to appreciate their sluggishness; the cavalry hurled dummy javelins at them; and the docility of the beasts had brought the horses to feel at home with them.[19]

Clearly Caesar could not train eight legions (tens of thousands of men) to fight elephants with the handful he sailed from Rome. He trained five cohorts against elephants and ordered them to station themselves in the formation wherever the elephants were set to attack.

The elephants of Scipio and Juba wore armor and carried towers. Juba brought reinforcements, raising the elephant division to at least sixty. With the Numidian reinforcements, Scipio felt he could attack Caesar with a significant numeric advantage. The battle of Thapsus played out in 46 BC. We have very detailed accounts of Thapsus because a friend of Caesar was either present or questioned eyewitnesses.[20] Plutarch says that

Caesar himself may not have participated in the battle because of an epileptic seizure, but his troops fought well.[21]

Sixty-four elephants were deployed on the right and left wings of Scipio's army, with light troops behind them. Caesar's five cohorts of specially trained soldiers moved into position opposing the pachyderms.

The initial charge of the elephants did not go well for Scipio and Juba, thanks in large part to Caesar's careful preparations. The volleys of sling stones and arrows caused chaos as the elephants were frightened. Most of them turned and trampled the light infantry behind them, rushing for home.[22] However, at least one elephant charged straight into Caesar's camp, angry. The story adds a personal element to the battle scene, as one soldier helped an unfortunate camp assistant who was assaulted by this maddened pachyderm.[23]

...the gallantry of a veteran soldier of the Fifth legion. On the left wing an elephant, maddened by the pain of a wound it had received, had attacked an unarmed sutler, pinned him underfoot, and then knelt upon him; and now, with its trunk erect and swaying, and trumpeting loudly, it was crushing him to death with its weight. This was more than the soldier could bear; he could not but confront the beast, fully armed as he was. When it observed him coming towards it with weapon poised to strike, the elephant abandoned the corpse, encircled the soldier with its trunk, and lifted him into the air. The soldier, perceiving that a dangerous crisis of this sort demanded resolute action on his part, hewed with his sword again and again at the encircling trunk with all the strength he could muster. The resulting pain caused the elephant to drop the soldier, wheel round, and with shrill trumpetings make all speed to rejoin its fellows.[24]

The Roman gladius (sword) weighed only two pounds, yet in testing has shown that it could penetrate flesh with a four-inch-deep wound: more than enough to damage the elephant's sensitive trunk.[25]

Caesar's legions captured all sixty-four enemy elephants with their towers and ornaments.[26] Apparently the tactics of missile fire had only frightened and wounded the beasts, not killed them, and their wounds were tended. Immediately after this victory, Caesar took all of these beasts, "equipped, armed and complete with towers and harness," and used them to terrify a rebellious town.[27]

Successful in every arena of combat, Caesar returned to Rome for a public triumph. Rather than attempting to ride in an elephant-drawn chariot, he simply walked among forty elephants along the steps of the capitol, each beast holding a torch in its trunk.[28]

What happened to these forty elephants is not entirely clear, but the various accounts might fit together. Caesar did hold public games to entertain the populace, using either twenty or forty elephants, depending on whether Pliny or Dio is more accurate. They fought against five hundred infantry and twenty cavalry in the arena. This cannot have been a fight to the death because both historians agree that men were riding on the elephant's backs and so to throw real javelins or hack at the elephants would certainly harm their riders as well. Of course it is feasible that after the battle spectacle, the riders dismounted and then the army attacked the pachyderms as Pompey had done. This is unlikely, however. For one thing, Caesar knew well how badly Pompey's reputation suffered for his cruelty to the elephants. Caesar's army in Africa took pains not to kill the enemy elephants, since sixty-four attacked and sixty-four joined his army henceforth.

The poet Juvenal referred to "Caesar's herd" and wrote that a Roman official was in charge of the "State-owned herds," called a *procurator ad elephantos*.[29] Julius Caesar seemed to be preparing an eastern campaign against the Parthians in eastern Europe, and the elephants could be very useful against this enemy that relied wholly on cavalry. Finally, after Caesar's assassination on March 15, 44 BC, both Antony and Octavius are mentioned in connection with elephants taken from Italy for the war against Brutus, so the elephants were not exterminated in the circus.

The Roman writer Aelian says the same herd of elephants that Julius Caesar had started was still breeding in Rome in 12 AD under Octavian (Augustus).[30]

35
Arrogant Emperors

Corruption and gridlock plagued the Roman senate until powerful generals became the policy-making branch of government, leading to the end of the Republic and the beginning of the Imperial age of Rome.

Pompey had failed in his bid to ride through Rome in an elephant-drawn chariot, but eventually the emperors would enjoy the god-like experience, if only in effigy. Tiberius had a statue of Caesar Augustus pulled around the city in a cart harnessed to elephants in 35 AD. Henceforth, it became fashionable for royalty and rich people to put images of their loved ones in carriages for pachyderm pulling.[1]

Where did these elephants come from? Many sources mention a herd of elephants that was kept near Rome through at least 200 AD, and these beasts were occasionally used against the Gauls or the Britons when the need arose.[2]

When Emperor Caligula fell to the assassins' blades, the Praetorian Guard forced his uncle Claudius to take power. Claudius had no military experience, and when an uprising threatened the Roman garrison near Londinium, Claudius felt compelled to earn some glory in Briton. Since Julius Caesar had used one elephant against the Britons, Claudius took several behemoths along. The ruler of the western world and his beasts traveled by ship from the Italian port of Ostia to Marseilles, in Gaul, in 44 AD. They marched north to the English Channel and then took boats across to meet Aulus Plautius, the governor of Gaul and Briton.[3] Claudius came up to reinforce the hard-pressed Plautius on the southern side of Thames, perhaps using the Richborough base, and they crossed Thames together.[4]

Unfortunately we hear nothing about the role of the pachyderms in driving the Britons back and saving the Roman garrison. It seems that the Emperor had a look around for a week or two and then loaded up the elephants and went home.

Emperor Nero owned an elephant that could walk up and down a tight-rope, while Germanicus trained elephants to wear dresses, toss flowers,

Ancient Triumphal Procession.

Some Roman emperors paraded through the streets in an elephant-drawn chariot. [*Strickland, Agnes attributed,* True Stories from Ancient History, *Philadelphia, Porter & Coates, circa 1900. Alta Edition.*]

and dance.[5] All of this silliness came from a herd of African Forest elephants that Julius Caesar had brought from Numidia and which Roman writers claim had been breeding well enough to form a stable population.[6] Considering the difficulties faced with breeding elephants even in the modern world, we must wonder if this was propaganda or if the Romans had some knowledge that we lack.

In the Roman world, elephants fell into disuse as military weapons during the Imperial period. The reasons for this are twofold. First, by the time of the emperors, Rome experienced the so-called Pax Romana: decades of relative calm and peace because no major enemies remained. Elephants became a biological curiosity to be enjoyed in the Circus.

The other key change in the Roman/elephant relationship was economic. Italians discovered the wonders of ivory. As a 1990 UNESCO history of Africa states, the Roman lust for ivory had caused the North African elephant to disappear by the end of second-century AD.[7]

Ivory came to be used for everything artistic in Rome: decorating ceilings, furniture, and even dice.[8] Emperor Caligula built a stable of ivory for his horse.[9] Craftsmen peddled all sorts of elephant-tusk carvings:

thrones, benches, beds, chariots, carriages, book covers, bird cages, and floor tiles.[10] Once the legions had overthrown Carthage, north Africa became little more than an ivory-trading hub for the empire.[11] As demand for ivory figurines grew, the number of elephants declined, forcing the trade to search farther south into Africa. The Romans even reestablished the old elephant-capturing ports Ptolemy on the Red Sea to trade with far away India to obtain ivory.[12] Ivory supplies became so poor that carvers began cutting elephant bones into layers as a substitute.[13] The progress of civilization during the Roman period sounds similar to our own times.

The last attempt of Rome to field war elephants can be described as darkly comical. In 193 AD, Emperor Pertinax died, and the Praetorians offered power to the highest bidder. The winner was a rich senator by the name of Didius Julianus.[14] A more powerful claimant to the empire was Septimius Severus, a general in the north, who immediately marched his legions toward Rome to take command.

The newly crowned Julianus did what he could to gather an army, including conscripting the Circus elephants. It was hoped that the troops under Severus would be frightened by the pachyderms. Instead, the frightened elephants threw off their mahouts and ran for home.

Emperors became less powerful and less sane during these years. Elagabalus (M. Aurelius Antoninus) loved chariots. He fashioned one chariot to be pulled by naked women, while his most dramatic means of transportation was a cart pulled by four elephants. Unfortunately, the vehicle knocked down a number of important tombstones in the Vatican region.[15] People could not take this fellow too seriously, so they murdered Elagabalus in the bathroom and threw his body into the Tiber River.[16]

The mighty war elephants that once supported the great armies of the world had become nothing more than clowns for entertainment and ivory trinkets for the wealthy.

36
Sackcloth, Ashes, and Prayer

While the Roman Republic fought Spaniards and Numidians in the western end of Europe and Africa, and the Maccabees brothers sought independence for Judea, the Parthians of Persia (modern Iran) were conquering the crumbling Seleucid empire.[1] Julius Caesar may have been planning a campaign against the Parthians when he was assassinated, but subsequent emperors chose to ignore the east.

While the Romans had run out of war elephants, the Parthians fielded them regularly. The first Roman emperor to face war elephants in battle was Trajan, who decided to press the Parthians. In 115 AD the legions of Trajan captured the Parthian capital of Ctesiphon on the Tigris River.[2] We do not hear about the elephants in the battle, but Trajan's famous column depicts the *carroballista*, described by Gaebel as the favorite anti-elephant weapon of Rome. "The ultimate ancient weapon against elephants was the Roman *carroballista*, a small catapult mounted on a cart drawn by two horses or mules."[3] This mini-catapult could rapidly fire darts that would wound pachyderms.

Rome again ignored the east for about a century, until Septimius Severus took Rome from the hapless high-bidding Senator Julianus. Severus ejected the Parthians from northern Mesopotamia and took Babylon.[4] The Romans created new provinces in the east and, by weakening the Parthians, left a new power to rise in Persia, the Sassanids.[5] This group would last four hundred years, until the Arab conquest.

Whereas the Parthians used some elephants, the Sassanids collected them *en masse* for fighting. In 227 AD the Sassanid king Artaxerxes invaded India and took hundreds of elephants.[6] Artaxerxes hoped to restore the Persian empire to its glory from the days of Cyrus, and his bravado so offended Roman emperor Alexander Severus that the Romans launched an invasion.[7] The legions were not well prepared, however, either for the cold winter marching, or for the seven hundred enemy war elephants carrying towers and archers. The Romans were defeated, losing thousands in the winter retreat, but Severus' propaganda machine turned it into a victory because he brought home eighteen captured pachyderms and claimed to have killed two hundred others.[8]

The barbarians became bolder in attacking Roman lands in western Europe, while the Sassanids pressured provinces in the Middle East. In 253 AD, Emperor Valerian divided the empire between east and west to provide command and control of legions in two continents.[9]

Along with a political and administrative shakeup, the Roman armies reorganized to counter the new enemies. Legions adopted large squadrons of cavalry and archers to face swift foes.[10] These changes may have been too late, at least for Valerian. When the Sassanids invaded Mesopotamia again, Emperor Valerian was captured. Some sources say that his skin was removed, stuffed with straw, and hung as a trophy in a temple.[11]

In 286 AD, Emperor Diocletian made the east/west administrative division deeper by naming a co-emperor to rule the east. Because eastern ruler Galerius defeated the Sassanids and put elephants on a monument declaring his victory, some have assumed that the Romans used war elephants in the battle.[12] More likely, the elephants signified the victory parade held in Antioch, when Galerius had captured elephants and their mahouts marching through the streets.[13]

The growth of Christianity in Rome, with the help of Constantine, abolished gladiator contests and the Circus fell into disuse.[14] Without the Circus, elephants were no longer needed in Rome, and it seems that they vanished from the capitol rather quickly. Within decades, coins issued during the reign of Constantius II portray "comical and unrealistic" elephants, perhaps indicating that no live models were available![15]

A Syrian book called *Aethiopica* written in the third or fourth century offers great detail of a battle in which Persian cataphracts charged an Ethiopian army.[16]

The main point of resistance, some way back, was a line of armoured elephants carrying on their backs towers manned by bowmen....The orders to the forward troops were to slip between the horses' legs of the attacking cataphracts and to rip open their bellies....Nevertheless many of the cataphracts succeeded in getting through this first line of defence and bore down on the elephants; but they were met by such a cloud of arrows aimed at their eyes that most of them were soon immobilized, and the survivors, having tried in vain to break through the solid barrier presented by the bodies of the elephants, retired in disorder.[17]

Ethiopian troops behind the elephants then counterattacked to eliminate the cavalry. These African elephants may represent the last of the Kushite military pachyderms.

Roman carroballistae hurled darts at enemy elephants with great effect. [*Courtesy of Max Schwartz. Reprinted with permission.*]

The growth of Christianity in Roman territories troubled the Zoroastrian Sassanid kings. Shapur II lashed out against Christians, believing them to be traitors or Roman spies. He sent three hundred elephants to level the town of Susa because it was filled with Christians.[18] The city was literally leveled by the beasts.

The Sassanid elephants participated in several sieges for which we have extensive accounts, although certain elements must be taken as exaggeration. In 338 AD, King Shapur II besieged the city of Nisibis. Theodoret, a Greek historian, describes how St. James, a local bishop, saved the city. James called upon God to send pests upon them, and God sent clouds of gnats and mosquitoes, which "filled the hollow trunks of the elephants, and the ears and nostrils of the horses and other animals. Finding the attack of these little creatures past endurance they broke their bridles, unseated their riders, and threw the ranks into confusion."[19]

Shapur failed again on the second try, but made better progress in his third attempt in 350 AD. He continued to bring elephants along, because the Roman defenders of the city were terrified of pachyderms: "In much earlier times Roman infantrymen had faced elephants firmly, but in the fourth century they were again a new, fearsome force in warfare."[20]

Ammianus describes them as "gleaming elephants with their cruel gaping jaws, pungent smell, and strange appearance." The Sassanid military adorned the elephant towers with flags and used them to instill confidence in their ranks.[21]

St. James continued to pray for miracles, but Shapur diverted a nearby river. This created a lake around Nisibis, and the weight of water caved in a 150-feet-length of the city wall. Rashly, wishing to take advantage of the breached wall, Shapur ordered an immediate assault, without scouting the water-logged terrain.[22]

First of all marched the heavy cavalry, accompanied by the horse-archers; next came the elephants, bearing iron towers upon their backs, and in each tower a number of bowmen; intermixed with the elephants were a certain amount of heavy-armed foot....The horses became quickly entangled in the ooze and mud which the waters had left behind them as they subsided; the elephants were even less able to overcome these difficulties, and as soon as they received a wound sank down—never to rise again—in the swamp.[23]

Julian "the Apostate," emperor a decade later, wrote several lines about the role of elephants in this assault. "...they [the Persians] tried the elephants...in battle line at equal distances from one another...carrying the towers...by the king's express command they charged at the wall and received a continuous fire of stones and arrows, while some of the elephants were wounded and perished by sinking into the mud."[24] Some of these missiles were not simple bow-fired arrows, but darts and bolts from catapults and ballistae.

The more spiritual view among the people was expressed in the sermon of Ephrem Syrus, a witness of the siege. "Elephants arrived and were defeated by sack-cloth, ashes and prayer."[25]

37
Breach of Faith

The Sassanid king Shapur II had been a constant problem in the eastern Roman empire. In 363 AD, the emperor Julian left Constantinople (modern Istanbul) with his legions to drive away the neo-Persian army.

To reach Ctesiphon, the old capital of the Parthians, his army had to cross the large Tigris River. Awaiting them on the opposite bank, though, were the Sassanid elephants. By the time Julian's forces came up with a plan to get across the Tigris, it was mid-June. Thus, they would not have time to siege the city and starve out the enemy before cold weather and winter would come. The Romans abandoned the campaign to return home.

The Sassanids had supplies and support from Ctesiphon and so were able to pursue the Roman army, to harass and kill stragglers.[1] On June 26, 363 AD, the Persians launched a surprise assault on the rear of the Roman column. Emperor Julian was not wearing his armor and was caught between heavy cavalry and the elephants. Julian was hit by a javelin, perhaps thrown from elephant back, and fainted. Although his guards carried him to safety, he died a few hours later, at the age of thirty-one.[2]

Killing the emperor emboldened the Persians. The next day the Sassanid elephants again charged the rear of the Roman column. They had success until some of the emperor's guards wounded the beasts with javelins. One ancient Persian writer, Al-Tabari, speaks of Shapur's "elephants covered with blankets," which implies that the pachyderms had very little protective armor.[3] The painful missiles caused the elephants to turn into their own troops and disrupt the Persian horse charge.

King Khusrau I of the Sassanids set his engineers to improve the Phasis Road in the north of his empire so that his elephants and cavalry could invade Scythia more quickly.[4] The problem with roads to the enemy, however, is that enemies like to use them too!

One region that had long been a part of the Roman empire, Armenia, became the first officially "Christian nation" in 301 AD, eleven years before Constantine thought of it. But Armenia fell under the control of the Zoroastrian Persians as Rome's power waned.

King Yazdegird II (438–457) of the Sassanids decreed that all Persian subjects must immediately adopt Zoroastrianism. Initially the Armenian nobles were cowed by the king's threats and agreed, but the people of Armenia replied to Yazdegird II that they would be politically loyal to his rule, but would not abandon their faith. Some of the Christians became overly zealous, destroying some Zoroastrian temples and attacking the Persian priests, and Yazdegird sent an army to quell the rebellion.

Constantinople could not help the Armenians because Attila the Hun was threatening at the time. The Roman empire in the west was coming unglued. Attacked by several barbarian tribes, Rome was sacked repeatedly and was no longer a western power by 472 AD.[5] This left only the eastern empire, known as the Byzantine empire, as a remnant of the old Roman order.

On Easter day, April 13, 451, a Sassanid army arrived with three hundred thousand troops to enforce Armenian compliance with the law. An unknown number of war elephants supported the Persian forces, carrying iron towers with archers. The Sassanid commander, Mushkan Nusalavurd, rode in a "barbed howdah."[6] Perhaps this iron tower had belts of sharp spikes around it to keep enemy troops from climbing up to attack the commander.

The Armenians did possess an army, made up of sixty-six thousand peasants and clergy. The Christian general, Vardan, led his forces well against the Persians at the Battle of Avarair: the Sassanids sustained far more casualties than the defenders. However, Vardan himself died in battle, and the Armenian army ran away. They continued to resist, using guerrilla tactics, until the Persians sued for peace in 484 AD. Invasions of the "White Huns" (Ephthalites) required the Sassanid forces to withdraw from Europe.[7]

We have no detailed accounts of Sassanid conflicts with the White Huns that involved elephants, but one nonviolent story does survive and tells of our pachyderms hard at work.

The Sassanid king Firuz, son of Yazdegird II, had gained a temporary peace with the White Huns by vowing that he and his army would not pass by a certain landmark/pillar. This vow essentially meant that he could not attack their cities, which lay beyond the landmark.

Using a bit of creative thinking and guile, the king brought up his army and fifty elephants. The beasts pulled down the pillar, the army harnessed it to the elephants, and the pachyderms dragged it in front of the army so that Firuz could destroy his enemies without breaking his vow![8]

The White Huns feigned a retreat until the Sassanid army rushed forward and fell into giant pits dug in the ground. Firuz and his army were destroyed. The ancient sources say that the gods had avenged his deceitful "breach of faith."

38
The Year of the Elephant

The story of Mohammed and the formation of the Islamic religion begins in 571 AD, known as "The Year of the Elephant." Mohammed came into the world that year in the city of Mecca, in present-day Saudi Arabia.

Religious tension had been building between Mecca and modern-day-Yemen, so that the Christian king Abraha raised an army and intended to destroy Mecca. The king's army contained several war elephants that were supposed to demolish the holy sites. Ethiopian armies had been putting elephants in the front line of their armies for centuries. Their leather howdahs could supposedly carry six men.[1] This is not impossible, as the African armies did not use heavy armor, and thus the elephant could carry more soldiers.

According to some of the histories, when the people of Mecca had fled the city, seeing the approach of Abraha's army, the lead elephant, named Mahmud, stopped and kneeled down, refusing to go further.[2] The rest of the elephants would not go without the leader, and so the whole formation came to a halt. Mahmud was beaten and cajoled, but would not take one more step toward Mecca.

According to the Koran, God (Allah) sent a flock of birds that dropped heavy pebbles on Abraha's army, killing many. Another translation indicates that smallpox struck the army. In any case, the king relented and ordered a retreat, leaving Mecca unmolested. The Koran says, "Hast thou not seen how thy Lord dealt with the army of the Elephant? Did he not cause their stratagem to miscarry?"[3] Thirty years later, Mohammed declared himself a divine prophet.

The armies of Constantinople often fought against Sassanid war elephants. After one victory in the early seventh century, the eastern emperor Herakleios staged a triumphal entry in a four-elephant-chariot.[4] Herakleios defeated Khusru Parviz who owned a thousand elephants, although the propagandists of the day did not belabor the point that nearly all of Khusru's pachyderms were used for hunting and hauling, not combat.[5]

Just as Muslims ascribed religious sensitivity to the elephants that refused to attack Mecca, so the Christians ascribed piety to some elephants visiting Byzantium (Constantinople).[6] John of Ephesus wrote that the elephants raised their trunks and signed the cross whenever they passed a Christian church, to thank God for helping them in battle![7] One must wonder if the mahouts taught the elephants some Christian sensibilities for the visit to Byzantium.

Civil wars weakened the Persian Sassanid kingdom. A general called Bahram received many Asian elephants from India to attack King Chosroes II. Despite a valiant fight by the elephant squadron, they were "surrounded and forced to surrender."[8] Civil wars may have weakened the Persians, but it was the furious onslaught of the Arabs that quickly destroyed them.

The following of Mohammed grew quickly. By 630 AD he had taken Mecca without a fight and was threatening to attack the Sassanid king in Persia. When the prophet died, his zealous adherents took up the cause and sought to spread the religion of Islam throughout the world, mainly by conquering nations. The believers of Mohammed were willing to fight to the death, while many foreign peoples preferred to adopt any religion if it brought peace.

The first Arab armies were relatively small and disorganized, but had high morale. Their first attempts to invade Persia failed, however, largely because of elephants.

In the spring of 634 AD, a small army led by King Yazdegird III met the Muslim raiders with one elephant. The Arab army was understandably frightened, having never seen an elephant before. To inspire the men, a Beni Bekr tribesman named Muthanna charged alone against the beast and killed it, but his bravery did not lead to victory or defeat. The battle was a draw.[9]

Six months later, another Arab army approached Persia and was opposed by an army with thirty elephants, a white one as the leader. The white elephant requires explanation, as it confuses westerners who assume that a white elephant would actually be white. In reality, only an albino elephant, which is extremely rare, is actually white. The more common "white" elephant simply has pale colorations at certain spots and other characteristics deemed to be "auspicious" and beautiful. When a white elephant is discovered, experts study the beast for months to check every aspect of its physique and temperament before officially declaring it to be white. All white elephants were claimed by the king or ruler and were believed to be specially blessed by the god(s). So when the Arabs saw this white elephant, it may simply have stood out from the rest by its size and majesty, as opposed to blinding them with its snow-like skin.

When the Arab horses charged at the Persian army, they stopped short, terrified by the behemoths. To try to instill confidence in his men (as Muthanna had done), Abu Obeidah dismounted his horse and ran to attack the white elephant. He struck the elephant once, and then the beast grabbed him in fury and crushed him underfoot.[10] The Muslim army fled.

When one elephant was eventually taken from the Persians, the Muslim commander sent it to Medina. "The strange animal astonished the simple natives, who asked one another wonderingly, 'Is this indeed one of God's works, or did human art make it?'"[11]

At the Battle of Cadesia in 636 AD, which would last three days, the Sassanids advanced successfully against the Arab cavalry, which refused to approach the elephants. The Arabs were better prepared this time. A group of archers distracted the beasts while Muslim soldiers ran forward to cut the straps holding the towers on the elephants' backs.[12] The elephant riders fell off and the howdahs were damaged, but the Persian infantry surged forward to help the wounded and recover the damaged towers. The day was viewed as a draw.

On day two, the Persians hoped to avoid battle because they had not finished repairing the "elephant furniture." In a scene reminiscent of Queen Semiramis, the Muslims attacked with horses and camels "dressed up to resemble elephants."[13] "In order to counter the deficiency that the elephants of the Persians placed against the Muslims, Qa'qa came up with a very ingenious device. He had some camels enveloped in fantastic housings and covered their heads with flowing vestments which gave them a strange and frightening appearance. On whichever side these artificial mammoths went, the horses of the Persians shied and became uncontrollable…"[14] On day two, the Persian cavalry did retreat, although it was not a total defeat.

On the third day the Sassanids had completed their equipment repair for the elephant squadron. However, the minor victory on day two had inspired confidence in the Arab army and brought some valuable information from defectors. New Persian "converts" told the Muslim commander that the best way to destroy the "black monsters" was to gouge their eyes and trunks.[15] No longer afraid of the elephants, the Muslim infantry aimed their attacks at the Persian elephants' eyes. A Syrian leader drove a spear into the eye of the leading white elephant, and when a second elephant took a missile in the eye, the whole pachyderm force stampeded in retreat.[16] The Arabs were victorious.

39
Early and Medieval Asia

From the Chiu Dynasty of China we find a humorous piece of prose about *Elephas maximus*.

The elephant is a vast creature. His body is very heavy and has the strength of bulls. His appearance is very queer. When we look at him from the front, we think we are looking at his posterior because he has a trunk which looks like his tail. When he walks it is, as it were, as if a mountain moved, but ah, how hard to know whether he is coming or going![1]

Written at about the time the Romans annihilated Carthage, the *Mahawamsa* or Ceylon Chronicle (of Sri Lanka) presents many stories about war elephants. The most detailed tells of Kandula the elephant, ridden by King Dutugamunu (circa 150 BC).[2] The Ceylon Chronicle is a lengthy poem, describing the king's desperate battle to take the fortified enemy city.

The city had three moats, and was guarded by a high wall. Its gate was covered with iron hard for foes to shatter. The elephant knelt on his knees and, battering with his tusks stone and mortar and brick, he attacked the iron gate. The Tamils from the watch-tower threw missiles of every kind, balls of red-hot iron and [vessels of] molten pitch. Down fell the smoking pitch upon Kandula's back. In anguish of pain he fled and plunged in a pool of water. 'This is no drinking bout!' cried Gothaimbara. 'Go, batter the iron gate! Batter down the gate!' In his pride the best of tuskers took heart and trumpeted loud. He reared up out of the water and stood on the bank defiant. The elephant-doctor washed away the pitch, and put on balm. The King mounted the elephant and rubbed his brow with his hand. 'Dear Kandula, I'll make you the lord of all Ceylon!' he said, and the beast was cheered and fed with the best of fodder. He was covered with a cloth, and he was armoured well with armour for his back of seven-fold buffalo hide. On the armour was placed a skin soaked in oil. Then, trumpeting like thunder, he came on, fearless of danger. He pierced the door with his tusks. With his feet he trampled the threshold. And the gate and the lintel crashed loudly to the earth.[3]

Execution by elephant continued into the twentieth century. [*Le Tour du Monde Magazine, 1868 Woodcut.*]

Another legendary story, with little documentation, tells of the brave Trung sisters of Vietnam, who freed their people from the Chinese in about 40 AD. Many paintings show them riding elephants into battle. The Chinese army later defeated their rebel force, and the pair committed suicide.[4]

In the Malaysian regions, in southern Sumatra, large sculptures known as the Pasemah statues show "warriors mounted on elephants, with bronze drums indicated on their backs, and they are also shown wearing bronze helmets and armed with bronze daggers."[5] Although early estimates dated them at the third or fourth centuries BCE, modern historians now place them between 0 and 500 AD.

Although the Indian study of elephant combat took shape in earlier centuries, it became more of a science in the centuries after the Christian era. Gajasiksa or Hasti Sastra, the martial strategy of elephants, was an important component of the study of military tactics.[6]

Although it is tempting to dismiss elephant head counts in early historical accounts as exaggerated, remember that in some cases the stated numbers indicate the "combat elephants" and at other times the "army elephants," of which the majority are simply supply carriers and transport vehicles. When the Chinese visitor Hieun Tsang visited India in about 630 AD and found sixty thousand elephants in the army, that is not necessarily a contradiction of another report of only five thousand elephants.[7] Only a fraction of pachyderms able to serve man are capable of joining the rigors of his wars.

Speaking of exaggerations, another purported "tall tale" dates from the early sixth century AD, when a Chinese traveler called Sung Yun visited India and wrote about his journey. One observation involves a weapon that many historians scoff at as silly. Sung Yun "speaks of fighting elephants with swords fastened to their trunks, with which they wrought great carnage...."[8] The author citing this passage immediately distanced himself from the idea, saying he found no support from other sources for such a claim. There are other sources, but not for several hundred years, and so the use of "trunk weapons" will be discussed in Chapter 45.

The technology for killing war elephants improved steadily with the advances in protecting them. As in all cases of military technology, the offense increases the power and stamina of weapons, while the defense undermines and counteracts those improvements. While plate metal armor grew stronger with flexible joints, archers improved the penetrating power of their missiles with stronger bows and arrows with metal shafts. Black iron was believed to be the best material for arrows, although reasons are not given. By oiling the arrow shaft, the projectile was said to enter more deeply. One archer named Arjuna purportedly killed an elephant with an iron arrow that sank into the beast all the way to the arrow's feathers: meaning that the missile almost disappeared into the poor animal.[9]

A few elephants carried devices called *yantras*, which were a kind of miniature ballista catapult. These were not very accurate and fell into disuse. Some cities did mount larger versions on their walls to deter elephants.[10]

On June 20, 712 AD, the Muslim leader Muhammed al-Qasim attacked the Hindu King of Sind, Dahir. The Indian army might well have looked like this:

> The traditional array of battle consisted of an open line of elephants covering the infantry, mostly bowmen, in the centre, with cavalry, covered by war chariots, on both flanks...The elephants were the distinctive feature of Indian warfare; they must be thought of as movable strong-points, giving stability to the line so long as they stood fast, and furnishing vantage-ground for the discharge of arrows and other missiles.[11]

As for the leader, "The king of Sind...met the army of Islam near Ar-Rur seated on a white elephant and with two female servants with him in the litter, one of whom was handing him betel-leaf and the other arrows, one by one...Dahir was hit with a volley of arrows and decapitated by a sword blow after his elephant's litter had caught fire from a *naft* arrow and the elephant had thrown himself in the water."[12]

There are several elements to this story of interest.

First of all, the three members of the Hindu howdah were the king and two female servants. Aside from the obvious peculiarity of women in the battle howdah, one had the predictable job of handing arrows to the king, but the other was apparently feeding him! Betel consumption is very common in Asia, and those "addicted" to it inevitably have lips and teeth stained black (if they do not brush regularly). The betel leaf is wrapped around a nut that produces a stimulating effect much like caffeine, adding the sense of strength, say its users.[13] It is not eaten, but sucked upon like hard candy and spit out like chewing tobacco. King Dahir must have hoped to increase his strength on the battlefield by taking this stimulant while firing his arrows from the elephant's back.

As an obvious target, probably being the only Hindu on elephant back with women in the howdah, the Muslim archers wounded Dahir, but the fatal blow came later, thanks to a "naft arrow." Flaming arrows had existed as weapons for millennia, but new discoveries brought "naft" or "naptha" to warfare and increased the potency of fire. The composition of the infamous "Greek fire" of Byzantium has not been discovered even to this day, but various flammable mixtures were used by armies of the Middle Ages. The naptha from the arrow splattered on King Dahir's howdah and started a conflagration. The elephant, naturally terrified of fire, wisely ran to a nearby river to escape the flames. Once in the river, the Hindu king was down at infantry level, where the enemy took his head.

The victorious forces of Islam around the world did not often use elephants for war for chiefly geographical and climatic reasons: few elephants were available and feeding them in nonfertile areas was cost-prohibitive. In 864 AD, Ya'qub defeated enemy elephants and captured some. However, "...he finally rejected the elephants, on the grounds that they were inauspicious beasts, since they were linked in pious minds with the Abyssinian Viceroy Abraha's expedition against Mecca in the so-called 'Year of the Elephant'!"[14] Bosworth goes on to note that Ya'qub was "hardly likely to be swayed by superstitious reverence, he just had no use for them in his army."

After a battle, even the victorious army emerges with numerous wounded soldiers and animals. Indian armies had skilled veterinary workers who would tend to the wounds of the beasts during the night.[15] We can only guess at the number of veterinarians used in ancient armies, and some physicians could treat both humans and animals. In modern Burma, which is viewed as having a nearly ideal corps of medical workers for the logging elephants, there is approximately one vet for every 85 elephants.[16] Since the accident rate in military training and transportation might be comparable to that of a logging camp, it is not unreasonable to think that an army with one hundred war elephants might employ two veterinarians with skill in pachyderm medicine. The *Gajashastra*, "a compendium of veterinary science of the elephant" at least two thousand years old, was found to be very accurate (not mythological) in its observations.[17]

It is equally true that mahouts gain skill in treating elephant wounds with years of practice. And elephants themselves have herbal and behavioral methods of treating sickness; they recognize and seek out certain plant species as possessing the remedy they need.

The Asian "white elephant" received the treatment of royalty and carried the king.

At festivals, the great beast was adorned sumptuously, its back covered by a fine striped or checkered carpet held secure by a girthband, clusters of jewels dangled from its ears, its bridle was set with gold and its head was crowned by a gold-chased tiara, a huge necklace encircled its neck and its legs were ringed by bangles of precious metals. Cords from which hung a large bell with a clapper or a row of small globular bells were tied above its knees, and the ringing or tinkling gave notice of its approach. The mahout, wearing a short tunic with sleeves, squatted on the elephant's neck, holding the royal standard in one hand and, in the other, a goad (ankusa) inset with precious stones. The king mounted the animal by means of a 'golden' ladder while it remained kneeling.[18]

While elephants appeared in the daily life of the Asian peoples, the peoples of Europe had all but forgotten pachyderms. The appearance of one elephant would cause quite a stir in the West, and came about, in part, because of the otherwise dark episodes of history called the Crusades.

40
Charlemagne and Frederick

On October 10, 732 AD, a Muslim army tried to conquer France from Spain, but Charles Martel and the Franks defeated them at the Battle of Tours. This ended the offensive operations of Muslims in western Europe. Forty years later the grandson of Charles Martel, Charlemagne ("Charles the Great"), invaded Spain to push the Muslims out, but failed. The newly named emperor of Europe was surrounded by enemies, with pagan Saxons in the east, Danes in the north, and Spanish Muslims in the west.

The Byzantine empire, what was left of the Roman empire in the eastern Mediterranean, also faced grave threats from the Muslims. Perhaps out of self-interest, Charlemagne sent two ambassadors to Baghdad to try diplomacy with the enemy.[1] He also sent along a Jewish merchant named Isaac, apparently to acquire some unusual items for the curious emperor. Charlemagne's biggest request, literally, was for Isaac to bring an elephant back to Europe.

The leader of the Muslim world in the late 700s AD was Abbasid Caliph Harun al-Rashid, also known as the King of the Persians and the "Commander of the Faithful."[2] This ruler became famous for his depiction in the classic book, *The Thousand and One Nights*. The Commander of the Faithful was very generous in his dealings with the ambassadors, but apparently had a difficult time procuring an elephant. It took a year or two to find a trained pachyderm for Charles the Great. This implies that the use of war elephants had not yet begun in the Muslim world.

We know very little about the elephant; some accounts say it was African, others an Indian beast. Since Harun sent along his own ambassador, Ibrahim, governor of Egypt, an African elephant is within the realm of possibility. The group and an elephant named Abul Abbas sailed west to Italy.

Some modern writers cast doubts on the whole affair (although it is found in credible sources) because they think that medieval ships could not carry an elephant.[3] It is hard to believe that the emperor of western Europe or the ruler of Egypt and Persia would have any difficulty building

Life-sized model of Indian elephant armor from a private collection. *[Photo by Alex Ramsay Photography. Life-sized model built by Hew Kennedy.]*

a ship capable of carrying a mere five tons. Even if Roman naval technology had faded dramatically in the "Dark Ages," the logistics of transporting one elephant across the Mediterranean cannot be a legitimate reason to doubt the ancient sources.

Isaac, Ibrahim, and the behemoth landed at Pisa in northern Italy, but waited through the winter before crossing the Alps in the spring. Charles the Great lived in Aachen, a German town near the modern border with Belgium. With the warming weather, a caravan reminiscent of Hannibal passed over the Alps, to arrive at Aachen on July 1 of 802 AD.[4]

Word had come to the townsfolk ahead of time about Isaac's elephant and other fabulous gifts from the east, so crowds of people lined the streets to see the exotic parade. Perhaps the most diplomatic gift from the Commander of the Faithful came with the Arab ambassador: a beautiful robe with "There is but one God" sewn on it, which was one religious point that both Muslim and Christian could agree upon.[5]

Charlemagne and Harun did not make peace, but they did send delegations back and forth a few times, which in itself was remarkable.

Abul Abbas the elephant became a celebrity in Europe, appearing at many public functions for the amazement of the crowds. Abul had a residence built in Augsburg, where he enjoyed frequent swims in the Rhine River.

In 804 the Danes invaded the northern edges of Charles' empire, and his army took Abul Abbas on the campaign. We have no record of how exactly Abul performed in battle, nor in what capacity he served, although being the only elephant in Europe and thus a prized possession, he likely did not see the heat of the action.[6]

After eight years in Germany, Abul Abbas died, perhaps of pneumonia caught while swimming in the cold waters of the Rhine.[7] "By the time he died in 810, his name—Abul Abbas—had become a household name in France and Germany and the Royal Frankish Annals recorded, "… the elephant which Harun, King of the Saracens sent, suddenly died."[8]

Harun of Persia had sent many ivory carvings to Charlemagne, but some believe that a fabulous ivory chess set left by Charlemagne were carved from the tusks of Abul Abbas after his death.

Prester John, a legendary figure of medieval times believed to have a basis in reality, claimed to rule a Christian nation that used warriors on elephants. Endless speculation has tried to locate this possible kingdom, and Ethiopia or India became the obvious favorite choices.[9] Europe's interest regarding elephants had climbed again with the visit of Abul Abbas to Charlemagne, and was reawakened after four hundred years by another pachyderm visitor.

Emperor Frederick II went crusading in the Holy Land against the Muslims in the thirteenth century and returned to Europe with an elephant.[10] Occasionally this beast was used to greet (and surprise) visiting dignitaries, such as Richard, the Earl of Cornwall.

Because young Frederick did not follow the Pope's dictates exactly when he went crusading in the east, the Roman Catholic church excommunicated him and ordered all loyal Christians to attack Germany. This meant that the emperor was constantly at war with Italy.

We do not know how this unnamed elephant performed in the battle near Milan, but we do have a few details about his marvelous entry into the captured city of Cremona in 1237. Frederick, who was well read, designed an imitation Roman triumph, as if he were a Caesar!

Frederick entered Cremona in triumph followed by the captured chariot, which paraded not only the Lombardic insignia but also the fettered Podesta of Milan. The chariot was drawn by Frederick's elephant, who 'on his back carried a wooden citadel, as well as trumpeters, along with the imperial banners, amidst the frantic applause of the multitude of spectators.'[11]

Whether Frederick designed the howdah himself based on something he saw during the Crusade or if he drew up a model based on readings from ancient history, who can say? It must have been a marvelous sight!

41
Plump and Ready

The "Ghaznavid Empire" that ruled eastern Iran, Afghanistan, and north India from the tenth through twelfth centuries AD relied heavily on slave soldiers (called *Mamluks*) and war elephants.[1] The Mamluks, usually Turks, were thought to be more loyal because they were bought (or captured) in childhood and knew no other life.

The first leader of the Ghaznavids was Sultan Mahmud, a multi-talented man. He was handsome (or ugly, depending on the source), medium height, had a muscular build, small eyes, and a chin with a scanty beard. Mahmud memorized the Koran and surpassed his peers in the martial arts of archery, spear fighting, and swordplay.[2] His mace weighed fifty-five kilograms and he could whirl it over his head and throw it a long distance.[3]

At the age of nineteen, Mahmud controlled an army. Defeated in his first battle, Mahmud returned a few months later and bested his foes, retaking his lost elephants. Brave in war, in his final years his body carried seventy-two scars and wounds. In one battle Mahmud killed so many opponents with his sword that only a bath of hot water could loose the hilt from the congealed blood cementing it to his hand.[4]

The long reign of Mahmud provides some of the most interesting details of elephant warfare, in excellent detail. When Mahmud's father died in 998, Mahmud defeated his brothers to take power. Once his throne was secure, he moved against India. King Jaipal faced him with a large army including "three hundred chain elephants."[5]

"Chain elephants" in a common sense can mean simply that there were a lot of elephants, a large group being called a chain. However, other specific cases plainly intend that the elephants carried a chain as a mace-style weapon. In this battle, it is not clear which meaning is intended. About this combat of November 27, 1001, Mahmud's personal biographer writes:

Noon had not yet arrived when the Musulmans [Muslims] had wreaked their vengeance on the infidel enemies of God, killing fifteen thousand of them, spreading them like a carpet over the ground, and making them food for beasts and birds of prey. Fifteen elephants fell on the field of battle, as their legs, being pierced with arrows, became as motionless as if they had been in a quagmire, and their trunks were cut with the swords of the valiant heroes.[6]

With only fifteen dead on the field, Mahmud was quick to adopt the surviving two hundred elephants into his own forces.

One opponent of Mahmud hid in a fortress called Taq, or the "Virgin Fort," cheekily named because it had never been penetrated. However, Mahmud's elephants succeeded.

The besiegers then crossed over in the face of a shower of stones and missiles, and attacked the gates of the fort, which crashed down under the furious charge of the elephants. The assailants rushed in to occupy the outer fortifications. The defenders fought bravely and contested every inch of the ground, but when Khalaf saw Mahmud's elephants trampling his men to death, he was so disconcerted that he offered submission, and surrendered the fort.[7]

Elephants may not have previously assailed this fortress; else the defenders might have followed the age-old Indian precaution of welding long spikes to the gates to hinder elephant charges. However, even if the fort had used spikes on the gates, the siege equipment borne by the elephants could have bypassed the defenses. The Ghaznavids invented special devices, "...five elephants fitted with rams and battering equipment for use against walls and buildings...."[8] No details are provided about this machine, but the odd number five may indicate that four elephants would carry the ram, while one beast pushed and pulled the ram that hung between the four. In other words, while human archers pelt the defenders, a group of four armored elephants rambles to the city gate with a heavy iron-tipped battering ram hanging by rope harnesses between them. They stop a few feet from the spiked gate. The fifth elephant, guided by its mahout, repeatedly pulls the ram back and then releases it so that the iron head crashes into the doors. The author's description here is merely an educated guess based on elephants "fitted with rams."

During the heavy snows of winter in 1007–1008 AD, Mahmud used his elephants against an invasion staged by the king of Cashgar, Ilak Khan.[9] This may be the only battle on record for war elephants fighting in deep snow; Hannibal's battle at the Trebbia River played out during a snow squall (and most of his elephants died there) but it was not deep. Mahmud's men moved out to meet the intruders in the mountains.

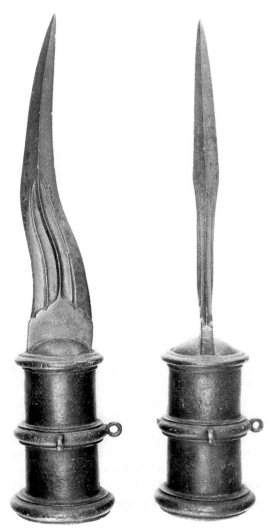

Tusk swords were often poisoned to make enemy soldiers afraid to approach the elephants. [XXVIM.40 © *The Board of Trustees of the Armouries.*]
Source: Royal Armories.

Mahmud rode a white elephant and believed it was a good luck charm, a "certain pledge of victory."[10] The charge of the elephants through the snow at the enemy was decisive.

...the execution wrought in their ranks by the Sultan's elephants completed their demoralisation. One of the elephants, lifting Ilak Khan's standard-bearer in his trunk, hurled him into the air and then catching him on his steel-clad tusks, cut the wretch in two, while others threw down riders from their horses and trampled them to death. The huge army of the Khan was seized with consternation and fled.[11]

This passage clearly refers to the tusk knives employed on some war elephants. There is no insurmountable difficulty in attaching weapons to an elephant's tusks; the real issue is whether the elephant can be trained not to injure itself on these weapons! If the elephant extends and swings his trunk during the combat, he might cut himself on the knives. Perhaps the safest place to fasten blades would be on the outer edges of the ivory, not the inside, so that the trunk can move freely between the tusks.

In India the Muslims often had to fight against elephants, and when those beasts were used effectively, the Muslims said they were "as headstrong as Satan."[12] In 1008 a confederation of Hindus rebelled under Anandapala, using headstrong pachyderms to expel the Muslims. The battle lasted from morning until evening with the Hindus beginning to take the advantage. Mahmud ordered his best warriors to attack the elephant carrying Anandapala. The Muslims used "naptha balls and flights of arrows" against this pachyderm, which panicked and fled. The Hindu army then disintegrated, having lost their commander.[13]

The use of burning naphtha balls thrown against rushing elephants to frighten them is mentioned by early Muslim historians as a feature of the warfare between the Rajputs and the Turkish invaders from the northwest.[14] Naptha arrows have been mentioned before, but the flaming balls are a new weapon. It seems that they were spherical weapons, perhaps baked clay, kept in pots of flammable oil and thrown from elephant back by warriors. Presumably they did not catch fire until they landed, unless the users had found a method of propelling them without injuring the hurler.

The core of Mahmud's army boasted between thirty-five thousand and fifty-five thousand men and one thousand elephants, although more could be fielded when necessary. The Ghaznavid military relied upon the cavalry, and commanders were each assigned an elephant to give them a better view of the battlefield.[15] The importance of elephants was such that as "royal beasts" they had to be turned over to the sultan when captured in battle: a part of his 20 percent of all booty.[16] Mahmud valued elephants so much that he often accepted them instead of cash tribute from his Hindu lands.

The elephants... were under the direct control of the Sultan. The elephant-drivers were mostly Hindus and their commander was called Muqaddam-il-Pilbanan. The Sultan personally reviewed the elephants every year and ordered lean and thins ones to be sent to India to recover their weight and strength. Almost all the elephants had either been captured in Indian wars of received as tribute from Hindu rajas.[17]

One sign of the extraordinary care that Mahmud took for his war elephants is this relocation system for the beasts. The enormous amount of food required by a pachyderm could not be fully supplied in the plains of Iran or mountains of Afghanistan, so his territories in India provided a periodic sabbatical for the elephants to regain any lost weight. Elephant keepers held the rank of general.[18]

At the peak of Mahmud's reign in 1023 AD he had fifty-four thousand cavalry and more than 1,300 elephants, each elephant with equipment and armor.[19] During one Indian invasion, saboteurs made a daring night raid, purportedly giving powerful intoxicants and drugs to Mahmud's war elephants. The beasts became delirious and went berserk, trampling the camp. Mahmud ordered the mahouts to kill the beasts, but several brave men were able to mount the crazed pachyderms and lead them away from camp until they could be controlled again.[20]

In 1025 Mahmud used four hundred behemoths against Alitigin, and "before battle, drums and other instruments were beaten in the Sultan's camp and the elephants' ornaments and accoutrements shaken and jangled to excite them and to shatter the enemy's nerve."[21] This perfectly illustrates the prebattle rituals used to enflame bulls to violence, just as the Seleucids did with "the juice of red berries." If, during training, drums are beaten to signify that violent work is coming, the elephants are eventually habituated to excitement at the sound of drums.[22] Another innovation of the Ghaznavid elephant riders was the *ayina-yi pil*, a metal skullcap to protect the elephant's head. These headpieces held dangling metal ornaments that the mahout could strike to clang like bells to frighten the enemy and encourage the elephants. [23]

Armies of this time invented an "exceptionally long spear called a *tomara* which was...used while fighting from an elephant."[24] The long spear was similar to the ancient sarissa, used by Alexander's phalanxes. Riders and mahouts could use the *tomara* to stab at opponents approaching on the ground. Since men in the howdah are seven to ten feet off the ground, a normal length spear will not reach foes on the earth!

Mahmud became sick with malaria and died in 1030 AD. His successor, Mas'ud, reviewed the elephant squadron of his inherited army and found that all 1670 elephants were "plump and ready for action" in Afghanistan.[25] It is not often that the well-rounded bellies of soldiers are a sign of preparedness for war!

Mas'ud was not successful at maintaining his Indian lands or keeping the elephant squadrons plump. In 1040 AD his army marched through the desert to repel Turkish invaders in the west, but they ran out of supplies and starved. What was left of his army was routed.

In 1117, Seljuqs invaded Afghanistan. The fifty war elephants initially panicked the Seljuq cavalry, but Amir Abual-Fadl rallied his men by using a dagger to rip open the lead elephant's belly, "unprotected by armor." The wounded beast retreated and the rest of the elephants followed, starting the rout of the Ghaznavid army.[26] Getting to the elephants without being shot by the archers on their backs was a difficulty. One source says that the invaders used a "*karwah*, a framework of bullock-hide stuffed with cotton which could be massed into a wall-like battleline, affording protection against an enemy charge or enemy arrows."[27] This soft shield was used to repel the Ghaznavid projectiles while approaching the elephants.

Another long-proven method of defeating armies (with or without war elephants) is by ambush or total surprise. Muhammed Ghori failed in his first invasion of India, but returned for a second try in the 1180s AD. When the Hindu leader Prithviraja appeared with a large army and perhaps three thousand elephants, the Sultan pretended to accept a truce to negotiate. That night the Muslims lit numerous campfires and set up their tents, and while the Indians slept, the invaders marched around and attacked at dawn from behind, winning decisively.[28]

42
Mongol Hordes

Genghis Khan, the famed warrior of the steppes, united the tribes of Mongolia with the goal of conquest in 1206 AD. After subduing China and learning the use of the burning substance called gunpowder, the "hordes" of cavalry swept into Muslim territory.

In modern-day Uzbekistan, the Khan surrounded the wealthy city of Samarkand. As usual, the invaders needed supplies and scoured the region for food and fodder for their many horses. When the people of the city realized that no relief forces would save them and food supplies ran short, they came up with a plan. The Turks of Samarkand hoped that they could break the siege by rushing out of the gates with their elephants, since horses are traditionally terrified of pachyderms.

However, the Mongol cavalry was different than most cavalry forces before it, more like the hit-and-run Parthians than traditional horsemen who were simply mounted soldiers. The Mongols were mobile archers and used the "double-recursive bow," which had greater range than traditional weapons. When the elephants charged out of the gates, the archers stampeded them with arrows, and the gates could not be closed because of the uncontrolled elephants trying to get back into the city. The Mongols charged through and took the city.

Although the pachyderms apparently survived the foolish charge, Genghis Khan was not terribly merciful. The mahouts asked the Khan for some food for their starving elephants. He asked "what did the elephants eat before we came?" They replied that the beasts ate the grass outside the city every night. Genghis told them they could set the beasts free outside to find their own food. Since the grasses had been eaten to the roots by the Mongol horses, the elephants starved.[1]

The Mongols often spread far into enemy territories, but never stayed. As a cavalry force they could not leave garrisons in cities: they simply pillaged and moved on. Whenever the great Khan or leader died, the hordes went home until the next leader emerged. The Mongols

64 Kubla Khan on four elephants

Marco Polo told of the magnificent howdah of Kublai Khan of the Mongols, carried by four elephants. This drawing is certainly an exaggeration. [*Ranking, John. Historical Researches on the Wars and Sports of the Mongols and Romans: In Which Elephants and Wild Beasts were Employed or Slain. London: Longman, Rees, Orme, Brown, and Green, 1826. Plate 64.*]

were not interested in acquiring war elephants, but did have to face them several times.

In 1277 the Hordes under Kublai Khan invaded Burma. The Mongols were surprised by the Burmese war elephants, and the famous cavalry began to panic. Nasiradin, the horse commander, ordered his army to ride into a nearby forest. Once in the trees, they tied their horses to the trees and dismounted to fight on foot. The archers waited for the elephants to draw close and then pelted them with a barrage of missiles. The elephants stampeded back through the Burmese infantry, and the Mongols remounted and attacked during the confusion, annihilating the enemy army.[2] Kublai, crippled by gout, was pleased to capture two hundred war elephants for his lavish entourage.

We know a great deal about Kublai Khan because the famous explorer Marco Polo lived with the Mongols for more than a decade and wrote a book about his travels. We are told that:

The Grand Khan took his station in a large wooden castle, borne upon the backs of four elephants, whose bodies were protected with coverings of thick leather hardened by fire, over which were housings of cloth of gold. The castle contained many cross-bow men and archers; and on the top of it was hoisted the imperial standard, adorned with representations of the sun and moon.[3]

The howdah was draped in tiger skins.[4] The four-elephant howdah illustration provided in this chapter is based on Marco Polo's description, but is highly improbable because of its size and weight. Four elephants might carry an impressively large howdah with a few guards and the Great Khan, but certainly not this palatial home with twenty men walking around in it! Aside from the sheer weight, the biggest problem would be mounting the howdah atop the elephants.

A more likely description of this massive howdah comes from Friar Odoric of Pordenone who saw Kublai Khan's journey from winter to summer capital. He wrote that "The king travelleth in a two-wheeled carriage, in which is formed a very goodly chamber, all of ligh-aloes and gold, and covered over with great and fine skins, and set with many precious stones. And the carriage is drawn by four elephants, well broken in and harnessed, and also by four splendid horses, richly caparisoned."[5] Thus, when Marco Polo said "borne on the backs of elephants" he did not mean carried, but dragged, which is far more believable.

Kublai did own smaller and less luxurious howdahs for hunting trips, carried by two elephants. Narrow passages prevented his four-behemoth-powered monstrosity from fitting on the roads.[6] Ah, the hard life of a traveler!

At one time, Kublai is said to have owned five thousand elephants.[7] Most were cargo carriers for his caravans, but they also pulled ships or barges up rivers by walking along the bank with ropes, much like the miniature locomotives pulling ships in locks of the Panama Canal.[8]

Kublai Khan showed little interest in maintaining the wars in the west, but wanted instead to control all of east Asia. As many as half a million Mongols (soldiers and their families) moved from Burma to the south and east into Champa, now Vietnam. Although the Hordes originally had the advantage of longer-ranged bows with which they could oppose enemy elephants, the Chams had learned crossbow warfare from China. They designed "two-man double-bow crossbow teams on the backs of elephants," an example of which is carved on the wall of a Khmer temple.[9] These powerful weapons had long range and an excellent vantage point for aiming at the invaders. Cham elephants had been trained to fight with their trunks and tusks, and frequently hurled enemy soldiers into the air and impaled them with their ivory.[10] The famous general Tran Hung Do inspired his outnumbered troops to drive out two successive invasions of the Mongols.

The Mongols failed repeatedly in attempts to take India. In 1298 they fell before an army fronted by 2,700 war elephants.[11]

Safe from the Mongols, India continued to prosper while the Hordes pillaged elsewhere. The violent methods of the Indian Sultans might leave the reader to wonder whether that stability of government was good.

For executing criminals or rebels, the Sultans designed special elephant tools.

The elephants which execute men have their tusks covered with sharp irons... with edges like those of knives. The driver mounts the elephant, and, when a person is thrown in front, the animal winds his trunk round him, hurls him into the air, and catching him on one of his tusks, dashes him to the ground, when he places one of his feet on the breast of the victim. After this he does as he is directed by the rider, under the order of the Sultan. If the Sultan desires the culprit to be cut in pieces, the elephant executes the command by means of the irons above described; if the Sultan desires the victim to be left alone, the elephant leaves him on the ground, and (the body) is then stripped of its skin.[12]

The elephants themselves, however, were well treated. The largest elephants were kept in special sheds near the palace. These beasts received special food called *kichu*, which is cooked in front of each elephant, sprinkled with sugar and salt, dipped in butter, and placed by hand in the beast's mouth. However, the elephants did not have freedom of movement: the stalls had chains everywhere to maintain control. The white elephant with "thirty spots of color" came in to see the Sultan every morning, as it was a "favorable omen" to look on the white elephant.[13] A breeding program went on in a different part of Delhi.

The Sultans were so enamored with elephants that enemies sometimes took advantage of this obsession. The Rai of Jaynagar delayed the Sultan Firuz Shah Tughlaq's army for several days in the late fourteenth century by releasing a beautiful wild elephant: the army spent three days trying to catch it before giving up and killing it. Then the Rai started rumors of eight marvelous pachyderms in a forest nearby, which occupied several more days for the Muslim army.[14] When these two stratagems succeeded, the Rai realized he could end the whole war by simply offering to send the sultan more of these marvelous elephant specimens each year. Tughlaq accepted a gift of twenty elephants and the promise of more to come each year and departed peacefully.

The Delhi sultans claimed to have three thousand war elephants, but only one thousand were trained for combat. Some modifications to the elephant armor appeared in the thirteenth and fourteenth centuries, especially to the headpiece. Flaps or side pieces were added to protect pachyderm ears.[15] Some helmets included a center spike on the forehead, which in combination with tusks would make the armored elephant look something like a triceratops dinosaur![16]

Improvements in elephant armor would soon become irrelevant. In 1388 the heavily armored pachyderms of Burma were defeated with crossbows and a frightening new device powered by Chinese powder: the cannon.[17]

43
Pyramids of Skulls

India stopped the Mongol Hordes in 1292 and 1299, but the nomadic conquerors had not given up.

Timur, meaning "Iron," led the Turkish Mongols on another world-shaking crusade to spread the Sunni version of Islam. He said, "As there is one God in heaven so there must be one king on earth. The entire world is not worth having more than one king." He took Samarkand in 1366, but arrows hit his right arm and leg leaving him lame, which is how he got the name Tamerlane, Timur the Lame. This disability did not improve his temperament in the least: he had the army create pyramids from seventy thousand severed heads in one vanquished city.[1]

In the spring of 1398, Tamerlane moved through Afghanistan and crossed the Indus river. When the city of Delhi refused to surrender and sent out an army to oppose him, on December 17, Tamerlane slaughtered tens of thousands of Indian prisoners to free up the guards for the coming battle.

The Sultan of Delhi had only 120 war elephants because years of civil war had weakened his power.[2] On the elephant's tusks were poisoned tipped daggers, and the howdahs carried archers, rocket men, grenade hurlers, and discus throwers.[3] New technologies appeared in the fourteenth century which immediately found use on the backs of elephants. The discus throwers undoubtedly used the *chakram*, a frisbee-like weapon (popularized on the Xena television show) with razor-sharp edges, sometimes even doused in poison.[4] Sikh warriors often wore six chakra on their turban head-coverings or on their arm, and could kill the enemy at eighty paces.[5] Grenade hurlers and rocket men used the newly discovered gunpowder from China in different ways. The rockets were large arrows with a slow-burning gunpowder fuse that would explode and send shrapnel outward ("rockets shod with iron which give repeated blows where they fall"). Grenades also exploded but they were thrown and not fired, and thus could be much larger and heavier.[6] Improved "Chinese snow" or gunpowder purified with saltpeter had greatly increased the efficiency of

Lifting heavy armor on to the elephant's back. [Photo courtesy of Mary Evans Picture Library]

explosive devices.[7] The pachyderms were the Indians' only advantage because the Turks outnumbered them by almost three to one.

Despite their overwhelming numeric advantage, the sight of war elephants terrified the Turks. Timur himself said in his autobiography:

It had been constantly dinned into the ears of my soldiers that…that these animals, in complete armour, marched into battle in front of their forces, and that arrows and swords were of no use against them…that in the battlefield they could take up the horse and the rider with their trunks and hurl them into the air.…They [his soldiers] had been with me in many campaigns, and had witnessed many a great battle, but the stories about the elephants of India had so affected them that they instantly replied that they would like to be placed with the ladies while the battle was in progress.[8]

Tamerlane had a psychological crisis on his hands. He immediately set to work on anti-elephant defenses to ease the fears of his soldiers.

First, the Turks built fence of sharp stakes to keep the elephants from raiding their camp. Second, all of the buffalo from the baggage train were tied together at the head and legs in a long line behind the palisade, with dry brambles tied to their heads. If the elephants charged the camp, the brambles were to be set aflame so that the screaming cows and fires would frighten the pachyderms.[9] Finally, Tamerlane had his smithies create hundreds of caltrops: spiked tetrahedra to throw down in front of the elephants at the beginning of battle.

These precautions calmed the fears of Tamerlane's men.

The battle began with the loud noise of the brass kettle drums on the backs of the Indian signal elephants. The Turks threw down the caltrops, which stopped the elephant charge. Mongol archers brought down the mahouts, and the soldiers hacked away at the pachyderm trunks. One brave fifteen-year-old boy, Timur's grandson, captured an elephant and brought it to Timur who "was affected to tears, for joy that God had given him such brave children."[10] The wounded beasts "of mighty form but craven spirit" stampeded through the Hindu army, and the Mongol cavalry pursued them into Delhi.[11]

Tamerlane purportedly wanted to see the captured elephants weep for losing the battle, and ordered that snuff be rubbed in their faces to make their eyes water.[12] For five days the Turks of Tamerlane plundered Delhi, leaving only disease and death in their wake.

Not one to pass up a new weapon, Timur adopted the surviving war elephants (with their drivers and howdah warriors) into his own army. He first used them against the Syrians, who were stomped and blown to bits by the grenade hurlers.[13] By the time his army reached Damascus, all Timur had to do was line up the elephants outside the city and the people surrendered. When Tamerlane took Baghdad in 1401, his men made pyramids of ninety thousand skulls.[14]

Tamerlane swept into Turkey and fought against Sultan Bayazid I, nicknamed "Lightning," in July of 1402. Timur's elephants wore armor, tusk swords, and carried men using "flame-throwers" on their backs.[15]

A Spanish emissary to Asia saw men arming elephants for battle and included this detail. "They attach a large ring to each tusk and fasten swords upon them, like the grooved swords we use in war, but theirs are shorter, being only as long as a man's arm."[16]

India fell under many unremarkable rulers for the next hundred years, but as always, elephants fought their wars. One interesting law dating from 1458 AD explains the rewards and punishments for good mahouts and their assistants. Victorious elephant warriors received promotions, money, armor, or umbrellas! However, the penalties for cowardice were harsh. "Whoever fights on an elephant and turns to flee on it shall be struck down from his elephant and beheaded, and his family shall be destroyed also."[17]

44
Thais, Burmese, Khmers, and Others

India requires much of our attention for elephant warfare in the second millennium AD because much of the action occurred there. However, other Asian lands used pachyderm warriors, to a lesser degree. These lands invented some new styles of tactics and armor for their behemoths.

Southern China, specifically the southern Han state (917–971 AD), possessed the only remaining Chinese battalion of war elephants, commanded by the "Legate Dirigent and Agitant of the Gigantic Elephants." The front-line elephant corps was successful in battle against Chu in 948, but Song dynasty crossbowmen defeated them in 971. "Chinese archery was an effective anti-elephant tactic, as Liu Fang found."[1] As for Liu Fang, he conquered north and central Vietnam from 602 to 605 AD. His Sui army came under attack by Champan (Vietnamese) troops mounted on war elephants. Fang had pits dug and covered the holes with grass, then feigned a retreat to lure some of the beasts into the traps. Using crossbows in combination with the traps, the enemy elephants stampeded. With a timely counterattack behind the fleeing pachyderms, the Champan army collapsed.[2]

Khmers used war elephants to drive the Chams out of Cambodia in the twelfth century. They added human gall to the alcohol given to war elephants before battle to "increase their courage" even into the nineteenth century. Khmer mahouts rode their elephants not from the neck but from the "crupper" near the elephant's tail and used a long goad to tap the elephant's rear legs as directions. The purpose of this unique reversal of positions was to put a professional warrior at the front.[3]

In May of 1388, Burmese general Si Lunfa attacked southwestern China with a huge army and one hundred armored elephants. The most intriguing detail of this battle is the inexpensive side armor provided for the beasts: "...bamboo tubes hung down both sides, with short spears in them to prevent thrusts from the side."[4] Reminiscent of a spiked bulldog collar, these sharp side bumpers would keep enemy infantry from attempting to mount the elephant to bring down its soldiers. However, this had

In Asia, opposing mahouts often fought each other with lances. *[Photo by Matt and Melissa Hamilton. Reprinted with permission.]*

little value against the Chinese who simply barraged the elephants with crossbow darts until they panicked and ran.[5] If the tradition of the Burmese Shans was followed, the general was buried with ten elephants, one hundred horses, and many slaves.[6]

In 1424 the two oldest sons of King Intharaja of Thailand fought each other from elephant back, with the winner to become the next ruler. Unfortunately for them, both were killed in the fight, leaving the youngest brother to become King Boromaraja II (1424–1448).[7] He defeated the Khmers at Angkor Wat, and in 1442 attacked enemies in the north of Thailand. The opponent in Lamphun hired Laotian spies to sneak into the Thai camp, where they cut off the tails of several war elephants. The beasts ran amok and while the camp was in chaos, the enemy attacked, forcing the army to retreat.[8]

Thais believed fervently in the power of amulets or talismans, and these symbols of power were worn by the elephants and horses as well as the soldiers. Monks would recite charms while drawing pictures of the sun and moon on the elephant's armor.[9]

In 2002 a beautiful movie called "The Legend of Suriyothai" dramatized the life of Queen Suriyothai of Thailand. In 1548 she and Princess Tepastri rode with King Manacharapad on war elephants against Burmese invaders.[10] In the short term they succeeded, but the persistent Burmese would conquer Thailand within two decades.

One Thai strategist, Naresuan, liked to hide elephants and cavalry in the jungle behind a battlefield. His infantry would feign flight to draw the enemy in pursuit, where the elephants could charge out of the jungle to attack the enemy flanks and rear.[11] These tactics helped Naresuan liberate Thailand from the Burmese in the 1580s, so that the common adage arose that "Thailand won its freedom on the backs of elephants."

In China in the late sixteenth century, well-trained elephants stood as guards outside the palace during early morning meetings of the Chinese court. They roamed freely in the palace grounds for most of the day, but when his majesty the emperor arrived, the elephants lined up on both sides of the gate. Once all members of the court had entered, the elephants stretched out their trunks to each other, in a symbolic gesture of locking the gate, as human guards might do by crossing their spears or axes at a doorway. Once the court recessed and the dignitaries departed, the elephants returned to their eating.[12]

In 1625 in the Chinese province of Guizhou, bandits attacked a town, but one of Guishou's work elephants was enjoying a bath in a muddy ditch beside the main road. The elephant attacked the passing thieves, throwing them into disarray, and the townspeople were able to drive the bandits away. The elephant received numerous wounds from poisoned arrows and died the next day, despite the best efforts of the locals to heal it. The townspeople made a burial mound and erected a monument with a lengthy inscription, including this piece:

With your unyielding stare and refusal to capitulate, in what way were you inferior to heroes and men of high worth? Whether we were to be in peace or in peril hung upon this one battle. While all others stood by doing nothing, you alone 'bared your arms for combat.'...The remnants of your ardent bravery are still alive.[13]

A famous story from 1659 describes a visit to the king of Bhutan (or Tibet, depending on the source), who owned fifty guard elephants and twenty-five guard camels, each carrying a swivel cannon that fired a half-pound ball.[14] In this same region, merchants had to travel cautiously and watch their goods at night because of elephant raiders. They said that "the elephant moves without noise...carrying off whatever food he can seize, as a sack of rice or flour, or a pot of butter...."[15] This type of incident continues even today in Thailand. During the dry season when food is scarce, local farmers pay trucks to haul their crops to town. Some elephants have become classic bandits, and perfected their techniques. One large elephant will stand in the road, forcing the truck to stop. Other elephants rush out from the forest and grab all of the sugar cane and tapioca from the back of the truck![16]

45
The Great Mahout

Akbar, a descendent of the Khans and Tamerlane, was born in 1542. His grandfather Babur started the era known as the Mughal, or Mogul, dynasty that controlled India for two hundred years.

Young Akbar was infatuated with elephants, so his father gave him a very quiet beast named Dilsankar.[1] Elephants earned impressive names during the Mughal era, such as Fateh Gaj (victory elephant), Futuh (unrivalled in fighting), and Asaman Shukoh (Heaven's dignity).[2] Akbar had a natural skill with even the most vicious elephants known as men slayers. One such story is written in great detail:

At the early age of fourteen he [Akbar] had acquired the difficult art of controlling vicious elephants. An elephant named Hawai, meaning 'Sky-rocket'…was notorious for his 'choler, passionateness, fierceness, and wickedness.' One day on the polo ground Akbar, who had drunk two or three cups of wine, took it to his head to mount the savage brute, who was compelled to execute 'wonderful manoeuvres'. Akbar then decided to have more excitement, and set Hawai to fight Ran Bagha, the 'Tiger in Battle,' another vicious giant. Ran Bagha, unable to withstand Hawai's furious onset, fled pursued by the victor, who justified his name by his speed. Akbar, to the terror of the onlookers, held on firmly, and the two maddened beasts, plunging down the steep bank of the Jumna, raced across the bridge of boats. The pontoons swayed and were submerged, the royal servants meantime swimming alongside in case their help should be needed. By good luck the elephants got safely across to the other side of the river and Ran Bagha continued his flight to save his life. Akbar, exercising the marvellous personal power over the brute creation which was one of his peculiar gifts was able to restrain Hawai in a moment."[3]

Akbar took power over the empire that same year, when his grandfather died, and ruled for almost fifty years (1556–1605), but his interest in elephants never waned. Perhaps by necessity, in choosing to ride the most intractable elephants, Akbar sometimes used two ankhus' on the beasts to force his will upon them.[4] Akbar must have possessed a thrill-seeker personality; always jumping upon a musth elephant with "the fumes of wrath circulating in its brain."[5]

Most of the Mughal elephants were female baggage haulers, sometimes pulling giant mortar cannons. Recognizing that gunpowder was the future of warfare, Akbar ordered his governors to collect and train elephants in proximity to gunfire so they would become accustomed to it. Gunners rode in howdahs with matchlock rifles, and eventually small cannons could be fired from the elephants backs.[6] Akbar invented guns that could be assembled and taken apart when needed, including *narnals* for one man, or *gajnals* to set in a howdah on a swivel.[7]

The Mughals improved mahout safety by providing armor for their whole bodies, except for their bare feet, needed to guide the elephant. The vulnerable eyes of the elephants could not be easily protected, but Akbar's designers found a good solution. If the elephant became unruly and disobedient, or enemies approached, the rider could release a piece of heavy canvas (weighted with metal balls) that was connected to the beast's head armor, covering its eyes.[8] The elephants themselves inherited *lamellar* armor, which consists of small overlapping plates laced together: relatively light and flexible, yet impenetrable.[9] The Indian elephant armor shown in this chapter's illustrations are an example of lamellar armor. New designs attached iron plates to the elephants' ears, while the Burmese idea of iron spikes to keep away enemy infantry was adopted, especially under the neck and trunk, where enemies tried to find unarmored vulnerable spots to stab the beasts.[10]

In 1556 Akbar's army easily defeated a much larger enemy with 1,500 elephants because the enemy leader Himu took an arrow through the head and his soldiers fled.[11] An eyewitness said that "musketeers and crossbowmen were placed on the backs of those enormous elephants, which were furnished with suits of mail (*kajim*) and defensive armour, and made ready for war. All the elephants had these war panoplies, and had their trunks armed with spears and knives."[12] Only eight years later, a brave queen named Durgautti fought against Asaph Khan. She was also hit in the eye with an arrow, but remained conscious and broke off the shaft to continue the elephant charge. However, as more arrows hit her, Durgautti asked the mahout to kill her. He refused but gave her a dagger and she killed herself.[13]

A campaign by Akbar in 1567 included two thousand war elephants.[14]

At the storming of the Hindu fortress Chitor in 1568, one of Akbar's elephants, named Jangia, had killed thirty men when its trunk was lopped off by a Rajput Hindu. The beast continued to fight, crushing fifteen more enemies before dying of its wounds.[15]

The year 1567 included the famous battle of Haldighati in which the last of the Rajput Hindus fought the Mughals. According to legend, a gray stallion named Chetak almost won the battle for the Hindus by "rearing and drumming his hooves on the forehead of the war elephant" ridden by the Mughal commander. Rana Pratap was able to kill the mahout, thus stopping the charge of the elephants. In some accounts, Chetak even lost half of a rear leg and hobbled to the rear, saving his rider. However, reinforcements arrived and the Hindus lost anyway.[16]

A unique tactic by one Gujar Khan was to disguise his elephants as giant yaks instead of the oft-tried disguising of camels or horses as elephants! Perhaps because the Mughal horses were trained to tolerate elephants, Gujar decided to give the horses something new to panic about. Using black yak skins to completely cover his pachyderms, including the black yak tail, his dark monsters terrified the enemy horses.[17]

When one of Akbar's brothers rebelled in Afghanistan, the Indian army marched on Kabul in 1582. Although his force included five thousand elephants, a majority were pack animals and not combat pachyderms.[18] Mughal armies put two elephants in the front of the column: one beast wore a headdress with a tall flag floating in the air, while an ornately caparisoned elephant followed with a "priceless relic" claimed to be a hair from the beard of the prophet Mohammed.[19] We have a detailed description of the war elephants in this army: "They wear plates of iron upon their foreheads, carry four archers, or else four gunners with great pieces. They go not in front of the army, lest, being hurt, they should disturb the ranks, and therefore are set in the rear: a sword is bound to their trunk, and daggers are fastened to their tusks."[20]

The "legendary" elephant sword is first mentioned in the writings of the Chinese explorer Sung Yun as a weapon used by the elephants in early sixth-century AD, more than nine centuries before Akbar. Why are historians so skeptical about the possibility of an elephant swinging a sword? Multiple sources attest to the use of "trunk weapons" by elephants throughout history. Pachyderms have swung scythes, swords, maces, and

---

Emperor Durjansal riding to war on a well-armored elephant that swings a chain weapon. The chains on the feet would be tightened and pegged into the ground if the elephant started to panic. [From *Philadelphia Museum of Art: Stella Kramrisch Collection*, 1994. *"Maharao Durjansal of Kotah on His Elephant Ranasangar"*, dated 1750–70, Kotah School, Rajasthan, opaque watercolor with gold and silver on paper, 15 3/4 in by 18 7/8 inches.] Source: Philadelphia Museum of Art.

Asian elephant lamellar armor, circa seventeenth century. *[XXVIA.102 © The Board of Trustees of the Armouries.]*
Source: Royal Armories.

chains, not to mention "weapons of opportunity" such as tree limbs and even enemy soldiers.

A Russian visitor to India (1466–1472), Afanasii Nikitin, describes seeing a battle (perhaps at Vijayanagar) where the elephants "were armored with long swords on their trunks and with steel plates."[21]

Ludovici di Varthema (1501–1568) says that elephant swords two fathoms in length (twelve feet) are attached to their trunks, although an editor adds, "more reasonable accounts describe them as blades projecting from sockets over the tusks."[22] We know that blades were used on tusks, but would the observers really mistake tusks for trunks? Further-

Close-up view of the lamellar armor: metal sewn into chain mail. *[XXVIA.102 © The Board of Trustees of the Armouries.]*
Source: Royal Armories.

more, a source with Akbar says that the elephants had *both* tusk weapons and trunk swords, which could not therefore be confused. Certainly the length of twelve feet (two fathoms) is hard to accept, unless we grant that perhaps the hilt (to be grappled by the elephant's trunk) was six feet long and the blade six feet as well. Topsel wrote that the elephant broad sword was two cubits long, which would be about thirty-six inches, but he intriguingly implies that the sword was connected to the armor on the beast's trunk.[23] If true, then the pachyderm would not have to grip a hilt, but simply swing its trunk in a normal fashion, avoiding any danger of dropping the weapon or cutting itself on the blade.

Sultan Muhammad Shah II used "armor-clad elephants with scythes attached to their trunks" in the years after Akbar.[24] A scythe presents less of a weight problem than a two-edged sword because the cutting blade is much thinner and lighter.

In a 1659 battle, Mughal ruler Aurangzeb was confronted with three elephants, "each of them dashing about with his trunk a chain of two or three men's weight." [25]

About thirty years later, "...the driver of an elephant belonging to Raja Ram Singh placed a heavy chain in its mouth and made it charge upon the enemy's advanced force....Wherever the elephant charged, the noise of the chain and the blows of his trunk struck terror into the enemy. The horses of two or three officers took fright, and threw their riders. Thus the army of the enemy was put to flight...."[26]

A long epic poem called the Alh-Khand, which was written in the eighteenth century but tells a much older story, describes that "...two maddened elephants, Jaura and Bhaura, swayed in mighty throes, as the men of Sirsa came...the elephants let loose and rushed upon the army. Amid the troops they whirled their chains, and hither and thither did they scatter them."[27]

The Russian traveler Nikitin, mentioned earlier, also recorded that he saw "three hundred elephants clad in Damask steel armour, carrying citadels equally fitted in steel, and each holding six warriors with guns and long muskets...Each elephant has two large probortsy and a heavy sword, weighing a kantar [about one hundred pounds] attached to its tusks, and large iron weights hanging from the trunk."[28] The translation is hard to understand, with no explanation of *probortsy* (perhaps tusk swords), though the iron weights in the trunk are certainly a heavy chain mace.

Aside from the literary references, we have marvelous paintings from the Mughal centuries showing elephants swinging heavy chains in battle. The war elephants bore beautiful armor, sometimes plated in silver and gold, as seen in the figure provided in this chapter. The watercolor portrays a combat between Syam Singhji and Durjansal in 1724.[29] The advantage to the chain (over a bladed weapon) is that it can be easily gripped in the trunk and it does not present so many dangers to the animal itself.

Research by scholars with expertise in Asian languages will certainly find more references to the legendary elephant sword. What is puzzling is: why is it legendary? Assuming that elephants can be ridden by soldiers, participate in battle, and pick up enemies in their trunks to kill them, why should the slight addition of a weapon in the beast's trunk seem so unbelievable? Even wild, untrained elephants swing tree limbs to beat dirt from their bodies and to threaten intruders!

War elephants (those that served directly for combat) had excellent care. Even while the army was marching, the best elephants had their own tents![30] After giving the beast a thorough bath including a scrub with pumice stone, "the keeper brings a pot full of red or yellow paint, and paints lines on its forehead, around the eyes, on the chest, and on the back, rubbing it then with coconut oil to strengthen the nerves, some keepers finally adding false tinsel on the forehead."[31]

The king frequently inspected the seven bravest elephants. Each wore rich regalia, and the king often lifted the trappings to see if the beasts were healthy, clean, and plump. In fact, each of the brave elephants had a personalized silken cord, which the mahouts used to measure the girth of the beast to show the king if it had sufficiently grown over time! They each had servants to care for them, and they received the best food, lots of sugar, and alcohol to drink.[32] The vast majority of the elephants lived in the suburbs or even other regions, "on call," but where they could cheaply forage for their own food.

The next notable Mughal ruler was Jahangir, who reportedly kept twelve thousand elephants. Unlike his father Akbar, who loved angry elephants, Jahangir showed great concern for the welfare and happiness of his pachyderms. He was particularly proud of ordering his men to warm up the bath water in the winter since cold water might make the beasts ill.[33] The peak of elephant warfare had been reached, however. There would be a steady decline in the number of pachyderms used in war from the late sixteenth century. Many historians agree "...elephants became less valuable and more vulnerable as the number of firearms increased."[34]

Gunpowder is first recorded from about 1044 AD in China, but battlefield uses were not found until 1233 AD. In one of Akbar's last battles, a rocket exploded in the bushes near the war elephants and caused a panic that disintegrated his army, perhaps the first sign that pachyderms would not enjoy the exploding technology.[35] Elephants were not immediately relegated to the scrap pile of obsolete weaponry, but they were gradually shifted to duties that would not bring them under cannon fire.[36]

One of Jehangir's wives, Queen Nur Jehan, rode an elephant in battle against an attacking Muslim force. Although enemy muskets caused many of her troops to flee, she kept firing with her arrows and reinspired her troops to counterattack. They won the battle.[37]

The next important Mughal ruler, Aurangzeb, loved elephant games so much that they nearly killed him as a teenager. Aurangzeb, on horseback, got too close to a pair of elephants that were fighting in a show. One of the beasts turned and, with a tusk, knocked Aurangzeb's horse over. Servants tried to intervene by lighting a round, spinning firework called a "Saint Catherine's wheel" to scare the beast away, but it continued to attack, ignoring the guards trying to protect the prince. It was the other elephant, angry at being ignored, that saved Aurangzeb by resuming the fight against his distracted opponent, and the prince escaped.[38]

A force of Uzbekh Muslims under Khailullah Khan used thousands of archers to barrage the elephant of Murad Bakhsh, a prince, and general of Aurangzeb. When his elephant sustained many wounds and was ready to run, the mahout cast a chain around the beast's legs because the general did not want to retreat. Bakhsh was able to kill most enemies that approached using his arrows, but one enemy "washed his hands of his life" and jumped under the elephant to cut the straps holding the howdah in place. Guards were able to intervene and the man was "cut to pieces." A rocket hit the howdah, and Bakhsh finally decided to run, jumping down and riding off on a horse. The mahout must have unchained the elephant's legs, because the howdah became a conversation piece in the capital, put on display to show the bravery of the prince whose tower "was stuck as thick with arrows as a porcupine with quills."[39] As can be imagined, the elephant sustained many injuries. Fortunately, the normal bow will not fire arrows that will usually kill an elephant. According to Akbar's biographer, one of his elephants survived with eighty-two arrow strikes and another beast with fifty-five![40]

One battle between Aurangzeb and Shuja Khan involved elephants on both sides and showed the utter brutality of war for man and beast.

The leading elephant, a very fierce one, attacked Shuja'at Khan, and he wounded it with his spear, but what does such an animal care for a spear? Shuja'at drew his sword and gave it two cuts, but what did it care for that? He then wounded it twice with his dagger, but even then it did not turn, but sought to bear down both the Khan and his horse....One of his attendants struck the elephant on his fore-legs with a two-handed sword, and brought him to his knees. Shuja'at and his attendant then threw his driver to the ground, and with the same dagger he wounded the elephant in the trunk and forehead so that he shrieked with pain and turned back. The animal had received so many wounds, that he fell on reaching the enemy's ranks.[41]

Simultaneously, with Aurangzeb in a howdah on the back of an elephant, a barrage of cannon fire took off one leg of both the mahout and the sultan's assistant behind him. This is the battle where three chain-swinging elephants charged toward the emperor's beast. He remained calm and ordered his guards to shoot down their mahouts. This ended the danger, and a royal mahout captured one of the "chain elephants" by mounting him and riding him back to camp. [42] One of the nice things about captured elephants is that they hold no political allegiances and will work for anyone who feeds them!

The history of the Far East was about to change. The western world wanted the wealth and resources of Asia and was prepared to use force to take it.

46
Beasts of Burden

In the last march of eastern elephants into western lands, in the year 1621, Turks known as the Zaporozhian Cossacks invaded through the Ukraine and into Poland. Four elephants supported a one hundred thousand man force under Sultan Osman II, but the Poles survived a siege and the Turks withdrew.[1]

While the east would no longer assault the west, the European colonial powers began to seek fortunes in far away places and sailed to Asia. Usually the British or Portuguese would negotiate for exclusive trade agreements (leaving out their rival powers), but if their requests were not granted quickly, the military option was immediately employed. Even with a small number of soldiers, the British and Portuguese were able to defeat large armies of Asians because of superior weapons and tactics.

When the Portuguese under Alfonso de Albuquerco attacked Malaysia, the sultan rode his elephant Juru Damang to drive them away, but the Portuguese muskets mowed down the Muslims en masse.[2] One story adds a bit of humor to this event. A Muslim teacher had been instructing the Raja in the doctrines of Islam for some days, but in the battle as men fell dead around the Raja's elephant, the teacher grabbed the side of the howdah and yelled, "Sultan, let us get back, this is no place to study the unity of God!"[3]

One tactical advantage held by western soldiers was the knowledge that Asian nations overemphasized the need for their commander and so "Europeans these forty years past (1745–1785) gained many a battle by pointing a four-pounder at the main elephant...."[4] Once a long-range weapon killed the Asian commander, the army fled.

In one battle, a Portuguese observer noted that two hundred elephants carried towers and had sword-like blade weapons "fastened to their teeth when they fight."[5] But blade weapons are little use in the distance combat of colonial rifles.

Elephant battery of heavy artillery along the Khyber Pass at Campbellpur, circa 1895. [*Courtesy of the Library of Congress.*]

Elephants and horses being trained not to panic at cannon-fire. *[Illustrated London News April 9, 1853. Reprinted with permission of The Illustrated London News Picture Library.]*

Rifles are not always fatal to elephants, because a substantial amount of powder must be expended to propel a bullet through the elephant skull. Several incidents are well-documented in England and the United States where musth or crazed elephants were shot dozens and even hundreds of times without killing the poor animal. The shot must be well-placed, or deeply penetrate, to kill the elephant. Gunpowder in the form of cannons was the more persistent foe of elephants, which would either run from the tremendous sound of the artillery piece, or die from its projectile.

The Indian sport known as *sath-maru*, or elephant wrestling, entertained crowds for hundreds of years, not ending until World War II.[6] Akbar built a special amphitheater for elephant fights in Agra.[7] To reduce the injuries of fighting elephants, they were often rubbed in butter, making them slippery so the opposing elephant could not easily grapple them with the trunk or scrape with a tusk.[8]

Tigers and elephants are often made to combat for the amusement of spectators; also, tigers and buffaloes, or alligators. The battle between intoxicated elephants is a sport suited only for the cruel-hearted, and too often indulged. The mahouts (the men who sit as drivers on the neck of the elephant) have frequently been the victims of the ignoble amusement of their noble masters; indeed, the danger they are exposed to is so great, that to escape is deemed a miracle. The fighting-elephants are males, and they are prepared for the sport by certain drugs mixed up with the wax from the human ear. The method of training elephants for fighting must be left to abler hands to describe.[9]

Fighting elephants learned that they could win by killing the mahout of the opponent and so would strike out at the rider.[10] In the 1660s, Francois Bernier lived in India and saw the elephant fights. The beasts were separated by a wall of earth four feet wide and five feet tall, with each struggling by trunk and tusk over the wall. When the wall collapsed, one elephant would run. The winner received money from the king, and if the losing mahout died, money might be sent to his family.[11]

The contests were not solely between elephant pairs, but often included tigers, bulls, or horses. "Some fight with wild horses, six horses to an elephant; which he kills by clasping his trunk about their necks; and pulling them to him, breaks their necks with his tusks...."[12]

As foreigners (farangs) visited Asia and traveled by elephant, they observed some of the routines of the mahout who lived and worked with his elephant. Because the pachyderm is comforted by the sound of the mahout's voice and may become alarmed or worried if long periods of silence ensue, the rider will talk to the elephant in a constant stream of words, even though the beast may have no idea what the meaning of those words is. Here is one example:

The mahout pulls one of the elephant's ears and says, in Hindi, "Go!" Slowly the elephant rises and lurches forward. "Active, Active," the mahout says, addressing the animal, "anyone would think you were the Queen of India. You need a manservant just to wash and massage you, another just to bring branches to eat, another just to exercise you. But I have to wait on you all by myself. Active, Active, where are the weddings and meals to earn your livelihood?" He continues, talking almost to himself, "When they are wild they run, but when they are tame they won't move...."[13]

The ancient ways had not been entirely forgotten. In 1751, an elephant wearing iron head plates attempted to batter down the gates of Fort Ponomaley in the War of Coromadel.[14] If the sources are to be believed, the presence of armored elephants reached its peak in the 18th century. Nizam-ul-Mulk of Hyderabad (1730) had more than a thousand pachyderms in his army, of which 225 had armour; while the Mughal army in

1739 owned two thousand behemoths, all of whom supposedly used armor for protection![15]

The French East India Company helped to organize Indian armies to oppose the British. The famous battle of Plassey, where the young British officer Robert Clive made a name for himself, included at least a handful of fighting elephants. The beasts wore chain mail and plate armor, but many fled or died under the first British artillery and gun barrage.[16]

The British used elephants mainly to pull artillery through difficult terrain. On one occasion during the crossing of a shallow river, a man fell off the side of an ammunition wagon and was about to be crushed by the rear wheel. An elephant that had been pushing the cart quickly grasped the wooden wheel with its trunk and lifted the cart so that the wagon passed over the man safely.[17] An illustration of the event is provided in Chapter 17.

In 1598, the Chinese emperor of Peking showed off at least sixty elephants to guests. "They were all covered with rich embroidered cloths, and their trappings, bridles, cruppers, etc., were ornamented with silver and gilt: on their backs was a fine wooden castle, spacious enough for eight persons."[18] China received a small supply of elephants, perhaps one each year, as tribute from Siam in the late seventeenth century. An envoy from Russia saw elephant-drawn chariots and more than a dozen well-trained pachyderms in the emperor's stable.[19] Manchu ruler Kien-lung (1736–1795) owned sixty and used an elephant-pulled chariot.

King Quang Trung of Vietnam drove the Chinese out of his territories in 1798 using elephants (brought to the battlefield by rafts) in a surprise preemptive attack that terrified the Chinese cavalry. Trung himself rode an armored elephant.[20]

Although the Chinese emperors still had pachyderms in 1834, they were gone by 1901.[21] China does still support a small number of wild elephants in the Yunnan province near Xishuangbanna, but for most Chinese the elephant is only a wonder of the zoo.

47
Mighty Engineers

The British utilized elephants as engineers while they ruled parts of Asia. Captain Sandys commanded 1,500 elephants, mainly as artillery-haulers, in the late eighteenth century. The Royal Engineers used elephants in the Indian army until 1895.[1] During this colonial era, elephants were so important to the British that an army veterinarian, William Gilchrist, wrote a book on elephant veterinary care.[2]

One of the best recorded wars using elephants as artillery-haulers is the British invasion of Abyssinia (Ethiopia) of 1868, when the army used forty-four elephants to pull cannons hundreds of miles across mountainous desert. Remarkably, only five beasts died during the adventure![3]

The British were not the only army using elephants to pull artillery pieces. During the siege of Paris, France, in 1870, elephants pulled heavy artillery across difficult terrain for the German forces.[4] Unofficial sources claim that "Jenny" the elephant from the Hamburg Zoo lifted and pulled heavy equipment for the Germans in World War I.

Nazis used elephants from the Hamburg Zoo to plow fields to conserve gas and tractors for war in World War II. While not common, elephants can effectively plow fields and do farm labor. In an unusual experiment in Africa in the late nineteenth century, the Belgians (with help from Indian mahouts) trained Congolese tribesmen to train and use African elephants to plow fields for cotton crops.[5]

When the Belgians first attempted to train elephants to work in Africa, what seemed to be a victory quickly turned into defeat. The first report said "The elephant experiment has now been proved a complete success... their ability to march over all styles of ground, soft, stony, sandy, boggy; to conquer all eccentricities of topography – hill and dale, river and jungle – while labouring under double their due weight of baggage, some 1,500 instead of seven hundred pounds; and this in a style that no other beast of burden could hope to emulate."[6] This glowing document was revised only days later when most of the elephants keeled over dead, having apparently starved and worked too hard! The author admitted that perhaps the double baggage was excessive and they should have given the beasts more time to eat.[7]

When the Japanese invaded Burma in 1942, the speed of their advance caught the British by surprise. The Japanese moved swiftly by hijacking mahouts and their elephants from defunct logging companies to carry soldiers and supplies through otherwise impassable jungles.

...once the artillery gun and the infantry musket became reasonably efficient, the days of elephants as front line combatants were numbered....Who could have foreseen that after an interval of many years elephants were destined to have perhaps their finest hour and to play their greatest part in war in the twentieth century, in spite of modern weapons on land and in the air. Both sides in Burma in the second world war were quick to realize how useful elephants could be in difficult country; oddly enough many of the elephants fought for both sides, but in different roles....[8]

While the Japanese used the elephants to carry supplies and personnel, the British used them in the additional role as field engineers in the construction of roads, bridges, and airfields. Both sides were able to use elephants effectively only because Burma had been full of trained logging elephants and their mahouts, and thus had an immediate pool of candidates with experience in the forests.

Another difference between the allied and the axis forces may have been the relative treatment of the elephants during these campaigns, although this Japanese account denies any cruelty:

The Burmese workers in the Burmese Construction Volunteer Corps were paid one rupee per head per day. We paid two rupees per elephant. Everyone took good care of the elephants. Even Japanese soldiers who beat up Burmese never took it out on the elephants. In the early stages, all our food and equipment came by elephant. We had about ten elephants per platoon. They'd be left free in the mountains in the evening, a chain hobbling their front legs. They'd search for wild bananas and bamboo overnight and cover themselves with dirt to keep from being eaten up by insects. In the morning the Burmese mahoots would track them down from their footprints. They'd usually be no more than one or two kilometers away. Then they'd get a morning bath in the river. Each mahoot would scrub his own elephant with a brush. The elephants looked so comfortable, rolling over and over in the river. It took about thirty minutes. Then they had full stomachs and were clean and in a good mood. Now you could put the saddle mount or pulling chains on them and they'd listen to commands and do a good day's work....we had to prepare an almost astronomical amount of lumber...The elephants pulled down the trees that we'd sawed almost through, moved them away, and stacked them up with their trunks.[9]

Loading small cannons onto elephant-back. [*Illustrated London News April 9, 1853. Reprinted with permission of The Illustrated London News Picture Library.*]

This interviewee, Abe Hiroshi, was convicted of war crimes (beating prisoners of war) and sentenced to life imprisonment.[10]

In 1944 many Burmese mahouts defected from the Japanese to the allied side; they had been press ganged (forcibly enlisted) by Japanese. The mahouts were worried about their elephants because the Japanese would not allow the beasts to roam free at night for food, fearing desertions. Chained near the camps, the beasts became thin. Another factor leading to defections was the total air superiority held by the allies in Asia by 1944. Some Royal Air Force pilots asked to be excused from bombing runs on elephants, but the supplies could not be allowed to reach the Japanese.[11] "...Allied planes were extremely active. Some Oozies must have been on the receiving end of an unpleasant air strafe (forty elephants killed on one occasion)....In all 1,652 elephants were recovered," but as many as four thousand were missing or dead.[12]

A veteran worker with the elephants, U Toke Gale wrote that "... during the period of the war from 1943 to 1945 many of the timber elephants died of overwork and under-nourishment, while some died at the hands of Japanese soldiers who shot them indiscriminately for their handsome tusks." He witnessed elephants working day and night without shade even in the hot season and said that far less than half of the elephants survived the war.[13] One distinctive wound on Japanese-used war elephants was nasty acid burns from carrying Japanese batteries on their backs.[14] While the Japanese used the elephants rigorously, one surviving beast called Lin Wang became a Chinese celebrity. After pulling cannons for the Japanese, "Grandpa Lin" was captured by the Chinese and moved to a zoo in Taiwan, where he lived to the age of eighty-six.[15]

Working for the allies, a fine description of elephant laborers in World War II is the best-selling book, *Elephant Bill*. The true story tells of Lt. Col. J.H. Williams, whose years in the logging industry enabled him to enlist the help of many mahouts and elephants to carry supplies to remote regions with his elephant Bandoola.[16]

The allied elephants in the Kabaw Valley built 270 log bridges and culvert crossings by using local materials. "This was a major engineer contribution to the XIVth Army victory, since it increased the flow of men, vehicles and supplies from a trickle to a mighty flood." When the retreating Japanese toppled hundreds of trees to block the allied pursuit, ten elephants cleared the road in one day.[17]

As pack animals the elephants could go through jungle impassable by any other means. The British discovered that a Bofors anti-aircraft gun could be disassembled, carried on the backs of eight elephants, and then reassembled at its destination. The allies were not entirely without fault in their use of elephants, however. General Wingate forced some mahouts at gunpoint to load four elephants to swim across the Chindit river, but so badly overloaded one beast that she sank and drowned.[18]

One frustration for impatient officers in the use of logging elephants came because of their union-style work day.[19] After years of laboring from breakfast to five o' clock in the evening, the pachyderms were not about to work one minute past five! They called it a day and left for the forest to find dinner. Elephants can be forced to work longer, as the Japanese tried, but the animals often die or kill their mahouts when the stress becomes too great.

Another difficulty with elephants is the classic intraspecies clash with horses and mules. The British and American forces used tens of thousands of equine beasts of burden in the Asian theater, which led to the occasional spontaneous rodeo show.

...there were those two damned elephants someone at Regimental Headquarters picked up and brought along. A mule can get used to almost anything, but he draws the line at an animal that hangs down at both ends. Sensible, not knowing whether an elephant is coming or going, the mule is inclined to play safe and take off, regardless of road, underbrush, leader, column, or common courtesy.[20]

To keep Allied planes and soldiers from shooting their laundry elephant, these soldiers provided it with identification and its own foxhole:

...1st Punjabis found an elephant standing sadly on a hilltop near MS 116, swathed in cloud and with a little bell fastened round its neck. It was escorted to Brigade Headquarters, where Brigadier Warren's orderly, who had experience as a mahout was entrusted with its care. A large '68' was painted on its back for recognition purposes just like a vehicle's tailboard, and it was employed taking the brigade's laundry down to the river with its hide as a scrubbing board. For a slit trench the elephant was provided with a shelter previously dug into a bank for a three-ton lorry and to this it wisely retired at the first sound of gunfire...It was last heard of in the stables of the Maharajah of Cooch Behar.[21]

The seizing of the Burma road by the Japanese had seriously threatened the whole Asian war effort because China could no longer receive allied supplies by sea or ground. The U.S. Air Transport Command was formed specifically to ferry supplies to China by air over the Himalaya mountains, the tallest in the world. A constant stream of aircraft made the dangerous journey, reminiscent of the later Berlin airlift. To quickly load the planes on the ground, General Tunner had elephants trained to move heavy drums of fuel into the cargo planes. It took some time to accustom the elephants to the sounds of airplanes, not only because of their innate nervousness, but because Royal Air Force planes had been strafing elephants and therefore were feared.[22] A photo of this super-sized ground crew reached hundreds of newspapers.[23] Some elephants substituted as tow trucks to pull disabled planes off the runways to pull vehicles out of deep mud on poor roads.[24]

48
Targets of Opportunity

The military of the United States of America has faced war elephants in only two wars: the Asian theater of World War II and the conflict in Vietnam. In Vietnam, pachyderms were used entirely in the role of support, carrying combatants and supplies through difficult jungle terrain.

New technologies have continuously increased the distances at which man can kill. We have progressed from rock, to spear, to arrow, to sling, to catapult, to cannon, to gun, to rocket, and finally to missiles; each innovation making death easier to deal at greater range. The size of the elephant, which protects it from most predators, works to its disadvantage in the modern world, as its massive body makes it an easy target.

The main line of supplies for the northern Vietnamese insurgents, the Ho Chi Minh Trail, opened in July of 1959 and would become the "most famous logistic system in military history." Composed of eight thousand miles of roads, the United States dropped more than two million tons of bombs to stop the munitions columns.[1] Even with 25 to 30% losses, the trail flow and speed of movement increased throughout the 1960s. Frustration with their inability to stem the tide of supplies and enemy soldiers led the United States to take more drastic measures.

The trail had many inlets and outlets to avoid bombing and congestion that might occur on a single stretch of ground. Some of the paths traversed very steep and dangerous terrain, which could be traveled only by elephant. A photograph by the Vietnam News Agency shows guerillas near Route 9 in Laos using elephants to haul supplies to the NVA.[2]

As pack animals, which is their general use where there are no roads, they will carry an immense bulk and weight on their backs amongst hills and swamps where by no other means could the goods be transported. Over a fairly easy country and elephant will carry half a ton for continuous marching, but if the route be hilly the load should be reduced to seven hundredweight. An elephant, especially a light one, is a good mount, and is exceedingly active and sure-footed over bad ground; in fact they never stumble and can be managed and guided with the greatest ease.[3]

The Vietcong 559th Transportation Group led by Lieutenant Pham Van Phan used several elephants for toting goods on the trail. Lieutenant Phan offered this account:

They're [elephants] not easy to manage, you know, especially when there's fighting going on. As soon as they left our base, one of them got bogged down in a swamp. After two hours of struggling hard to save it, one of the soldiers suggested we kill it, take its tusks, and distribute the meat to the surrounding villages. But we felt we couldn't do that: these elephants have done a lot for the regiment. Seeing the huge animal sink deeper and deeper into the mire, I lost all hope to save it. Thuan, the commander of the unit, sent men to fell trees in the forest to fill up the swamp. The elephant quickly understood: it grabbed hold of the logs with its forelegs and gradually pulled itself from the mud and out of danger. We were all overjoyed and set off immediately...but somehow we were detected and our convoy was shelled. We were worried that our animals, because of their size, were not safe. The lead elephant ran amuck. Fearing it would be killed, Thuan sent me to tell the mahout to get it quickly under control. As it was in the lead, the whole convoy depended on it. Thuan gave order to all the mahouts to hide behind the large ears of the elephants while they moved on open ground. At last we got out of the dangerous area. I still wonder how no elephants were hit.[4]

A semifictional account of the Vietnam War called *The Story of a Mahout and His War Elephant* offers more detailed scenes from this difficult sort of lifestyle.[5]

United States intelligence and reconnaissance recognized that the enemy had adopted elephants as transportation vehicles, and thus pachyderms became legitimate "targets of opportunity" for both air and ground forces. Some pilots and soldiers wanted clarification on these orders, but even the clarification remained unclear.

A New York Times report from Saigon on June 21, 1966, wrote that "United States Marine pilots also strafed a column of eleven pack elephants in the mountains thirty-five miles southwest of Danang in South Vietnam yesterday. Five of the animals were killed and five others seen to fall. Again there were no secondary explosions." The lack of secondary explosions simply meant that the beasts were not carrying munitions.

The following year, during a briefing of Helicopter Squadron 265, the pilots were told not to call in air strikes on "friendly elephants." When the commander asked how they would know a friendly elephant from a

An African elephant examining a car, used for perspective on the size of a tusker. [*Photo courtesy of Gerhard Geldenhuys*]
Source: Photographer Gerhard Geldenhuys. Model release (car occupant) Steve Lawson.

hostile elephant, the reply was to look for mud on their bellies: a sign that they had been on the trail.[6]

When sighted, if the helicopter crew believed the elephants were hostile, they would usually request that jets come in to destroy the beasts, but sometimes the gunners in the choppers could do it themselves.[7] Rather than using the mud method of identification, the commander for one helicopter crew determined that since no friendly villages were in the area, the beasts must be hostile, so four adults and a calf were gunned down.[8]

Visual sightings of enemy soldiers and elephants were not the only way of locating them for bombing runs. The United States developed a number of sensors, including "sniffers," that could detect high levels of methane (which the elephant's simple digestive system produces prodigiously) and infrared and heat detectors. Frequently, air strikes based on sensor detection hit elephants rather than troop columns. Even aside from direct attempts to destroy pachyderms, the widespread use of defoliant chemicals to destroy the forest canopy took away a major source of food and must have had a major impact on the elephant population of Vietnam.

The one incident during the Vietnam conflict in which the United States military attempted to utilize a war elephant was the inspiration for the Disney movie "Operation Dumbo Drop" in the mid-1990s.

In 1967, a mountain village friendly to the United States wanted elephants to help them haul logs to the local sawmill, and the U.S. Military Assistance Command (USMACV) wanted to help them get some. However, the remote region was surrounded by the Vietcong and so marching the elephant to the village was not practical. One plan was to use multiple helicopters to carry crated elephants underneath in a cargo net and carry them to the village. [9] The other plan was to push parachute-harnessed behemoths out of the back of a C-130E cargo plane!

The Air Force insisted that any living, large animals must be tranquilized and fully secured to pallets, and that a weapon powerful enough to kill the beast be mounted inside the aircraft in case of an emergency. The whole plan might have gone unnoticed by international media except that special fast-working tranquilizers had to be acquired to sedate the elephants. Once the Royal Society for the Prevention of Cruelty to Animals in Britain heard about air-dropping pachyderms, the media jumped on the story. [10]

There are two widely different versions of the outcome of the operation. The first version printed in 1980 by Michael Kukler says that one elephant was walked into the cargo plane, but when the engines revved up and the plane began to take off from the runway, the elephant panicked. Lest the shifting of the animal cause the plane to crash, they tranquilized the pachyderm.

Once the beast was tranquilized, it relaxed and released a gas so strong the that average human nose could not stand. It made a noise so loud it almost shattered your eardrums and shook the plane. It went BAROOOM and this is how the operation got its name. [11]

Next, says Kukler, the plane turned right back around and evacuated its ill-smelling, drugged passenger.

The more detailed and perhaps more credible version comes from Jim Morris, who writes that twenty-eight reporters were on hand to watch the helicopters carry away four drugged elephants to the village.

The army had cameras rolling for this major public relations venture, and the short film survives in the National Archives.[12] Unfortunately two things conspired to prevent this story from becoming a big media event. First, Martin Luther King was killed that day, relegating all other news to footnotes. Second, the media attention had attracted the Vietcong, who were waiting in ambush near the destination and killed three of the four elephants. The fourth elephant ran away.[13] Air Force cameras did not record this grisly end to Operation Barooom.

Currently, there is only one place on Earth that continues to use war elephants: Myanmar, or Burma. Myanmar has been ruled by a military junta called the State Peace and Development Council (SPDC) for the last fifteen years. The government represses minority views and minority tribes, including the Karen and Mon peoples of southern Burma. The Karen National Liberation Army uses elephants to carry supplies from other regions to support their insurgency.[14] The forces move in groups of twenty to thirty, sometimes using ex-logging elephants "as 'porters' for ammunition, weapons and tired troops."[15]

The four-thousand-year history of cooperation between man and elephant in warfare has ended.

Epilogue

The common wisdom among military scholars is to dismiss combat elephants as a foolish novelty with no real effect in battle. Field Marshal Montgomery blames King Porus, who fought against Alexander the Great, for leading India into the dark age of elephant futility, though Porus neither invented the art nor found it to be futile.[1] Lynn Montross posits that "...with the possible exception of the Hydaspes, it is difficult to find a battle in which the huge beasts played a decisive part," though the book you have just read shows that pachyderms played decisive roles in dozens of battles.[2] The 2005 work *Warfare in Ancient Greece* says of war elephants that "Neither the Romans nor indeed the Parthians ever really bothered with them....," when in fact the Romans used elephants in more conflicts than mighty Carthage.[3]

The problem with common wisdom is that it is often wrong. Once a theory becomes generally accepted, no one bothers to challenge the truth of it. *War Elephants* challenges the view that pachyderms were a useless or counterproductive part of ancient or modern armies. Yes, when misused, misplaced, or mistimed in battle, the elephants did run back over their own armies, wreaking damage and death. However, when properly trained, placed, and led into combat, the beasts proved to be highly effective.

The question of whether elephants *should* be used for war is a different matter. Personally, I would prefer that pachyderms not be turned into vicious killers.

Now that humans rule the earth, it is humans who must work to preserve parts of the non-human world. Elephants are falling out of the public view, and thus losing what protection we might offer.

It was the war effort and need for combat elephants that led to the world's earliest 'national parks,' because "...elephants had to be hunted and captured alive, special forest tracts were designated as elephant preserves, and inhabited by trackers, hunters, and tamers..."[4] Thus, land and beast were preserved because of the economic and military value of pachyderms.

Now, by forbidding any economic use of elephants, we strip their land and confine them to zoos where they will not breed. In this era influenced by animal rights pressures, all "uses" of elephants are frowned upon. In consequence, elephants are removed from the circuses, zoo keepers are seperated from elephants ("protected contact"), and zoos can rarely acquire new elephants from the wild. So the gene pool by which elephants might breed is isolated and stunted; the beasts in zoos are getting older without mating; and there are even less "jobs" for elephants. Because humans rule the earth [for better or worse], and humans view labor and money as the key to existence, elephants only "matter" if they support the human economy. By removing elephants from the human economy: ending logging in Asian forests; stopping circus entertainment; outlawing tourist rides; and etc., well-meaning animal lovers have contributed to the faster extinction of the elephant species.

Are animal lovers correct, ethically, in demanding these changes? Perhaps. But their efforts for the long-term good may spell the short term demise of the objects they hope to preserve. We care about things that we know: our friends, family, and possessions. We know them because they are around, we see and sense them. We do not care much about things we do not know: outer space, insects, trigonometry. By isolating people from elephants, we are forgetting them. By forgetting them, we doom them to annihilation.

Elephants have been observed repeatedly acting in ways that seem to be emotional. They sometimes die of grief when a companion elephant or human trainer dies.[5] Pachyderms gather around sick or wounded elephants and try to lift them up or feed them. They pass around the bones of dead elephants as if remembering or pondering the idea of death.[6] Among the animals, I wonder if elephants are not the closest to humans in their variety of emotional states.

By allowing elephants to slip away toward extinction, humankind has forgotten its close relationship with pachyderms. To lose such magnificent creatures would be among the greatest shames of human history.

Endnotes

INTRODUCTION

1. Fazl, Abu-l. *The Akbarnama of Abu-l Fazl*. Bibliotheca India series. Translator H. Beveridge. Calcutta: Asiatic Society of Bengal, 1912, p. 111.
2. Armandi, P. *Histoire Militaire des Elephants*. Paris: Librairie D'Amyot, 1843.

1. USEFUL ORPHAN

1. Scigliano, Eric. *Love, War, and Circuses: The Age-Old Relationship between Elephants and Humans*. Boston: Houghton Mifflin, 2002, p. 117.
2. Kenoyer, Jonathan Mark. *Ancient Cities of the Indus Valley Civilization*. New York: Oxford University Press, 1998, p. 166.
3. Mehta, Ved. *Portrait of India*. New Haven: Yale University Press, 1993, p. 222.
4. Wood, J.G. *Sketches and Anecdotes of Animal Life*, second series. London: G. Routledge, 1858, pp. 6 and 7.
5. Elvin, Mark. *The Retreat of the Elephants: An Environmental History of China*. New Haven: Yale University Press, 2004, p. 15.
6. Fernando, Joseph M.P. "Genetics, Ecology, and Conservation of the Asian Elephant." Doctor of Philosophy of Biology dissertation at the University of Oregon, 1998, p. 93.
7. Kendall, Timothy. *Kerma and the Kingdom of Kush 2500–1500 BC: The Archaeological Discovery of an Ancient Nubian Empire*. Washington, DC: National Museum of Art, 1996.
8. Barnett, R.D. "Early Greek and Oriental Ivories." In *The Journal of Hellenic Studies*, Vol. 68, 1948, p. 1ff.
9. Singh, Sarva Daman. *Ancient Indian Warfare with Special Reference to the Vedic Period*. Leiden: E.J. Brill, 1965, p. 73.
10. Downs, James F. "The Origin and Spread of Riding in the Near East and Central Asia." In *American Anthropologist*, new series, Vol. 63 n. 6, December 1961, p. 1197. Also Littauer, M.A. and Crouwel, J.H. *Wheeled Vehicles and Ridden Animals in the Ancient Near East*. Leiden, Netherlands: E.J. Brill, 1979, p. 66.

11. Ranking, John. *Historical Researches on the Wars and Sports of the Mongols and Romans: In Which Elephants and Wild Beasts Were Employed or Slain.* London: Longman, Rees, Orme, Brown, and Green, 1826, pp. 86 and 87.
12. Bishop, Carl W. "The Elephant and Its Ivory in Ancient China." In *Journal of the American Oriental Society*, Vol. 41, 1921, p. 299.
13. Morewood-Dowsett, J. "Supplement: Elephant Past and Present." In *Journal of the Royal African Society*, Vol. 38 n. 152, July 1939, p. 21.
14. Stopford, J.G.B. "A Neglected Source of Labour in Africa." In *Journal of the Royal African Society,* Vol. 1 n. 4, July 1902, p. 451.
15. Morewood-Dowsett, Supplement, p. 22.
16. Hart, Lynette and Sundar. "Family Traditions for Mahouts of Asian Elephants." In *Anthrozoos*, Vol. 13 n.1, 2000, p. 35.
17. Stopford, "Neglected Source", pp. 448 and 449.
18. Levin, Bernard. *Hannibal's Footsteps.* London: Hodder and Stoughton, 1987, p. 55.

2. EARLY CONTESTS

1. Morewood-Dowsett, J. "Supplement: Elephant Past and Present." In *Journal of the Royal African Society*, Vol. 38 n. 152, July 1939, p. 22.
2. Spinage, C.A. *Elephants.* London: T & A.D. Poyser Ltd., 1994, p. 265.
3. Hart, Lynette and Sundar. "Family Traditions for Mahouts of Asian Elephants." In *Anthrozoos*, Vol. 13 n.1, 2000, p. 35; and *The Hutchinson Dictionary of Ancient and Medieval Warfare.* Chicago: Fitzroy Dearborn, 1998, p. 110.
4. Spinage, *Elephants*, p. 137.
5. Bradford, Alfred S. *With Arrow, Sword, and Spear: A History of Warfare in the Ancient World.* Westport, CT: Praeger, 2001, p. 128.
6. Singh, Sarva Daman. *Ancient Indian Warfare with Special Reference to the Vedic Period.* Leiden: E.J. Brill, 1965, p. 169.
7. Singh, *Ancient*, p. 83.
8. Singh, *Ancient*, p. 81.
9. Spinage, *Elephants*, p. 75.
10. Dikshitar, V.R. Ramachandra. *War in Ancient India.* Delhi: Motilal Banarsidass, 1987, pp. 168 and 169.
11. Wood, J.G. *Sketches and Anecdotes of Animal Life*, second series. London: G. Routledge, 1858, pp. 77–79.
12. Emerson, Gertrude. *Voiceless India.* Westport: Greenwood Press, 1971. Reprint of 1930 ed., p. 118.
13. Namboodiri, Nibha, ed. *Practical Elephant Management: A Handbook for Mahouts.* Elephant Welfare Association, 1997. Online at www.elephantcare.org/mancover.htm
14. Wynter, Philip. "Elephants at War: In Burma, Big Beasts Work for Allied Army." In *Life Magazine*, April 10, 1944, p. 19.

15. Singh, *Ancient*, p. 79.
16. Singh, *Ancient*, p. 80.
17. Singh, *Ancient*, p. 117.
18. Pant, G.N. *Horse & Elephant Armour*. Delhi: Agam Kala Prakashan, 1997, p. 185.

3. BEAUTY AND THE BEASTS

1. James, Jamie. "Enigma: The Myth of Semiramis." *Opera News*, January 16, 1993, p. 18.
2. Fraser, Antonia. *The Warrior Queens*. New York: Alfred A. Knopf, 1989, p. 28.
3. James, "Enigma", p. 19.
4. Fraser, *Warrior*, p. 29.
5. Murphy, Edwin. *The Antiquities of Asia: A Translation with Notes of Book II of the Library of History of Diodorus Siculus*. New Brunswick, NJ: Transaction Publishers, 1989, p. 23.
6. Fernando, Joseph M.P. "Genetics, Ecology, and Conservation of the Asian Elephant." Doctor of Philosophy of Biology dissertation at the University of Oregon, 1998, p. 90.
7. Murphy, *Antiquities*, pp. 25 and 26.

4. FILL OF BLOOD

1. Sykes, Percy. *A History of Persia* in two volumes. 3rd edition. London: Macmillan, 1951, p. 153.
2. Center for Iranian Studies. "Ethiopia: Relations with Persia." In *Encyclopaedia Iranica*. Online at www.iranica.com/articles/v9fl/v9f103.html.
3. Huart, Clement. *Ancient Persia and Iranian Civilization*. New York: Knopf, 1927, p. 44.
4. Mayor, Adrienne. *Greek Fire, Poison Arrows & Scorpion Bombs: Biological and Chemical Warfare in the Ancient World*. New York: Overlook Duckworth, 2003, pp. 158 and 159.
5. Rawlinson, George. *The Five Great Monarchies of the Ancient Eastern World* in three volumes. 2nd edition. New York: Scribner, Welford and Co., 1871, Vol. 3, p. 387.
6. Sykes, Percy. *A History of Persia* in two volumes. 3rd edition. London: Macmillan, 1951, p. 153; also Mayor, Greek Fire, 159.
7. Tafazzoli, Ahmad. "Elephant: A Demonic Creature and a Symbol of Sovereignty." In *Monumentum*, Vol. 2, 1975, p. 395.
8. Wood, J.G. *Sketches and Anecdotes of Animal Life*, second series. London: G. Routledge, 1858, p. 28.

9. Op. cit., Sykes, p. 158.
10. Higham, Robin. "The International Commission for Military History-Meeting, Tehran, 6-16 July 1976." In *Military Affairs*, Vol. 40 n. 4, December 1976, p. 153.
11. Barnett, R.D. "Early Greek and Oriental Ivories." In *The Journal of Hellenic Studies*, Vol. 68, 1948, p. 1ff.
12. MacMunn, George. *The Martial Races of India*. Quetta, Pakistan: Gosha-e-Adab, 1977, p. 21.

5. IMPROVEMENTS

1. Laufer, Berthold. *Ivory in China*. Anthropology Leaflet #21, Chicago: Field Museum of Natural History, 1925, pp. 11 and 12.
2. Bishop, Carl W. "The Elephant and Its Ivory in Ancient China." In *Journal of the American Oriental Society*, Vol. 41, 1921, p. 302.
3. Singh, Sarva Daman. *Ancient Indian Warfare with Special Reference to the Vedic Period*. Leiden: E.J. Brill, 1965, p. 74.
4. Laufer, *Ivory*, p. 10.
5. McCrindle, John W. *Ancient India as Described by Megasthenes and Arrian*. New Delhi, India: Munshiram Manoharlal Publishers, 2000, p. 30.
6. Basham, A.L. *The Wonder That Was India*. 3rd revised edition. Vol. I. New York: Taplinger, 1968, p. 130.
7. Pant, G.N. *Horse & Elephant Armour*. Delhi, India: Agam Kala Prakashan, 1997, p. 3.
8. Barker, Phil. *Armies of the Macedonian and Punic Wars*. England: War Games Research Group, 1971, p. 35.
9. Stone, George Cameron. *A Glossary of the Construction, Decoration and Use of Arms and Armor in All Countries and in All Times*. New York: Jack Brussel, 1934, p. 8.
10. Wood, J.G. *Sketches and Anecdotes of Animal Life*, second series. London: G. Routledge, 1858, pp. 57-59.
11. Pant, *Horse*, p. 91.
12. MacMunn, George. *The Martial Races of India*. Quetta, Pakistan: Gosha-e-Adab, 1977, p. 29.
13. Paradine-Palmer, Greta. *Jhools in the Dust*. York, England: Wilton 65, 2002, p. 116.
14. Wilford, John Noble. "Greek Myths: Not Necessarily Mythical." In *The New York Times*, July 4, 2000.
15. Mayor, Adrienne. *The First Fossil Hunters: Paleontology in Greek and Roman Times*. Princeton: Princeton University Press, 2000, pp. 55 and 56.
16. Mayor, *First*, p. 35.

6. THE ELEPHANT MYSTERY

1. Anglim, Simon et al. *Fighting Techniques of the Ancient World*. New York: Thomas Dunne Books, 2002, p. 33.
2. Briant, Pierre. *From Cyrus to Alexander: A History of the Persian Empire*. Translated by Peter T. Daniels. Winona Lake, IN: Eisenbrauns, 2002. p. 757.
3. Tafazzoli, Ahmad. "Elephant: A Demonic Creature and a Symbol of Sovereignty." In *Monumentum*, Vol. 2, 1975, p. 395.
4. Polyaenus, quoted in Jimenez, Ramon L. *Caesar Against the Celts*. Edison, NJ: Castle Books, 1996, pp. 156 and 157.
5. Durschmied, Erik. *From Armageddon to the Fall of Rome*. London: Hodder & Stoughton, 2002, pp. 142 and 143.
6. Everson, Tim. *Warfare in Ancient Greece: Arms and Armour from the Heroes of Homer to Alexander the Great*. London: Sutton Publishing, 2004, p. 202.
7. Briant, *From Cyrus*, p. 426.
8. Green, Peter. *Alexander of Macedon, 356-323 BC*. Berkeley: University of California Press, 1991, p. 288; also Sykes, Percy. *A History of Persia* in two volumes. 3rd edition. London: Macmillan, 1951, p. 256.
9. Aristotle. *The Works of Aristotle, Volume IV, Historia Animalium*, New York: Oxford University Press, 1910, Book IX, Section 610a, number 15.
10. Rennie, James [though stated as Anonymous]. *The Elephant Principally Viewed in Relation to Man, a new edition*. London, Charles Knight & Co., 1844, p. 171.
11. Pant, G.N. *Horse & and Elephant Armour*. Delhi, India: Agam Kala Prakashan, 1997, p. 3.
12. *Alexander the Great*. Makers of History series, Vol. VI. New York: A.L. Fowle, 1906, p. 176.
13. Cummings, Lewis V. *Alexander the Great*. Boston: Houghton Mifflin, 1940, p. 214.
14. Ashley, James R. *The Macedonian Empire*. Jefferson, NC: McFarland, 1998, p. 258.
15. Aelian. *Aelian on the Characteristics of Animals*. In three volumes. Translated by A.F. Scholfield. Cambridge: Harvard University Press, 1971, Vol. III, p. 89, and Eltringham, Dr. S.K. consultant. *The Illustrated Encyclopedia of Elephants: From Their Origins and Evolution to Their Ceremonial and Working Relationship with Man*. New York: Crescent Books, 1991, p. 140. (0517061368).
16. Adams, Jack. *Wild Elephants in Captivity*. Carson, CA.: Center for the Study of Elephants, 1981, p. 146; and Guerrero, Diana. "Elephant Management in the United States." Arkanimals.com/WildSide/Elefnt4.html, copyright 1995.

17. Scullard, H.H. *The Elephant in the Greek and Roman World*. Cambridge: Thames and Hudson, 1974, p. 65.

18. Briant, *From Cyrus,* p. 201, 756.

7. THE HORROR

1. Pliny. *Natural History* in 10 volumes. Volume III, Libri VIII-XI. Edited by H. Rackham, 2nd edition. Cambridge: Harvard University Press, 1983, pp. 105–107.

2. Fildes, Alan and Fletcher, Joann. *Alexander the Great*. Los Angeles: J. Paul Getty Museum, 2002, p. 102.

3. Pope, William Christopher. *Alexander the Great in India*. Masters Thesis for the University of Houston at Clear Lake, May, 1996, p. 24.

4. Paradine-Palmer, Greta. *Jhools in the Dust*. York, England: Wilton 65, 2002, pp. 81, 139.

5. Sykes, Percy. *A History of Persia* in two volumes. 3rd edition. London: Macmillan, 1951, p. 273.

6. Plutarch. *Plutarch's Lives of Illustrious Men*. In three volumes. New York: John W. Lovell Co., 1880, Vol. 2, p. 489.

7. Hammond, N.G.L. *The Genius of Alexander the Great*. Chapel Hill, NC.: University of North Carolina Press, 1997, p. 166.

8. Rollin, Charles. *The Ancient History of the Egyptians, Carthaginians, Assyrians, Babylonians, Medes and Persians, Grecians, and Macedonians...*in two volumes. Cincinnati: Applegate, Pounsford & Co., 1868, Vol. 1, p. 584.

9. Starnaman, Craig D. *Alexander, Porus, and the Battle of the Hydaspes*. Master's Thesis at Michigan State University, 1990, p. 81.

10. MacMunn, George. *The Martial Races of India*. Quetta, Pakistan: Gosha-e-Adab, 1977, p. 29.

11. Paradine-Palmer, *Jhools,* p. 116.

12. Pope, *Alexander,* p. 50.

13. Pant, G.N. *Horse & Elephant Armour*. Delhi: Agam Kala Prakashan, 1997, p. 93.

14. Pseudo-Callisthenes. *The Romance of Alexander the Great*. New York: Columbia University Press, 1969, pp. 119 and 120.

15. Ducrey, Pierre. *Warfare in Ancient Greece*. New York: Schocken Books, 1986, p. 103, 106.

16. Groning, Karl and Saller, Martin. *Elephants: A Cultural and Natural History*. Germany: Konemann, 1999, p. 201.

17. Arrian. *Anabasis Alexandri Books V–VII, and Indica*. Translator: Brunt, P.A. Cambridge, MA.: Harvard University Press., 1983, pp. 53 and 54.

18. Plutarch. *Plutarch's Lives of Illustrious Men*. Translator: Dryden, John. In three volumes. New York: John W. Lovell Co., ca. 1880, p. 490.

19. Rapson, E.J. ed. *The Cambridge History of India*. Delhi, India: S. Chand & Co., 1962, Vol. 1, p. 364.

20. Scullard, H.H. *The Elephant in the Greek and Roman World.* Aspects of Greek and Roman Life series. Cambridge: Thames and Hudson, 1974, p. 71.

8. ALEXANDER'S OPINION

1. Rufus, Quintus Curtius. *The Life and Death of Alexander the Great, King of Macedon.* London: S.S., 1674 ed., p. 399.
2. Scullard, H.H. *The Elephant in the Greek and Roman World.* Aspects of Greek and Roman Life series. Cambridge: Thames and Hudson, 1974, p. 72.
3. Bosworth, A.B. *The Legacy of Alexander.* New York: Oxford University Press, 2002, p. 108.
4. Dinerstein, Eric. *Smithsonian.* "Nepal's 'Land Rovers' Cover Themselves with Dust, and Glory." June, 1988, Vol. 19, n.6, p.76.
5. Alexander, Shana. *The Astonishing Elephant.* New York: Random House, 2000, p. 84.
6. Tarn, W.W. *Hellenistic Military & Naval Developments.* Chicago: Ares Publishers, 1975, pp. 93 and 94.
7. Brunt, P.A. "Notes on Aristobulus of Cassandria." In *The Classical Quarterly,* new series, Vol. 24 n. 1, May 1974, p. 68.
8. Diodorus. *Diodorus of Sicily* in 12 volumes. Cambridge: Harvard University Press, 1957, Vol. 8, p. 389.
9. Murphy, Edwin. *The Antiquities of Asia: A Translation with Notes of Book II of the Library of History of Diodorus Siculus.* New Brunswick, NJ: Transaction Publishers, 1989, p. 111.
10. Heckel, Waldemar. "Resistance to Alexander the Great." In *The Greek World in the Fourth Century,* edited by Lawrence A. Tritle. New York: Routledge, 1997, p. 212.
11. Scullard, *Elephant,* p. 73.
12. Rennie, James. *The Elephant Principally Viewed in Relation to Man.* New revised edition. London: Charles Knight, 1844, p. 212.
13. Tarn, W.W. "Alexander: The Conquest of the Far East." In *The Cambridge Ancient History, Vol. VI Macedon, 401-301 B.C.* Editor J.B. Bury et al. New York: Macmillan, 1933, p. 422.

9. DEATH ON THE NILE

1. Rennie, James [though stated as anonymous]. *The Elephant Principally Viewed in Relation to Man.* New revised ed. London: Charles Knight, 1844, p. 212.
2. Adams, Jack. *Wild Elephants in Captivity.* Carson, CA.: Center for the Study of Elephants, 1981, pp. 124 and 125.

3. Will, Edouard. "The Succession to Alexander." In *The Cambridge Ancient History, second edition.* Vol. VII Part I, The Hellenistic World. Editor F.W. Walbank. Cambridge: Cambridge University Press, 2001, p, 25.

4. Trautmann, Thomas R. "Elephants and the Mauryas." In *India: History and Thought.* Edited by S. N. Mukherjee. Calcutta, India: Subarnarekha, 1982, p. 267.

5. Kincaid, C.A. *Successors of Alexander the Great.* Chicago: Ares Publishers, 1980, p. 11.

6. Scullard, H.H. *The Elephant in the Greek and Roman World.* Aspects of Greek and Roman Life series. Cambridge: Thames and Hudson, 1974. p. 78.

7. Anglim, Simon et al. *Fighting Techniques of the Ancient World.* New York: Thomas Dunne Books, 2002, p. 126.

8. Maihafer, Harry. "River Crossing Imperiled." In *Military History*, Vol. 5, n. 4, February 1989, p. 29.

9. Tarn, W.W. *Hellenistic Military & Naval Developments.* Chicago: Ares Publishers, 1975, p. 94.

10. Welles, C. Bradford. *Alexander and the Hellenistic World.* Toronto: A.M. Hakkert Co., 1970, p. 53.

11. Billows, Richard A. *Antigonos the One-Eyed and the Creation of the Hellenistic State.* Berkeley: University of California Press, 1990, pp. 59–60.

12. Tarn, W.W. "Greece: 335 to 321 B.C." In *The Cambridge Ancient History, Vol. VI Macedon, 401–301 B.C.* Editor J.B. Bury et al. New York: Macmillan, 1933, p. 467.

13. Adams, W. Lindsay. "The Successors of Alexander." In *The Greek World in the Fourth Century.* New York: Routledge, 1997, p. 233.

14. Bosworth, A.B. *The Legacy of Alexander.* New York: Oxford University Press, 2002, pp. 82 and 83.

15. Scullard, *Elephant*, p. 79.

16. Diodorus. *Diodorus of Sicily in Twelve Volumes.* Vol. 9. Cambridge: Harvard University Press, 1969, pp. 108 and 109.

17. Groning, Karl and Saller, Martin. *Elephants: A Cultural and Natural History.* Germany: Konemann, 1999, p. 204.

18. Kincaid, *Successors*, p. 16.

19. Digby, Simon. *War-Horse and Elephant in the Dehli Sultanate: A Study of Military Supplies.* Orient Monographs. Karachi, Pakistan: Oxford University Press, 1971, p. 51.

20. Toynbee, J.M.C. *Animals in Roman Life and Art.* Ithaca, NY: Cornell University Press, 1973, p. 39.

10. ELEPHANTS MARCHING

1. Plutarch. *Plutarch's Lives of Illustrious Men.* In three volumes. New York: John W. Lovell Co., ca. 1880, Vol. 2, p. 319.

2. Billows, Richard A. *Antigonus the One-Eyed and the Creation of the Hellenistic State*. Berkeley: University of California Press, 1990. pp. 27 and 29.

3. Heckel, Waldemar. "Resistance to Alexander the Great." In *The Greek World in the Fourth Century: From the Fall of the Athenian Empire to the Successors of Alexander*, edited by Lawrence A. Tritle. New York: Routledge, 1997, p. 199.

4. Ramsay, William Mitchell. "Geography and History in a Phyrgo-Pisidian Glen." In *Geographical Journal*, Vol. 41, n. 4, April 1923, p. 288.

5. Morewood-Dowsett, J. "Supplement: Elephant Past and Present." In *Journal of the Royal African Society*, Vol. 38, n. 152, July 1939, p. 28.

6. Pickard-Cambridge, A.W. "The Rise of Macedonia." In *The Cambridge Ancient History, Vol. VI Macedon, 401–301 B.C.* Editor J.B. Bury et al. New York: Macmillan, 1933, pp. 210 and 211.

7. Tarn, W.W. "The Heritage of Alexander." In *The Cambridge Ancient History, Vol. VI Macedon, 401–301 B.C.* New York: Macmillan, 1933, p. 477.

8. Diodorus. "The Armies of Eumenes and Antigonus at the Battle of Paraetacene." In *The Hellenistic World from Alexander to the Roman Conquest*. New York: Cambridge University Press, 1994, p. 53. [Note: Diodorus says 114 elephants in one place, but 125 in another.]

9. Devine, A.M. "Diodorus' Account of the Battle of Paraitacene." In *The Ancient World*, Vol. XII nos 3–4, December 1985, p. 79.

10. Tarn, W.W. *Hellenistic Military & Naval Developments*. Chicago: Ares Publishers, 1975. [Reprint from 1930], p. 97.

11. Bosworth, A.B. *The Legacy of Alexander: Politics, Warfare, and Propaganda under the Successors*. New York: Oxford University Press, 2002. p. 142.

12. Adcock, F.E. *The Greek and Macedonian Art of War*. Berkeley: University of California Press, 1957, p. 78.

13. Diodorus, "Armies", pp. 337–339.

14. Bosworth, *Legacy*, pp. 144 and 145.

15. Plutarch, *Lives*, p. 314.

16. Diodorus, "Armies", p. 341.

17. Kruse, Gosta. *Trunk Call*. London: Elek Books, 1962, p. 76.

18. Bosworth, *Legacy*, p. 153.

19. Devine, A.M. "Diodorus' Account of the Battle of Gabiene." In *The Ancient World*, Vol. XII nos 3–4, December 1985, p. 92.

20. Delbruck, Hans. *Warfare in Antiquity*. History of the Art of War series. Vol. I. Translated by Walter J. Renfroe, Jr. Lincoln: University of Nebraska, 1990, p. 240.

21. Parke, H.W. *Greek Mercenary Soldiers*. Chicago: Ares Publishers, 1981, p. 207.

22. Plutarch, *Lives*, p. 317.

23. Heckel, Waldemar. *The Marshals of Alexander's Empire*. New York: Routledge, 1992, p. 56.
24. Bosworth, *Legacy*, pp. 166 and 167.
25. Barker, Phil. *Armies of the Macedonian and Punic Wars*. England: War Games Research Group, 1971, p. 6.
26. Montross, Lynn. *War Through the Ages*. Revised and enlarged 3rd edition. New York: Harper & Bros., 1960, p. 43.
27. Appian. "Seleucus and the Foundation of the Seleucid Empire." In *The Hellenistic World from Alexander to the Roman Conquest*. New York: Cambridge University Press, 1994, p. 87.
28. Durant, Will. *The Life of Greece*. The Story of Civilization, part II. New York: Simon and Schuster, 1966, p. 558.

11. SIEGE

1. Gaebel, Robert E. *Cavalry Operations in the Ancient Greek World*. Norman: University of Oklahoma Press, 2002, pp. 212–13.
2. Ducrey, Pierre. *Warfare in Ancient Greece*. New York: Schocken Books, 1986, p. 106.
3. Hammond, N.G.L. and Walbank, F.W. *A History of Macedonia: 336–167 BC*. Vol. III. Oxford: Clarendon Press, 1988, pp. 156–7.
4. Green, Peter. *Alexander of Macedon, 356–323 BC*. Berkeley: University of California Press, 1991, pp. 19 and 20.
5. Spinage, C.A. *Elephants*. London: T & A.D. Poyser Ltd., 1994, p. 154.
6. Rennie, James [though stated as Anonymous]. *The Elephant as he exists in a wild state, and as he has been made subservient, in peace and in war, to the purposes of man*. New York: Harper & Brothers, 1848, p. 213.

12. CAVALRY KILLERS

1. Bevan, Edwyn Robert. *The House of Seleucus*. Two volumes in one. Chicago: Ares, 1985, p. 48.
2. Gaebel, Robert E. *Cavalry Operations in the Ancient Greek World*. Norman: University of Oklahoma Press, 2002, p. 219.
3. Tarn, W.W. "The Heritage of Alexander." In *The Cambridge Ancient History, Vol. VI Macedon, 401–301 B.C.* New York: Macmillan, 1933, p. 484.
4. Plutarch. *Plutarch's Lives of Illustrious Men*. Vol. III. New York: John W. Lovell Co., ca. 1880, pp. 208 and 209.
5. Billows, Richard A. *Antigonos the One-Eyed and the Creation of the Hellenistic State*. Berkeley: University of California Press, 1990, p. 127.
6. Scullard, H.H. *The Elephant in the Greek and Roman World*. Cambridge: Thames and Hudson, 1974, pp. 80 and 81.

7. Delbruck, Hans. *Warfare in Antiquity*. Vol. I. Lincoln: University of Nebraska, 1990, pp. 240 and 241.
8. Diodorus. *Diodorus of Sicily* in 12 volumes. Cambridge: Harvard University Press, 1957, p. 61.
9. Warry, John. *Warfare in the Classical World*. New York: Barnes and Noble Books, 1993, p. 93.
10. Fernando, Joseph M.P. "Genetics, Ecology, and Conservation of the Asian Elephant." Doctor of Philosophy of Biology dissertation at the University of Oregon, 1998, p. 88.
11. Adcock, F.E. *The Greek and Macedonian Art of War*. Berkeley: University of California Press, 1957, p. 55.
12. Rennie, James. *The Elephant as he exists in a wild state....* New York: Harper & Brothers, 1848, p. 214.
13. Reid, Robert W. *Military History*. "Diabolical in its Simplicity: the Ancient, Durable Caltrop." August, 1998, Vol. 15, n.3, p. 21.
14. Errington, R. Malcolm. *A History of Macedonia*. Berkeley: University of California Press, 1990, p. 141.
15. Grainger, John D. *Seleukos Nikator*. New York: Routledge, 1990, pp. 92 and 93.
16. Appian. "Seleucus and the Foundation of the Seleucid Empire." In *The Hellenistic World from Alexander to the Roman Conquest*. New York: Cambridge University Press, 1994, p. 88.
17. Griffith, G.T. *The Mercenaries of the Hellenistic World*. New York: AMS Press (reprint), 1977, p. 56.
18. Rollin, Charles. *The Ancient History of the Egyptians, Carthaginians, Assyrians, Babylonians, Medes and Persians, Grecians, and Macedonians...in 2 volumes*. Cincinnati: Applegate, Pounsford & Co., 1868, v. 2, p. 40.
19. Parke, H.W. *Greek Mercenary Soldiers*. Chicago: Ares Publishers, 1981, p. 217.
20. Tarn, "Heritage", pp. 499 and 500.
21. Bevan, *House*, p. 295; also Sastri, K.A. Nilakanta ed. *A Comprehensive History of India*. Vol. 2. Bombay: Orient Longmans, 1957, p. 2.
22. Rawlinson, George. *The Sixth Great Oriental Monarchy*. New York: Scribner, Welford & Armstrong, 1873, p. 61.
23. Bhattacharjee, Arun. *History of Ancient India*. New Delhi, India: Sterling Publishers, 1979, p. 172.
24. Tarn, W.W. *Hellenistic Military & Naval Developments*. Chicago: Ares Publishers, 1975, p. 94.
25. Sastri, K.A. Nilakanta ed. *A Comprehensive History of India*. Vol. 2. Bombay: Orient Longmans, 1957, pp. 5, 64.
26. Peddie, John. *The Roman War Machine*. London: Sutton Publishing, 1994, p. 85.
27. Stadter, Philip A. "The Ars Tactica of Arrian: Tradition and Originality." In *Classical Philology*, Vol. 73, n. 2, April 1978, p. 124.

28. Hammond, N.G.L. and Walbank, F.W. *A History of Macedonia: 336–167 BC.* Vol. III. Oxford: Clarendon Press, 1988, p. 178.
29. Grainger, *Seleukos*, p. 118.
30. Bar-Kochva, Bezalel. *The Seleucid Army.* Cambridge: Cambridge University Press, 1976, p. 76.
31. Albright, William F. *From the Stone Age to Christianity.* 2nd ed. Garden City, NY: Doubleday, 1957, p. 339.
32. Plutarch, *Lives*, p. 228.
33. Kincaid, C.A. *Successors of Alexander the Great.* Chicago: Ares Publishers, 1980, p. 42.
34. Billows, *Antigonus*, pp. 178, 182.
35. Billows, *Antigonus*, pp. 184 and 185.
36. Diodorus, *Diodorus*, Vol. 12, p. 5.
37. Tarn, *Heritage*, p. 504.
38. Gaebel, *Cavalry*, p. 226.
39. Fuller, J.F.C. *Armament and History.* New York: Charles Scribner's Sons, 1945, p. 32.
40. Ducrey, Pierre. *Warfare in Ancient Greece.* New York: Schocken Books, 1986, p. 103.
41. Scullard, *Elephant*, p. 98.

13. THE ELEPHANT INDUSTRY

1. Gowers, William. "The African Elephant in Warfare." In *African Affairs*, Vol. 46 issue 182, January 1947, p. 43.
2. Bar-Kochva, Bezalel. *The Seleucid Army.* Cambridge: Cambridge University Press, 1976, p. 79.
3. Eggert, Lori S. "The Evolution and Conservation of the African Forest Elephant." Doctor of Philosophy in Biology dissertation at the University of California in San Diego, 2002, p. 96.
4. Pliny. *Natural History* in ten volumes. Vol. III, Libri VIII–XI. Edited by H. Rackham, 2nd edition. Cambridge: Harvard University Press, 1983, pp. 23–25.
5. Associated Press. "Toledo Celebrates: It's a 275 Pound Boy: Elephant Birth in Captivity Quite Rare." Cincinnati Enquirer, May 3, 2003. Found on Internet page [http://www.enquirer.com/editions/2003/ 05/03/loc_oh-elephantbirth03.html] on August 16, 2003.
6. Sekunda, Nick. *Seleucid and Ptolemaic Reformed Armies 168-145 BC*, in two volumes. Stockport, England: Montvert Publications, 1994, p. 27.
7. Fernando, Joseph M.P. "Genetics, Ecology, and Conservation of the Asian Elephant." Doctor of Philosophy of Biology dissertation at the University of Oregon, 1998, p. 1.
8. Hammond, N.G.L. and Walbank, F.W. *A History of Macedonia: 336–167 BC.* Vol. III. Oxford: Clarendon Press, 1988, p. 205.

9. Bevan, Edwyn Robert. *The House of Seleucus.* Two volumes in one, reprint of 1902 edition. Chicago: Ares, 1985, p. 215.
10. Shipley, Graham. *The Greek World After Alexander: 323-30 BC.* New York: Routledge, 2000, p. 288.
11. Grainger, *Seleukos*, pp. 166.
12. Lobban, R.A. and De Liedekerke, Valerie. "Elephants in Ancient Egypt and Nubia." In *Anthrozoos*, Vol. 13, n. 4, 2000, pp. 233 and 234.
13. Crowfoot, J.W. "Some Red Sea Ports in the Anglo-Egyptian Sudan." In *Geographical Journal*, Vol. 37, n. 5, May 1911, p. 525.
14. Phillips, Jacke. "Punt and Aksum: Egypt and the Horn of Africa." In *The Journal of African History*, Vol. 38, n. 3, 1997, p. 447.
15. Rollin, Charles. *The Ancient History of the Egyptians, Carthaginians, Assyrians, Babylonians, Medes and Persians, Grecians, and Macedonians... in two volumes.* Cincinnati: Applegate, Pounsford & Co., 1868, Vol. 2, p. 54.
16. Casson, Lionel. "Ptolemy II and the Hunting of African Elephants." In *Transactions of the American Philological Association*, Vol. 123, 1993, p. 259.
17. De Beer, Gavin. *Hannibal: Challenging Rome's Supremacy.* New York: Viking Press, 1969, p. 102.
18. Jennison, George. *Animals for Show and Pleasure in Ancient Rome.* Manchester, England: Manchester University Press, 1937, p. 37.
19. Welsby, Derek A. *The Kingdom of Kush: the Napatan and Meroitic Empires.* London: British Museum Press, 1996, p. 43.
20. Welsby, *Kingdom*, pp. 43 and 44.
21. Welsby, *Kingdom*, p. 146.
22. Hintze, Fritz. "The Meroitic Period." In *Africa in Antiquity: The Arts of Ancient Nubia and the Sudan.* New York: The Brooklyn Museum, 1978, p. 89.
23. Blundell, H. Weld. "Exploration in the Abai Basin, Abyssinia." In *Geographical Journal*, Vol. 27, n. 6, June 1906, p. 542.
24. Casson, "Ptolemy", p. 252.
25. Bevan, Edwyn. *The House of Ptolemy: A History of Egypt under the Ptolemaic Dynasty.* Chicago: Ares Publishers, 1985. Reprint of 1927, 1968 edition, p. 176.
26. Rennie, James [though stated as Anonymous]. *The Elephant as he exists in a wild state, and as he has been made subservient, in peace and in war, to the purposes of man.* New York: Harper & Brothers, 1848, p. 105.
27. Pliny, *Natural*, p. 21.
28. Gudger, E.W. "Bullets and Spear-Heads Embedded in the Tusks of Elephants." In *The Scientific Monthly*, Vol. 35, n. 4, October 1932, pp. 323–327.
29. Rice, E.E. *The Grand Procession of Ptolemy Philadelphus.* New York: Oxford University Press, 1983, pp. 91 and 92.

30. Casson, "Ptolemy", p. 251.
31. Strachan, Mr. "An Account of the Taking and Taming of Elephants in Zeylan [Ceylon/Sri Lanka], by Mr. Strachan, a Physician, Who Lived 17 Years There." In *Philosophical Transactions*, Vol. 23, 1702–1703, p. 1054.
32. Casson, "Ptolemy", p. 253.
33. Pliny, *Natural*, Vol. 3, p. 19.
34. Casson, "Ptolemy", pp. 249 and 250.
35. Casson, "Ptolemy", p. 254.
36. Jennison, George. *Animals for Show and Pleasure in Ancient Rome*. Manchester, England: Manchester University Press, 1937, pp. 38 and 39.
37. Lobban, "Elephants", p. 240.
38. Sekunda, *Seleucid*, Vol. 2, p. 77.
39. Scullard, H.H. *The Elephant in the Greek and Roman World*. Aspects of Greek and Roman Life series. Cambridge: Thames and Hudson, 1974, pp. 130 and 131.
40. Kincaid, C.A. *Successors of Alexander the Great: Ptolemy I, Pyrrhus of Epirus, Hiero of Syracuse, Antiochus III*. Chicago: Ares Publishers, 1980, p. 117.
41. Scott, Kenneth. "The Significance of Statues in Precious Metals in Emperor Worship." In *Transactions and Proceedings of the American Philological Association*, Vol. 62, 1931, p. 101.

14. UNMITIGATED GAULS

1. Jouguet, Pierre. *Macedonian Imperialism and the Hellenization of the East*. New York: Knopf, 1928, p. 179.
2. Sekunda, Nick. *Seleucid and Ptolemaic Reformed Armies 168–145 BC*, in two volumes. Stockport, England: Montvert Publications, 1994, p. 19.
3. Abbott, Jacob. *Pyrrhus*. Makers of History series, Illustrated edition. New York: A.L. Fowle, 1906, p. 204.
4. Swain, Joseph Ward. *The Ancient World*, Vol. 2, The World Empires: Alexander and the Romans after 334 B.C. New York: Harper & Row, 1950, p. 42.
5. Tarn, W.W. "The First Syrian War." In *The Journal of Hellenic Studies*, Vol. 46 part 2, 1926, pp. 155 and 156.
6. Grainger, John D. *Seleukos Nikator: Constructing a Hellenistic Kingdom*. New York: Routledge, 1990, p. 213.
7. Scullard, H.H. *The Elephant in the Greek and Roman World*. Aspects of Greek and Roman Life series. Cambridge: Thames and Hudson, 1974, p. 121.
8. Bevan, Edwyn Robert. *The House of Seleucus*. Two volumes in one, reprint of 1902 edition. Chicago: Ares, 1985, p. 143.

9. Reinach, Sal. "Elephant foulant aux pieds un Galata." In *Bulletin du Corre-spondance Hellenique*. Vol. 9, 1885, p. 485.

10. Pease, Arthur Stanley. "Notes on Some Uses of Bells among the Greeks and Romans." In *Harvard Studies in Classical Philology*. Vol. 15, 1904, p. 40.

11. Saxtorph, Niels M. *Warriors and Weapons of Early Times in Color*. New York: Macmillan, 1972, p. 160.

12. Pease, "Notes", pp. 41 and 42.

13. Rostovtzeff, M. *The Social and Economic History of the Hellenistic World*. Vol. I. London: Oxford, 1953, p. 433 Plate LIII.

15. THE ELEPHANT OF SURPRISE

1. Scullard, H.H. *The Elephant in the Greek and Roman World*. Aspects of Greek and Roman Life series. Cambridge: Thames and Hudson, 1974, p. 102. From Macaulay's *Lays of Ancient Rome*.

2. Alexander, Shana. *The Astonishing Elephant*. New York: Random House, 2000, p. 86.

3. Kincaid, C.A. *Successors of Alexander the Great: Ptolemy I, Pyrrhus of Epirus, Hiero of Syracuse, Antiochus III*. Chicago: Ares Publishers, 1980, p. 56.

4. Plutarch. *Plutarch's Lives of Illustrious Men*. Translator: Dryden, John. Vol. II. New York: John W. Lovell Co., ca. 1880, p. 9.

5. Rollin, Charles. *The Ancient History of the Egyptians, Carthaginians, Assyrians, Babylonians, Medes and Persians, Grecians, and Macedonians... in two volumes*. Cincinnati: Applegate, Pounsford & Co., 1868, Vol. 2, p. 22.

6. Roberts, Timothy R. *Ancient Rome*. Chronicles of the Roman World series. New York: Friedman/Fairfax Publishers, 2000, p. 55.

7. Garoufalias, Petros. *Pyrrhus: King of Epirus*. London: Stacey International, 1979, pp. 23–26.

8. Kincaid, *Successors*, p. 64.

9. Hammond, N.G.L. and Walbank, F.W. *A History of Macedonia: 336–167 BC*. Vol. III. Oxford: Clarendon Press, 1988, p. 246.

10. Pease, Arthur Stanley. "Notes on Some Uses of Bells among the Greeks and Romans." In *Harvard Studies in Classical Philology*. Volume 15, 1904, pp. 39 and 40.

11. Fernando, Joseph M.P. "Genetics, Ecology, and Conservation of the Asian Elephant." Doctor of Philosophy of Biology dissertation at the University of Oregon, 1998, p. 41.

12. Eltringham, Dr. S.K. consultant. *The Illustrated Encyclopedia of Elephants: From Their Origins and Evolution to Their Ceremonial and Working Relationship with Man*. New York: Crescent Books, 1991, p. 122.

13. Casson, Lionel. "Ptolemy II and the Hunting of African Elephants." In *Transactions of the American Philological Association*, Vol. 123, 1993, p. 253.

14. Casson, Lionel. *The Ancient Mariners: Seafarers and Sea Fighters of the Mediterranean in Ancient Times*. Minerva Press, 1959, p. 215.

15. Glover, R.F. "The Tactical Handling of the Elephant." In Greece & Rome, Vol. 17, n. 49, January 1948, p. 10.

16. Strachan, Mr. "An Account of the Taking and Taming of Elephants in Zeylan [Ceylon/Sri Lanka], by Mr. Strachan, a Physician, Who Lived 17 Years There." In *Philosophical Transactions*, Vol. 23, 1702–1703, p. 1054.

17. Warry, John. *Warfare in the Classical World*. New York: Barnes and Noble Books, 1993, pp. 103 and 104.

18. Spinage, C.A. *Elephants*. London: T & A.D. Poyser Ltd., 1994, p. 283.

19. Groning, Karl and Saller, Martin. *Elephants: A Cultural and Natural History*. Germany: Konemann, 1999, p. 218.

20. Dio [Cassius Dio Cocceianus]. *Dio's Roman History with an English Translation by Earnest Cary, Ph.D. on the Basis of the Version of Herbert Baldwin Foster, Ph.D. in Nine Volumes*. Cambridge, MA: Harvard University Press, 1954, Vol. I., pp. 325–327.

21. Florus, Lucius Annaeus. *Epitome of Roman History*. New York: G.P. Putnam's Sons, 1929, p. 61.

22. Delbruck, Hans. *Warfare in Antiquity*. History of the Art of War series. Vol. I. Translated by Walter J. Renfroe, Jr. Lincoln: University of Nebraska, 1990, original 1920, p. 563.

23. Morris, William O'Connor. *Hannibal: Soldier, Statesman, Patriot*. New York: G.P. Putnam's Sons, 1903, p. 7.

24. Dionysius of Halicarnassus. *The Roman Antiquities* in seven volumes. Translator Earnest Cary. Cambridge: Harvard University Press, 1950, p. 391; also Kincaid, p. 73.

25. Adcock, F.E. *The Greek and Macedonian Art of War*. Berkeley: University of California Press, 1957, p. 49.

16. FLAMING PIGS

1. Sillar, F.C. and Meyler, R.M. *Elephants: Ancient and Modern*. New York: Viking, 1968, p. 68.

2. Dio [Cassius Dio Cocceianus]. *Dio's Roman History with an English Translation by Earnest Cary, Ph.D. on the Basis of the Version of Herbert Baldwin Foster, Ph.D. in nine volumes*. Cambridge, MA: Harvard University Press, 1954, Vol. 1, p. 333.

3. Dionysius of Halicarnassus. *The Roman Antiquities* in seven volumes. Translator Earnest Cary. Cambridge: Harvard University Press, 1950, pp. 389–391.

4. Groning, Karl and Saller, Martin. *Elephants: A Cultural and Natural History*. Germany: Konemann, 1999, p. 218.

5. Scullard, H.H. *The Elephant in the Greek and Roman World*. Aspects of Greek and Roman Life series. Cambridge: Thames and Hudson, 1974, pp. 109 and 110.

6. Robinson, Charles Alexander. *Ancient History: From Prehistoric Times to the Death of Justinian*. New York: Macmillan, 1961, p. 459.

7. Heitland, W.E. *The Roman Republic*. Cambridge: Cambridge University Press, 1923, p. 158.

8. Grant, Michael. *From Alexander to Cleopatra: The Hellenistic World*. New York: History Book Club, 2000 reprint of 1982 edition, p. 35.

9. Kincaid, C.A. *Successors of Alexander the Great: Ptolemy I, Pyrrhus of Epirus, Hiero of Syracuse, Antiochus III*. Chicago: Ares Publishers, 1980, p. 80.

10. Havell, H.L. *Republican Rome*. Hertfordshire, England: Oracle Publishing, 1996 reprint of 1914 work, p. 144.

11. Warry, John. *Warfare in the Classical World*. New York: Barnes and Noble Books, 1993, p. 107.

12. Roberts, Timothy R. *Ancient Rome*. Chronicles of the Roman World series. New York: Friedman/Fairfax Publishers, 2000, p. 58.

13. Heitland, *Roman*, p. 159.

14. De Beer, Gavin. *Hannibal: Challenging Rome's Supremacy*. New York: Viking Press, 1969, p. 78.

15. Florus, Lucius Annaeus. *Epitome of Roman History*. New York: G.P. Putnam's Sons, 1929, pp. 61–63.

16. Dionysius, *Roman*, p. 423.

17. Wynter, Philip. "Elephants at War: In Burma, Big Beasts Work for Allied Army." In *Life Magazine*, April 10, 1944, p. 19.

18. Toynbee, J.M.C. *Animals in Roman Life and Art*. Ithaca, NY: Cornell University Press, 1973, p. 34.

19. Groning, *Elephants*, p. 218.

20. Mayor, Adrienne. *Greek Fire, Poison Arrows & Scorpion Bombs: Biological and Chemical Warfare in the Ancient World*. NY: Overlook Duckworth, 2003, p. 200.

21. Garlan, Yvon. "War and Siegecraft." In *The Cambridge Ancient History, second edition*. Vol. VII, Part I, The Hellenistic World. Editor F.W. Walbank. Cambridge: Cambridge University Press, 2001, p. 359.

22. Rowland, Emory. "Military Use of Elephants in the Greek and Roman Period." Internet article located at www.barca.fsnet.co.uk/elephants-war-greek.htm, dated 12/1/86.

23. Fuller, J.F.C. *Armament and History: A Study of the Influence of Armament on History from the Dawn of Classical Warfare to the Second World War*. New York: Charles Scribner's Sons, 1945, p. 33.

24. Toynbee, *Animals*, p. 34.

25. Scullard, *Elephants*, p. 115.
26. Rostovtzeff, M. *The Social and Economic History of the Hellenistic World*. Vol. 1. London: Oxford, 1953, p. 383.
27. Dorey, T.A. and Dudley, D.R. *Rome Against Carthage*. London: Secker & Warburg, 1971, p. xvi.
28. Warry, *Warfare*, p. 107; also Mayor, *Greek Fire*, p. 202.
29. Garoufalias, Petros. *Pyrrhus: King of Epirus*. London: Stacey International, 1979, p. 120.
30. Payne, Robert. *The Roman Triumph*. New York: Abelard-Schuman, 1962, p. 50.
31. Errington, R.M. "Rome and Greece to 205 B.C." In *The Cambridge Ancient History, second edition*, Vol. VIII, "Rome and the Mediterranean to 133 BC." Editor A.E. Astin. New York: Cambridge University Press, 2001, p. 82.
32. Langer, William L. ed. *Western Civilization: Paleolithic Man to the Emergence of European Powers*, Vol. 1, New York: American Heritage, 1968, p. 219.
33. Nardo, Don. *The Battle of Zama*. Battles of the Ancient World series. San Diego: Lucent Books, 1996, p. 30.
34. Crawford, Michael. *The Roman Republic*. Second edition. Cambridge: Harvard University Press, 1993, pp. 45 and 46.

17. CHAOS IN THE STREETS

1. Scullard, H.H. *The Elephant in the Greek and Roman World*. Aspects of Greek and Roman Life series. Cambridge: Thames and Hudson, 1974, p. 100.
2. Errington, R. Malcolm. *A History of Macedonia*. Translator C. Errington. Berkeley: University of California Press, 1990, p. 165.
3. Griffith, G.T. *The Mercenaries of the Hellenistic World*. New York: AMS Press (reprint), 1977, p. 63.
4. Hammond, N.G.L. and Walbank, F.W. *A History of Macedonia: 336–167 BC*. Vol. III. Oxford: Clarendon Press, 1988, p. 264.
5. Glover, R.F. "The Tactical Handling of the Elephant." In *Greece & Rome*, Vol. 17, n. 49, January 1948, p. 7.
6. Montagu, John Drogo. *Battles of the Greek & Roman Worlds*. Mechanicsburg, PA.: Stackpole Books, 2000, p. 116.
7. Rollin, Charles. *The Ancient History of the Egyptians, Carthaginians, Assyrians, Babylonians, Medes and Persians, Grecians, and Macedonians...in two volumes*. Cincinnati: Applegate, Pounsford & Co., 1868, Vol. 2, p. 73.
8. Scullard, *Elephant*, p. 118.
9. Garoufalias, *Pyrrhus*, p. 138.

10. Kincaid, C.A. *Successors of Alexander the Great: Ptolemy I, Pyrrhus of Epirus, Hiero of Syracuse, Antiochus III*. Chicago: Ares Publishers, 1980, p. 101.
11. Montagu, *Battles*, pp. 116 and 117.
12. Gabbert, Janice J. *Antigonus II Gonatas: A Political Biography*. New York: Routledge, 1997, p. 31.
13. Anglim, Simon et al. *Fighting Techniques of the Ancient World: 3000 BC-500 AD: Equipment, Combat Skills, and Tactics*. New York: Thomas Dunne Books, 2002, p. 163.

18. WAR ELEPHANTS OF CARTHAGE

1. Rollin, Charles. *The Ancient History of the Egyptians, Carthaginians, Assyrians, Babylonians, Medes and Persians, Grecians, and Macedonians...in two volumes*. Cincinnati: Applegate, Pounsford & Co., 1868, Vol. 1, pp. 74 and 75.
2. Bath, Tony. *Hannibal's Campaigns*. NY Barnes and Noble, 1992, p. 11.
3. Robinson, Charles Alexander. *Ancient History: From Prehistoric Times to the Death of Justinian*. New York: Macmillan, 1961, pp. 472 and 473.
4. Scullard, H.H. "Carthage and Rome." In *The Cambridge Ancient History, second edition*, Vol. VII part 2. "The Rise of Rome to 220 B.C." Editor F.W. Walbank. Cambridge: Cambridge University Press, 2002, pp. 492–494.
5. Langer, William L. ed. *Western Civilization: Paleolithic Man to the Emergence of European Powers*, Vol. 1, New York: American Heritage, 1968, p. 219.
6. Connolly, Peter. *Hannibal and the Enemies of Rome*. London: Macdonald Educational, 1978, p. 41.
7. Dupuy, Trevor Nevitt. *The Military Life of Hannibal: Father of Strategy*. New York: Franklin Watts, 1969, p. 15.
8. Gowers, William. "The African Elephant in Warfare." In *African Affairs*, Vol. 46 issue 182, January 1947, p. 43.; Jennison, George. *Animals for Show and Pleasure in Ancient Rome*. Manchester, England: Manchester University Press, 1937, pp. 197 and 198.
9. Wise, Terence and Hook, Richard. *Armies of the Carthaginian Wars 265–146 BC*. Men-at-Arms series. London: Osprey, 1993, p. 12.
10. Baker, G.P. *Hannibal*. NY: Dodd, Mead, 1929, p. 29.
11. Connolly, *Hannibal*, p. 45.
12. Wise, Terence and Hook, Richard. *Armies of the Carthaginian Wars 265-146 BC*. Men-at-Arms series. London: Osprey, 1993, p. 12.
13. Scullard, H.H. *The Elephant in the Greek and Roman World*. Aspects of Greek and Roman Life series. Cambridge: Thames and Hudson, 1974, p. 149.

14. Kincaid, C.A. *Successors of Alexander the Great: Ptolemy I, Pyrrhus of Epirus, Hiero of Syracuse, Antiochus III*. Chicago: Ares Publishers, 1980, p. 117.

15. Snowden, Frank M. Jr. "The Negro in Classical Italy." In *The American Journal of Philology*. Vol. 68, n. 3, 1947, p. 284.

16. Gowers, William. "The African Elephant in Warfare." In *African Affairs*, Vol. 46 issue 182, January 1947, p. 43.

17. May, Elmer C. et al. *Ancient and Medieval Warfare*. Wayne, NJ.:Avery Publishing, 1984, p. 46.

18. Caven, Brian. *The Punic Wars*. NY: Barnes and Noble Books, 1992, p. 4.

19. Scullard, "Carthage", p. 547.

20. Scullard, *Elephant*, p. 149.

21. Heitland, W.E. *The Roman Republic*. Cambridge: Cambridge University Press, 1923, p. 198.

22. Baker, *Hannibal*, p. 42.

23. Havell, H.L. *Republican Rome*. Hertfordshire, England: Oracle Publishing, 1996, p. 172.

24. Polybius. *The Rise of the Roman Empire*. Translator Ian Scott-Kilvert. New York: Penguin, 1979, p. 74.

25. Morris, William O'Connor. *Hannibal: Soldier, Statesman, Patriot*. New York: G.P. Putnam's Sons, 1903, pp. 16 and 17.

26. Soren, David et al. *Carthage: Uncovering the Mysteries and Splendors of Ancient Tunisia*. New York: Simon and Schuster, 1990, p. 104.

27. Morris, *Hannibal*, p. 21.

28. Scullard, H.H. *A History of the Roman World: 753 to 146 BC*. 5th ed. New York: Routledge, 2003, p. 172.

29. Griffith, G.T. *The Mercenaries of the Hellenistic World*. New York: AMS Press (reprint), 1977, p. 214.

30. Soren, *Carthage*, p. 106.

31. Gowers, "African", p. 45.

32. Polybius, *Rise*, p. 79.

33. Dorey, T.A. and Dudley, D.R. *Rome Against Carthage*. London: Secker & Warburg, 1971, p. 13.

34. Diodorus. *Diodorus of Sicily* in 12 volumes. Translator Francis R. Walton. Cambridge: Harvard University Press, 1957, Vol. 11, p. 109.

35. Diodorus, Vol. 9, p. 111.

36. Goldsworthy, Adrian. *The Punic Wars*. London: Cassell, 2000, p. 90.

19. PROUD MAHOUTS

1. Charles-Picard, Gilbert and Colette. *Daily Life in Carthage at the Time of Hannibal*. New York: Macmillan, 1966, pp. 200 and 201.

2. Heitland, W.E. *The Roman Republic*. Vols. 1 and 2. Cambridge: Cambridge University Press, 1923, p. 199.

3. Caven, Brian. *The Punic Wars*. NY: Barnes and Noble Books, 1992, p. 45.

4. Polybius. *The Rise of the Roman Empire*. Translator Ian Scott-Kilvert. New York: Penguin, 1979, pp. 85 and 86.

5. Delbruck, Hans. *Warfare in Antiquity*. History of the Art of War series. Vol. I. Translated by Walter J. Renfroe, Jr. Lincoln: University of Nebraska, 1990, p. 305.

6. Griffith, G.T. *The Mercenaries of the Hellenistic World*. New York: AMS Press, 1977, p. 215.

7. Scullard, H.H. *The Elephant in the Greek and Roman World*. Aspects of Greek and Roman Life series. Cambridge: Thames and Hudson, 1974, p. 152.

8. Scullard, H.H. *A History of the Roman World: 753 to 146 BC*. Fifth edition. New York: Routledge, 2003, p. 174.

9. Dio [Cassius Dio Cocceianus]. *Dio's Roman History with an English Translation by Earnest Cary, Ph.D. on the Basis of the Version of Herbert Baldwin Foster, Ph.D. in nine volumes*. Cambridge, MA: Harvard University Press, 1954, Vol. I., p. 439.

10. West, Robert Francis. *Animal Suffering in Roman Literature*. Master of Arts Thesis for the University of Calgary in Alberta, Canada, in February 1997, p. 3.

11. Shelton, Jo-Ann. "The Identification of Elephants with Enemies: Why Elephants Were Abused in Ancient Rome." Fifteen page Internet essay at cla.calpoly.edu/~jlynch/Elephants.htm cited June 18, 2003, p. 4.

12. West, Robert Francis. *Animal Suffering in Roman Literature*. Master of Arts Thesis for the University of Calgary in Alberta, Canada, in February 1997, p. 3.

20. CRUELTY AND INHUMANITY

1. De Beer, Gavin. *Hannibal: Challenging Rome's Supremacy*. New York: Viking Press, 1969, p. 88.

2. Gabriel, Richard A. and Metz, Karen S. *From Sumer to Rome: The Military Capabilities of Ancient Armies*. New York: Greenwood Press, 1991, p. 45.

3. Scullard, H.H. *A History of the Roman World: 753 to 146 BC*. Fifth edition. New York: Routledge, 2003, p. 184.

4. Heitland, W.E. *The Roman Republic*. Vols. 1 and 2. Cambridge: Cambridge University Press, 1923, p. 216.

5. Griffith, G.T. *The Mercenaries of the Hellenistic World*. New York: AMS Press (reprint), 1977, pp. 220 and 221.

6. Church, Alfred J. *The Story of Carthage*. New York: G.P. Putnam's Sons, 1891, p. 171.

7. Warmington, B.H. *Carthage*. Baltimore: Penguin, 1964, p. 202.

8. Warry, John. *Warfare in the Classical World*. New York: Barnes and Noble Books, 1993, p. 115.

9. Dodge, Theodore Ayrault. *Hannibal*. New York: Da Capo Press, 1995, p. 134.

10. Lancel, Serge. *Hannibal*. Translator Antonia Nevill. Malden, MA: Blackwell, 1998, p. 17.

11. Scullard, H.H. "Carthage and Rome." In *The Cambridge Ancient History, second edition*, Vol. VII, part 2. "The Rise of Rome to 220 B.C." Editor F.W. Walbank. Cambridge: Cambridge University Press, 2002 reprint of 1989 work, p. 567.

12. Baker, G.P. *Hannibal*. NY: Dodd, Mead, 1929, pp. 65 and 66.

13. Scullard, "Carthage", p. 568.

14. Bradford, Ernle. *Hannibal*. New York: Dorset Press, 1991, p. 13.

15. Tarn, W.W. *Hellenistic Military & Naval Developments*. Chicago: Ares Publishers, 1975, p. 98.

21. THE LION'S BROOD

1. Dorey, T.A. and Dudley, D.R. *Rome Against Carthage*. London: Secker & Warburg, 1971, p. 31.

2. Hallward, B.L. "Hannibal's Invasion of Italy." In *The Cambridge Ancient History, Vol. VIII Rome and Meditterranean 218–133 B.C*. Bury, J.B. ed. New York: Macmillan, 1933, p. 27.

3. Prevas, John. *Hannibal Crosses the Alps: The Enigma Re-Examined*. Rockville Centre, NY: Sarpedon, 1998, p. 35.

4. Scullard, H.H. "The Carthaginians in Spain." In *The Cambridge Ancient History, second edition*, Vol. VIII, "Rome and the Mediterranean to 133 BC." Editor A.E. Astin. New York: Cambridge University Press, 2001, p. 22.

5. Healy, Mark. *Cannae 216 BC: Hannibal Smashes Rome's Army*. Campaign Series. London: Osprey, 1994, p. 7.

6. Livy. *The War with Hannibal: Books XXI-XXX of the History of Rome from Its Foundation*. Translated by Aubrey de Selincourt; editor Betty Radice. New York: Penguin, 1965, p. 23.

7. Hallward, B.L. "Scipio and Victory." In *The Cambridge Ancient History, Vol. VIII Rome and Meditterranean 218–133 B.C*. Bury, J.B. ed. New York: Macmillan, 1933, p. 91.

8. Lancel, *Hannibal*, p. 9.

9. Lancel, *Hannibal*, p. 38.

10. Dupuy, Trevor Nevitt. *The Military Life of Hannibal: Father of Strategy*. New York: Franklin Watts, 1969, p. 12.

11. Anglim, Simon et al. *Fighting Techniques of the Ancient World: 3000 BC-500 AD: Equipment, Combat Skills, and Tactics*. New York: Thomas Dunne Books, 2002, p. 163.

12. Durschmied, Erik. *From Armageddon to the Fall of Rome: How the Myth Makers Changed the World*. London: Hodder & Stoughton, 2002, p. 168.

13. Livy, *War*, p. 25.
14. Lancel, *Hannibal*, p. 43.
15. May, Elmer C. et al. *Ancient and Medieval Warfare*. Wayne, NJ.: Avery Publishing, 1984, p. 52.
16. Livy, *War*, p. 26.
17. Polybius. *The Rise of the Roman Empire*. Translator Ian Scott-Kilvert. New York: Penguin, 1979, p. 191.

22. DANGEROUS WATERS

1. Creasy, Edward S. *Fifteen Decisive Battles of the World*. New York: Heritage Press, 1969, p. 50.
2. Diodorus. *Diodorus of Sicily* in 12 volumes. Translator Francis R. Walton. Cambridge: Harvard University Press, 1957, Vol. 11, p. 181.
3. Payne, Robert. *Ancient Rome*. New York: IBooks, 2001, p. 81.
4. Roberts, Timothy R. *Ancient Rome*. Chronicles of the Roman World series. New York: Friedman/Fairfax Publishers, 2000, p. 72.
5. Hallward, B.L. "Hannibal's Invasion of Italy." In *The Cambridge Ancient History, Vol. VIII Rome and Meditterranean 218–133 B.C.* Bury, J.B. ed. New York: Macmillan, 1933, p. 34.
6. Scullard, H.H. *A History of the Roman World: 753 to 146 BC*. Fifth edition. New York: Routledge, 2003, p. 204.
7. Rostovtzeff, M. *The Social and Economic History of the Hellenistic World*. Vol. 1. London: Oxford, 1953, p. 383.
8. Curchin, Leonard A. *Roman Spain: Conquest and Assimilation*. New York: Routledge, 1991, p. 25.
9. Healy, Mark. *Cannae 216 BC: Hannibal Smashes Rome's Army*. Campaign Series. London: Osprey, 1994, p. 12.
10. Ramsay, William Mitchell. "Geography and History in a Phyrgo-Pisidian Glen." In *Geographical Journal*, Vol. 41, n. 4, April 1923, p. 288 ff.
11. Dodge, Theodore Ayrault. *Hannibal: A History of the Art of War among the Carthaginians and Romans down to the Battle of Pydna, 168 B.C., with a Detailed Account of the Second Punic War*. New York: Da Capo Press, 1995, p. 199.
12. Williams, Heathcote. *Sacred Elephant*. New York: Harmony Books, 1989, pp. 84 and 85.
13. Alexander, Shana. *The Astonishing Elephant*. New York: Random House, 2000, p. 90.
14. Hallward, "Hannibal's", p. 37.
15. Scullard, H.H. *The Elephant in the Greek and Roman World*. Aspects of Greek and Roman Life series. Cambridge: Thames and Hudson, 1974, p. 152.
16. Dodge, *Hannibal*, p. 190.

17. Polybius. *The Rise of the Roman Empire*. Translator Ian Scott-Kilvert. New York: Penguin, 1979, p. 219.
18. Anglim, Simon et al. *Fighting Techniques of the Ancient World: 3000 BC-500 AD: Equipment, Combat Skills, and Tactics*. New York: Thomas Dunne Books, 2002, p. 125.
19. O'Bryhim, S. "Hannibal's Elephants and the Crossing of the Rhone." In *The Classical Quarterly, new series*. Vol. 41, n. 1, 1991, p. 122.
20. O'Bryhim, "Hannibal's", p. 124.
21. Polybius, *Rise*, p. 219.
22. Cottrell, Leonard. *Hannibal: Enemy of Rome*. New York: Da Capo Press, 1992, p. 46.

23. TREACHEROUS PATHS

1. Healy, Mark. *Cannae 216 BC: Hannibal Smashes Rome's Army*. Campaign Series. London: Osprey, 1994, p. 15.
2. Dodge, Theodore Ayrault. *Hannibal: A History of the Art of War among the Carthaginians and Romans down to the Battle of Pydna, 168 B.C., with a Detailed Account of the Second Punic War*. New York: Da Capo Press, 1995 edition of 1891 work, p. 229.
3. Hoyte, John. *Trunk Road for Hannibal: With an Elephant over the Alps*. London: Geoffrey Bles, 1960, p. 97, 168.
4. Groning, Karl and Saller, Martin. *Elephants: A Cultural and Natural History*. Germany: Konemann, 1999, p. 222.
5. Hoyte, *Trunk*, pp. 96 and 97.
6. Zeuner, Wolfgang. "Hot on the Heels of Hannibal." In *Geographical Magazine*, Vol. 62, n.10, Oct. 1990, p. 23.
7. Kruse, Gosta. *Trunk Call*. London: Elek Books, 1962, pp. 114–117.
8. Dodge, *Hannibal*, p. 242.
9. De Beer, Gavin. *Hannibal: Challenging Rome's Supremacy*. New York: Viking Press, 1969, p. 167.
10. Warry, John. *Warfare in the Classical World*. New York: Barnes and Noble Books, 1993, p. 117; also Dodge, *Hannibal*, p. 230.
11. Polybius. *The Rise of the Roman Empire*. Translator Ian Scott-Kilvert. New York: Penguin, 1979, p. 224.
12. Goldsworthy, Adrian. *The Punic Wars*. London: Cassell, 2000, p. 168.
13. Prevas, John. *Hannibal Crosses the Alps: The Enigma Re-Examined*. Rockville Centre, NY: Sarpedon, 1998, pp. 129–30.
14. Hoyte, *Trunk*, p. 183.
15. Hallward, B.L. "Hannibal's Invasion of Italy." In *The Cambridge Ancient History, Vol. VIII Rome and Mediterranean 218–133 B.C.* Bury, J.B. ed. New York: Macmillan, 1933, p. 38.

16. Livy. *The War with Hannibal: Books XXI-XXX of the History of Rome from Its Foundation*. Translated by Aubrey de Selincourt; editor Betty Radice. New York: Penguin, 1965, p. 62.

17. Allen, Tom. "Through the Alps to the Gates of Rome." In *Greece and Rome: Builders of Our World*. Washington, D.C.: National Geographic Society, 1977, pp. 317 and 318.

18. Hallward, "Hannibal's", p. 38.

19. Gabriel, Richard A. *Great Captains of Antiquity*. Contributions in Military Studies series no. 204. Westport, CT: Greenwood Press, 2001, p. 130.

20. Polybius, *Rise*, p. 228.

21. Florus, Lucius Annaeus. *Epitome of Roman History*. New York: G.P. Putnam's Sons, 1929, p. 97.

24. THE BEST LAID PLANS

1. Dio [Cassius Dio Cocceianus]. *Dio's Roman History with an English Translation by Earnest Cary, Ph.D. on the Basis of the Version of Herbert Baldwin Foster, Ph.D. in Nine Volumes*. Cambridge, MA: Harvard University Press, 1954, Vol. II, p. 97.

2. Montagu, John Drogo. *Battles of the Greek & Roman Worlds*. Mechanicsburg, PA.: Stackpole Books, 2000, p. 178.

3. Dodge, Theodore Ayrault. *Hannibal: A History of the Art of War among the Carthaginians and Romans down to the Battle of Pydna, 168 B.C., with a Detailed Account of the Second Punic War*. New York: Da Capo Press, 1995 edition of 1891 work, p. 92.

4. Robinson, Charles Alexander. *Ancient History: From Prehistoric Times to the Death of Justinian*. New York: Macmillan, 1961, p. 480.

5. Polybius. *The Rise of the Roman Empire*. Translator Ian Scott-Kilvert. New York: Penguin, 1979, p. 242.

6. Gowers, William. "African Elephants and Ancient Authors." In *African Affairs*, Vol. 47 issue 188, July 1948, p. 179; also Day, Michael. "Jumbo Discovery-Africa is home to not one but two species of elephants." In *New Scientist*, Vol. 166, n. 2232, p. 15, April 1, 2000.

7. Peddie, John. *Hannibal's War*. Phoenix Mill, England: Sutton Publishing, 1997, p. 208.

8. Toynbee, Arnold J. *Hannibal's Legacy: The Hannibalic War's Effects on Roman Life*. Two volumes. New York: Oxford University Press, 1965, p. 37.

9. Jackson, Peter. *Endangered Species: Elephants*. Secaucus, NJ: Chartwell Books, 1990, p. 54.; also Scullard, H.H. *The Elephant in the Greek and Roman World*. Aspects of Greek and Roman Life series. Cambridge: Thames and Hudson, 1974, plate XXII h.

10. Toynbee, *Hannibal's*, pp. 34 and 35.

11. Lucretius. *Lucretius on the Nature of Things*. Translator John Selby Watson. London: Bell and Daldy, 1872, p. 239.

12. Gowers, William. "The African Elephant in Warfare." In *African Affairs*, Vol. 46 issue 182, January 1947, p. 43.

13. De Beer, Gavin. *Hannibal: Challenging Rome's Supremacy*. New York: Viking Press, 1969, p. 106.

14. Montross, Lynn. *War Through the Ages*. Revised and enlarged 3rd edition. New York: Harper & Bros., 1960, p. 56.

15. Anglim, Simon et al. *Fighting Techniques of the Ancient World: 3000 BC-500 AD: Equipment, Combat Skills, and Tactics*. New York: Thomas Dunne Books, 2002, pp. 165 and 166.

16. Hallward, B.L. "Hannibal's Invasion of Italy." In *The Cambridge Ancient History, Vol. VIII Rome and Meditterranean 218-133 B.C.* Bury, J.B. ed. New York: Macmillan, 1933, pp. 41 and 42.

17. Hildinger, Erik. *Swords Against the Senate: The Rise of the Roman Army and the Fall of the Republic*. Cambridge, MA.: Da Capo, 2002, p. 22.

18. Dodge, *Hannibal*, p. 270.

19. Allen, Tom. "Through the Alps to the Gates of Rome." In *Greece and Rome: Builders of Our World*. Washington, DC: National Geographic Society, 1977, p. 317.

20. Polybius. *The Rise of the Roman Empire*. Translator Ian Scott-Kilvert. New York: Penguin, 1979, p. 247.

21. Scullard, H.H. "Ennius, Cato, and Surus." In *The Classical Review, new series*. Vol. 3, n. 3–4, December 1953, p. 140.

25. STALEMATE

1. Hallward, B.L. "Hannibal's Invasion of Italy." In *The Cambridge Ancient History, Vol. VIII Rome and Meditterranean 218–133 B.C.* Bury, J.B. ed. New York: Macmillan, 1933, p. 45.

2. Delort, Robert. *The Life and Lore of the Elephant*. New York: Harry N. Abrams Publishers, 1992, p. 85.

3. Pliny. *Natural History* in 10 volumes. Vol. III, Libri VIII–XI. Edited by H. Rackham, 2nd edition. Cambridge: Harvard University Press, 1983, p. 11.

4. Scullard, H.H. *The Elephant in the Greek and Roman World*. Aspects of Greek and Roman Life series. Cambridge: Thames and Hudson, 1974, p. 175.

5. Armstrong, Donald. *The Reluctant Warriors*. New York: Thomas Y. Crowell, 1966, p. 40.

6. Masson, Georgina. *A Concise History of Republican Rome*. London: Thames and Hudson, 1973, p. 56.

7. Diodorus. *Diodorus of Sicily* in 12 volumes. Translator Francis R. Walton. Cambridge: Harvard University Press, 1957, Vol. 11, p. 171.

8. Salmon, E.T. "The Strategy of the Second Punic War." In *Greece & Rome*, second series, Vol. 7, n. 2, October 1960, p. 137.

9. Nardo, Don. *The Battle of Zama*. Battles of the Ancient World series. San Diego: Lucent Books, 1996, p. 55.

10. Montgomery, Viscount (Field-Marshal Montgomery of Alamein). *A History of Warfare*. Cleveland: World Publishing, 1968, pp. 91 and 92.

11. Nepos, Cornelius. *Lives of Famous Men (de Viris Illustribus)*. Translator Gareth Schmeling. Lawrence, KS: Coronado Press, 1971, p. 119. [on Hannibal]

12. Vanoyeke, V. "Les elephants d'Hannibal contre les legions romaines." In *Historia*, Vol. 578, February 1995, p. 60.

13. Gowers, William. "The African Elephant in Warfare." In *African Affairs*, Vol. 46 issue 182, January 1947, p. 46.

14. Montagu, John Drogo. *Battles of the Greek & Roman Worlds*. Mechanicsburg, PA: Stackpole Books, 2000, p. 186.

15. Church, Alfred J. *The Story of Carthage*. New York: G.P. Putnam's Sons, 1891, p. 233.

16. Heitland, W.E. *The Roman Republic*. Cambridge: Cambridge University Press, 1923, p. 288.

17. Peddie, John. *Hannibal's War*. Phoenix Mill, England: Sutton Publishing, 1997, p. 158.

18. Plutarch. *Plutarch's Lives of Illustrious Men*. Translator: Dryden, John. In three volumes. New York: John W. Lovell Co., ca. 1880, Vol. 1, p. 471.

19. Plutarch, *Plutarch's*, Vol. 1, pp. 474 and 476.

20. Plutarch, *Plutarch's*, Vol. 1, p. 493.

21. Scullard, *Elephant*, p. 164.

22. Peddie, *Hannibal's*, p. 174.

23. Plutarch, *Plutarch's*, Vol. 1, pp. 496.

24. Gabriel, Richard A. and Metz, Karen S. *From Sumer to Rome: The Military Capabilities of Ancient Armies*. New York: Greenwood Press, 1991, pp. 45 and 46.

26. HASDRUBAL

1. Diodorus. *Diodorus of Sicily* in 12 volumes. Translator Francis R. Walton. Cambridge: Harvard University Press, 1957, Vol. 11, p. 199.

2. Montagu, John Drogo. *Battles of the Greek & Roman Worlds*. Mechanicsburg, PA: Stackpole Books, 2000, pp. 185–187.

3. Robinson, Charles Alexander. *Ancient History: From Prehistoric Times to the Death of Justinian*. New York: Macmillan, 1961, p. 483.

4. Gabriel, Richard A. *Great Captains of Antiquity*. Contributions in Military Studies series no. 204. Westport, CT: Greenwood Press, 2001, p. 151.

5. Hart, B.H. Liddell. *A Greater Than Napoleon: Scipio Africanus*. New York: Biblo and Tannen, 1971, pp. 96 and 97.

6. Polybius. *The Rise of the Roman Empire*. Translator Ian Scott-Kilvert. New York: Penguin, 1979, p. 412-416.

7. Hallward, B.L. "Scipio and Victory." In *The Cambridge Ancient History, Vol. VIII Rome and Meditterranean 218–133 B.C.* Bury, J.B. ed. New York: Macmillan, 1933, p. 87.

8. Delort, Robert. *The Life and Lore of the Elephant*. New York: Harry N. Abrams Publishers, 1992, p. 88.

9. Dio [Cassius Dio Cocceianus]. *Dio's Roman History with an English Translation by Earnest Cary, Ph.D. on the Basis of the Version of Herbert Baldwin Foster, Ph.D. in nine volumes*. Cambridge, MA: Harvard University Press, 1954, p. 211.

10. Gudger, E.W. "Bullets and Spear-Heads Embedded in the Tusks of Elephants." In *The Scientific Monthly*, volume 35 no. 4, October 1932, pp. 324–7.

11. De Beer, Gavin. *Hannibal: Challenging Rome's Supremacy*. New York: Viking Press, 1969, p. 107.

12. May, Elmer C. et al. *Ancient and Medieval Warfare*. Wayne, NJ.: Avery Publishing, 1984, p. 59.

13. Durschmied, Erik. *From Armageddon to the Fall of Rome: How the Myth Makers Changed the World*. London: Hodder & Stoughton, 2002, p. 201.

14. Masson, Georgina. *A Concise History of Republican Rome*. London: Thames and Hudson, 1973, p. 61.

15. Henderson, Bernard W. "The Campaign of the Metaurus." In *The English Historical Review*. Vol. 13, n. 51, July 1898, pp. 429-432

16. Warry, John. *Warfare in the Classical World*. New York: Barnes and Noble Books, 1993, p. 123.

17. Henderson, "Metaurus", p. 421.

18. Henderson, Bernard W. "The Campaign of the Metaurus continued." In *The English Historical Review*, Vol. 13, n. 52, October 1898, p. 626.

19. Montagu, *Battles*, p. 190.

20. Polybius, *Rise*, p. 425.

21. Hoyte, John. *Trunk Road for Hannibal: With an Elephant over the Alps*. London: Geoffrey Bles, 1960, p. 27.

22. Arnold, Thomas. *The Second Punic War*. London: Macmillan, 1886, pp. 329–332.

23. Meiklejohn, K.W. "Roman Strategy and Tactics from 509 to 202 BC" part two. In *Greece & Rome*, Vol. 8, n. 22, October 1938, p. 16.

27. ROME'S GENIUS

1. Meiklejohn, K.W. "Roman Strategy and Tactics from 509 to 202 BC" part two. In *Greece & Rome*, Vol. 8, n. 22, October 1938, p. 16 and 17.

2. Fournie, Daniel A. "Clash of Titans at Zama." In *Military History*, Vol. 16, n. 6, February 2000, p. 29.

3. Jennison, George. *Animals for Show and Pleasure in Ancient Rome*. Manchester, England: Manchester University Press, 1937, p. 196.

4. Montgomery, Viscount (Field-Marshal Montgomery of Alamein). *A History of Warfare*. Cleveland: World Publishing, 1968, p. 93.

5. Herbert, Henry William. *The Captains of the Roman Republic…* New York: Charles Scribner, 1854, p.125.

6. Kagan, Donald. *On the Origins of War and the Preservation of Peace*. New York: Doubleday, 1995, p. 232.

7. Payne, Robert. *Ancient Rome*. New York: IBooks, 2001, p. 83.

8. Wise, Terence and Hook, Richard. *Armies of the Carthaginian Wars 265-146 BC*. Men-at-Arms series. London: Osprey, 1993, p. 14.

9. Hallward, B.L. "Scipio and Victory." In *The Cambridge Ancient History, Vol. VIII Rome and Mediterranean 218-133 B.C.* Bury, J.B. ed. New York: Macmillan, 1933, p. 104.

10. Fournie, "Clash", p. 30.

11. Cottrell, Leonard. *Hannibal: Enemy of Rome*. New York: Da Capo Press, 1992, p. 235.

12. Nardo, Don. *The Battle of Zama*. Battles of the Ancient World series. San Diego: Lucent Books, 1996, p. 66.

13. Roberts, Timothy R. *Ancient Rome*. Chronicles of the Roman World series. New York: Friedman/Fairfax Publishers, 2000, p. 76.

14. Lucretius. *Lucretius on the Nature of Things*. Translator John Selby Watson. London: Bell and Daldy, 1872, p. 240.

15. Morris, William O'Connor. *Hannibal: Soldier, Statesman, Patriot*. New York: G.P. Putnam's Sons, 1903, p. 314.

16. Gabriel, Richard A. *Great Captains of Antiquity*. Contributions in Military Studies series no. 204. Westport: Greenwood Press, 2001, pp. 175 and 176.

17. Warry, John. *Warfare in the Classical World*. New York: Barnes and Noble Books, 1993, p. 124.

18. Polybius. *The Rise of the Roman Empire*. Translator Ian Scott-Kilvert. New York: Penguin, 1979, p. 475.

19. Montagu, John Drogo. *Battles of the Greek & Roman Worlds*. Mechanicsburg, PA: Stackpole Books, 2000, p. 195.

20. Durschmied, Erik. *From Armageddon to the Fall of Rome: How the Myth Makers Changed the World*. London: Hodder & Stoughton, 2002, pp. 206 and 207.

21. Saxtorph, Niels M. *Warriors and Weapons of Early Times in Color*. New York: Macmillan, 1972, p. 160.

22. Hart, B.H. Liddell. *A Greater Than Napoleon: Scipio Africanus*. New York: Biblo and Tannen, 1971, reprint of 1927 work, pp. 178 and 179.

23. Scullard, H.H. *The Elephant in the Greek and Roman World*. Aspects of Greek and Roman Life series. Cambridge: Thames and Hudson, 1974, p. 169.

24. Montagu, *Battles*, p. 195.

25. Delbruck, Hans. *Warfare in Antiquity*. History of the Art of War series. Vol. I. Translated by Walter J. Renfroe, Jr. Lincoln: University of Nebraska, 1990, p. 374.
26. Raven, Susan. *Rome in Africa*. Third edition. New York: Routledge, 1993, p. 44.
27. Dio [Cassius Dio Cocceianus]. *Dio's Roman History with an English Translation by Earnest Cary, Ph.D. on the Basis of the Version of Herbert Baldwin Foster, Ph.D. in nine volumes*. Cambridge, MA: Harvard University Press, 1954, p. 273.
28. Scullard, H.H. *A History of the Roman World: 753 to 146 BC*. Fifth edition. New York: Routledge, 2003, p. 238.
29. Badian, E. *Roman Imperialism in the Late Republic*. Ithaca, NY: Cornell University Press, 1968, p. 11.
30. Blond, Georges. *The Elephants*. Translator Frances Frenaye. NY: Macmillan, 1961, p. 38.
31. Jurmain, Suzanne. *From Trunk to Tail: Elephants Legendary and Real*. New York: Harcourt, Brace, Jovanovich, 1978, p. 52.
32. Hallward, B.L. and Charlesworth, M.P. "The Fall of Carthage." In *The Cambridge Ancient History, Vol. VIII Rome and Meditterranean 218-133 B.C.* Bury, J.B. ed. New York: Macmillan, 1933, p. 484.

28. AFRICA VERSUS ASIA

1. Bevan, Edwyn Robert. *The House of Seleucus*. Two volumes in one, reprint of 1902 edition. Vol. II. Chicago: Ares, 1985, pp. 168–70.
2. Scullard, H.H. *The Elephant in the Greek and Roman World*. Aspects of Greek and Roman Life series. Cambridge: Thames and Hudson, 1974, p. 134, 138.
3. Phillips, Jacke. "Punt and Aksum: Egypt and the Horn of Africa." In *The Journal of African History*, Vol. 38, n. 3, 1997, pp. 445 and 446.
4. Bar-Kochva, Bezalel. *The Seleucid Army: Organization and Tactics in the Great Campaigns*. New York: Cambridge University Press, 1976, p. 119.
5. Bevan, *House*, Vol. 2, pp. 289 and 290.
6. Warry, John. *Warfare in the Classical World*. New York: Barnes and Noble Books, 1993, p. 93, 95.
7. Glover, R.F. "The Tactical Handling of the Elephant." In *Greece & Rome*, Vol. 17, n.49, January 1948, p. 3.
8. Maxwell-Stuart, P.G. "I Maccabees 6:34 Again." In *Vetus Testamentum*, Vol. 25, n. 2, April 1975, p. 231.
9. Anderson, H. "3 Maccabees: A New Translation and Introduction." In *The Old Testament Pseudipigrapha, Vol. 2*. James Charlesworth, editor. Garden City, NY: Doubleday, 1985, p. 523, 525.

10. Ducrey, Pierre. *Warfare in Ancient Greece*. Janet Lloyd, translator. New York: Schocken Books, 1986, p. 106.

11. "Kazakhs soothe fraught elephant nerves with vodka." April 26, 1999, Reuters, on CNN.com.

12. "Drunk Elephants Kill Six People." Reuters, Dec. 17, 2002, on bbcnews.com.

13. Rosenthal, Monroe and Mozeson, Keith. *Wars of the Jews: A Military History from Biblical to Modern Times*. Hippocrene Jewish History series. New York: Hippocrene Books, 1990, p. 87.

14. Cannon, Teresa and Davis, Peter. *Aliya: Stories of the Elephants of Sri Lanka*. Melbourne, Australia: Airavata Press, 1995, p. 95.

15. *Encyclopedia Judaica*. New York: Macmillan, 1971, p. 1348.

16. Brooks, Richard. *Atlas of World Military History*. New York: Barnes and Noble Books, 2000, p. 21.

17. Scullard, *Elephant*, pp. 139 and 140.

18. Scullard, *Elephant*, p. 142.

19. Bevan, *House*, Vol. 2, pp. 318 and 319.

20. Tarn, W.W. *Hellenistic Military & Naval Developments*. Chicago: Ares Publishers, 1975, p. 99.

21. Toynbee, J.M.C. *Animals in Roman Life and Art*. Ithaca, NY: Cornell University Press, 1973, p. 33.

22. Op. cit., Morewood-Dowsett, p. 26.

23. Chamoux, Francois. *Hellenistic Civilization*. Translator Michel Roussel. Malden, MA.: Blackwell Publishing, 2003, p. 288.

24. Musti, Domenico. "Syria and the East." In *The Cambridge Ancient History, second edition*. Vol. VII, part I, The Hellenistic World. Editor F.W. Walbank. Cambridge: Cambridge University Press, 2001, p. 213 note.

25. Bevan, *House*, Vol. 2, p. 23.

26. Langer, William L. ed. *Western Civilization: Paleolithic Man to the Emergence of European Powers*, Vol. 1, New York: American Heritage, 1968, p. 211.

27. Bar-Kochva, Bezalel. *The Seleucid Army: Organization and Tactics in the Great Campaigns*. New York: Cambridge University Press, 1976, p. 154.

28. Grant, Michael. *From Alexander to Cleopatra: The Hellenistic World*. New York: History Book Club, 2000, p. 72.

29. Toynbee, *Animals*, p. 33.

29. DAY OF SLAUGHTER

1. Havell, H.L. *Republican Rome*. Hertfordshire, England: Oracle Publishing, 1996, p. 283.

2. Holleaux, Maurice. "Rome and Macedon: The Romans Against Philip." In *The Cambridge Ancient History, Vol. VIII, Rome and the Mediterranean 218–133 BC*. Cambridge: Cambridge University Press, 1930, pp. 155–158.

3. Gowers, William. "The African Elephant in Warfare." In *African Affairs*, Vol. 46 issue 182, January 1947, p. 45.

4. Delbruck, Hans. *Warfare in Antiquity*. History of the Art of War series. Vol. I. Translated by Walter J. Renfroe, Jr. Lincoln: University of Nebraska, 1990, original 1920, p. 562.

5. Livy. *Livy*.[History of Rome] In 14 volumes. Cambridge, MA: Harvard University Press, 1961, Vol. 9, p. 107.

6. Scullard, H.H. *The Elephant in the Greek and Roman World*. Aspects of Greek and Roman Life series. Cambridge: Thames and Hudson, 1974, p. 179.

7. Plutarch. *Plutarch's Lives of Illustrious Men*. Translator: Dryden, John. In three volumes. New York: John W. Lovell Co., ca. 1880, Vol. 1, p. 574.

8. Holleaux, *Rome*, p. 174.

9. Heitland, W.E. *The Roman Republic*. Vol.2. Cambridge: Cambridge University Press, 1923, pp. 26 and 27.

10. Anglim, Simon et al. *Fighting Techniques of the Ancient World: 3000 BC-500 AD: Equipment, Combat Skills, and Tactics*. New York: Thomas Dunne Books, 2002, p. 49.

11. Hammond, N.G.L. and Walbank, F.W. *A History of Macedonia: 336–167 BC*. Vol. III. Oxford: Clarendon Press, 1988, p. 437.

12. Montagu, John Drogo. *Battles of the Greek & Roman Worlds*. Mechanicsburg, PA.: Stackpole Books, 2000, p. 127.

13. Livy, *Livy*, Vol. 9, p. 361.

14. Pliny. *Natural History* in 10 volumes. Vol. III, Libri VIII-XI. Edited by H. Rackham, 2nd edition. Cambridge: Harvard University Press, 1983, p. 11.

15. Dio [Cassius Dio Cocceianus]. *Dio's Roman History with an English Translation by Earnest Cary, Ph.D. on the Basis of the Version of Herbert Baldwin Foster, Ph.D. in nine volumes*. Cambridge, MA: Harvard University Press, 1954, Vol. 2, p. 307.

16. Livy, *Livy*, Vol. 10, p. 127; also Bevan, Edwyn Robert. *The House of Seleucus*. Two volumes in one, reprint of 1902 edition. Chicago: Ares, 1985, p. 69.

17. Livy, *Livy*, Vol. 10, p. 167.

18. Havell, *Republican*, p. 293.

19. Montagu, *Battles*, p. 129.

20. Havell, *Republican*, p. 294.

21. Frontinus. *Stratagems; Aqueducts of Rome*. Loeb Classical Library series. Translator Charles E. Bennett. Cambridge: Harvard University Press, 1997 reprint of 1925 work, p. 321.

22. Gabriel, Richard A. and Metz, Karen S. *From Sumer to Rome: The Military Capabilities of Ancient Armies*. New York: Greenwood Press, 1991, p. 68.

23. Rattenbury, R.M. "An Ancient Armoured Force." In *The Classical Review*, Vol. 56, n. 3, November 1942, p. 113.

24. Bar-Kochva, Bezalel. *Judas Maccabaeus: The Jewish Struggle Against the Seleucids*. New York: Cambridge University Press, 1989, p. 13.

25. Sekunda, *Seleucid*, p. 28.

26. Livy, *Livy*, Vol. 10, p. 405.

27. Jennison, George. *Animals for Show and Pleasure in Ancient Rome*. Manchester, England: Manchester University Press, 1937, pp. 196 and 197.

28. Dio, *Dio's Roman History*, p. 319.

29. Bar-Kochva, *Seleucid*, p. 171.

30. Kincaid, C.A. *Successors of Alexander the Great: Ptolemy I, Pyrrhus of Epirus, Hiero of Syracuse, Antiochus III*. Chicago: Ares Publishers, 1980, p. 179.

31. Rennie, James [though stated as Anonymous]. *The Elephant Principally Viewed in Relation to Man, a new edition*. London, Charles Knight & Co., 1844, p. 229.

30. WEAPONS OF MASSIVE DESTRUCTION

1. Bar-Kochva, Bezalel. *The Seleucid Army*. New York: Cambridge University Press, 1976, p. 80.

2. Livy. *Livy*.[History of Rome] In 14 volumes. Cambridge, MA: Harvard University Press, 1961, Vol. 9, p. 70.

3. Payne, Robert. *Ancient Rome*. New York: IBooks, 2001, p. 92.

4. Morkholm, Otto. *Antiochus IV of Syria*. Classica et Mediaevalia Dissertations VIII. Norway: Gyldendalske Boghandel, 1966, pp. 26 and 27.

5. Kincaid, C.A. *Successors of Alexander the Great: Ptolemy I, Pyrrhus of Epirus, Hiero of Syracuse, Antiochus III*. Chicago: Ares Publishers, 1980, p. 181.

6. Green, Peter. *Alexander to Actium: The Historical Evolution of the Hellenistic Age*. Berkeley: University of California Press, 1990, p. 422.

7. Havell, H.L. *Republican Rome*. Hertfordshire, England: Oracle Publishing, 1996 reprint of 1914 work, pp. 302 and 303.

8. Benecke, P.V.M. "The Fall of the Macedonian Monarchy" and "Rome and the Hellenistic States." In *The Cambridge Ancient History, Vol. VIII, Rome and the Mediterranean 218–133 BC*. Cambridge: Cambridge University Press, 1930, pp. 255 and 256.

9. Scullard, H.H. *The Elephant in the Greek and Roman World*. Aspects of Greek and Roman Life series. Cambridge: Thames and Hudson, 1974, p. 182.

10. Gowers, William. "The African Elephant in Warfare." In *African Affairs*, Vol. 46 issue 182, January 1947, p. 47; also Scullard, *Elephant*, p. 182.

11. Hammond, N.G.L. and Walbank, F.W. *A History of Macedonia: 336-167 BC.* Vol. III. Oxford: Clarendon Press, 1988, pp. 519-521.

12. Roth, Jonathan P. *The Logistics of the Roman Army at War (264 BC-AD 235).* Vol. 22 in the Columbia Studies in the Classical Tradition series. Boston: Brill, 1999, pp. 61-64.

13. Scullard, *Elephant*, p. 182.

14. Hammond, *History*, p. 541.

15. Dio, Vol. 2, p. 337.

16. Hyland, Ann. *Equus: The Horse in the Roman World.* London: B.T. Batsford Ltd., 1990 (0713462604), p. 108.

17. Hammond, *History*, p. 542.

18. Hammond, *History*, pp. 527 and 528.

19. Wood, J.G. *Sketches and Anecdotes of Animal Life*, second series. London: G. Routledge, 1858, p. 63.

20. Plutarch. *Plutarch's Lives of Illustrious Men.* Translator: Dryden, John. In three volumes. New York: John W. Lovell Co., ca. 1880, Vol. 1, p. 410.

21. Hammond, *History*, p. 540.

22. Rollin, Charles. *The Ancient History of the Egyptians, Carthaginians, Assyrians, Babylonians, Medes and Persians, Grecians, and Macedonians...in two volumes.* Cincinnati: Applegate, Pounsford & Co., 1868, p. 223.

23. Hammond, N.G.L. "The Battle of Pydna." In *The Journal of Hellenic Studies*, Vol. 104, 1984, p. 46.

24. Hammond, *History*, p. 555.

25. Scullard, *Elephant*, p. 184.

26. Webster, Graham. *The Roman Imperial Army of the First and Second Centuries A.D.* London: Adam & Charles Black, 1969, p. 36.

27. Reiter, William. *Aemilius Paullus: Conqueror of Greece.* London: Croom Helm, 1988, p. 138.

28. Langer, William L. ed. *Western Civilization: Paleolithic Man to the Emergence of European Powers*, Volume 1, New York: American Heritage, 1968, p. 223.

29. Scullard, *Elephant*, pp. 184 and 185.

31. GUERRILLA WAR

1. Morkholm, Otto. *Antiochus IV of Syria.* Classica et Mediaevalia Dissertations VIII. Norway: Gyldendalske Boghandel, 1966, p. 35.

2. Sekunda, Nick. *Seleucid and Ptolemaic Reformed Armies 168-145 BC*, in two volumes. Stockport, England: Montvert Publications, 1994, p. 4.

3. Morkholm, *Antiochus*, p. 133.

4. Healy, Mark. *Warriors of the Old Testament: Joshua, King David, Nebuchadnezzar, Judas Maccabeus.* London: Brockhampton Press, 1998, p. 147.

5. Dio [Cassius Dio Cocceianus]. *Dio's Roman History with an English Translation by Earnest Cary, Ph.D. on the Basis of the Version of Herbert Baldwin*

Foster, Ph.D. in nine volumes. Cambridge, MA: Harvard University Press, 1954, p. 361.

6. Bevan, E.R. "Syria and the Jews." In *The Cambridge Ancient History, Vol. VIII, Rome and the Mediterranean 218–133 BC.* Cambridge: Cambridge University Press, 1930, p. 506.

7. Welles, C. Bradford. *Alexander and the Hellenistic World.* Toronto: A.M. Hakkert Co., 1970, p. 125.

8. Healy, *Warriors,* pp. 154–156.

9. Tarn, W.W. *Hellenistic Civilisation,* 2nd ed. London: Edward Arnold, 1930, pp. 186 and 187.

10. Payne, Robert. Ancient Rome. New York: IBooks, 2001, p. 83.

11. Bevan, Edwyn Robert. *The House of Seleucus.* Two volumes in one, reprint of 1902 edition. Chicago: Ares, 1985, p. 186.

12. Cary, M. *A History of the Greek World From 323 to 146 B.C.* New York: Barnes and Noble, 1965, pp. 220 and 221.

13. Green, Peter. *Alexander to Actium: The Historical Evolution of the Hellenistic Age.* Berkeley: University of California Press, 1990, pp. 436 and 437.

14. Ibid., p. 439.

15. Sekunda, *Seleucid,* p. 9–11, 28.

16. Bar-Kochva, Bezalel. *Judas Maccabaeus: The Jewish Struggle Against the Seleucids.* New York: Cambridge University Press, 1989, p. 322.

17. Sillar, F.C. and Meyler, R.M. *Elephants: Ancient and Modern.* New York: Viking, 1968, p. 83.

18. Josephus, Flavius. *The Works of Josephus.* Complete and unabridged, new updated edition. Translated by William Whiston. Peabody, MA: Hendrickson Publishers, 1989, p. 331.

19. Sekunda, *Seleucid,* p. 27.

20. Bevan, *House,* pp. 221 and 222.

21. Sekunda, *Seleucid,* p. 72.

22. Sekunda, *Seleucid,* p. 72.

23. Rennie, James [though stated as Anonymous]. *The Elephant as he exists in a wild state, and as he has been made subservient, in peace and in war, to the purposes of man.* New York: Harper & Brothers, 1848, p. 217.

32. THE RUNNING OF THE BULLS

1. Scullard, H.H. *The Elephant in the Greek and Roman World.* Aspects of Greek and Roman Life series. Cambridge: Thames and Hudson, 1974, p. 190.

2. Schulten, A. "The Romans in Spain." In *The Cambridge Ancient History, Vol. VIII, Rome and the Mediterranean 218–133 BC.* Cambridge: Cambridge University Press, 1930, p. 307.

3. Schulten, "Romans", p. 315.

4. Montagu, John Drogo. *Battles of the Greek & Roman Worlds*. Mechanicsburg, PA.: Stackpole Books, 2000, p. 202.

5. Scullard, *Elephant*, p. 190.

6. Munro, Richard K. "Roman Conquest of Spain." In *Military History*, Vol. 17, n. 2, p. 34, June 2000.

7. Scullard, *Elephant*, p. 191.

8. Gabriel, Richard A. and Metz, Karen S. *From Sumer to Rome: The Military Capabilities of Ancient Armies*. New York: Greenwood Press, 1991, p. 74.

9. Peddie, John. *The Roman War Machine*. London: Sutton Publishing, 1994, p. 87.

10. Munro, "Roman", p. 34.

11. Hallward, B.L. and Charlesworth, M.P. "The Fall of Carthage." In *The Cambridge Ancient History, Vol. VIII Rome and Meditterranean 218–133 B.C.* Bury, J.B. ed. New York: Macmillan, 1933, p. 475.

12. McDonnell, Myles. "The Speech of Numidicus at Gellius, N.A. 1.6." In *The American Journal of Philology*, Vol. 108, n. 1, Spring 1987, p. 86.

13. Curchin, Leonard A. *Roman Spain: Conquest and Assimilation*. New York: Routledge, 1991, p. 36.

14. Sekunda, Nicholas. *Republican Roman Army 200-104BC*. Men-at-Arms series. Oxford: Osprey Publishing, 2002, p. 40.

15. Benedict, Coleman H. "The Romans in Southern Gaul." In *The American Journal of Philology*, Vol. 63, n. 1, 1942, pp. 44 and 45.

16. Toynbee, J.M.C. *Animals in Roman Life and Art*. Ithaca, NY: Cornell University Press, 1973, pp. 49 and 50.

17. Toynbee, *Animals*, p. 37.

18. Jennison, George. *Animals for Show and Pleasure in Ancient Rome*. Manchester, England: Manchester University Press, 1937, p. 143.

19. Sallust. *Sallust*. Translator J.C. Rolfe. Cambridge: Harvard University Press, 1985, p. 141.

20. Robinson, Charles Alexander. *Ancient History: From Prehistoric Times to the Death of Justinian*. New York: Macmillan, 1961, p. 508.

21. Sallust, pp. 218 and 219.

22. Fentress, Elizabeth W.B. *Numidia and the Roman Army: Social, Military and Economic Aspects of the Frontier Zone*. Oxford, England: BAR International Series #53, 1979, p. 61.

23. Montagu, *Battles*, p. 206.

24. Payne, Robert. *The Roman Triumph*. New York: Abelard-Schuman, 1962, p. 93.

25. Heitland, W.E. *The Roman Republic*. Volumes 1 and 2. Cambridge: Cambridge University Press, 1923, Vol. 2, p. 361.

26. Robinson, *Ancient*, pp. 508 and 509.

33. POMPEY'S CIRCUS

1. Pliny. *Natural History* in 10 volumes. Volume III, Libri VIII-XI. Edited by H. Rackham, 2nd edition. Cambridge: Harvard University Press, 1983, p. 49.
2. Montgomery, Viscount (Field-Marshal Montgomery of Alamein). *A History of Warfare*. Cleveland: World Publishing, 1968, p. 100.
3. Payne, Robert. *Ancient Rome*. New York: IBooks, 2001, p. 108.
4. Toynbee, J.M.C. *Animals in Roman Life and Art*. Ithaca, NY: Cornell University Press, 1973, p. 39.
5. Plutarch. *Plutarch's Lives of Illustrious Men*. Translator: Dryden, John. In three volumes. New York: John W. Lovell Co., ca. 1880, Vol. 2, p. 368.
6. West, Robert Francis. *Animal Suffering in Roman Literature*. Master of Arts Thesis for the University of Calgary in Alberta, Canada, in February 1997, p. 3.
7. West, *Animal*, p. 4.
8. Shelton, Jo-Ann. "Elephants, Pompey, and the Reports of Popular Displeasure in 55 BC." In *Veritatis Amicitiaeque Causa: Essays in Honor of Anna Lydia Motto and John R. Clark*. Editors Shannon N. Byrne and Edmund P. Cueva. Wauconda, IL: Bolchazy-Carducci Publishers, 1999, pp. 255 and 256.
9. Shelton, "Elephants", p. 259.

34. THE HERD OF JULIUS CAESAR

1. Payne, Robert. *Ancient Rome*. New York: IBooks, 2001, p. 111.
2. Nearing, Homer, Jr. "Local Caesar Traditions in Britain." In *Speculum*, Vol. 24, n. 2, April 1949, p. 222n.
3. Montgomery, Viscount (Field-Marshal). *A History of Warfare*. Cleveland: World Publishing, 1968, p. 103.
4. Auguet, Roland. *Cruelty and Civilization: The Roman Games*. London: George Allen and Unwin, 1972, p. 110.
5. Polyaenus, quoted in Jimenez, Ramon L. *Caesar Against the Celts*. Edison, NJ: Castle Books, 1996, pp. 156 and 157.
6. Gowers, William. "The African Elephant in Warfare." In *African Affairs*, Vol. 46, issue 182, January 1947, p. 49.
7. Jimenez, Ramon L. *Caesar Against the Celts*. Edison, NJ: Castle Books, 1996, pp. 157 and 158.
8. Gowers, "African", p. 49.
9. Jimenez, *Caesar*, p. 158.
10. Montgomery, *History*, p. 105.
11. Scullard, H.H. *The Elephant in the Greek and Roman World*. Aspects of Greek and Roman Life series. Cambridge: Thames and Hudson, 1974, pp. 194 and 195.

12. Florus, Lucius Annaeus. *Epitome of Roman History*. New York: G.P. Putnam's Sons, 1929, p. 289.
13. Caesar, Julius. *Alexandrian, African and Spanish Wars*. Translated by A.G. Way. Cambridge, MA: Harvard University Press, 1955, p. 187.
14. Gabriel, Richard A. and Metz, Karen S. *From Sumer to Rome: The Military Capabilities of Ancient Armies*. New York: Greenwood Press, 1991, p. 73.
15. Greep, S.J. "Lead Sling-Shot from Windridge Farm, St Albans and the Use of the Sling by the Roman Army in Britain." In *Britannia*. Volume 18, 1987, pp. 192 and 193.
16. Pritchett, W. Kendrick. *The Greek State at War*. Vol. 5. Berkeley: University of California, 1991, pp. 58 and 59.
17. Gabriel, *Sumer*, p. 75.
18. Lucan (Lucanus, Marcus Annaeus). "Pharsalia (aka The Civil War), AD 61-65. Found at www.fullbooks.com/Pharsalia–Civil-War-.html
19. Caesar, *Alexandrian*, p. 259.
20. Gowers, "African", p. 47.
21. Montagu, John Drogo. *Battles of the Greek & Roman Worlds*. Mechanicsburg, PA: Stackpole Books, 2000, p. 235.
22. Spaulding, Oliver Lyman et al. *Warfare: A Study of Military Methods from the Earliest Times*. Washington, D.C.: Infantry Journal Press, 1937, p. 183.
23. Roth, Jonathan P. *The Logistics of the Roman Army at War (264 BC-AD 235)*. Vol. 22 in the Columbia Studies in the Classical Tradition series. Boston: Brill, 1999, p. 106.
24. Caesar, *Alexandrian*, p. 277.
25. Gabriel, Richard A. and Metz, Karen S. *From Sumer to Rome: The Military Capabilities of Ancient Armies*. New York: Greenwood Press, 1991, p. 64.
26. Toynbee, J.M.C. *Animals in Roman Life and Art*. Ithaca, NY: Cornell University Press, 1973, p. 38.
27. Caesar, *Alexandrian*, p. 281.
28. Levick, B.M. "Antiquarian or Revolutionary? Claudius Caesar's Conception of His Principate." In *The American Journal of Philology*, Vol. 99, n. 1, Spring 1978, p. 100.
29. Toynbee, *Animals*, p. 47.
30. Jennison, George. *Animals for Show and Pleasure in Ancient Rome*. Manchester, England: Manchester University Press, 1937, p. 65.

35. ARROGANT EMPERORS

1. Toynbee, J.M.C. *Animals in Roman Life and Art*. Ithaca, NY: Cornell University Press, 1973, p. 42.
2. Gowers, William. "The African Elephant in Warfare." In *African Affairs*, Vol. 46, issue 182, January 1947, p. 48.

3. Spaulding, Oliver Lyman et al. *Warfare: A Study of Military Methods from the Earliest Times.* Washington, D.C.: Infantry Journal Press, 1937, pp. 207 and 208.

4. Hind, J.G.F. "The Invasion of Britain in A.D. 43: An Alternative Strategy for Aulus Plautius." In *Britannia,* Vol. 20, 1989, p. 18.

5. Toynbee, *Animals,* pp. 48 and 49.

6. Jennison, George. *Animals for Show and Pleasure in Ancient Rome.* Manchester, England: Manchester University Press, 1937, p. 65.

7. Mokhtar, G. ed. *Ancient Civilizations of Africa.* General History of Africa, Vol. II. Berkeley: UNESCO, 1990, p. 293.

8. Thorley, J. "The Development of Trade between the Roman Empire and the East under Augustus." In *Greece & Rome,* second series, Vol. 16, n. 2, October 1969, pp. 220 and 221.

9. Clutton-Brock, Juliet. *A Natural History of Domesticated Mammals,* 2nd ed. New York: Cambridge Univ. Press, 1999.

10. Jackson, Peter. *Endangered Species: Elephants.* Secaucus, NJ: Chartwell Books, 1990, p. 85.

11. Barton, I.M. *Africa in the Roman Empire.* Accra, Ghana: Ghana Universities Press, 1972, p. 51.

12. Thorley, Development, p. 220.

13. Law, R.C.C. "The Garamantes and Trans-Saharan Enterprise in Classical Times." In *The Journal of African History.* Vol. 8, n. 2, 1967, p. 196.

14. Gibbon, Edward. *The History of the Decline & Fall of the Roman Empire* in three volumes. New York: Heritage Press, 1946, Vol. I, pp. 83 and 84.

15. Fowden, Garth. "Constantine's Porphyry Column: The Earliest Literary Allusion." In *The Journal of Roman Studies,* Vol. 81, 1991, p. 119.

16. Payne, Robert. *Ancient Rome.* New York: IBooks, 2001, p. 219.

36. SACKCLOTH, ASHES, AND PRAYER

1. Bevan, E.R. "Syria and the Jews." In *The Cambridge Ancient History, Vol. VIII, Rome and the Mediterranean 218-133 BC.* Cambridge: Cambridge University Press, 1930, p. 34.

2. Robinson, Charles Alexander. *Ancient History: From Prehistoric Times to the Death of Justinian.* New York: Macmillan, 1961, p. 599.

3. Gaebel, Robert E. *Cavalry Operations in the Ancient Greek World.* Norman: University of Oklahoma Press, 2002, p. 229 footnote.

4. Mommsen, Theodor. *The Provinces of the Roman Empire from Caesar to Diocletian.* Two volumes. New York: Barnes and Noble, 1996, Vol. 2, p. 79.

5. Dodgeon, Michael H. and Lieu, Samuel N.C. eds. *The Roman Eastern Frontier and the Persian Wars (AD 226-363).* New York: Routledge, 1994, p. 1.

6. Sykes, Percy. A History of Persia in two volumes. 3rd edition. London: Macmillan, 1951, p. 394.
7. Rawlinson, George. The Seventh Great Oriental Monarchy; or the Geography, History and Antiquities of the Sassanian or New Persian Empire. Two volumes. New York: Dodd, Mead & Co., ca. 1875, p. 42.
8. Payne, Robert. Ancient Rome. New York: IBooks, 2001, p. 186.
9. Ibid., pp. 232 and 233.
10. Montgomery, Viscount (Field-Marshal). A History of Warfare. Cleveland: World Publishing, 1968, p. 124.
11. Rawlinson, Seventh, p. 87.
12. Winfrey, Laurie Platt. The Unforgettable Elephant. New York: Walker and Co., 1980, p. 34.
13. Rothman, Margret S. Pond. "The Thematic Organization of the Panel Reliefs on the Arch of Galerius." In American Journal of Archaeology, Vol. 81, n. 4, Autumn 1977, p. 442.
14. Scigliano, Eric. Love, War, and Circuses: the Age-Old Relationship between Elephants and Humans. Boston: Houghton Mifflin, 2002, p. 133.
15. Toynbee, J.M.C. Animals in Roman Life and Art. Ithaca, NY: Cornell University Press, 1973, p. 45.
16. Sandy, Gerald N. Heliodorus. Boston: Twayne, 1982, p. 1.
17. Rattenbury, R.M. "An Ancient Armoured Force." In The Classical Review, Vol. 56, n. 3, November 1942, p. 114.
18. Ghirshman, R. "The Town Which Three Hundred Elephants Rased to the Ground." In The Illustrated London News, Vol. 5816, October 7, 1950, p. 571.
19. Dodgeon, Roman, p. 167.
20. Ferrill, Arthur. The Fall of the Roman Empire: The Military Explanation. Thames & Hudson, 1986.
21. Huart, Clement. Ancient Persia and Iranian Civilization. New York: Knopf, 1927, p. 151.
22. Sykes, Percy. A History of Persia in two volumes. 3rd edition. London: Macmillan, 1951, p. 414.
23. Rawlinson, Seventh, pp. 163 and 164.
24. Dodgeon, Roman, p. 201.
25. Dodgeon, Roman, p. 196.

37. BREACH OF FAITH

1. Rawlinson, George. The Seventh Great Oriental Monarchy; or the Geography, History and Antiquities of the Sassanian or New Persian Empire. Two volumes. New York: Dodd, Mead & Co., ca. 1875, p. 224.
2. Rawlinson, Seventh, pp. 226–228.
3. Dodgeon, Michael H. and Lieu, Samuel N.C. eds. The Roman Eastern Frontier and the Persian Wars (AD 226-363). New York: Routledge, 1994, p. 285.

4. Yarshates, Ehsan, ed. *The Cambridge History of Iran*. Cambridge: Cambridge University Press, 1983. Vol. 3-2, p. 765.

5. Payne, Robert. *Ancient Rome*. New York: IBooks, 2001, p. 259.

6. Chalabian, Antranig. "In 451, the Armenians were the First Christians to Take up Arms in Defending Their Right to Worship." In *Military History*, Vol. 13, n.5, Dec. 1996. Found online at ancienthistory.about. com/library/prm/ blarmeniana.htm in July 2005.

7. Chalabian, "451."

8. Rawlinson, *Seventh*, p. 324.

38. THE YEAR OF THE ELEPHANT

1. Nicolle, David. *Rome's Enemies (5): The Desert Frontier*. Men-at-Arms series. Oxford: Osprey, 2003.

2. Sillar, F.C. and Meyler, R.M. *Elephants: Ancient and Modern*. New York: Viking, 1968, p. 29.

3. Sykes, Percy. *A History of Persia* in two volumes. 3rd edition. London: Macmillan, 1951, p. 509.

4. Kazhdan, Alexander P. ed. et al. *The Oxford Dictionary of Byzantium*. New York: Oxford University Press, 1991. Vol. 1, p. 684.

5. Sykes, *History*, p. 486.

6. Kazhdan, *Oxford*, p. 684.

7. Jurmain, Suzanne. *From Trunk to Tail: Elephants Legendary and Real*. New York: Harcourt, Brace, Jovanovich, 1978, p. 67.

8. Rawlinson, George. *The Seventh Great Oriental Monarchy; or the Geography, History and Antiquities of the Sassanian or New Persian Empire*. Two volumes. New York: Dodd, Mead & Co., ca. 1875, Vol. 2, p. 152.

9. Nafziger, George F. and Walton, Mark W. *Islam at War: A History*. Westport, CT: Praeger, 2003, p. 21.

10. Rawlinson, *Seventh*, pp. 216 and 217.

11. Rawlinson, *Seventh*, p. 214.

12. Rawlinson, *Seventh*, p. 220.

13. Rawlinson, *Seventh*, p. 221.

14. Salam, Zahid-Ivan. *Jihad and the Foreign Policy of the Khilafah State*. London: Khilafah Publications, 2001, online at www.khilafah.com, p. 14.

15. Salam, *Jihad*, p. 14.

16. Sykes, Percy. *A History of Persia* in two volumes. 3rd edition. London: Macmillan, 1951, Vol. 1, p. 495.

39. EARLY AND MEDIEVAL ASIA

1. Sillar, F.C. and Meyler, R.M. *Elephants: Ancient and Modern*. New York: Viking, 1968, p. 11.

2. Jayewardene, Jayantha. "Elephants in Sri Lankan History and Culture." Found on website Art Sri Lanka at www.artsrilanka.org/essays/elephants/ on January 22, 2005.

3. Basham, A.L. *The Wonder that was India.* 3rd revised edition. Vol. I. New York: Taplinger, 1968, pp. 459 and 460.

4. Scigliano, Eric. *Love, War, and Circuses: The Age-Old Relationship between Elephants and Humans.* Boston: Houghton Mifflin, 2002, p. 120.

5. Wales, H.G. Quaritch. *Ancient South-East Asian Warfare.* London: Bernard Quaritch Ltd., 1952, pp. 20 and 21.

6. Dikshitar, V.R. Ramachandra. *War in Ancient India.* Delhi: Motilal Banarsidass, 1987, pp. 171 and 172.

7. Bhattacharjee, Arun. *History of Ancient India.* New Delhi, India: Sterling Publishers, 1979, pp. 325 and 326.

8. Basham, *Wonder,* p. 130.

9. Singh, Sarva Daman. *Ancient Indian Warfare with Special Reference to the Vedic Period.* Leiden: E.J. Brill, 1965, p. 105.

10. Singh, *Ancient,* p. 113.

11. Moreland, W.H. and Chatterjee, Atul Chandra. *A Short History of India.* Second edition. London: Longmans, Green and Co., p. 119.

12. Wink, Andre. *Al Hind: The Making of the Indo-Islamic World.* Vol. 1. New York: E.J. Brill, 1990, pp. 204 and 205.

13. Fowler, Stephen. "Betel Nut: An Essay." In *Juice Magazine,* Issue 1, online at www.epistola.com/sfowler/scholar/scholar-betel.html cited 1/20.2005.

14. Bosworth, C.E. "The Armies of the Saffarids." In *Bulletin of the School of Oriental and African Studies, University of London,* Vol. 31, n. 3, 1968, p. 548.

15. Auboyer, Jeannine. *Daily Life in Ancient India from Approximately 200 BC to 700 AD.* Translator Simon W. Taylor. New York: Macmillan, 1965, pp. 286 and 287.

16. Lair, Richard C. *Gone Astray: The Care and Management of the Asian Elephant in Domesticity.* Rome, Italy: Food and Agriculture Organization of the United Nations (FAO), 1997, p. 192.

17. Bandopadhyay, A. "Reappraisal of an Ancient Text on Elephants." In *Current Science,* Vol. 77, n. 1, July 10, 1999, pp. 9 and 10.

18. Auboyer, *Daily,* p. 260.

40. CHARLEMAGNE AND FREDERICK

1. Runciman, Steven. "Charlemagne and Palestine." In *The English Historical Review,* Oct. 1935, Vol. 50, n. 200, p. 608.

2. Collins, Roger. *Charlemagne.* Toronto: University of Toronto Press, 1998, p. 152.

3. Hodges, Richard. "Charlemagne's Elephant." In *History Today*, Dec. 2000, Vol. 50, n. 12.
4. "Abul-Abbas." Entry in Wikipedia, free online encyclopedia, www.wikipedia.org.
5. Mandaville, John. "An Elephant for Charlemagne." In *Aramco World*, February 1977, online at www.saudiaramcoworld.com/issue/197702/an.elephant.for.charlemagne.htm
6. Chamberlin, Russell. *Charlemagne: Emperor of the Western World*. London: Grafton Books, 1986, p. 216.
7. "Abul-Abbas." Entry in Wikipedia, free online encyclopedia, www.wikipedia.org.
8. Mandaville, "Elephant".
9. Bar-Ilan, Meir. "Prester John: Fiction and History." In *History of European Ideas*, Vol. 20, n.1–3, 1995, pp. 291–298. Also online at faculty.biu.ac.il/~barilm/presjohn.html
10. Bedini, Silvio A. *The Pope's Elephant: An Elephant's Journey from Deep in India to the Heart of Rome*. New York: Penguin, 1997, p. 30.
11. Heckscher, William S. "Bernini's Elephant and Obelisk." In *The Art Bulletin*, Vol. 29, n. 3, Sept. 1947, p. 167.

41. PLUMP AND READY

1. Powell, John ed. *Magill's Guide to Military History*, Vol. 2, Corunna-Janissaries. Pasadena, CA: Salem Press, 2001, p. 600.
2. Nazim, Muhammed. *The Life and Times of Sultan Mahmud of Ghazna*. New Delhi, India: Munshiram Manoharlal, 1971, pp. 35, 151.
3. Lal, Kishor.Saran. *Early Muslims in India*. New Delhi: Book & Books, 1984, p. 29.
4. Nazim, *Life*, p. 155.
5. Dow, Alexander. "Mahometans in India: Bloody Invasions under Mahmud." In *The Great Events by Famous Historians*, edited by Rossiter Johnson, Vol. 5. Online at http://www.fullbooks.com/The-Great-Events-by-Famous-Historians-Volume4.html
6. Al Biruni, Abu Rihan. *Tarikhu-L Hind*. Second edition. Calcutta: Susil Gupta, 1952, p. 22.
7. Nazim, *Life*, pp. 68 and 69.
8. Bosworth, C.E. *The Ghaznavids: Their Empire in Afghanistan and Eastern Iran, 994–1040*. New Delhi: Munshiram Manoharlal, 1992, p. 118.
9. Frye, R.N. *The Cambridge History of Iran*. Vol. 4. Cambridge: Cambridge University Press, 1983, p. 171.
10. Ranking, John. *Historical Researches on the Wars and Sports of the Mongols and Romans: In Which Elephants and Wild Beasts Were Employed or Slain...* London: Longman, Rees, Orme, Brown, and Green, 1826, pp. 103 and 104.

11. Nazim, *Life,* p. 51.
12. Al Biruni, *Tarikhu,* p. 24.
13. Goel, Sita Ram. *Heroic Hindu Resistance to Muslim Invaders (636 AD to 1206 AD).* Voice of India, New Delhi. Internet book at voi.org/books/hhrmi/index.htm. Chapter 3, Frustration of the Ghaznavids.
14. Dowson, John and Elliot, H.M., eds. *The History of India as Told by Its Own Historians. The Muhammadan Period.* 3rd ed. Calcutta: Susil Gupta (India) Private Ltd. 1960, Vol. 1.
15. Powell, *Magill's,* p. 600.
16. Frye, R.N. *The Cambridge History of Iran.* Volume 4. Cambridge: Cambridge University Press, 1983, p. 180.
17. Nazim, *Life,* p. 139.
18. Frye, *Cambridge,* p. 186.
19. Bosworth, *Ghaznavids,* pp. 116, 127.
20. Ranking, *Historical,* p. 277.
21. Bosworth, Ghaznavids, p. 116.
22. Powell, *Magill's,* p. 600.
23. Bosworth, *Ghaznavids,* p. 117.
24. Nicolle, David. *Arms and Armour of the Crusading Era, 1050–1350, Islam, Eastern Europe and Asia.* Revised and updated edition. Vol. II. Mechanicsburg, PA: Stackpole Books, 1999, p. 326.
25. Bosworth, Ghaznavids, p. 116.
26. Bosworth, Clifford Edmund. *The Later Ghaznavids: Splendour and Decay: The Dynasty in Afghanistan and Northern India, 1040–1186.* New Delhi: Munshiram Manoharlal, 1992, p. 96.
27. Bosworth, *Later,* p. 116.
28. Misra, Ram Gopal. *Indian Resistance to Early Muslim Invaders up to 1206 A.D.* Meerut City, India: Anu Books, pp. 92 and 93.

42. MONGOL HORDES

1. Turnbull, Stephen. *Genghis Khan & the Mongol Conquests 1190–1400.* Essential Histories series. New York: Routledge, 2003, pp. 21 and 22.
2. Benson, Douglas S. *Six Emperors: Mongolian Aggression in the Thirteenth Century.* Chicago: Douglas S. Benson, 1995, p. 359.
3. Ranking, John. *Historical Researches on the Wars and Sports of the Mongols and Romans: In Which Elephants and Wild Beasts Were Employed or Slain.* London: Longman, Rees, Orme, Brown, and Green, 1826, p. 60.
4. Laufer, Berthold. *Ivory in China.* Anthropology Leaflet #21, Chicago: Field Museum of Natural History, 1925, p. 18.
5. Impey, Lawrence. "Shangtu, the Summer Capital of Kublai Khan." In *Geographical Review,* Vol. 15, n.4, Oct. 1925, p. 588.
6. Ranking, *Historical,* p. 78.
7. Spinage, C.A. *Elephants.* London: T & A.D. Poyser Ltd., 1994, p. 36.

8. Ranking, *Historical*, p. 90.
9. Nicolle, David. *Arms and Armour of the Crusading Era, 1050–1350, Islam, Eastern Europe and Asia*. Revised and updated edition. Vol. II. Mechanicsburg, PA: Stackpole Books, 1999, pp. 330 and 331, 495.
10. Turnbull, Stephen. *Genghis Khan & the Mongol Conquests 1190–1400*. Essential Histories series. New York: Routledge, 2003, p. 82.
11. Ranking, *Historical*, p. 84.
12. Dowson, John ed. *The History of India as Told by Its Own Historians*. *The Muhammadan Period*. Reprint of 1871 edition. Vol. 3. New York, AMS Press, 1966, p. 618.
13. Ibid., Vol. 4, pp. 109 and 110.
14. Ibid., Vol. 3, pp. 313 and 314.
15. Nicolle, David. *Arms and Armour of the Crusading Era, 1050–1350, Islam, Eastern Europe and Asia*. Revised and updated edition. Vol. II. Mechanicsburg, PA: Stackpole Books, 1999, pp. 237, 266, 448, 466.
16. Chadwick, Douglas H. *The Fate of the Elephant*. San Francisco: Sierra Club, 1994, p. 282.
17. Laufer, *Ivory*, p. 14.

43. PYRAMIDS OF SKULLS

1. Roberts, J. Howard. "Brilliant and Brutal: Tamerlane Conquered a Vast Empire." In *Military History*, Vol. 13, n. 5, Dec. 1996, pp. 12–16.
2. Rawlinson, H.G. *India: A Short Cultural History*. Editor C.G. Seligman. New York: D. Appleton-Century Co., 1952, p. 238.
3. Chaliand, Gerard. *The Art of War in World History: From Antiquity to the Nuclear Age*. Berkeley: University of California Press, 1994, p. 485; also Dowson, Vol. 3, pp. 498 and 499.
4. Ranking, John. *Historical Researches on the Wars and Sports of the Mongols and Romans: In Which Elephants and Wild Beasts Were Employed or Slain*. London: Longman, Rees, Orme, Brown, and Green, 1826, p. 280.
5. Paul, E. Jaiwant. '*By My Sword and Shield*': *Traditional Weapons of the Indian Warrior*. New Delhi, India: Roli Books, 2004, p. 86.
6. Paul, *By My Sword*, pp. 133 and 134.
7. Di Cosmo, Nicola, ed. *Warfare in Inner Asian History (500–1800)*. Section 8, Vol. 6. Handbook of Oriental Studies series. Leiden, The Netherlands: Brill, 2002, p. 273.
8. Dowson, John ed. *The History of India as Told by Its Own Historians*. Reprint of 1871 edition. New York, AMS Press, 1966, Timur, pp. 437–439.
9. Ranking, *Historical*, pp. 133 and 134.
10. Ranking, *Historical*, pp. 133 and 134.
11. Dowson, *Timur*, pp. 115 and 116.
12. Cooper, Jilly. *Animals in War: Valiant Horses, Courageous Dogs, and Other Unsung Animal Heroes*. Guilford CT: Lyons Press, 2002, p. 147.

13. Ranking, *Historical*, p. 144.
14. Ranking, *Historical*, p. 150.
15. Craig, Simon. "Battle of Ankara: Collision of Empires." In *Military History*, Vol. 19 n. 3, August 2002, p. 63.
16. Richardson, Thom. "The Elephant Tusk Swords." In *Royal Armouries Yearbook*. Vol. 4, 1999, p. 133.
17. Wales, H.G. Quaritch. Ancient Southeast Asian Warfare. London: Bernard Quaritsch, 1952, pp. 186 and 187.

44. THAIS, BURMESE, KHMERS, AND OTHERS

1. *The Hutchinson Dictionary of Ancient and Medieval Warfare*. Chicago: Fitzroy Dearborn, 1998, p. 110.
2. Graff, David Andrew. *Medieval Chinese Warfare, 300–900*. Warfare and History series. Routledge, 2002, p. 145.
3. Wales, H.G. Quaritch. *Ancient Southeast Asian Warfare*. London: Bernard Quaritsch, 1952, p. 143.
4. Elvin, Mark. *The Retreat of the Elephants: An Environmental History of China*. New Haven: Yale University Press, 2004, p. 15.
5. Goodrich, L. Carrington and Chia-Sheng, Feng. "The Early Development of Firearms in China." In *Isis*, Jan. 1946, Vol. 36, n.2, pp. 121 and 122.
6. Burn, Richard ed. *The Cambridge History of India*, Vol. IV, The Mughul Period. Delhi: S. Chand & Co., 1963, p. 487.
7. Kimball, Charles. "Ayutthayan Siam." On the Guide to Thailand website at www.guidetothailand.com/thailand-history/ayuttuya.htm
8. Stearn, Duncan. "The Rise of Ayutthaya, part two, 1395–1448." In *Pattaya Mail*, Vol. 10, n. 47, November 2002. Online at http://www.pattayamail.com/486/columns.shtml#hd6
9. Wales, *Ancient*, p. 133.
10. Scigliano, Eric. *Love, War, and Circuses: The Age-Old Relationship between Elephants and Humans*. Boston: Houghton Mifflin, 2002, p. 120.
11. Wales, *Ancient*, pp. 168 and 169.
12. Elvin, *Retreat*, pp. 16 and 17.
13. Elvin, *Retreat*, pp. 268 and 269.
14. Ranking, John. *Historical Researches on the Wars and Sports of the Mongols and Romans: In Which Elephants and Wild Beasts Were Employed or Slain...* London: Longman, Rees, Orme, Brown, and Green, 1826, p. 106.
15. Op. cit., Tavernier, Vol. 2, pp. 262 and 263.
16. Wannabovorn, Sutin. "Elephants Turn to Thievery." Associated Press, January 5, 2004 (or 2005).

45. THE GREAT MAHOUT

1. Das, Asok Kumar. "The Elephant in Mughal Painting." In *Marg*, Vol. 50, n.3, March 1999, pp. 36–54.
2. Pant, G.N. *Horse & Elephant Armour*. Delhi: Agam Kala Prakashan, 1997, p. 101, note 73.
3. Smith, Vincent A. *Akbar: The Great Mogul 1542–1605*. 2nd revised ed. Oxford: Clarendon Press., 1919, pp. 52 and 53.
4. Smith, *Akbar*, pp. 73 and 74.
5. Alter, Stephen. *Elephas Maximus: A Portrait of the Indian Elephant*. Orlando: Harcourt, 2004, p. 158.
6. Nicolle, David. *Mughal India, 1504–1761*. Men-at-Arms series. Editor Lee Johnson. London: Osprey, 1993, p. 16.
7. Rizvi, S.A.A. *The Wonder that was India*. Vol. II. London: Sidgwick & Jackson, 1987, p. 179.
8. Pant, *Horse*, pp. 113 and 119, note 51.
9. Paul, E. Jaiwant. *'By My Sword and Shield': Traditional Weapons of the Indian Warrior*. New Delhi, India: Roli Books, 2004, pp. 89–91.
10. Ranking, John. *Historical Researches on the Wars and Sports of the Mongols and Romans: In Which Elephants and Wild Beasts Were Employed or Slain*. London: Longman, Rees, Orme, Brown, and Green, 1826, pp. 12 and 13.
11. Burn, Richard, ed. *The Cambridge History of India*, Vol. IV, The Mughul Period. Delhi: S. Chand & Co., 1963, p. 72.
12. Richardson, Thom and Stevens, Donna. "The Elephant Armour." In *Royal Armouries Yearbook*. Vol. 1, 1996, p. 102.
13. Jones, David E. *Women Warriors: A History*. Washington, DC: Brassey's, 1997, p. 43; also Ranking, *Historical*, p. 279.
14. Streusand, Douglas E. *The Formation of the Mughal Empire*. Delhi: Oxford University Press, 1989, p. 55.
15. Leong, Jeffrey Say Seck. "Storming the Last Hindu Fortress." In *Military History*, Vol. 15, n.6, Feb. 1999, pp. 58–64.
16. Overdorf, Jason. "Saving the Rajas' Horse." In *Smithsonian*, Vol. 35, n.3, June 2004, pp. 80–89.
17. Abu-L-Fazl. *The Akbarnama of Abu-L-Fazl: A History of the Reign of Akbar*, Vol. 3. Translated by H. Beveridge. Calcutta: Royal Asiatic Society of Bengal, 1939, p. 176.
18. Smith, *Akbar*, p. 361.
19. Dubois, J.A. *Hindu Manners, Customs, and Ceremonies*. H.K. Beauchamp, translator. Oxford: Clarendon Press, 1899, p. 680.
20. Ranking, *Historical*, p. 279.
21. Morris, A.S. "The Journey Beyond Three Seas." In *Geographical Journal*, Vol. 133, n. 4, Dec. 1967, p. 505.
22. Stone, George Cameron. *A Glossary of the Construction, Decoration and Use of Arms and Armor in All Countries and in All Times*. New York: Jack Brussel, 1934, p. 216.

23. Newton, R. *Bible Animals and the Lessons Taught by Them*. London: Thomas Nelson and Sons, 1889, p. 250; also Wood, J.G. *Wood's Bible Animals*. Guelph, Ontario: J.W. Lyon & Co., 1877, p.364–5.

24. Rawlinson, *India*, p. 256.

25. Dowson, John ed. *The History of India as Told by Its Own Historians, The Muhammadan Period, Aurangzeb. The Posthumous Papers of the Late Sir H.M. Eliot*. Third edition. Calcutta: Susil Gupta, 1960, pp. 13–15.

26. Dowson, *Aurangzeb*, p. 110.

27. Grierson, George A. (translator). "The Lay of Brahma's Marriage: An Episode of the Alh-Khand." In *Bulletin of the School of Oriental Studies, Univerity of London*, Vol. 2, n.4, 1923, p. 597.

28. Richardson, Thom. "The Elephant Tusk Swords." In Royal Armouries Yearbook. Vol. 4, 1999, p. 134.

29. Kramrisch, Stella. *Painted Delight: Indian Paintings from Philadelphia Collections*. Philadelphia: Philadelphia Museum of Art, 1986, painting #53.

30. Ranking, *Historical*, p. 286.

31. Op. cit., Tavernier, Vol. 1, pp. 304 and 305.

32. Op. cit., Tavernier, Vol. 1, p. 386.

33. Op. cit., Alter, p. 159.

34. Streusand, Douglas E. *The Formation of the Mughal Empire*. Delhi: Oxford University Press, 1989, p. 55.

35. Chelladhurai, A. "The History of Rocketry in India." Online at users. pandora.be/epan/Files/History% 20of%20Rocketry%20in%20India.pdf

36. Hintze, Andrea. *The Mughal Empire and Its Decline: An Interpretation of the Sources of Social Power*. Brookfield, MA: Ashgate, 1997, p. 60.

37. Jones, *Women*, p. 44.

38. Hansen, Waldemar. *The Peacock Throne: The Drama of Mogul India*. New York: Holt, Rinehart and Winston, 1972, p. 122.

39. Dowson, *Aurangzeb*, p. 26.

40. Abu-L-Fazl, *Akbarnama*, pp. 473 and 474.

41. Dowson, John ed. *The History of India as Told by Its Own Historians, The Muhammadan Period, Jahangiri. The Posthumous Papers of the Late Sir H.M. Eliot*. Third edition. Calcutta: Susil Gupta, 1959, pp. 84 and 85.

42. Burn, *Cambridge*, pp. 224 and 225.

46. BEASTS OF BURDEN

1. Sorobey, Ronald B. "Cossack Pirates of the Black Sea." In *Military History* magazine, June 2003, Vol. 20, issue 2.

2. Wales, H.G. Quaritch. *Ancient Southeast Asian Warfare*. London: Bernard Quaritsch, 1952, p. 80.

3. Brown, C.C. "A Malay Herodotus." In *Bulletin of the School of Oriental and African Studies, University of London*, Vol 12, n.3/4, 1948, p. 735.

4. Ness, Gayl D. and Stahl, William. "Western Imperialist Armies in Asia." In *Comparative Studies in Society and History*, Vol. 19, n. 1, Jan. 1977, p. 10.
5. Davies, E.L.B. Meurig. "Elephant Tactics: Amm. Marc. 25.1.14; Sil. 9.581 −3; Lucr. 2.537−9." In *The Classical Quarterly*, new series, Vol. 1 n. 3/4, July-Oct. 1951, pp. 153−155.
6. Chadwick, Douglas H. *The Fate of the Elephant*. San Francisco: Sierra Club, 1994, p. 282.
7. Rennie, James [though stated as Anonymous]. *The Elephant as he exists in a wild state, and as he has been made subservient, in peace and in war, to the purposes of man*. New York: Harper & Brothers, 1848, p. 164.
8. Cline, Marie I. *Meet India: Everyday Facts about India*. Albuquerque: University of New Mexico, 1943, p. 105.
9. Ali, Mrs. Meer Hassan. *Observations on the Musselmauns of India*. Edited by W. Crooke. 2nd edition, 1917. Found online at www.fullbooks.com/Observations-on-the-Mussulmauns-of-India1.html
10. Rennie, *Elephant*, p. 166.
11. Bernier, Francois. *Travels in the Mogul Empire, AD 1656−1668*. 2nd revised edition. Delhi, India: Low Price Publications, 1999, p. 277.
12. Ranking, *Historical*, pp. 284 and 285.
13. Mehta, Ved. *Portrait of India*. New Haven, CT: Yale University Press, 1993, p. 519 and 520.
14. Rennie, *Elephant*.
15. Pant, G.N. *Horse & Elephant Armour*. Delhi: Agam Kala Prakashan, 1997, p. 97.
16. Harrington, Peter. *Plassey, 1757: Clive of India's Finest Hour*. Praeger Illustrated Military History series. Westport, CT: Praeger, 2005, p. 47.
17. Menault, Ernest. *The Intelligence of Animals with Illustrative Anecdotes*. Anonymous translator (from the original French). New York: Charles Scribner, 1870, p. 266−7.
18. Ranking, John. *Historical Researches on the Wars and Sports of the Mongols and Romans: In Which Elephants and Wild Beasts Were Employed or Slain*. London: Longman, Rees, Orme, Brown, and Green, 1826, pp. 91 and 92.
19. Laufer, Berthold. *Ivory in China*. Anthropology Leaflet #21, Chicago: Field Museum of Natural History, 1925, p. 19.
20. Tucker, Spencer. C. "The First Tet Offensive." In *Vietnam Magazine*, Feb. 2003, found online at www. historynet.com/vn/blfirsttetoffensive/
21. Laufer, *Ivory*, pp. 18, 20.

47. MIGHTY ENGINEERS

1. Spinage, C.A. *Elephants*. London: T & A.D. Poyser Ltd., 1994, p. 270.
2. Gaidoz, H. "Les Elephans a la Guerre." In *Revue des deux mondes*, Vol. 4, 1874, p. 497.

3. Gaidoz, "Les Elephans", pp. 499–504.
4. Gaidoz, "Les Elephans", p. 506.
5. Bevan, Edwyn. *The House of Ptolemy: A History of Egypt under the Ptolemaic Dynasty*. Chicago: Ares Publishers, 1985, p. 388.
6. Rankin, L.K. "The Elephant Experiment in Africa: A Brief Account of the Belgian Elephant Expedition." In *Proceedings of the Royal Geographical Society and Monthly Record of Geography*, Vol. 4, n. 5, May 1882, p. 285.
7. Spinage, *Elephants*, p. 278.
8. Croft, John. "Gentlemen–The Elephants." In *The Army Quarterly and Defence Journal*, Vol. 113, n.2, 1983, pp. 193 and 194.
9. Cook, Haruko Taya and Theodore F. *Japan at War: An Oral History*. New York: New Press, 1992. Interview with Abe Hiroshi, "Building the Siam Railroad." pp. 100 and 101.
10. Beckman, Stephanie, compiler. "Singapore Cases-Details of Trial Records." University of California Berkeley War Crimes Study Center. Cases #235/1034 Banno case. Found online at //ist-socrates.berkeley.edu/~warcrime/Japan/singapore/Trials/Banno.htm
11. Cooper, Jilly. *Animals in War: Valiant Horses, Courageous Dogs, and Other Unsung Animal Heroes*. Guilford CT: Lyons Press, 2002, p. 154.
12. Croft, "Gentlemen", p. 195.
13. "Notes on the Thai-Burma Railway." In *Journal of Kyoto Seika University* , no. 22. On Web site www.Kyoto-seika.ac.jp/johokan/kiyo/pdf-data/no22/david.pdf.
14. Cooper, Jilly. *Animals in War: Valiant Horses, Courageous Dogs, and Other Unsung Animal Heroes*. Guilford CT: Lyons Press, 2002, p. 154.
15. British Broadcasting Corporation. "War veteran elephant dies." In *BBC News World Edition, Asia-Pacific*. Dated February 26, 2003. Found online at newswww.bbc.net.uk/2/low/asia-pacific/2800737.stm
16. Croft, "Gentlemen", p. 194.
17. Croft, "Gentlemen", p. 196.
18. Cooper, *Animals*, p. 152.
19. Wynter, Philip. "Elephants at War: In Burma, Big Beasts Work for Allied Army." In *Life Magazine*, April 10, 1944, p. 18.
20. Thrapp, Don L. "The Mules of Mars." In *The Quartermaster Review*, May-June 1946. Found online at www.qmmuseum.lee.army.mil/WWII/mules_of_mars.htm
21. Latimer, John. *Burma: The Forgotten War*. London: John Murray Publishers Ltd., 2004. Quotation cited from a book review on the Stone & Stone Bookstore Web site, as the book is not yet available in the U.S., found at http://www.sonic.net/~bstone/archives/050102.shtml
22. Cooper, *Animals*, p. 154.

23. Glines, C.V. "Flying the Hump." In *Air Force Magazine*. Journal of the Air Force Association. Vol. 74, n.3, March, 1991. Online at www.afa.org/magazine/1991/0391hump_print.html

24. Alexander, Shana. *The Astonishing Elephant*. New York: Random House, 2000, p. 83.

48. TARGETS OF OPPORTUNITY

1. Beckett, Ian F.W. *Encyclopedia of Guerilla Warfare*. Santa Barbara, CA: ABC-CLIO, 1999, p. 104.

2. Page, Tim. *Another Vietnam: Pictures of the War from the Other Side*. Washington, DC: National Geographic Society, 2002, pp. 120, 109.

3. Stopford, J.G.B. "A Neglected Source of Labour in Africa." In *Journal of the Royal African Society*, Vol.1, n. 4, July 1902, pp. 448 and 449.

4. Prados, John. *The Blood Road: The Ho Chi Minh Trail and the Vietnam War*. New York: John Wiley & Sons, 1999, p. 44.

5. Hung, Vu. *The Story of a Mahout and His War Elephant*. Hanoi: Foreign Languages Publishing House, 1976.

6. Prados, *Blood*, p. 221.

7. Halvarg, David. *The War Against the Greens: The "Wise Use" Movement, the New Right, and the Browning of America*. Revised and updated. Boulder, CO: Johnson Books, 2004.

8. Winter Soldier Investigation, testimony given in Detroit, Michigan, Jan. 31- Feb. 2, 1971. On internet at lists.village.Virginia.edu/sixties/HTML_docs/ Resources/Primary/Winter_Soldier/WS_30_Misc.html

9. Morris, Jim. *Fighting Men: Stories of Soldiering*. New York: Dell, 1993, p. 62.

10. Ibid., pp. 64–5.

11. Kukler, Michael A. *Operation Barooom*. Gastonia, NC: Michael A. Kukler, 1980, p. 1.

12. Department of Defense, Department of the Air Force. "Elephants for Chu Lai, Trang-Phuc and Chu Lai AB, Vietnam." Records of U.S. Air Force Commands, Activities, and Organizations, 1900–1991. ARC Identifier 70766, Record Group 342. Record found online at arcweb.archives.gov

13. Op. cit., Morris, p. 70.

14. Online article at membrane.com/burma2.html cited January 2005.

15. Falise, Thierry. "A Camp for Displaced Karen in Southeastern Burma is the Base for a Christian Militia." In *Youth Crusaders: The Nation*. May 17, 1998. Online at www.stud.uni-hannover.de/archiv/ius-l/msg00402.html

EPILOGUE

1. Montgomery, Viscount. *A History of Warfare*. Cleveland: World Publishing, 1968, pp. 395–6.

2. Montross, Lynn. *War Through the Ages*. Revised and enlarged 3rd edition. New York: Harper & Bros., 1960, p. 53.

3. Everson, Tim. *Warfare in Ancient Greece: Arms and Armour from the Heroes of Homer to Alexander the Great*. London: Sutton Publishing, 2004, p. 206.

4. Hart, Lynette and Sundar. "Family Traditions for Mahouts of Asian Elephants." In *Anthrozoos*, v. 13 n.1, 2000, p. 34; also Alter, Stephen. *Elephas Maximus: A Portrait of the Indian Elephant*. Orlando: Harcourt, 2004, p. 205.

5. "Indian Elephant Dies of Grief." May 5, 1999, Associated Press, on [cnn.com].

6. Joubert, Dereck. "Eyewitness to an Elephant Wake." In *National Geographic*, May 1991, pp. 39–41.

Glossary

Abyssinia. An antiquated name of Ethiopia, Africa.

Ahriman's devils. A term of disparagement by Zoroastrians and ancient Persians for elephants.

Anatolia. An ancient name for modern Turkey.

Ankh or ankhus. The most common tool of the elephant-rider: a hook mounted on a bamboo rod, used to give the elephant direction.

Ballista or carroballista. An ancient weapon reminiscent of a large crossbow used to fire darts at the enemy.

Behemoth. A Biblical word for a giant beast in the book of Job. It is often used of elephants.

Bull elephant. The male elephant.

Caltrops. Traps, often set in the ground, to harm the enemy.

Cataphract. Heavily armored cavalry, used specifically of armored horses (not elephants).

Chakram. A discus-style bladed weapon of India, hurled at the enemy.

Champa. Ancient name for Vietnam.

Circus. The Circus was an auditorium used in ancient Rome for popular gladiatorial games.

Cow elephant. The female elephant.

Diadochi. Greek word meaning successors.

Elephantarch. Greek title for a commander of war elephants.

Elephantomachai. Greek word for soldiers specially trained and armored to fight against elephants.

Elephas Maximus. The Asian elephant.

Flaming pig strategy. A tactic of using noisy pigs to frighten enemy elephants. Often the pigs were dipped in tar and lit afire to make them squeal more.

Gajnal. An Asian swivel-gun mounted on an elephant's back during the Mughal era of India.

Gladius. The sword most popular in Roman legions. The gladius was two-edged and relatively short, meant for stabbing, not slashing.

Hamstringing. The tactic of disabling enemy horses and elephants by cutting the tendons in their legs, making them unable to run.

Howdah. Any platform placed on an elephant's back, usually a seat or small tower.

Ivory. The tusk material of elephants, which is easily carved and very beautiful.

Javelin. A lightweight pole weapon to be thrown at the enemy.

Karwah. Unusual and soft Asian defensive shield, carried in front to block enemy arrows.

Keddah. A man-made enclosure built to "round-up" elephant herds as captives.

Koonkie. An elephant (usually female) specially trained to assist in capturing wild elephants.

Kraal. See keddah. May be related to our English word "corral."

Lamellar. A type of armor used in Asia combining different styles of metal to create a semi-flexible protection for humans, horses, and elephants.

Loxodonta. "Long teeth," describing the African elephant by its magnificent tusks. Two species are now acknowledged. *Loxodonta Africanus* is the well-known African Bush or Savannah elephant. *Loxodonta Cyclotis* is the lesser known and smaller African Forest elephant.

Lucanian oxen. A Roman term for elephants, which they first encountered in the region of Lucania, Italy during the invasion of Pyrrhus.

Mahout. An elephant rider, who usually rides on the elephant's neck.

Mamluks. Turkish slave children raised as professional mercenary soldiers.

Must or Musth. A periodic hormonal condition that affects bull elephants, creating extreme aggression.

Naptha or naft. An ancient fire weapon, perhaps an oil used on arrows and in a primitive flame thrower.

Narnals. Small guns, used by India, that are mounted on an elephant's back.

Oozie. Burmese name for an elephant rider or mahout.

Pachyderm. Means "thick-skinned." Has become synonymous with elephant.

Palisade. A fence or row of stakes used as a defensive measure to stop enemy advances.

Phalanx. An effective but relatively immobile group of tightly-packed and armored Greek soldiers with long spears (sarissae).

Punic. A Roman term for the Carthaginians, who were of Phoenician descent.

Quilted armor. Using layers of blankets or textiles as an inexpensive form of body protection.

Regalia. Beautiful trappings or ornamentation used to impress crowds. Often used on elephants.

Saint Catherine's Wheel. A pyrotechnic or firework-style device used in Asia during professional elephant fights (with spectators) to distract out-of-control elephants.

Sarissa. A long pole weapon, ten to twenty feet in length, used mainly by the Greek phalanx.

Stiphos. Ancient Syrian (Seleucid) soldiers assigned to protect the legs of their war elephants.

Successor Wars. The long civil wars between the generals left behind when Alexander the Great died.

Suffetes. Leaders of ancient Carthage, a naval and political power centered in North Africa.

Trumpeting. A term used of the loud wails or outbursts made by angry or frightened elephants.

Trunk sword. A bladed weapon carried in an elephant's trunk. Believed to be mere legend by many.

Tusk swords. Bladed weapons mounted on an elephant's tusks. Used mainly in Asia under the Mughals.

Tusker. A nickname for bull elephants with sizable ivory tusks.

Velites. Roman light infantry, used mainly to harass the enemy with javelins.

Bibliography

Abbott, Jacob. *Pyrrhus*. Illustrated ed., Makers of History series. New York: A.L. Fowle, 1906.

"Abul-Abbas." Entry in Wikipedia, online encyclopedia at www.wikipedia.org cited Jan. 2005.

Abu-L-Fazl. *The Akbarnama of Abu-L-Fazl: A History of the Reign of Akbar*. Vol. 3. Translated by H. Beveridge. Calcutta: Royal Asiatic Society of Bengal, 1939.

Adams, Jack. *Wild Elephants in Captivity*. Carson, CA: Center for the Study of Elephants, 1981.

Adams, W. Lindsay. "The Successors of Alexander." In *The Greek World in the Fourth Century: From the Fall of the Athenian Empire to the Successors of Alexander*, ed. Lawrence A. Tritle. New York: Routledge, 1997.

Adcock, F.E. *The Greek and Macedonian Art of War*. Berkeley: University of California Press, 1957.

Aelian. *Aelian on the Characteristics of Animals*. Translated by A.F. Scholfield. Cambridge: Harvard University Press, 1971.

Albright, William Foxwell. *From the Stone Age to Christianity*. 2nd ed. Garden City, NJ: Doubleday, 1957.

Alexander the Great. Makers of History series, illustrated ed. New York: A.L. Fowle, 1906.

Alexander, Shana. *The Astonishing Elephant*. New York: Random House, 2000.

Ali, Mrs. Meer Hassan. *Observations on the Musselmauns of India*. Edited by W. Crooke. 2nd edition, 1917. Online at www.fullbooks.com/Observations-on-the-Musselmauns-of-India1.html, Jan. 2005.

Allen, Tom. "Through the Alps to the Gates of Rome." In *Greece and Rome: Builders of Our World*. Washington, DC: National Geographic Society, 1977, pp. 294–371.

Anderson, H. "3 Maccabees: A New Translation and Introduction." In *The Old Testament Pseudipigrapha, volume two*. James Charlesworth, editor. Garden City, NY: Doubleday, 1985.

Anglim, Simon et al. *Fighting Techniques of the Ancient World: 3000 BC-500 AD: Equipment, Combat Skills, and Tactics*. New York: Thomas Dunne Books, 2002.

Anson, Edward Madden IV. *Eumenes of Cardia*. Doctor of Philosophy dissertation at Univerity of Virginia, 1975.

Aristotle. *The Works of Aristotle, Vol. IV, Historia Animalium*, translated by D'Arcy W. Thompson. New York: Oxford University Press, 1910.

Armandi, P. *Histoire Militaire des Elephants*. Paris: Librairie D'Amyot, 1843.

Armstrong, Donald. *The Reluctant Warriors*. New York: Thomas Y. Crowell, 1966.

Arnold, Thomas. *The Second Punic War*. London: Macmillan, 1886.

Arrian. *Anabasis Alexandri Books V–VII, and Indica*. Translator: Brunt, PA. Cambridge, MA: Harvard University Press., 1983.

"Asculum." Internet analysis of Battle of Asculum between Pyrrhus and Romans. www.wargamer.com/greatbattles/Asculum.asp cited June 2003.

Ashley, James R. *The Macedonian Empire: The Era of Warfare under Philip II and Alexander the Great, 359-323 BC*. Jefferson, NC: McFarland, 1998.

Associated Press. "Toledo Celebrates: It's a 275 Pound Boy: Elephant Birth in Captivity Quite Rare." *Cincinnati Enquirer*, May 3, 2003. Found on Internet page www.enquirer.com/editions/2003/05/03/loc_oh-elephantbirth03.html on August 16, 2003.

Astin, A.E. *Scipio Aemilianus*. Oxford: Clarendon Press, 1967.

Auboyer, Jeannine. *Daily Life in Ancient India from Approximately 200 BC to 700 AD*. Translator Simon W. Taylor. New York: Macmillan, 1965.

Auguet, Roland. *Cruelty and Civilization: The Roman Games*. London: George Allen and Unwin, 1972.

Austin, M.M. *The Hellenistic World from Alexander to the Roman Conquest: A Selection of Ancient Sources in Translation*. New York: Cambridge University Press, 1994.

Avi-Yonah, Michael. *Hellenism and the East: Contacts and Interrelations from Alexander to the Roman Conquest*. University Microfilms, 1978.

Badian, E. *Roman Imperialism in the Late Republic*. Ithaca, NY: Cornell University Press, 1968.

Baker, G.P. *Hannibal*. New York: Dodd, Mead, 1929.

Bandopadhyay, A. "Reappraisal of an Ancient Text on Elephants." In *Current Science*, Vol. 77, n. 1, July 10, 1999.

Bar-Ilan, Meir. "Prester John: Fiction and History." In *History of European Ideas*, Vol. 20, n.1-3, 1995. Also online at faculty.biu.ac.il/~barilm/presjohn.html

Barker, Phil. *Armies of the Macedonian and Punic Wars*. England: War Games Research Group, 1971.

Bar-Kochva, Bezalel. *Judas Maccabaeus: The Jewish Struggle Against the Seleucids*. New York: Cambridge University Press, 1989.

Bar-Kochva, Bezalel. *The Seleucid Army: Organization and Tactics in the Great Campaigns*. New York: Cambridge University Press, 1976.

Barnett, R.D. "Early Greek and Oriental Ivories." In *The Journal of Hellenic Studies*, Vol. 68, 1948.

Barton, I.M. *Africa in the Roman Empire*. Accra, Ghana: Ghana Universities Press, 1972.

Basham, A.L. *The Wonder that was India*. 3rd revised edition. Vol. I. New York: Taplinger, 1967.

Basham, A.L. ed. *A Cultural History of India*. Oxford: Clarendon Press, 1975.

Bath, Tony. *Hannibal's Campaigns*. NY Barnes and Noble, 1992.

Beckett, Ian F.W. *Encyclopedia of Guerilla Warfare*. Santa Barbara, CA: ABC-CLIO, 1999.

Beckman, Stephanie, compiler. "Singapore Cases - Details of Trial Records." University of California Berkeley War Crimes Study Center. Cases #235/1034 Banno case. Found online at //ist-socrates.berkeley.edu/~warcrime/Japan/singapore/Trials/Banno.htm

Bedini, Silvio A. *The Pope's Elephant: An Elephant's Journey from Deep in India to the Heart of Rome*. New York: Penguin, 1997.

Benecke, P.V.M. "The Fall of the Macedonian Monarchy" and "Rome and the Hellenistic States." In *The Cambridge Ancient History, Vol. VIII, Rome and the Mediterranean 218-133 BC*. Cambridge: Cambridge University Press, 1930.

Benedict, Coleman H. "The Romans in Southern Gaul." In *The American Journal of Philology*, Vol. 63, n. 1, 1942.

Bernier, Francois. *Travels in the Mogul Empire, AD 1656-1668*. Translator Archibald Constable, 2nd revised edition by Vincent A. Smith. Delhi, India: Low Price Publications, 1999.

Bevan, Edwyn Robert. *The House of Ptolemy: A History of Egypt under the Ptolemaic Dynasty*. Chicago: Ares Publishers, 1985. Reprint of 1927 edition.

Bevan, Edwyn Robert. *The House of Seleucus*. Two volumes in one, reprint of 1902 edition. Chicago: Ares, 1985.

Bevan, Edwyn Robert. "Syria and the Jews." In *The Cambridge Ancient History, Vol. VIII, Rome and the Mediterranean 218-133 BC*. Cambridge: Cambridge University Press, 1930.

Bhattacharjee, Arun. *History of Ancient India*. New Delhi: Sterling Publishers, 1979.

Billows, Richard A. *Antigonos the One-Eyed and the Creation of the Hellenistic State*. Berkeley: University of California Press, 1990.

Bishop, Carl W. "The Elephant and Its Ivory in Ancient China." In *Journal of the American Oriental Society*, Vol. 41, 1921.

Blond, Georges. *The Elephants*. Translator Frances Frenaye. New York: Macmillan, 1961.

Blundell, H. Weld. "Exploration in the Abai Basin, Abyssinia." In *Geographical Journal*, Vol. 27, n. 6, June 1906.

Bosworth, A.B. *The Legacy of Alexander: Politics, Warfare, and Propaganda under the Successors*. New York: Oxford University Press, 2002.

Bosworth, Clifford Edmund. "Armies of the Prophet: Strategy, Tactics and Weapons in Islamic Warfare." In *The World of Islam*, Bernard Lewis editor. London: Thames and Hudson, 1992.

Bosworth, Clifford Edmund. "The Armies of the Saffarids." In *Bulletin of the School of Oriental and African Studies, University of London*, Vol. 31, n. 3, 1968.

Bosworth, Clifford Edmund. *The Ghaznavids: Their Empire in Afghanistan and Eastern Iran, 994-1040*. New Delhi: Munshiram Manoharlal, 1992.

Bosworth, Clifford Edmund. *The Later Ghaznavids: Splendour and Decay: The Dynasty in Afghanistan and Northern India, 1040-1186*. New Delhi: Munshiram Manoharlal, 1992.

Boyle, J.A., ed. *The Cambridge History of Iran*. Vol. 5. Cambridge: Cambridge University Press, 1983.

Bradford, Alfred S. *With Arrow, Sword, and Spear: A History of Warfare in the Ancient World*. Westport, CT: Praeger, 2001.

Bradford, Ernle. *Hannibal*. New York: Dorset Press, 1991.

Briant, Pierre. *From Cyrus to Alexander: A History of the Persian Empire*. Translated by Peter T. Daniels. Winona Lake, IN: Eisenbrauns, 2002.

British Broadcasting Corporation. "War veteran elephant dies." In *BBC News World Edition, Asia-Pacific*. Dated February 26, 2003. Found online at newswww.bbc.net.uk/2/low/asia-pacific/2800737.stm

Brooks, Richard. *Atlas of World Military History*. New York: Barnes and Noble Books, 2000.

Brown, C.C. "A Malay Herodotus." In *Bulletin of the School of Oriental and African Studies, University of London*, Vol. 12, n.3/4, 1948.

Brunt, P.A. "Notes on Aristobulus of Cassandria." In *The Classical Quarterly*, new series, Vol. 24, n. 1, May 1974.

Burn, Richard ed. *The Cambridge History of India*, Vol. IV, The Mughul Period. New Delhi: S. Chand & Co., 1963.

Caesar, Julius. *Alexandrian, African and Spanish Wars*. Translated by A.G. Way. Cambridge, MA: Harvard University Press, 1955.

Cannon, Teresa and Davis, Peter. *Aliya: Stories of the Elephants of Sri Lanka*. Melbourne, Australia: Airavata Press, 1995.

Cary, M. *A History of the Greek World From 323 to 146 B.C.* New York: Barnes and Noble, 1965.

Casson, Lionel. *The Ancient Mariners: Seafarers and Sea Fighters of the Mediterranean in Ancient Times*. New York: Minerva Press, 1959.

Casson, Lionel. *The Periplus Maris Erythraei*. Princeton, NJ.: Princeton University Press, 1989.

Casson, Lionel. "Ptolemy II and the Hunting of African Elephants." In *Transactions of the American Philological Association*, Vol. 123, 1993.

Caven, Brian. *The Punic Wars*. New York: Barnes and Noble Books, 1992.

Center for Iranian Studies. "Ethiopia: Relations with Persia." In *Encyclopaedia Iranica*. Online at www.iranica.com/articles/v9fl/v9f103.html

Chadwick, Douglas H. *The Fate of the Elephant*. San Francisco: Sierra Club, 1994.

Chakravorty, B. "Comparative Study of the Rajput and Mughal Military Systems." In *The Journal of the United Service Institution of India.* Vol. 101, n. 424, 1971.

Chalabian, Antranig. "In 451, the Armenians Were the First Christians to Take Up Arms in Defending Their Right to Worship." In *Military History,* Vol. 13, n.5, Dec. 1996.

Chaliand, Gerard. *The Art of War in World History: From Antiquity to the Nuclear Age.* Berkeley: University of California Press, 1994.

Chamoux, Francois. *Hellenistic Civilization.* Translator Michel Roussel. Malden, MA.: Blackwell Publishing, 2003.

"Charlemagne's Elephant." In *History Today,* on the Web site for History Bookshop.com, online at www.historybookshop.com/articles/commentary/charlemagne-elephant-ht.asp

Charles-Picard, Gilbert and Colette. *Daily Life in Carthage at the Time of Hannibal.* New York: Macmillan, 1966.

Cheema, G.S. *The Forgotten Mughals: A History of the Later Emperors of the House of Babar (1707-1857).* New Delhi: Manohar, 2002.

Chelladhurai, A. "The History of Rocketry in India." Online at users.pandora.be/epan/Files/History%20of%20Rocketry%20in%20India.pdf

Church, Alfred J. *The Story of Carthage.* New York: G.P. Putnam's Sons, 1891.

Cline, Marie I. *Meet India: Everyday Facts about India.* Albuquerque: University of New Mexico, 1943.

Collins, Andrew. *Gateway to Atlantis: The Search for the Source of a Lost Civilization.* New York: Carroll & Graf, 2000.

Conder, Claude Reignier. *Judas Maccabaeus and the Jewish War of Independence.* New edition. Strand, England: A.P. Watt & Son, 1894.

Connolly, Peter. *Hannibal and the Enemies of Rome.* London: Macdonald Educational, 1978.

Cook, Haruko Taya and Theodore F. *Japan at War: An Oral History.* Interview with Abe Hiroshi, "Building the Siam Railroad." New York: New Press, 1992.

Cooper, Jilly. *Animals in War: Valiant Horses, Courageous Dogs, and Other Unsung Animal Heroes.* Guilford, CT: Lyons Press, 2002. Reprint of 1983 work.

Cottrell, Leonard. *Hannibal: Enemy of Rome.* New York: Da Capo Press, 1992.

Craig, Simon. "Battle of Ankara: Collision of Empires." In *Military History,* Vol. 19, n. 3, August 2002.

Crawford, Michael. *The Roman Republic.* 2nd ed. Cambridge: Harvard University Press, 1993.

Creasy, Edward S. *Fifteen Decisive Battles of the World.* New York: Heritage Press, 1969.

Crowfoot, J.W. "Some Red Sea Ports in the Anglo-Egyptian Sudan." In *Geographical Journal,* Vol. 37, n. 5, May 1911.

Ctesias. *Ancient India as Described by Ktesias the Knidian.* Abridgement of *Indika* by J.W. McCrindle. London: Trubner, 1882.

Cummings, Lewis V. *Alexander the Great*. Boston: Houghton Mifflin, 1940.

Cummings, Robert J. "Africa Between the Ages." In *African Studies Review*, Vol. 29, n.3, Sept. 1986.

Curchin, Leonard A. *Roman Spain: Conquest and Assimilation*. New York: Routledge, 1991.

Davis, Paul K. *100 Decisive Battles from Ancient Times to the Present*. Santa Barbara: ABC-CLIO, 1999.

Day, Michael. "Jumbo Discovery—Africa is home to not one but two species of elephants." In *New Scientist*, Vol. 166, n. 2232, April 1, 2000.

De Beer, Gavin. *Hannibal: Challenging Rome's Supremacy*. New York: Viking Press, 1969.

Delbruck, Hans. *Warfare in Antiquity*. History of the Art of War series. Vol. I. Translated by Walter J. Renfroe, Jr. Lincoln: University of Nebraska, 1990, original 1920.

Delort, Robert. *The Life and Lore of the Elephant*. New York: Harry N. Abrams Publishers, 1992.

Department of Defense, Department of the Air Force. "Elephants for Chu Lai, Trang-Phuc and Chu Lai AB, Vietnam." Records of U.S. Air Force Commands, Activities, and Organizations, 1900-1991. ARC Identifier 70766, Record Group 342. Record found online at arcweb.archives.gov

Desai, Vishakha N. *Life at Court: Art for India's Rulers, 16th-19th Centuries*. Boston: Museum of Fine Arts, 1985.

Devine, A.M. "Diodorus' Account of the Battle of Gabiene." In *The Ancient World*, Vol. XII, nos 3-4, December 1985.

Devine, A.M. "Diodorus' Account of the Battle of Paraitacene." In *The Ancient World*, Vol. XII, nos 3-4, December 1985.

Dhavalikar, M.K. "Ganesa: Myth and Reality." In *Ganesh: Studies of an Asian God*. Editor Robert L. Brown. State University of New York Press, 1991.

Digby, Simon. *War-Horse and Elephant in the Dehli Sultanate: A Study of Military Supplies*. Orient Monographs. Karachi, Pakistan: Oxford University Press, 1971.

Dikshitar, V.R. Ramachandra. *War in Ancient India*. Delhi: Motilal Banarsidass, 1987.

Dinerstein, Eric. "Nepal's 'Land Rovers' Cover Themselves with Dust, and Glory." *Smithsonian*. Vol. 19, n.6, June, 1988.

Dio [Cassius Dio Cocceianus]. *Dio's Roman History with an English Translation by Earnest Cary, Ph.D. on the Basis of the Version of Herbert Baldwin Foster, Ph.D. in nine volumes*. Cambridge, MA: Harvard University Press, 1954.

Diodorus. "The Armies of Eumenes and Antigonus at the Battle of Paraetacene." In *The Hellenistic World from Alexander to the Roman Conquest: A Selection of Ancient Sources in Translation*. Editor M.M. Austin. New York: Cambridge University Press, 1994.

Diodorus. *Diodorus of Sicily* in 12 volumes. Translator Francis R. Walton. Cambridge, MA: Harvard University Press, 1957.

Dionysius of Halicarnassus. *The Roman Antiquities* in seven volumes. Translator Earnest Cary. Cambridge, MA: Harvard University Press, 1950.

Dodge, Theodore Ayrault. *Hannibal: A History of the Art of War among the Carthaginians and Romans Down to the Battle of Pydna, 168 B.C., with a Detailed Account of the Second Punic War.* New York: Da Capo Press, 1995 edition of 1891 work.

Dodgeon, Michael H. and Lieu, Samuel N.C. eds. *The Roman Eastern Frontier and the Persian Wars (AD 226-363).* New York: Routledge, 1994.

Dorey, T.A. and Dudley, D.R. *Rome Against Carthage.* London: Secker & Warburg, 1971.

Dow, Alexander. "Mahometans in India: Bloody Invasions under Mahmud." In *The Great Events by Famous Historians*, edited by Rossiter Johnson, volume five. Online at http://www.fullbooks.com/The-Great-Events-by-Famous-Historians-Volume4.html

Downs, James F. "The Origin and Spread of Riding in the Near East and Central Asia." In *American Anthropologist*, new series, Vol. 63, n. 6, December 1961.

Dowson, John ed. *The History of India as Told by Its Own Historians.* Reprint of 1871 edition. New York, AMS Press, 1966. In eight volumes.

Dowson, John and Elliot, H.M., eds. *The History of India as Told by Its Own Historians.* 3rd ed. Calcutta: Susil Gupta Private Ltd. 1960.

"Drunk Elephants Kill Six People." Reuters, Dec. 17, 2002, on bbcnews.com.

Dubois, J.A. *Hindu Manners, Customs, and Ceremonies.* H.K. Beauchamp, translator. Oxford: Clarendon Press, 1899.

Ducrey, Pierre. *Warfare in Ancient Greece.* Janet Lloyd, translator. New York: Schocken Books, 1986.

Dupuy, Trevor Nevitt. *The Military Life of Hannibal: Father of Strategy.* New York: Franklin Watts, 1969.

Durant, Will. *The Life of Greece.* The Story of Civilization, part II. New York: Simon and Schuster, 1966.

Durschmied, Erik. *From Armageddon to the Fall of Rome: How the Myth Makers Changed the World.* London: Hodder & Stoughton, 2002.

Eggert, Lori S. "The Evolution and Conservation of the African Forest Elephant." Doctor of Philosophy in Biology dissertation at the University of California in San Diego, 2002.

Eltringham, Dr. S.K. consultant. *The Illustrated Encyclopedia of Elephants: From Their Origins and Evolution to Their Ceremonial and Working Relationship with Man.* New York: Crescent Books, 1991.

Elvin, Mark. *The Retreat of the Elephants: An Environmental History of China.* New Haven: Yale University Press, 2004.

Emerson, Gertrude. *Voiceless India.* Westport: Greenwood Press, 1971. Reprint of 1930 ed.

Encyclopedia Judaica. New York: Macmillan, 1971.

Errington, R.M. "From Babylon to Triparadeisos: 323-320 B.C." In *The Journal of Hellenic Studies*, Vol. 90, 1970.

Errington, R.M. *A History of Macedonia*. Translator C. Errington. Berkeley: University of California Press, 1990.

Errington, R.M. "Rome Against Philip and Antiochus." In *The Cambridge Ancient History, second edition*, Vol. VIII, "Rome and the Mediterranean to 133 BC." Editor A.E. Astin. New York: Cambridge University Press, 2001.

Errington, R.M. "Rome and Greece to 205 B.C." In *The Cambridge Ancient History, second edition*, Vol. VIII, "Rome and the Mediterranean to 133 BC." Editor A.E. Astin. New York: Cambridge University Press, 2001.

Everson, Tim. *Warfare in Ancient Greece: Arms and Armour from the Heroes of Homer to Alexander the Great*. London: Sutton Publishing, 2004.

Fentress, Elizabeth W.B. *Numidia and the Roman Army: Social, Military and Economic Aspects of the Frontier Zone*. Oxford, England: BAR International Series #53, 1979.

Fernando, Joseph M.P. "Genetics, Ecology, and Conservation of the Asian Elephant." Doctor of Philosophy of Biology dissertation at the University of Oregon, 1998.

Fernando, S.B.U. "Training Working Elephants." In *Animal Training: A Review and Commentary on Current Practice*. Hertfordshire, England: Universities Federation for Animal Welfare, 1990.

Ferrill, Arthur. *The Fall of the Roman Empire: The Military Explanation*. London: Thames & Hudson, 1986.

Fildes, Alan and Fletcher, Joann. *Alexander the Great: Son of the Gods*. Los Angeles: J. Paul Getty Museum, 2002.

Filson, Stormie. "Battle of Gaugamela: Conquest of a Continent." *Military History*, October 2000, Vol. 17, n.4.

Findlay, Ronald. "Globalization and the European Economy: Medieval Origins to the Industrial Revolution." Online paper at Columbia University.

Florus, Lucius Annaeus. *Epitome of Roman History*. New York: G.P. Putnam's Sons, 1929.

Fournie, Daniel A. "Although Overshadowed by His Brother Hannibal Barca, Hasdrubal Showed Equal Tactical Genius." In *Military History*. Vol. 16, n. 3, August 1999.

Fournie, Daniel A. "Clash of Titans at Zama." In *Military History*, Vol. 16, n. 6, February 2000.

Fowden, Garth. "Constantine's Porphyry Column: The Earliest Literary Allusion." In *The Journal of Roman Studies*, Vol. 81, 1991.

Frank, Tenney. "Pyrrhus." In *The Cambridge Ancient History, Vol. VII, The Hellenistic Monarchies and the Rise of Rome*. Editor S.A. Cook et al. Cambridge: Cambridge University Press, 1928.

Franke, P.R. "Pyrrhus." In *The Cambridge Ancient History, second edition*, Vol. VII, part 2. "The Rise of Rome to 220 B.C." Editor F.W. Walbank. Cambridge: Cambridge University Press, 2002.

Fraser, Antonia. *The Warrior Queens*. New York: Alfred A. Knopf, 1989.

Frontinus. *Stratagems; Aqueducts of Rome*. Loeb Classical Library series. Translator Charles E. Bennett. Cambridge, MA: Harvard University Press, 1997. Reprint of 1925 work.

Frye, R.N. *The Cambridge History of Iran*. Vol. 4. Cambridge: Cambridge University Press, 1983.

Fuller, J.F.C. *Armament and History: A Study of the Influence of Armament on History from the Dawn of Classical Warfare to the Second World War*. New York: Charles Scribner's Sons, 1945.

Fuller, J.F.C. *The Generalship of Alexander the Great*. New York: Minerva Press, 1968.

Gabbert, Janice J. *Antigonus II Gonatas: A Political Biography*. New York: Routledge, 1997.

Gabriel, Richard A. and Metz, Karen S. *From Sumer to Rome: The Military Capabilities of Ancient Armies*. New York: Greenwood Press, 1991.

Gabriel, Richard A. *Great Captains of Antiquity*. Contributions in Military Studies series no. 204. Westport, CT: Greenwood Press, 2001.

Gaebel, Robert E. *Cavalry Operations in the Ancient Greek World*. Norman: University of Oklahoma Press, 2002.

Gaidoz, H. "Les Elephans a la Guerre." In *Revue des deux mondes*, Vol. 4, 1874.

Garlan, Yvon. "War and Siegecraft." In *The Cambridge Ancient History, second edition*. Vol. VII, part I, The Hellenistic World. Editor F.W. Walbank. Cambridge: Cambridge University Press, 2001.

Garoufalias, Petros. *Pyrrhus: King of Epirus*. London: Stacey International, 1979.

Ghirshman, R. "The Town Which Three Hundred Elephants Rased to the Ground." In *The Illustrated London News*, Vol. 5816, October 7, 1950.

Gibbon, Edward. *The History of the Decline & Fall of the Roman Empire* in three volumes. New York: Heritage Press, 1946.

Glines, C.V. "Flying the Hump." In *Air Force Magazine*. Journal of the Air Force Association. Vol. 74 n.3, March, 1991. Online at www.afa.org/magazine/1991/0391hump_print.html

Glover, R.F. "The Tactical Handling of the Elephant." In *Greece & Rome*, Vol. 17, n. 49, Jan. 1948.

Goel, Sita Ram. *Heroic Hindu Resistance to Muslim Invaders (636 AD to 1206 AD)*. New Delhi: Voice of India, online at voi.org/books/hhrmi/index.htm

Goldsworthy, Adrian. *The Punic Wars*. London: Cassell, 2000.

Goodrich, L. Carrington and Chia-Sheng, Feng. "The Early Development of Firearms in China." In *Isis*, Vol. 36, n.2, Jan. 1946.

Gowers, William. "The African Elephant in Warfare." In *African Affairs*, Vol. 46, issue 182, January 1947.

Gowers, William. "African Elephants and Ancient Authors." In *African Affairs*, Vol. 47, issue 188, July 1948.

Graff, David Andrew. *Medieval Chinese Warfare, 300-900*. Warfare and History series. New York: Routledge, 2002.

Grainger, John D. "An Empire Builder: Seleukos Nikator." In *History Today*, Vol. 43, n.5, May 1993.

Grainger, John D. *Seleukos Nikator: Constructing a Hellenistic Kingdom*. New York: Routledge, 1990.

Grant, Michael. *The Army of the Caesars*. New York: Charles Scribner's Sons, 1974.

Grant, Michael. *From Alexander to Cleopatra: The Hellenistic World*. New York: History Book Club, 2000 reprint of 1982 edition.

Green, Peter. *Alexander of Macedon, 356-323 BC*. Berkeley: University of California Press, 1991.

Green, Peter. *Alexander to Actium: The Historical Evolution of the Hellenistic Age*. Berkeley: University of California Press, 1990.

Greenhut, Jeffrey. "Armies of India from the Aryans to the Marathas." In *The Journal of the United Service Institution of India*. Vol. 106, n. 442, 1976.

Greep, S.J. "Lead Sling-Shot from Windridge Farm, St Albans and the Use of the Sling by the Roman Army in Britain." In *Britannia*. Vol. 18, 1987.

Grierson, George A. (translator). "The Lay of Brahma's Marriage: An Episode of the Alh-Khand." In *Bulletin of the School of Oriental Studies, University of London*, Vol. 2, n.4, 1923.

Griffith, G.T. *The Mercenaries of the Hellenistic World*. New York: AMS Press, 1977.

Groning, Karl and Saller, Martin. *Elephants: A Cultural and Natural History*. Germany: Konemann, 1999.

Gudger, E.W. "Bullets and Spear-Heads Embedded in the Tusks of Elephants." In *The Scientific Monthly*, Vol. 35, n. 4, October 1932.

Hallward, B.L. "Hannibal's Invasion of Italy." In *The Cambridge Ancient History, Vol. VIII Rome and Mediterranean 218-133 B.C*. Bury, J.B. ed. New York: Macmillan, 1933.

Hallward, B.L. "Scipio and Victory." In *The Cambridge Ancient History, Vol. VIII Rome and Mediterranean 218-133 B.C*. Bury, J.B. ed. New York: Macmillan, 1933.

Hallward, B.L. and Charlesworth, M.P. "The Fall of Carthage." In *The Cambridge Ancient History, Vol. VIII Rome and Mediterranean 218-133 B.C*. Bury, J.B. ed. New York: Macmillan, 1933.

Halvarg, David. *The War Against the Greens: The "Wise Use" Movement, the New Right, and the Browning of America*. Revised and updated. Boulder, CO: Johnson Books, 2004.

Hammond, N.G.L. "The Battle of Pydna." In *The Journal of Hellenic Studies*, Vol. 104, 1984.

Hammond, N.G.L. "The Campaign and the Battle of Cynoscephalae in 197 BC." In *The Journal of Hellenic Studies*, Vol. 108, 1988.

Hammond, N.G.L. *The Genius of Alexander the Great*. Chapel Hill: University of North Carolina Press, 1997.

Hammond, N.G.L. and Walbank, F.W. *A History of Macedonia: 336-167 BC*. Vol. III. Oxford: Clarendon Press, 1988.

Hansen, Waldemar. *The Peacock Throne: The Drama of Mogul India*. New York: Holt, Rinehart and Winston, 1972.

Harrington, Peter. *Plassey, 1757: Clive of India's Finest Hour*. Praeger Illustrated Military History series. Westport, CT: Praeger, 2005.

Hart, B.H. Liddell. *A Greater Than Napoleon: Scipio Africanus*. New York: Biblo and Tannen, 1971, reprint of 1927 work.

Hart, Lynette and Sundar. "Family Traditions for Mahouts of Asian Elephants." In *Anthrozoos*, Vol. 13, n.1, 2000.

Havell, H.L. *Republican Rome*. Hertfordshire, England: Oracle Publishing, 1996 reprint of 1914 work.

Healy, Mark. *Cannae 216 BC: Hannibal Smashes Rome's Army*. Campaign Series. London: Osprey, 1994.

Healy, Mark. *Warriors of the Old Testament: Joshua, King David, Nebuchadnezzar, Judas Maccabeus*. London: Brockhampton Press, 1998.

Heathcote, T.A. *The Indian Army: The Garrison of British Imperial India, 1822-1922*. Historic Armies and Navies series. New York: Hippocrene Books, 1974.

Heckel, Waldemar. *The Marshals of Alexander's Empire*. New York: Routledge, 1992.

Heckel, Waldemar. "Resistance to Alexander the Great." In *The Greek World in the Fourth Century: From the Fall of the Athenian Empire to the Successors of Alexander*, edited by Lawrence A. Tritle. New York: Routledge, 1997.

Heckscher, William S. "Bernini's Elephant and Obelisk." In *The Art Bulletin*, Vol. 29, n. 3, Sept. 1947.

Heitland, W.E. *The Roman Republic*. Vols. 1-2. Cambridge: Cambridge University Press, 1923.

Henderson, Bernard W. "The Campaign of the Metaurus." In *The English Historical Review*. Vol. 13, n. 51, July 1898.

Henderson, Bernard W. "The Campaign of the Metaurus continued." In *The English Historical Review*, Vol. 13, n. 52, October 1898.

Higham, Robin. "The International Commission for Military History - Meeting, Tehran, 6-16 July 1976." In *Military Affairs*, Vol. 40, n. 4, December 1976, p. 153.

Hildinger, Erik. *Swords Against the Senate: The Rise of the Roman Army and the Fall of the Republic*. Cambridge, MA.: Da Capo, 2002.

Hind, J.G.F. "The Invasion of Britain in A.D. 43: An Alternative Strategy for Aulus Plautius." In *Britannia*, Vol. 20, 1989.

Hintze, Andrea. *The Mughal Empire and Its Decline: An Interpretation of the Sources of Social Power*. Brookfield, MA: Ashgate, 1997.

Hintze, Fritz. "The Meroitic Period." In *Africa in Antiquity: The Arts of Ancient Nubia and the Sudan*. New York: The Brooklyn Museum, 1978.

Hodges, Richard. "Charlemagne's Elephant." In *History Today*, Dec. 2000, Vol. 50, n. 12.

Holleaux, Maurice. "Rome and Macedon: The Romans Against Philip" and "Rome and Antiochus." In *The Cambridge Ancient History, Vol. VIII, Rome and the Mediterranean 218-133 BC*. Cambridge: Cambridge University Press, 1930.

Hopkins, E.W. "Interpretation of Mahabharata iii.42.5." In *Journal of the American Oriental Society*, Vol. 14, 1888.

Hoyte, John. *Trunk Road for Hannibal: With an Elephant over the Alps*. London: Geoffrey Bles, 1960.

Huart, Clement. *Ancient Persia and Iranian Civilization*. New York: Knopf, 1927.

Hung, Vu. *The Story of a Mahout and His War Elephant*. Hanoi: Foreign Languages Publishing House, 1976.

The Hutchinson Dictionary of Ancient and Medieval Warfare. Chicago: Fitzroy Dearborn, 1998.

Impey, Lawrence. "Shangtu, the Summer Capital of Kublai Khan." In *Geographical Review*, Vol. 15, n.4, Oct. 1925.

"Indian Elephant Dies of Grief." May 5, 1999, Associated Press.

Jackson, Peter. *Endangered Species: Elephants*. Secaucus, NJ: Chartwell Books, 1990.

Jayewardene, Jayantha. "Elephants in Sri Lankan History and Culture." Found on Web site Art Sri Lanka at www.artsrilanka.org/essays/elephants/on January 22, 2005.

Jennison, George. *Animals for Show and Pleasure in Ancient Rome*. Manchester, England: Manchester University Press, 1937.

Jimenez, Ramon L. *Caesar Against the Celts*. Edison, NJ: Castle Books, 1996.

Jones, David E. *Women Warriors: A History*. Washington, D.C.: Brassey's, 1997.

Josephus, Flavius. *The Works of Josephus*. Complete and unabridged, new updated edition. Translated by William Whiston. Peabody, MA: Hendrickson Publishers, 1989.

Jouguet, Pierre. *Macedonian Imperialism and the Hellenization of the East*. New York: Knopf, 1928.

Jurmain, Suzanne. *From Trunk to Tail: Elephants Legendary and Real*. New York: Harcourt, Brace, Jovanovich, 1978.

Kagan, Donald. *On the Origins of War and the Preservation of Peace*. New York: Doubleday, 1995.

Kazhdan, Alexander P. ed. et al. *The Oxford Dictionary of Byzantium*, Vol. 1. New York: Oxford University Press, 1991.

Kelly, Christopher. "A Grand Tour: Reading Gibbon's 'Decline and Fall.'" In *Greece & Rome*, 2nd series, Vol. 44, n. 1, April 1997.

Kendall, Timothy. *Kerma and the Kingdom of Kush 2500-1500 BC: The Archaeological Discovery of an Ancient Nubian Empire*. Washington, DC: National Museum of Art, 1996.

Kenoyer, Jonathan Mark. *Ancient Cities of the Indus Valley Civilization*. New York: Oxford University Press, 1998.

Kimball, Charles. "Ayutthayan Siam." On the Guide to Thailand Web site at www.guidetothailand.com/thailand-history/ayuttuya.htm

Kincaid, C.A. *Successors of Alexander the Great: Ptolemy I, Pyrrhus of Epirus, Hiero of Syracuse, Antiochus III*. Chicago: Ares Publishers, 1980.

Kramrisch, Stella. *Painted Delight: Indian Paintings from Philadelphia Collections*. Philadelphia: Philadelphia Museum of Art, 1986.

Kruse, Gosta. *Trunk Call*. London: Elek Books, 1962.

Kukler, Michael A. *Operation Barooom*. Gastonia, NC: Michael A. Kukler, 1980.

Kumar, Baldev. *The Early Kusanas*. New Delhi: Sterling Publ., 1973.

Lahiri-Choudhury, Dhriti K. ed. *The Great Indian Elephant Book: An Anthology of Writings on Elephants in the Raj*. Oxford: Oxford University Press, 1999.

Lahiri-Choudhury, D.K. "The Indian elephant in a changing world." In *Contemporary Indian Tradition*, edited by Carla M. Borden. Washington DC: Smithsonian Institution, 1989.

Lair, Richard C. *Gone Astray: The Care and Management of the Asian Elephant in Domesticity*. Rome, Italy: Food and Agriculture Organization of the United Nations (FAO), 1997.

Lal, Kishor.Saran. *Early Muslims in India*. New Delhi: Book & Books, 1984.

Lamb, Harold. *Cyrus the Great*. Garden City, NJ: Doubleday, 1960.

Lancel, Serge. *Hannibal*. Translator Antonia Nevill. Malden, MA.: Blackwell, 1998.

Langer, William L. ed. *Western Civilization: Paleolithic Man to the Emergence of European Powers*, Volume 1, New York: American Heritage, 1968.

Latimer, John. *Burma: The Forgotten War*. London: John Murray Publishers Ltd., 2004. Quotation cited from a book review on the Stone & Stone Bookstore website, as the book is not yet available in the U.S., found at http://www.sonic.net/~bstone/archives/050102.shtml

Laufer, Berthold. *Ivory in China*. Anthropology Leaflet #21, Chicago: Field Museum of Natural History, 1925.

Law, R.C.C. "The Garamantes and Trans-Saharan Enterprise in Classical Times." In *The Journal of African History*. Vol. 8, n. 2, 1967.

Lazenby, J.F. *Hannibal's War: A Military History of the Second Punic War*. Norman, OK.: University of Oklahoma Press, 1998.

Leong, Jeffrey Say Seck. "Storming the last Hindu Fortress." In *Military History*, Vol. 15, n. 6, Feb. 1999.

Levick, B.M. "Antiquarian or Revolutionary? Claudius Caesar's Conception of His Principate." In *The American Journal of Philology*, Vol. 99, n. 1, Spring 1978.

Levin, Bernard. *Hannibal's Footsteps*. London: Hodder and Stoughton, 1987.

Littauer, M.A. and Crouwel, J.H. *Wheeled Vehicles and Ridden Animals in the Ancient Near East*. Leiden, Netherlands: E.J. Brill, 1979.

Livy. *Livy.*[History of Rome] In 14 volumes. Cambridge, MA: Harvard University Press, 1961.

Livy. *The War with Hannibal: Books XXI-XXX of the History of Rome from Its Foundation*. Translated by Aubrey de Selincourt; editor Betty Radice. New York: Penguin, 1965.

Lobban, R.A. and De Liedekerke, Valerie. "Elephants in Ancient Egypt and Nubia." In *Anthrozoos*, Vol. 13, n. 4, 2000.

Louis, Henry. "On the River Telubin." In *Geographical Journal*, Vol. 4, n. 3, Sept. 1894.

Lucan (Lucanus, Marcus Annaeus). "Pharsalia (aka The Civil War), AD 61-65." Found at www.fullbooks.com/Pharsalia-Civil-War-.html

Lucretius. *Lucretius on the Nature of Things*. Translator John Selby Watson. London: Bell and Daldy, 1872.

Lynn, John A. *Battle: A History of Combat and Culture*. Boulder, CO: Westview Press, 2003.

MacMunn, George. *The Martial Races of India*. Quetta, Pakistan: Gosha-e-Adab, 1977.

Mahaffy, John Pentland. *The Empire of Alexander the Great*. New York: Barnes & Noble, 1995 reprint of 1898 work.

Mahomet, Sake Deen (1759–1851). *The Travels of Dean Mahomet: An Eighteenth-Century Journey through India*. Edited by Michael H. Fisher. Berkeley: University of California, 1997.

Maihafer, Harry J. "River Crossing Imperiled." In *Military History*, Vol. 5, n. 4, February 1989.

Mandaville, John. "An Elephant for Charlemagne." In *Aramco World*, February 1977, online at http://www.saudiaramcoworld.com/issue/197702/an.elephant.for.charlemagne.htm

Mansei, A. "Mountain Guns in the Naga Hills, 1879-80." War Department, Ordnance Office, *Proceedings of the Royal Artillery Institution*. #263. March 9, 1883.

Marcellinus, Ammianus. "The Siege of Amida." In *Ammianus Marcellinus*. Translated by John Rolfe. London, 1935. Online at www.deremilitari.org/RESOURCES/SOURCES/ammianus.htm

Masson, Georgina. *A Concise History of Republican Rome*. London: Thames and Hudson, 1973.

Maxwell-Stuart, P.G. "I Maccabees 6:34 Again." In *Vetus Testamentum*, Vol. 25, n. 2, April 1975.

May, Elmer C. et al. *Ancient and Medieval Warfare*. Wayne, NJ: Avery Publishing, 1984.

Mayor, Adrienne. *The First Fossil Hunters: Paleontology in Greek and Roman Times*. Princeton: Princeton University Press, 2000.

Mayor, Adrienne. *Greek Fire, Poison Arrows & Scorpion Bombs: Biological and Chemical Warfare in the Ancient World*. New York: Overlook Duckworth, 2003.

McCrindle, John W. *Ancient India as Described by Megasthenes and Arrian*. New Delhi: Munshiram Manoharlal Publishers, 2000 edition of 1926 work.

McDonnell, Myles. "The Speech of Numidicus at Gellius, N.A. 1.6." In *The American Journal of Philology*, Vol. 108, n. 1, Spring 1987.

Mehta, Ved. *Portrait of India*. New Haven, CT: Yale University Press, 1993.

Meiklejohn, K.W. "Roman Strategy and Tactics from 509 to 202 BC" part two. In *Greece & Rome*, Vol. 8, n. 22, October 1938.

Michelet, J. *History of the Roman Republic*. Translated by William Hazlitt. London: David Bogue, 1847.

Mielczarek, Mariusz. *Cataphracti and Clibanarii: Studies on the Heavy Armoured Cavalry of the Ancient World*. Lodz, Poland: Oficyna Naukowa, 1993.

Mokhtar, G. ed. *Ancient Civilizations of Africa*. General History of Africa Vol. II. Berkeley: UNESCO, 1990.

Mommsen, Theodor. *The Provinces of the Roman Empire from Caesar to Diocletian*. Two volumes. New York: Barnes and Noble Books, 1996, from 1909 corrected edition.

Montagu, John Drogo. *Battles of the Greek & Roman Worlds*. Mechanicsburg, PA: Stackpole Books, 2000.

Montgomery, Viscount (Field-Marshal Montgomery of Alamein). *A History of Warfare*. Cleveland: World Publishing, 1968.

Montross, Lynn. *War through the Ages*. Revised and enlarged 3rd edition. New York: Harper & Bros., 1960.

Moreland, W.H. and Chatterjee, Atul Chandra. *A Short History of India*. Second edition. London: Longmans, Green and Co., n.d.

Morewood-Dowsett, J. "Supplement: Elephant Past and Present." In *Journal of the Royal African Society*, Vol. 38, n. 152, July 1939.

Morkholm, Otto. *Antiochus IV of Syria*. Classica et Mediaevalia Dissertations VIII. Norway: Gyldendalske Boghandel, 1966.

Morris, A.S. "The Journey Beyond Three Seas." In *Geographical Journal*, Vol. 133, n.4, Dec. 1967.

Morris, William O'Connor. *Hannibal: Soldier, Statesman, Patriot*. New York: G.P. Putnam's Sons, 1903.

Munro, Richard K. "Roman Conquest of Spain." In *Military History*, Vol. 17, n. 2. June, 2000.

Murphy, Edwin. *The Antiquities of Asia: A Translation with Notes of Book II of the Library of History of Diodorus Siculus*. New Brunswick, NJ: Transaction Publishers, 1989.

Murray, G.W. and Warmington, E.H. "Trogodytica: The Red Sea Littoral in Ptolemaic Times." In *Geographical Journal*, Vol. 133, n. 1, March 1967.

Murray, Neil. *The Love of Elephants*. Secaucus, NJ: Chartwell Books, 1990.

Musti, Domenico. "Syria and the East." In *The Cambridge Ancient History, second edition*. Vol. VII. part I, The Hellenistic World. Editor F.W. Walbank. Cambridge: Cambridge University Press, 2001, pp. 175–220.

Namboodiri, Nibha, ed. *Practical Elephant Management: A Handbook for Mahouts*. Elephant Welfare Association, 1997. Online at http://www.elephantcare.org/mancover.htm

Narain, A.K. "Ganesa: The Idea and the Icon." In *Ganesh: Studies of an Asian God*. Editor Robert L. Brown. State University of New York Press, 1991.

Nardo, Don. *The Battle of Zama*. Battles of the Ancient World series. San Diego: Lucent Books, 1996.

Nazim, Muhammed. *The Life and Times of Sultan Mahmud of Ghazna*. New Delhi: Munshiram Manoharlal, 1971 (originally 1931).

Nearing, Homer, Jr. "Local Caesar Traditions in Britain." In *Speculum*, Vol. 24, n. 2, April 1949.

Nepos, Cornelius. *Lives of Famous Men (de Viris Illustribus)*. Translator Gareth Schmeling. Lawrence, KS: Coronado Press, 1971.

Ness, Gayl D. and Stahl, William. "Western Imperialist Armies in Asia." In *Comparative Studies in Society and History*, Vol. 19, n. 1, Jan. 1977.

Nicholls, Frank. "Tame Elephants." In *The Great Indian Elephant Book: An Anthology of Writings on Elephants in the Raj* by Dhriti K. Lahiri-Choudhury, editor. New York: Oxford University Press, 1999.

Nicolle, David. *Arms and Armour of the Crusading Era, 1050-1350, Islam, Eastern Europe and Asia*. Revised and updated edition. Vol. II. Mechanicsburg, PA: Stackpole Books, 1999.

Nicolle, David. *Mughal India, 1504-1761*. Men-At-Arms series. Editor Lee Johnson. London: Osprey, 1993.

Nicolle, David. *Rome's Enemies (5): The Desert Frontier*. Men-at-Arms series. Oxford: Osprey, 2003.

O'Bryhim, S. "Hannibal's Elephants and the Crossing of the Rhone." In *The Classical Quarterly, new series*. Vol. 41, n. 1, 1991.

Page, Tim. *Another Vietnam: Pictures of the War from the Other Side*. Washington, DC: National Geographic Society, 2002.

Pant, G.N. *Horse & Elephant Armour*. New Delhi: Agam Kala Prakashan, 1997.

Paradine-Palmer, Greta. *Jhools in the Dust*. York, England: Wilton 65, 2002.

Parke, H.W. *Greek Mercenary Soldiers: From the Earliest Times to the Battle of Ipsus*. Reprint of 1933 edition. Chicago: Ares Publishers, 1981.

Paul, E. Jaiwant. *'By My Sword and Shield': Traditional Weapons of the Indian Warrior*. New Delhi: Roli Books, 2004.

Payne, Robert. *Ancient Rome*. New York: IBooks, 2001.

Payne, Robert. *The Roman Triumph*. New York: Abelard-Schuman, 1962.

Pease, Arthur Stanley. "Notes on Some Uses of Bells among the Greeks and Romans." In *Harvard Studies in Classical Philology*. Vol. 15, 1904.

Peddie, John. *Hannibal's War*. Phoenix Mill, England: Sutton Publishing, 1997.

Peddie, John. *The Roman War Machine*. London: Sutton Publishing, 1994.

Peek, Ian Denys. *One Fourteenth of an Elephant: A Memoir of Life and Death on the Burma-Thailand Railway*. London: Doubleday, 2004.

Phillips, Jacke. "Punt and Aksum: Egypt and the Horn of Africa." In *The Journal of African History*, Vol. 38, n. 3, 1997.

Pickard-Cambridge, A.W. "The Rise of Macedonia." In *The Cambridge Ancient History, Vol. VI Macedon, 401-301 B.C.* Editor J.B. Bury et al. New York: Macmillan, 1933.

Pliny. *Natural History* in 10 volumes. Vol. III, Libri VIII-XI. Edited by H. Rackham, 2nd edition. Cambridge: Harvard University Press, 1983.

Plutarch. *Plutarch's Lives of Illustrious Men*. Translator: Dryden, John. In three volumes. New York: John W. Lovell Co., ca. 1880.

Polybius. *The Rise of the Roman Empire*. Translator Ian Scott-Kilvert. New York: Penguin, 1979.

Pope, William Christopher. *Alexander the Great in India*. Masters Thesis for the University of Houston at Clear Lake, May, 1996.

Powell, John ed. *Magill's Guide to Military History*, Vol. 2, Corunna-Janissaries. Pasadena, CA: Salem Press, 2001.

Prados, John. *The Blood Road: The Ho Chi Minh Trail and the Vietnam War*. New York: John Wiley & Sons, 1999.

Prevas, John. *Hannibal Crosses the Alps: The Enigma Re-Examined*. Rockville Centre, NY: Sarpedon, 1998.

Pritchett, W. Kendrick. *The Greek State at War*. Vol. 5. Berkeley: University of California, 1991.

Pseudo-Callisthenes. *The Romance of Alexander the Great*. Translated from the Armenian version by Albert M. Woloojian. New York: Columbia University Press, 1969.

Ramsay, William Mitchell. "Geography and History in a Phyrgo-Pisidian Glen." In *Geographical Journal*, Vol. 41, n. 4, April 1923.

Rankin, L.K. "The Elephant Experiment in Africa: A Brief Account of the Belgian Elephant Expedition." In *Proceedings of the Royal Geographical Society and Monthly Record of Geography*, Vol. 4, n. 5, May 1882.

Ranking, John. *Historical Researches on the Wars and Sports of the Mongols and Romans: In Which Elephants and Wild Beasts Were Employed or Slain*. London: Longman, Rees, Orme, Brown, and Green, 1826.

Rapson, E.J. ed. *The Cambridge History of India*. New Delhi: S. Chand & Co., 1962.

Rattenbury, R.M. "An Ancient Armoured Force." In *The Classical Review*, Vol. 56, n. 3, November 1942.

Raven, Susan. *Rome in Africa*. Third edition. New York: Routledge, 1993.

Rawlinson, George. *The Five Great Monarchies of the Ancient Eastern World* in three volumes. Second edition. New York: Scribner, Welford and Co., 1871.

Rawlinson, George. *The Sixth Great Oriental Monarchy; or the Geography, History, & Antiquities of Parthia*. New York: Scribner, Welford and Armstrong, 1873.

Rawlinson, George. *The Seventh Great Oriental Monarchy; or the Geography, History and Antiquities of the Sassanian or New Persian Empire*. Two volumes. New York: Dodd, Mead & Co., ca. 1875.

Rawlinson, H.G. *India: A Short Cultural History*. Editor C.G. Seligman. New York: D. Appleton-Century Co., 1938, 1952.

Rees, P.A. "Asian Elephants in Zoos Face Global Extinction: Should Zoos Accept the Inevitable?" In *Oryx*, Vol. 37, n. 1, January, 2003.

Reicke, Bo. *The New Testament Era: The World of the Bible from 500 BC to AD 100*. Philadelphia: Fortress Press, 1987.

Reid, J.S. "Lucretiana: Notes on Books I and II of the De Rerum Natura." In *Harvard Studies in Classical Philology*. Vol. 22, 1911.

Reid, Robert W. *Military History*. "Diabolical in Its Simplicity: The Ancient, Durable Caltrop." Vol.15, n.3, August, 1998.

Reinach, Sal. "Elephant foulant aux pieds un Galata." In *Bulletin du Correspondance Hellenique*. Vol. 9, 1885.

Reiter, William. *Aemilius Paullus: Conqueror of Greece*. London: Croom Helm, 1988.

Renault, Mary. *The Nature of Alexander*. New York: Pantheon Books, 1975.

Rennie, James [though stated as Anonymous]. *The Elephant as he exists in a wild state, and as he has been made subservient, in peace and in war, to the purposes of man*. New York: Harper & Brothers, 1848.

Rennie, James [though stated as Anonymous]. *The Elephant Principally Viewed in Relation to Man, a new edition*. London: Charles Knight & Co., 1844.

Rice, E.E. *The Grand Procession of Ptolemy Philadelphus*. New York: Oxford University Press, 1983.

Richardson, Thom. "The Elephant Tusk Swords." In *Royal Armouries Yearbook*. Vol. 4, 1999.

Richardson, Thom and Stevens, Donna. "The Elephant Armour." In *Royal Armouries Yearbook*. Vol. 1, 1996.

Rizvi, S.A.A. *The Wonder that was India*. Vol. II. London: Sidgwick & Jackson, 1987.

Roberts, J. Howard. "Brilliant and Brutal: Tamerlane Conquered a Vast Empire." In *Military History*, Vol. 13, n. 5, Dec. 1996.

Roberts, Timothy R. *Ancient Rome*. Chronicles of the Roman World series. New York: Friedman/Fairfax Publishers, 2000.

Robinson, Charles Alexander. *Ancient History: From Prehistoric Times to the Death of Justinian*. New York: Macmillan, 1961.

Roe, Thomas. "Voyage into the East Indies." In *The Travels of Sig. Pietro della Valle* by Mario Schipano, London: J. Macock, 1665.

Rollin, Charles. *The Ancient History of the Egyptians, Carthaginians, Assyrians, Babylonians, Medes and Persians, Grecians, and Macedonians...in two volumes.* Cincinnati: Applegate, Pounsford & Co., 1868.

Rostovtzeff, M. *The Social and Economic History of the Hellenistic World.* Vol. I. London: Oxford, 1953.

Roth, Jonathan P. *The Logistics of the Roman Army at War (264 BC - AD 235).* Vol. 22 in the Columbia Studies in the Classical Tradition series. Boston: Brill, 1999.

Rothman, Margret S. Pond. "The Thematic Organization of the Panel Reliefs on the Arch of Galerius." In *American Journal of Archaeology,* Vol. 81, n. 4, Autumn 1977.

Rowland, Emory. "Military Use of Elephants in the Greek and Roman Period." Internet article located at www.barca.fsnet.co.uk/elephants-war-greek. htm, dated 12/1/86.

Rufus, Quintus Curtius. *The Life and Death of Alexander the Great, King of Macedon.* London: S.S., 1674.

Runciman, Steven. "Charlemagne and Palestine." In *The English Historical Review,* Vol. 50, n. 200, Oct. 1935.

Salam, Zahid-Ivan. *Jihad and the Foreign Policy of the Khilafah State.* London: Khilafah Publications, 2001, online at www.khilafah.com

Sallust. *Sallust.* Translator J.C. Rolfe. Cambridge, MA: Harvard University Press, 1985.

Salmon, E.T. "The Strategy of the Second Punic War." In *Greece & Rome,* second series, Vol. 7, n. 2, October 1960.

Sandy, Gerald N. *Heliodorus.* Boston: Twayne, 1982.

Sarkar, Jagadish. "Men and Beasts in Medieval Indian Warfare." In *Journal of Indian History.* 1973. Golden Jubilee edition. pp. 463–494.

Sastri, K.A. Nilakanta ed. *A Comprehensive History of India.* Vol. 2. Bombay: Orient Longmans, 1957.

Saxtorph, Niels M. *Warriors and Weapons of Early Times in Color.* New York: Macmillan, 1972.

Schafer, Edward H. "War Elephants in Ancient and Medieval China." In *Oriens,* Vol. 10, 1957.

Schneck, William C. *Engineer.* "The Origins of Military Mines: Part I." Vol. 28, n.3, July 1998.

Schulten, A. "The Romans in Spain." In *The Cambridge Ancient History, Vol. VIII, Rome and the Mediterranean 218-133 BC.* Cambridge: Cambridge University Press, 1930.

Scigliano, Eric. *Love, War, and Circuses: The Age-Old Relationship between Elephants and Humans.* Boston: Houghton Mifflin, 2002.

Scott, Kenneth. "The Significance of Statues in Precious Metals in Emperor Worship." In *Transactions and Proceedings of the American Philological Association,* Vol. 62, 1931.

Scullard, H.H. "Carthage and Rome." In *The Cambridge Ancient History, second edition*, Vol. VII, part 2. "The Rise of Rome to 220 B.C." Editor F.W. Walbank. Cambridge: Cambridge University Press, 2002 reprint of 1989 work.

Scullard, H.H. "The Carthaginians in Spain." In *The Cambridge Ancient History, second edition*, Vol. VIII, "Rome and the Mediterranean to 133 BC." Editor A.E. Astin. New York: Cambridge University Press, 2001.

Scullard, H.H. *The Elephant in the Greek and Roman World*. Aspects of Greek and Roman Life series. Cambridge: Thames and Hudson, 1974.

Scullard, H.H. "Ennius, Cato, and Surus." In *The Classical Review, new series*. Vol. 3, n. 3-4, December 1953.

Scullard, H.H. *A History of the Roman World: 753 to 146 BC*. Fifth edition. New York: Routledge, 2003.

Sekunda, Nicholas. *Republican Roman Army 200-104BC*. Men-at-Arms series. Oxford: Osprey Publishing, 2002.

Sekunda, Nicholas. *Seleucid and Ptolemaic Reformed Armies 168-145 BC*, in two volumes. Stockport, England: Montvert Publications, 1994.

Shaw, Brent D. "War and Violence." In *Late Antiquity: A Guide to the Postclassical World*. Editor G.W. Bowersock et al. Cambridge, MA: Harvard University Press, 1999.

Shelton, Jo-Ann. "Elephants, Pompey, and the Reports of Popular Displeasure in 55 BC." In *Veritatis Amicitiaeque Causa: Essays in Honor of Anna Lydia Motto and John R. Clark*. Editors Shannon N. Byrne and Edmund P. Cueva. Wauconda, IL.: Bolchazy-Carducci Publishers, 1999.

Shelton, Jo-Ann. "The Identification of Elephants with Enemies: Why Elephants Were Abused in Ancient Rome." Fifteen page Internet essay at cla.calpoly.edu/~jlynch/Elephants.htm, cited June 18, 2003.

Shipley, Graham. *The Greek World After Alexander: 323-30 BC*. New York: Routledge, 2000.

Sillar, F.C. and Meyler, R.M. *Elephants: Ancient and Modern*. New York: Viking, 1968.

Singh, Kesri. Citation in "The Mewar Encyclopedia" under the entry "Haldighati, Battle of." Online at www.mewarindia.com/ency/hal.html

Singh, Sarva Daman. *Ancient Indian Warfare with Special Reference to the Vedic Period*. Leiden, The Netherlands: E.J. Brill, 1965.

Smith, G. Elliot. *Elephants and Ethnologists*. New York: E.P. Dutton, 1924.

Smith, Vincent A. *Akbar: The Great Mogul 1542-1605*. 2nd revised ed. Oxford: Clarendon Press, 1919.

Snowden, Frank M. Jr. "The Negro in Classical Italy." In *The American Journal of Philology*. Vol. 68, n. 3, 1947.

Soren, David et al. *Carthage: Uncovering the Mysteries and Splendors of Ancient Tunisia*. New York: Simon and Schuster, 1990.

Sorobey, Ronald B. "Cossack Pirates of the Black Sea." In *Military History* magazine, Vol. 20, issue 2, June 2003.

Spaulding, Oliver Lyman et al. *Warfare: A Study of Military Methods from the Earliest Times*. Washington, D.C.: Infantry Journal Press, 1937.

Spinage, C.A. *Elephants*. London: T & A.D. Poyser Ltd., 1994.

Stadter, Philip A. "The Ars Tactica of Arrian: Tradition and Originality." In *Classical Philology*, Vol. 73, n. 2, April 1978.

Stanley-Millson, Caroline. *Asian Affairs*. "Asian Working Elephants in South India." Vol. 22, n.1, February, 1991.

Starnaman, Craig D. *Alexander, Porus, and the Battle of the Hydaspes*. Master's Thesis at Michigan State University, 1990.

Stearn, Duncan. "The Rise of Ayutthaya, part two, 1395-1448." In *Pattaya Mail*, Vol. 10, n. 47, November 2002. Online at http://www.pattayamail.com/486/columns.shtml#hd6

Stewart, John. "The Elephant in War." In *MHQ: The Quarterly Journal of Military History*, Vol. 3, n. 3, Spring 1991.

Stone, George Cameron. *A Glossary of the Construction, Decoration and Use of Arms and Armor in All Countries and in All Times*. New York: Jack Brussel, 1934.

Stopford, J.G.B. "A Neglected Source of Labour in Africa." In *Journal of the Royal African Society*, Vol. 1, n. 4, July 1902.

Strachan, Mr. "An Account of the Taking and Taming of Elephants in Zeylan [Ceylon], by Mr. Strachan, a Physician, Who Lived 17 Years There." In *Philosophical Transactions*, Vol. 23, 1702-1703.

Streusand, Douglas E. *The Formation of the Mughal Empire*. New Delhi: Oxford University Press, 1989.

Swain, Joseph Ward. *The Ancient World, Vol 2, The World Empires: Alexander and the Romans After 334 B.C.* New York: Harper & Row, 1950.

Sykes, Percy. *A History of Persia* in two volumes. 3rd edition. London: Macmillan, 1951.

Tafazzoli, Ahmad. "Elephant: A Demonic Creature and a Symbol of Sovereignty." In *Monumentum*, Vol. 2, 1975.

Tarn, W.W. "Alexander: The Conquest of the Far East." In *The Cambridge Ancient History, Vol. VI Macedon, 401-301 B.C.* Editor J.B. Bury et al. New York: Macmillan, 1933, pp. 387–437.

Tarn, W.W. "The First Syrian War." In *The Journal of Hellenic Studies*, Vol. 46, part 2, 1926.

Tarn, W.W. "Greece: 335 to 321 B.C." In *The Cambridge Ancient History, Vol. VI Macedon, 401-301 B.C.* Editor J.B. Bury et al. New York: Macmillan, 1933.

Tarn, W.W. *Hellenistic Civilisation*, 2nd ed. London: Edward Arnold, 1930.

Tarn, W.W. *Hellenistic Military & Naval Developments*. Chicago: Ares Publishers, 1975. [Reprint from 1930]

Tarn, W.W. "The Heritage of Alexander." In *The Cambridge Ancient History, Vol. VI Macedon, 401-301 B.C.* Editor J.B. Bury et al. New York: Macmillan, 1933.

Tavernier, Jean Baptiste. *Travels in India (1676)*. In two volumes. Translator V. Ball. London: Macmillan, 1889.

Taylor, Ira Donathan. "The Logistics of the Roman Army in North Africa." Doctor of Philosophy dissertation, University of Arkansas, 1997.

Tennent, J. Emerson. "Elephant Shooting." In *The Great Indian Elephant Book: An Anthology of Writings on Elephants in the Raj* by Dhriti K. Lahiri-Choudhury, editor. New York: Oxford University Press, 1999.

Thorley, J. "The Development of Trade between the Roman Empire and the East under Augustus." In *Greece & Rome*, second series, Vol. 16, n. 2, October 1969.

Thrapp, Don L. "The Mules of Mars." In *The Quartermaster Review*, May-June 1946. Found online at http://www.qmmuseum.lee.army.mil/WWII/mules_of_mars.htm

Toynbee, Arnold J. *Hannibal's Legacy: The Hannibalic War's Effects on Roman Life*. Two volumes. New York: Oxford University Press, 1965.

Toynbee, J.M.C. *Animals in Roman Life and Art*. Ithaca, NY: Cornell University Press, 1973.

Trautmann, Thomas R. "Elephants and the Mauryas." In *India: History and Thought*. Edited by S. N. Mukherjee. Calcutta, India: Subarnarekha, 1982.

Tucker, Spencer. C. "The First Tet Offensive." In *Vietnam Magazine*, Feb. 2003, found online at www.historynet.com/vn/blfirsttetoffensive/

Turnbull, Stephen. *Genghis Khan & the Mongol Conquests 1190-1400*. Essential Histories series. New York: Routledge, 2003.

Ueda-Sarson, Luke. *Alexander's Elephants*. Internet essay of seven pages (2002?), cited June 18, 2003. www.ne.jp/asahi/luke/ueda-sarson/Al-Ele.html

Vanoyeke, V. "Les elephants d'Hannibal contre les legions romaines." In *Historia*, Vol. 578, February 1995.

Vollrath, F. and Douglas-Hamilton, I. "African Bees to control African Elephants." *Naturwissenschaften*, Vol. 89 (11), November, 2003.

Wales, H.G. Quaritch. *Ancient Southeast Asian Warfare*. London: Bernard Quaritsch, 1952.

Walsh, P.G. "Massinissa." In *The Journal of Roman Studies*, Vol. 55, n. 1-2, 1965.

Wannabovorn, Sutin. "Elephants Turn to Thievery." Associated Press, January 5, 2004 (or 2005).

Warmington, B.H. *Carthage*. Baltimore: Penguin, 1964.

Warry, John. *Warfare in the Classical World*. New York: Barnes and Noble Books, 1993.

Webster, Graham. *The Roman Imperial Army of the First and Second Centuries A. D.* London: Adam & Charles Black, 1969.

Welles, C. Bradford. *Alexander and the Hellenistic World*. Toronto: A.M. Hakkert Co., 1970.

Welsby, Derek A. *The Kingdom of Kush: the Napatan and Meroitic Empires*. London: British Museum Press, 1996.

West, Robert Francis. *Animal Suffering in Roman Literature*. Master of Arts Thesis for the University of Calgary in Alberta, Canada, in February 1997.

Wheatley, Pat. "Antigonus Monophthalmus in Babylonia, 310-308 B.C." In *The Journal of Near Eastern Studies*, Vol. 61, n.1, 2002.

Wilford, John Noble. "Greek Myths: Not Necessarily Mythical." In *The New York Times*, July 4, 2000.

Will, Edouard. "The Succession to Alexander." In *The Cambridge Ancient History, second edition*. Vol. VII, part I, The Hellenistic World. Editor F.W. Walbank. Cambridge: Cambridge University Press, 2001.

Williams, Heathcote. *Sacred Elephant*. New York: Harmony Books, 1989.

Winfrey, Laurie Platt. *The Unforgettable Elephant*. New York: Walker and Co., 1980.

Wink, Andre. *Al Hind: The Making of the Indo-Islamic World*. Vol. 1: Early Medieval India and the Expansion of Islam, 7th-11th Centuries. New York: E.J. Brill, 1990.

Wise, Terence and Hook, Richard. *Armies of the Carthaginian Wars 265-146 BC*. Men-at-Arms series. London: Osprey, 1993.

Wynter, Philip. "Elephants at War: In Burma, Big Beasts Work for Allied Army." In *Life Magazine*, April 10, 1944.

Yalichev, Serge. *Mercenaries of the Ancient World*. London: Constable, 1997.

Yarshates, Ehsan, ed. *The Cambridge History of Iran*. Vol. 3. Cambridge: Cambridge University Press, 1983.

Zvelebil, K.V. "'Elephant Language' of the Mahouts of Mudumalai Wildlife Sanctuary." In *Journal of the American Oriental Society*, Vol. 99, n. 4, Oct.–Dec. 1979.

Index

CPSIA information can be obtained
at www.ICGtesting.com
Printed in the USA
LVHW011045070721
692012LV00021B/1482